SYMPATHY FOR THE EVIL

SYMPATHY FOR THE EVIL

In Norway, Terrorists' Rights Are More Important Than National Security and The Welfare of Its Citizens

KRISTINA VANAHEIM

Copyright © 2021 by **Kristina Vanaheim**
All rights reserved.
Sympathy For the Evil/ Kristina Vanaheim. 1st Edition.
ISBN: 9798484998104
Cover Design by The Unique Book Cover

*This book is dedicated to my fellow Norwegians.
The ordinary men and women who see the
writing on the wall but have no voice.*

I think there is a very big difference between the U.S. and Canada, which are immigrant countries, and countries like Norway and probably Austria and others, who have, you know, people have been living there for thousands of years. But I think that we have the same core. The same core is that if you believe in your Western ideas, you should believe that everybody is equal.

That you don't have any special rights because your parents have been living here forever. We don't have other rights than people who are living… It's by the things that you contribute to your society, that is the most important part of what you're doing.

Norwegian Prime Minister Erna Solberg,
Munich Security Conference February 16, 2020

The Labor Party believes that terrorist rights are more important than the nation's security.

Progress Party and Ministry of Justice Sylvi Listhaug,
Facebook Post March 8, 2018.

Europe is committing suicide. Or at least its leaders have decided to commit suicide. Whether the European people choose to go along with this is, naturally, another matter.

Douglas Murray, The Strange Death of Europe.
Published in 2017

If you are going to sin, sin against God, not the bureaucracy. God will forgive you, but the bureaucracy won't.

Hyman Rickover, United States Navy Admiral,
Quoted in the New York Times, November 3, 1986.

Norwegian authorities should perhaps choose to enter into negotiations with Pakistan, a country we have given billions of kroner in aid throughout the years: Either you accept Aisha Shezadi Kausar, or we turn off the *pengekranen*, the money spigot. It is time for Norway to take back the values of the country. And in that country, there is no room for either Islamists, left-wing, or right-wing extremists. It is time to put the foot down for all forms of extremism.

Norwegian author Hege Storhaug,
Human Rights Service, May 18, 2021

Contents

Introduction 1
Chapter 1: The American Boy Who Loved Norway 7
Chapter 2: You've Made Your ISIS Husband's Bed, Now Lie in It 13
Chapter 3: Do Not Return. Wait for Your Reward from Allah 27
Chapter 4: The Filthy, Shameless Acts of Western Culture 44
Chapter 5: The Road to Syria Was Paved with Bad Intentions 56
Chapter 6: Bureaucracy Is the Art of Making the Possible Impossible 70
Chapter 7: When Norwegian Journalists Become Social Justice Activists . 81
Chapter 8: The Formation of the Prophet Ummah 94
Chapter 9: I Swear by Allah I Didn't Know He Was a Terrorist 120
Chapter 10: Michael Moore's Norwegian Fairy Tale 132
Chapter 11: Beating Up Jews Awakened Youths Politically 149
Chapter 12: The World Needs Another Osama bin Laden 160
Chapter 13: Sometimes A Government Has to Make Moral Decisions .. 179
Chapter 14: Oh, What a Tangled Web We Weave... 197
Chapter 15: God Will Forgive Your Sins. The Bureaucracy Won't 214
Chapter 16: Radical Islam Will Never Leave Norway 226
Chapter 17: The Shadow Has Fallen Upon Norway 244
Chapter 18: You Are Always in My Heart, Norway 254
Notes 267

Introduction

*Norway. A Beautiful, Peaceful Country.
What if I told You a Different Story?*

A F JORD TRAVEL NORWAY travel brochure describes Norway as a beautiful, peaceful country located far north in mainland Europe. The land to the north offers unique, natural phenomena, such as the fantastic fjords, the long and rugged coast, the magic northern lights, and the exotic midnight sun. The stunning country is part of the Scandinavian peninsula and hosts mainland Europe's northernmost point: The North Cape. It is considered one of the safest and happiest countries with one of the lowest crime rates in the world. Norway consistently ranks high on the World Happiness Report and ranked number one on the OECD Better Life Index and the Democracy Index in 2019. The country's values are egalitarian ideals, with the Nordic welfare model, universal health care, and a comprehensive social security system. And we were Vikings!

Norway is all that and so much more. I know because I grew up in that beautiful and peaceful country. And Fjord Travel's Norway short account of my homeland is what I remember and cherish. And thankfully, none of those spectacular natural features of Norway went away. They are still there and will stay there for generations to come, just as they were there for generations before us. And so will my good memories. Memories I treasure and hold on to for dear life and take with me till the end of days.

But what if I told you a different story than Fjord Travel Norway? A dark side. One that the media, politicians, and authorities don't want you to know. A story that will reveal ranking high on the World Happiness Report and the Democracy Index is worthless when those who govern Norway put their country and citizens last. Or that those rankings may look good on paper and show the world. But is it based on reality? Not the way I see it. And you may also see Norway with different eyes after you read *Sympathy for the Evil*.

What is *Sympathy for the Evil* about?

Sympathy for the Evil is the unforgettable story of a Norwegian woman and her American son going up against the stonewalling Norwegian Directorate of Immigration. While the two are fighting a hellish bureaucracy, social justice warrior politicians, the left-wing media activists, high-profile immigration attorneys, and immigrant crusaders have joined forces to bring an ISIS woman safely back on Norwegian soil. Come hell or high water. And they are deceiving the Norwegian people with one lie after another.

We follow Heidi and Eric on their journey from the United States to Norway. Heidi, Eric, Robert, Sonja, and their families and friends are real people, but their names are fictitious. I could not have written the book without them. However, I could have written about the jihads in Norway that were allowed free reign and got the kid-glove treatment. But the purpose of the story is to show Good versus Evil. And how Evil often wins.

To protect Heidi and Eric's identities, I have not cited any sources in the chapters about them. I base their journey on one article from the only national newspaper that published their story. And then quickly forgot about them. Other accounts are from articles from a local newspaper in Heidi's hometown and their Facebook page supporting Eric. Based on factual stories, I took the liberty to imagine how conversations would have played out between the family members.

Parallel with Eric and Heidi's story is the ISIS woman's road to radicalism, journey to Syria, and her cunning fight to come back to the country she betrayed. The ISIS woman, Sumaira, and her child are a big focus of the story. I ridicule Sumaira, the government, Sumaira's defense attorney, and the politicians about the lies they told. I mock the child's alleged disease, but unfortunately, that's part of the story and how the Norwegian politicians and media deceived their people. I would never make fun of Cystic Fibrosis's horrible illness; however, I mock the lies they told about the child having it. And in no way would I want a child hurt in any way. I melt just as any snowflake when I see a hurting child. With that said, readers will learn politicians' priorities, and they are not always ethnic Norwegian children or Norway and its people.

Some may think I am too hard on the ISIS woman and should forgive and give people a chance. I am a forgiving person, but when I compare the treatment of ISIS women and innocent Norwegians like Heidi and her American son Eric, I have no sympathy for her. Or the other ISIS women who will most likely soon be brought back to the country they betrayed. With the help of the government, costing the tax payers millions.

I struggled back and forth if I should reveal the ISIS woman's full name. Mainstream media in Norway had taken the utmost measures to protect her, and they still do. She was only a stay-at-home mom and housewife for her three ISIS husbands, you see, so they take great care to protect her. That is the story the delusional media touts anyway. In the end, I decided to use her real name. It is now out in certain media outlets, and I ended up saying: Tough luck. I have a big heart, but that heart is now broken in a lot of places. I did not wish jihad on Norway or the United States, nor did I want a holy war. And neither did Eric and Heidi. The ISIS woman did. And she won in the end.

I base other characters and stories on newspaper accounts and other sources: Possibly ninety percent factual and heavily cited, and ten percent rants. Some may say it's the other way around. I ridicule many in *Sympathy for the Evil*. And I have fun doing it because it does not take much to amuse me. It is not personal, and I apologize, but not really. Nobody gets a pass; Norwegian politicians and the mainstream media, defense attorneys, journalists, leftists, the Norwegian bureaucracy, and immigration officials. Then Michael Moore gets reamed out, and Big Bad Tech, Jack Dorsey, Democrats, CNN, the *New York Times*, Antifa, Blitz, Norway's Green Party, radical Islam, and many others. Most of the time, it's sarcasm and irony, but there's always some truth behind it.

I have a weird sense of humor and an imaginary mind, so that my ill-timed humor may be amusing to a few and cringeworthy to most. I have gone through the manuscript a thousand times, rewritten, deleted, and added to it, and I came to a point where I just had to say enough. If I had waited any longer, I would have been in the afterlife in the halls of Valhalla drinking with the gods. Although that does not sound like a bad thing, the way this world is today.

I find the last chapter tedious, as I wouldn't say I like to write about myself. But I decided to include it anyway. I also went up against the stonewalling immigration authorities in Norway and it is therefore part of the story. I attempted to shorten it, but after thousands of hours working on the book, I started during the Covid-19 pandemic, I was over it and couldn't think any longer. My advice as a self-published writer and to those who wants to start a journey on their first book: Have a plan. Organize your sources and citations from the beginning. Do not wait until the book is complete unless you want to experience hell on earth trying to figure things out. When I started out writing being laid off work and quarantined, I had no idea I would complete an entire manuscript of almost 125,000 words. But as weeks of lockdown turned into months, that is what happened.

In Norway, Terrorists Are Harbored and Protected

*Sympathy for the Ev*il also uncovers how jihad is allowed to flourish on Norwegian soil; terrorists are harbored and protected; and radical Islam is gaining a stronghold in the small Nordic country, inhabited by a little of four million ethnic Norwegians. It exposes the inability and unwillingness of politicians and authorities to deal with it, the cover-up and lying by omission from the mainstream media, and the injustice a few native good Norwegians are facing when returning to their home country. It reveals incompetent leadership, ill-advised mass immigration on steroids, the vilifying and silencing of those on the right, kid-glove treatment of dangerous criminals, and a policy that puts Norway and Norwegians last.

You will learn a lot about ISIS and the terror it inflicted on the world. The genocide against the Yazidi people is covered and reveals a good reason never to forgive or forget anyone who joined the terror organization to fight a holy war. I also write about Hoda Muthana, an infamous ISIS woman from Alabama, and the twisted turn of events in her saga to come back to the United States. A turn of events suppressed by the media in the United States. Michael Moore gets nearly half a chapter. I am not sure if he still lives in his imaginary world about the Scandinavian utopia, but seeing his tweets lately, he is still the same old Michael Moore.

At the end of the Introduction, I must add that this is not a book to understand radical Islam. There are plenty of books out there that does just that. It is also not a book about good Muslims. It is a book about the radical ideology infiltrating Norway and, in this case, the extreme, which ranges from ISIS recruiters to Islam Net to radical teachings in the mosques. None of that belongs in peaceful and democratic Norway. What this book is essentially about is my *extreme* worries about my home country.

A Word About Translation and Hege Storhaug

Hege Storhaug is a Norwegian author and founder of the Human Rights Service. I mention Hege several times in the book and cite stories written by her and her talented writers at Human Rights Service. I ordered Ms. Storhaug's book *Den 11 Landeplage* last year. The English version is *Islam. Europe Invaded. America Warned.* I did not finish the book until recently since I was busy writing, imagining I would be a bestselling author like her. Since we are writing about comparable subjects concerning radical Islam in Norway, I found some similarities that I wanted to point out. She cites a speech made by Islam Net's founder Fahad Qureshi, similar to chapter four in *Sympathy for the Evil*. I have the utmost respect for Ms. Storhaug, and I do not want anyone to think I copied it from her book. I read her book after the fact, and although my account is based on a MEMRI video I found online, I wanted to point it out for clarification.

Most of the sources I used in *Sympathy for the Evil*, including newspapers, were written in Norwegian. I have translated them to the best of my ability, especially taking great care when quoting people. I ridicule the Norwegian mainstream media, but they are talented journalists, and their stories have been a tremendous help in writing *Sympathy for the Evil*. If they weren't so biased and brainwashed my people, they may have been some of the best journalists in the world.

I would consider myself lucky if somebody read *Sympathy for the Evil*. It is my first book, and I am not a professional writer. I am also not a scholar, expert on world affairs or politics, or social critic expert. I write what I think in plain language, and I mean what I write. I did not hire a proofreading company or an editor. Number one, I couldn't afford it. Number two, I did not want to reveal my identity. Number three, I would be distraught if they told me my book was the worst they ever read, and I would probably have taken a long walk on a short pier. I have gone over the manuscript so many times that I became blind to errors you may find. Nonetheless, I had fun writing it, and I have already started on my next book. I am uncovering the madness one book at a time.

I did, however, hire a company based in England to make a cover for the book: The Unique Book Cover. I sent them a photo of the flag and some ideas, and I could not be more pleased with the job they did.

I Have Second Thoughts

It's mid-September 2021, and *Sympathy for the Evil* is ready to be published on Amazon. In the past few weeks, I have at times had serious doubts if I should publish the book. First and foremost, *Sympathy for the Evil* is controversial in so many ways. It is a critical view of radical Islam and its infiltration into Norwegian society. Second, it is a highly unfavorable account of the government, politicians, and the media in Norway. A cardinal sin. And a challenging task for someone who loves their country and is brought up not to rock the boat. It paints a bleak picture of the future of once a peaceful and democratic country. All reasons I write under a penname.

If truth be told, I still have second thoughts, but after spending over a year and thousands of hours on the book, I have decided to take a leap of faith and publish it.

Thank you so much for reading *Sympathy for the Evil*.

CHAPTER 1
The American Boy Who Loved Norway

North Carolina, United States of America, 2015

There's utter silence on the other line. "Mamma, we're coming home. Mamma, are you there? Ingrid, mamma, can you hear me? We're coming home. Eric, Robert, and I are coming home." Heidi hears sobbing and someone trying to talk. And finally, she hears her mom's familiar voice, and Heidi knows she is crying tears of joy. The moment Ingrid had waited for since Heidi left Norway in 1982 has finally come. Her daughter is coming home! And she is bringing her two American sons with her. Ingrid's affectionate grandsons that she loves above all. And this time, it's not on a summer vacation. All three want to settle in Norway, in the same town Heidi grew up in and a stone's throw away from Ingrid.

"My dearest Heidi, this is the best day of my life," Ingrid says between sobs. "When did you find out? Did they say you can travel to Norway? Did they give you permission to stay here?"

"Yes, mamma, they called us from the Norwegian Consulate today and told us we could go to Norway and start our lives there. I can't believe it, but we're coming home. Soon, maybe even a few months from now. We have to sell the house and give our notice to work, and if all goes well, we may be in Norway by August."

"Heidi, I don't think I will sleep tonight. I have waited for this for years, and you know that. And now, a few months seem too long for you to get here. But I will wait for you and Eric and Robert. I will wait. Did you tell your brother yet?"

"No, I will call Leif next. I hope he's awake. I can't wait to tell him, and Eric and Robert can't wait to move to Norway. Eric especially. Remember, he wanted to move there ever since he was a little boy. When we used to come home on summer vacations, now his dream has come through. Our dream. He is beside himself."

"I know Heidi. I lived it. Remember when he came to visit one summer, and he insisted on bringing a bottle of air back to Amerika so his friends at school could smell the fresh Norwegian mountain air."

"I know, mamma. We all remember that. Who could forget? I only wish Brian was here and he was coming with us to Norway. We miss him so much."
"Me too, Heidi. I can't believe he is gone."

Heidi talks with her mother a little longer, and after hanging up the phone, she goes outside on the front porch at her home on the outskirts of a North Carolina city. She recalls the days' event and what is ahead for her and her two sons Eric and Robert. It is March and still cold out, but she loves to feel the cool breeze caress her face. It reminds her of her homeland. She is excited and sad at the same time. Excited that she is moving back home and sad that Brian is gone. And she is sorry her life in the United States is over. A life Heidi has loved even though the longing for her home country was always there. A life she built with a good husband in a loving marriage that gave them two amazing sons she would do anything for.

She's had the best of both worlds, she thinks. Two American-born sons, half American and half Norwegian, that are now willing to take a big chance with her, giving up everything they have built together in the United States and moving to Norway. But she knows they do not feel forced to follow her. They feel a connection to Norway, perhaps as strong as her, and have no worries about starting a new life in the land of the midnight sun.

The more she thinks of what lies ahead, the more excited she gets. And to be able to give this tremendous gift to her mom in her twilight years is worth all the worries. Her precious mom, now nearing her nineties, spending her days in a nursing home. And she wants nothing more at the end of her life to get her daughter and two grandsons back.

Heidi's thoughts wander back to 1982. The day she sat on a Scandinavian Airlines plane en route from Norway towards the enchanted land she had grown up watching on NRK, the Norwegian Broadcasting Corporation, and the only television channel at the time. She was finally visiting the country that had brought the music she loved to listen to when she grew up, and the movies were showing a life a young Norwegian girl could only dream of. The captivating nation she was now going to spend one year as an au pair. And being a young woman, only twenty years old, she had no idea what was in store for her sitting on that plane.

When she first met Brian, she did not know he would sweep her off her feet and that she would marry him and spend the next thirty-three years in the United States, thousands of miles away from her home country. But she did not regret a minute of it. And she and Brian had two sons that they would give the world to. Robert was born in 1983, and nine years later, Eric came into this world. She thought of her younger son Eric, that had always been so fascinated by Norway. They would go on vacations to visit her family in Møre and Romsdal; grandparents, uncles, aunts, and many cousins. Ever since he was a little boy, Eric wanted to live in Norway and would tell her time and time again he would move there when he grew up. He wanted all of them to move there. Together. His father, brother Robert, and his mother. She remembered how crushed he would be if she went on her own when he had to go to school and could not come with her.

Their whole life fell apart in 2013 when Brian unexpectedly died. She does not know how she could have gone through her grief without her sons, and now the three of them are closer than ever. She remembers the first conversation they had about moving to Norway a year after Brian had died. They just threw it out there. Like, 'what if we did?' Later, that conversation turned into serious discussions, and before she knew it, they decided to make it a reality. They had no family left in the United States, and after losing Brian, she would want nothing more than to move back to be close to her family and her mom, as long as Robert and Eric would come with her.

She thinks of the conversation she had with the consular officer from the Norwegian Consulate earlier in the day. The bureaucrat brought great news. She had sent their applications for residence permits to the Norwegian Directorate of Immigration, UDI. And they can move to Norway, awaiting approval. She went over all necessary administrative processes they had to go through to establish residency in Norway and wished them luck. She was okay, just wired to be bureaucratic. It came with the job. Heidi already knew the deal. They were informed when they all visited the Consulate together a few months back. Go to Norway, bring all necessary papers, get a job and they are all good to go. She worried a lot about the move but wasn't too concerned about making it work. She, Eric, and Robert had impeccable work records, no arrest record, and a strong will to make a life in the country they all loved, not wanting to be a burden on anyone. And she was Norwegian, after all. There should be no problems, except for having to go through mountains of paperwork.

Before starting the application process for residency, she had found out that she no longer had Norwegian citizenship. When she became an American citizen in 1991, a year before Eric was born, she did not know that she would lose the right to her Norwegian nationality. The United States allows dual citizenship, and she assumed Norway did too. Heidi never contacted Norwegian immigration authorities and had kept her Norwegian passport until Folkeregisteret; the Norwegian Population Register swiftly removed her name in 2014. She had started the application process to move to Norway and was then removed from the register as if she never existed. Although the registration in Norway did not occur until 2014, 23 years after she got her U.S. citizenship, the decision had a retroactive effect.

After getting over the initial shock of no longer being a citizen of Norway and losing all her rights to live in her home country, she reluctantly accepted that she would have to apply for residency like any foreigner would. But these were only formalities and a hurdle she and her sons would have to go through, and it would be all worth it in the end.

It was March 2015, and her journey back to Norway had just begun.

No Special Connection to Norway

It is August 2015, and Heidi, Robert, and Eric have arrived in Heidi's hometown, a small village in Møre and Romsdal, on the western coast of Norway. The district is the most northerly of the famous west coast fjords, and the scenery is second to none. The region boasts deep fjords, alpine mountains, gentle valleys, countless green islands, vast forest, the wild Atlantic coast, impressive mountain roads, numerous lakes, barren mountain plateaus, charming mountain farms, and the highest waterfalls in Norway.[1] It was undeniably paradise for Eric and Robert, who both loved the outdoors and fishing.

Three long years are behind them, and they are finally back in Heidi's home country and eager to start a new life in a new land. Eric, who had always longed to live in Norway, was finally in his right element and looked forward to settling in the country where his mother was born. He was on fire, she later recalled. As soon as the Consulate gave them the green light to make a move, they sold their house and belongings not needed in Norway, and all three left their jobs and their life in the USA behind.

Heidi was exhausted but relieved they had made it this far. Her mom was in seventh heaven now that her daughter was finally home, and Heidi had applied for a job at the nursing home where her 90-year-old mother lived. They had followed all advice given to them by the Consulate, and now the wait began for residence permits arriving in the mail. All three had checked in with the police station, which is required when you arrive in Norway as an "immigrant." They had opened bank accounts and received tax identification cards, and they were all looking for jobs. She hoped the application process wouldn't take too long so that they could get peace of mind. Dealing with immigration authorities was, at times, nerve-wracking. But she had faith in the Norwegian system, even the Directorate of Immigration, and she knew it would work out in the end.

Møre and Romsdal, Norway, September 2016

"Mom, you need to see this. I can't believe it." Heidi hears Eric approaching the house. He had gone down to the mailbox, something he had done every day for weeks. He wanted to be the first to open letters from UDI, as they were still waiting for their residence permit, more than a year after they arrived in Norway. "What's the matter, honey." Eric storms into the living room, tears welling from his eyes, holding a white envelope and a letter in his hand. "Mom, they rejected me. UDI rejected my application.

They don't want me here. They're kicking me out of the country." "Honey, you must have read it wrong. They can't do that to you. They can't do that to us," says Heidi, but she has a sinking feeling in her stomach.

Eric hands Heidi the letter, and she reads it with shock and tears in her eyes. She was overcome with a gnawing fear the last couple of months. Why was UDI taking so long? Their application should only be a formality and should not take almost two years to complete. The waiting was almost unbearable, and now her fears were confirmed. UDI had finally decided, and the authorities had rejected Eric's family immigration and residence permit application. She can barely believe the cold-hearted news explaining the rejection, delivered in a language only a callous bureaucrat can manage:

> A foreigner who was born to parents, at least one of whom was a Norwegian citizen at the time of the applicant's birth, is entitled to a residence permit.

With that said, UDI concludes the following:

> The applicant has no special connection to Norway, nor are there strong human considerations within the understanding of the Immigration Act, which would speak in favor of making an exception to the general conditions for a residence permit.

Furthermore, the UDI writes that they have taken into account that the applicant has already resided in the country for one year, and that the Norwegian-born mother has previously had Norwegian citizenship and that Eric has relatives in Norway, but still conclude:

> However, this does not in itself correspond to a special connection to Norway in the sense of the Immigration Act.

The final decision from UDI is that Eric must leave Norway and return to the United States.

Heidi has to sit down. She looks at Eric, who is beyond distraught, and she feels her entire world is falling apart. How can they be so heartless? How can the bureaucrats at UDI punish her and her family for a seemingly innocent decision made years ago when they could approve Eric with the stroke of a pen? How can they deny Eric a stay when she and Robert were approved?

She knew they could make exceptions to the rules. She had read about it in the Norwegian media many times. When the press blew up an immigrant story loud enough, politicians would act. Why were they punishing her, a Norwegian? And that the only reason they denied Eric a family reunification because she was an American citizen at the time of his birth was too hard to comprehend. There had to be something they could do.

"I'm calling Leif. He can help us. We'll fix this, Eric. There is no way they can deport you from Norway." She tried to console Eric as only a mother can do, but deep inside, she had a nagging feeling this was only the beginning of a long struggle. And she had no idea how it would end.

CHAPTER 2
You've Made Your ISIS Husband's Bed, Now Lie in It

Oslo District Court, Room 250, March 2, 2021

> He did not say much about it before he went down to Syria. But eventually, we talked a lot on the phone. He told what he was doing, that it was warfare. And that they were bombing the roads. I did not react negatively to it because I was so in love. And what he stood for was things I stood for myself. At the time, I had a pretty radical mindset around this violent jihad. I was quite positive about it. I just laughed and giggled when he spoke.[1]

Thirty-year-old Sumaira Ghafoor speaks those heinous words in Oslo District Court on a cold winter day in Norway. The radical Muslim, who many Norwegians only had seen in the media covered in a black niqab, showing her eyes only, was now wearing Western clothes. Dressed in beige trousers, a matching jacket, and a white blouse, her dark hair is layered and shoulder-length. And instead of a veil covering her face, she is wearing a beige scarf around her neck. Before the trial, she had appeared nervous and looked down at the floor, walking from the press area until she entered room 250 in Oslo District Court. When taking the witness stand after the prosecutor's introductory speech, she answered question after question, revealing shocking information never before heard in a Norwegian court of law. It was apparent to many watching the court drama that day that the woman went to Syria on her own accord.

And knowing that the Norwegian government spent millions of taxpayer monies bringing the ISIS woman back to Norway, misleading the Norwegians on a falsehood that her child was sick made her statements even more outrageous. Adding to the courtroom spectacle was Sumaira's defense attorney Nils Christian Nordhus, for some reason sporting what could only be described as a Muhammad beard, speaking her case. And one would wonder what his audacious mind was thinking. Did he believe the words coming out of his mouth, one sentence more desperate than the next? "We are trying to capture the forced situation she has been in. She is a victim of human trafficking; it must lead to acquittal."[2]

The trial of the ISIS woman, never before seen in Norway and watched closely by many, was a bone of contention in many corners of this Nordic land. The opinion among Norwegians if the ISIS woman should be allowed back in Norway resembled that of the United States 2020 presidential election. There is no middle ground. You are either on one side of the fence or the other.

The defendant, who had pleaded not guilty, was the first woman to stand trial in Norway, accused of actively joining a terrorist organization. And the first traitor to be actively brought back by the government to the land she deceived. And, knowing Norway, she won't be the last. The once enchanted land in Northern Europe that had taken her in so generously and with open arms twenty-six years ago. The prosecutor reads the basis for indictment:

> The Public Prosecutor's Office with this place an indictment against 'unnamed person' in Oslo District Court for having participated in a terrorist organization that took steps to achieve its purpose by unlawful means, under section 147 (d) of the Penal Code 1902 for the period until September 30, 2015. And under section 136 (a) for the period from October 1, 2015; for having participated in a terrorist organization that took steps to achieve its purpose by unlawful means.[3]

Prosecutor Geir Evanger, a stout man with a shaved head and a nicely trimmed beard and mustache, continues his statement and the basis for indictment. Known for wearing red suspenders in court, perhaps now hidden under the black robe he wears. Part of the work attire during court hearings in Norway, required by the Courts of Justice Act:

> From 2013 until March 2019, she participated in the terrorist organization ISIL in Syria. After traveling from Norway to Syria in the winter of 2013, she moved in with her husband Bastian Vasquez, with whom she later had a child. Vasquez was affiliated with and had sworn allegiance to ISIL, and he participated in armed missions for the organization. By taking care of their children and taking care of various tasks at home, she created the conditions for Vasquez to take an active part in the fighting for ISIL.
> During her marriage to Vasquez, she also spoke positively about ISIL and life in Syria to women in Norway intending to marry foreign fighters in the organization. After Vasquez died in connection with the production of bombs for ISIL in 2015, she received financial support from the organization before she married in late autumn 2015 and had children with an 'unnamed person,' also affiliated with ISIL. The second husband

> participated actively in armed missions for the organization and was also a Sharia judge in ISIL. By taking care of their children and taking care of various home tasks, she facilitated that her second husband participated actively in combat action for ISIL. After the second husband died in battle for ISIL in March 2017, she married an 'unnamed person' affiliated with ISIL and a friend of her second husband. Until she was taken out by Kurdish forces and brought to the al-Hol camp, she stayed in ISIL-controlled areas with people affiliated with the organization.[4]

"I ask the defendant if you admit guilt after the indictment?" The defendant answered no. "Then you can sit down, and you will have the opportunity to explain yourself later today."[5]

Sumaira, accused of participating in the al-Nusra Front and ISIS terror organizations, came to Norway from Pakistan with her family when she was four years old. She grew up on the east side of Oslo, surrounded by a large family; her mother, father, and many brothers and sisters. Higher education was important to her father and instilled in his children. The parents are Muslims, and although they are not strict followers of the religion, allegedly, her father insisted on abiding by the tradition of an arranged marriage. Her parents had chosen a cousin in Pakistan with whom she was to marry. Sumaira told the court that the love for foreign fighter Bastian Vasquez made her travel to Syria. Her journey to the war-torn country started in the autumn of 2010 when she studied computer technology at Oslo University College, now called Oslo Met. The Norwegian Broadcasting Corporation, NRK, writes that she seemed well integrated into Norwegian society.[6]

As relentless social justice activists, the state-owned taxpayer-funded propaganda media house has in dozens of articles portrayed her as just a regular young Norwegian woman doing what everyday young Norwegian women do. Never questioning her motive for joining ISIS or put her in a negative light, rather a victim of her circumstances, than a jihad woman who chose her destiny.

She did group assignments at school listing her interest in Photoshop, shopping, and portrait photography. They are delighted to tell you she played actively in soccer and is a Manchester United fan. And the parents could not make themselves clean out things from her girls' room after leaving for Syria. The red Manchester United pillow is still in her bed.[7] Those are usually sentiments heard in media from grieving parents talking about losing a child to murder or kidnappings. Or the parents of Louisa Jespersen from Denmark and Maren Ueland from Norway. Two young, beautiful, Scandinavian women full of life, beheaded by ISIS sympathizers in the High Atlas Mountains in Morocco in 2018. The same year the woman on the stand in Oslo District Court still supported ISIS. Yet, NRK will go to great lengths humanizing even the most vicious criminals, as long as it fits their narrative. And they tell us, almost like an afterthought, that Sumaira and her fellow students gather several times in the school's prayer room. Suddenly the most normal thing in the world, unheard of when I grew up in Evangelical Lutheran, Norway. A mostly homogeneous and peaceful country at the time with a little over four million people.

In the summer of 2011, one year after starting college, she joined the organization Islam Net, and she tells the court of the controversial group based in Oslo: "I was told that I had to wear a hijab. I said I would rather not, just because I was told. I learned a lot about how to behave within that direction of Islam." Growing up in a family not practicing Islam, she slowly began gaining interest in the religion when joining Islam Net. At times she would not go home because her parents, whom she calls liberal when it came to faith, were critical of her wearing an *abaya* with her *hijab* and *niqab*.[8]

The abaya is a long robe or cloak covering a woman's body. Not to be confused with the robe some of us women are known to wear, lounging around in the mornings, to the despair of many husbands worldwide. There have even been sightings of women at mailboxes wearing the robe, but they may be urban legends. The hijab is the headscarf, and the niqab is a veil covering the face apart from the eyes. These oppressive garments are often seen in Norway's streets, as Islam is taking a stronghold. Despite being a country that consistently ranks at the top among the world countries for gender equality, caring about human rights, and best countries for women to live.

There were battles at home when her parents caught her wearing the repressive outfits, and it was during this period, she lost many friends and flunked in several subjects at school. She ended up in a conflict with Islam Net and cut off contact. Sumaira said she met Bastian Vasquez on Facebook in 2012 when she wanted to break from Islam Net:

> My parents wanted me to focus more on school, and they could not understand why I took a lower-paying job. When I get pressure from people, I leave. I didn't have so many friends anymore because I had started wearing the hijab. I only had the girls from Islam Net around me, and when I lost that, I got to know the girls from the Prophet Ummah and Bastian.[9]

After joining the radical Salafi-jihadist group Prophet Ummah, Sumaira immediately experienced a difference between what she learned from Islam Net and the Prophet Ummah:

> At Islam Net, you learned that you have an internal war with yourself and to take care of yourself. The Prophet Ummah stands more for physical warfare. At the time, I had a pretty radical mindset around the idea of a holy war. I was pretty optimistic about it. I would contact many

well-known Islamists on Facebook. They were called something else, though, on social media. [10]

Sumaira admits she had an affair with Ubaydullah Hussain, another pillar of the Norwegian society and the leader of the Prophet Ummah. A month and a half after meeting, Bastian Vasquez proposed to Sumaira, and she finally introduced him to her parents. Her father immediately took a dislike to Vasquez and did not give him his marriage blessing. In October 2012, not long after the failed meeting with Sumaira's parents, Vasquez traveled to Syria:

> He did not say much about it before he went down. But eventually, we talked a lot on the phone. He told what he was doing that it was warfare, and they were bombing the roads. I did not react negatively to it because I was so in love that what he stood for was things I stood for myself. I just laughed and giggled when he spoke.[11]

Defying her father, Sumaira and Bastian married via video link WhatsApp. By then, they had already started talking about her joining him in Syria. Sumaira had told Bastian about her other plans, or rather her father's plans, and that she did not want to marry a cousin from Pakistan, as the family wanted. "I had plans to move to Egypt, but when he said I should come to him instead, I chose to go to him. I missed him so much, so I wanted to be with him and take care of him."[12]

Vasquez had told her he was going to Syria to fight against the Assad regime. Supposedly, she did not know what the Al-Nusra Front was *really* doing. "I learned it eventually, but not in detail. There was not much in the media at that time. So, a lot of what I learned was what he told me. Then it was a lot based on what he explained." Sumaira was happy that Vasquez wanted her to move to Syria. He had promised her that they would live in a large villa with a swimming pool:

> If I had not met him, I would not have gone anywhere. Vasquez broke many religious rules while in Norway, and I thought he would respect my choices. I'm not sure if I thought about the consequences. I had a slight idea but did not know it would turn out this way. It's not easy to explain now because I do not know what I was thinking. Now, it is incomprehensible to me how I thought back then.[13]

Sumaira didn't think she would be one of several wives, and she was never beaten or yelled at during her childhood. What one has to do with the other is unknown. She expected to have regular contact with those at home, even though she disobeyed their wishes and left without telling anyone in the family. She collected between 40,000 and 60,000 kroner for airline tickets and other expenses and bought clothes for her and Vasquez before leaving for

Syria. Sumaira admitted to being radicalized and did not reflect on Vasquez participating in warfare:

> I was pretty radical at the time and did not think clearly. Seeing how we met and became acquainted; I did not believe that what I was doing was dangerous. I wanted to help the civilian population. But when I came down to Syria, it became clear this was not how I imagined. He had said he killed generals and set off roadside bombs but had I not been so in love, I would not have gone down, even if I had the radical mindset. It's not something I stand for today. Of course, I am responsible for that, but I do not understand why I made those choices.[14]

In February 2013, five months after Vasquez had left Norway, Sumaira arrived in Syria. Vasquez had joined the jihadist militia group al-Nusra Front, also known as Jabhat al-Nusra. It did not take long before he said to put on her niqab, and Vasquez would not let her wear any green clothes. Bastian started buying black cloaks for her:

> When we entered the house, the first thing he told me was that I should start cooking. I was a little shocked. I had said on the phone that I could not cook. I thought he would respect that it would not be the perfect food, but I was often told that I was not good in the kitchen. Everyone ate, and he went out. I washed clothes and cleaned the house. If he was in combat, he placed me with the Syrian family we borrowed the house from. If he went out during the day, it was to plant roadside bombs. I was not allowed to go out by myself. Most of the time, I was inside the house, without anyone to talk to.[15]

Sumaira says the first time she wanted to go home was in May 2013. It was after the first time Vasquez had been violent towards her:

> Through many things with Bastian, I realized I was in the wrong place. I wanted to go home, but he refused to support my choice. He took my mobile phone and removed a SIM card. I couldn't communicate with the outside world. Until then, I had had occasional contact with the family. I could not speak freely for fear of punishment from my husband.[16]

Prosecutor Evanger asks Sumaira what triggered her decision to return to Norway and her family. And to the surprise of nobody, it wasn't that her husband planted roadside bombs and blew people to smithereens. It was all about her. She tells of several episodes of violence where Vasquez beat her, kicked her, and locked her inside. "It was because he was not how I had perceived him. He was a completely different person."[17]

The prosecutor asks Sumaira what happened when Vasquez left Jabhat al-Nusra to join an even more extreme terrorist group, ISIS, the Islamic State of Iraq, and Syria. "A while after joining, he told me himself. I knew little about ISIS at the time because I did not have access to the internet. I only got to know things if he told me something, but he eventually stopped talking about what he was doing."[17] NRK spoke to Prosecutor Evanger after Sumaira's testimony:

> We believe that she knew what she was going for and went into it with open eyes. Once she went down to Syria and actively contributes, there is no decisive legal factor indicating that we cannot convict participation. We think that she knew pretty well that her room for maneuver would be limited and that there would be less contact with others.
> But the fact that Bastian Vasquez would eventually become violent would have been problematic for her to predict. We believe that she had extreme thoughts before she left and thought violent jihad was okay. She says so herself. We had intercepted conversations between her and Bastian Vasquez before leaving, which supports this. The mothers were invaluable supporters. Children needed to be born for recruitment to ensure the next generation of ISIS recruits when someone dropped out. It is the tasks at home and the role as a mother that assume criminal responsibility.[18]

In interrogations before the trial, Sumaira explained that taking care of Vasquez meant being involved in a holy war. Prosecutor Evanger asked her on the stand if she felt she was waging a holy war. "Only because I was his wife down there. Since I was married to him, it sounded right to be present with him and take care of him." Attorney Nordhus believes that the woman is a victim of terrorism.[19] Proving the old Russian proverb, "God wanted to punish mankind, so he created lawyers." "We believe that giving birth to a child can never be a criminal offense. We think that what she has done is to take the children from the terrorist regime down there. She did not want them to be there, and she succeeded in the end." The defense attorney stressed that she went to Syria to avoid being married to a cousin from Pakistan. He also points out that the woman became active in Islam Net through Oslo University College:

> She has made clear that Islam Net did not send her to Syria. But through them, she comes in contact with the Prophet's Ummah and later Bastian Vasquez. She is clear that the situation is complex, and she takes responsibility. But she would not have left if it were not for getting away from stress and pressure. She knew she would live with Vasquez and that he was with Jabhat al-Nusra. Their fight against Assad was considered by many to be legitimate. But what is also clear is that her stay in Syria will be something entirely different than she had imagined. And we should not punish those forced to remain.[20]

Orphanages and Arms Purchases

> I don't know if you have changed your mind? says the man. I have not changed my mind. Then you are crazy. If you do, I do it, the woman answers.

The cellphone conversation, intercepted by the Norwegian Police Security Service, PST, was static, but the words were legible and the tone cheerful and flirty. Sumaira tells Bastian Vasquez that her father nags her to marry a cousin in Pakistan. She has told him no several times, and she is thinking about *hijra*.[21] What Sumaira was thinking about, *hijra* or *hegira*, was to depart or migrate. Hijra is often referred to the journey of the Islamic Prophet Muhammed and his followers from Mecca to Medina in the year 622.[22]

A few days after the trial had started, NRK released intercepted phone conversations from the Norwegian Police Security Service between Sumaira Ghafoor and Sebastian Vasquez. To downplay the seriousness of the discussions, NRK chose the headline: "Woman accused of terrorism in intercepted conversations: Talked about orphanages and arms purchases." In the first conversations with foreign fighter Bastian Vasquez, the accused ISIS woman said she wanted to start an orphanage in Syria, writes NRK. Eventually, she expressed that she also wanted weapon and weapons training.[23] Understandably, since recent studies have shown that the way kids behave today, weapons and weapons training are necessary when running an orphanage.

In August 2012, the Norwegian Police Security Service started the first investigation against people who had traveled to Syria to join rebel groups. In connection with the foreign war investigation, PST intercepted several Norwegian and Syrian telephone numbers. Sooner or later, Bastian Vasquez also appeared in the conversations. Through these, they discovered that Vasquez had many and lengthy discussions with a Norwegian-speaking woman. That woman is 30-year-old Sumaira Ghafoor, who is now on trial in Oslo District Court. Vasquez had already ended up on the police radar after posting a video in January 2012 in which he threatened the Norwegian royal family, the prime minister, and Norwegian soldiers. Minor stuff. The police issued an indictment, but Vasquez never appeared in court. In October 2012, Vasquez traveled to Syria to join the Nusra Front, a branch of al-Qaeda that fought against Bashar al-Assad's government forces.[24] How he was able to leave the country while being under an indictment is not known.

Prosecutor Geir Evanger believes the woman's knowledge of what she went to is crucial and says the intercepted conversations are significant evidence. "It sheds light on what kind of dialogue and contact the accused and Bastian Vasquez had before she left, and what she knew about what she went to." The woman's fervent defender, Nils Christian Nordhus, has a different opinion and disagrees that the conversations are punishable: "We think that these conversations are entirely in line with what our client has explained all along. The court will decide whether she eventually, during her stay in Syria, ended up in a situation where she is exploited and forced to continue living."[25]

Vasquez promises her that she will get a house and a garden if she comes to Syria. Sumaira thinks she can start an orphanage when she comes down. "There are many children who do not have parents and stuff down there. Then we can start up an orphanage or something like that for them." They then discuss how much money she should take with her. Sumaira says she has about 16,000 kroner but hopes to save up about 25,000 kroner before she travels. Vasquez thinks you can bring up to 50,000 kroner to Turkey. Sumaira tells him they are trying to find a sister for a brother but finds it difficult to find someone for hijra. "It is not very easy, but I have found a sister who will possibly go along as well." The prosecution believes Sumaira tried to get women to marry Norwegian foreign fighters in Syria. Prosecutor Geir Evanger asked the accused woman in court what she meant. She said she is unsure today but thinks it was a Somali man who wanted to get married.[26]

> I've bought a *sykt sykt våpen*, a sick, sick weapon.
> Are you kidding? Have you used it?
> Pow, pow, pow, ha-ha! AK-47, best you can find on the market. There are still Russian letters on it. Everything is just nonsense, I swear. Collect lots of money and come here, we start a new life with family, children, everything you want. As soon as I have a 'scholar,' I'll show up. As soon as I have someone who can marry us, I'll call you right away. Then I put you on speaker.[27]

Sumaira tells Vasquez she needs a few more months to save money for the orphanage, writes NRK.[28] They seem very hung up on Sumaira's orphanage plan, a noble idea for the jihadists. Join ISIS, slaughter Yazidi's men and older women, keep the younger women as sex slaves for years. And to atone for their sins, but only temporarily, open an orphanage for the Yazidi children until they are big enough to be kept as sex slaves. It sounds farfetched, but not when discovering what ISIS did to the Yazidi people.

Sumaira and Bastian Vasquez next conversation is December 7, 2012:

> A boss with a big vest with lots of magazines, bomb belts, a giant beard, bodyguards, and a Finlandshette called people to jihad. It was completely sick. Everyone was there, and he made everyone laugh. That was the highlight of my day, man.[29]

Bastian Vasquez knew his Norwegian language. *Finlandshette*, or Finnish hood, is what they call a balaclava in Norway. During the Crimean War of 1854, handmade balaclavas were sent to British troops to keep them warm. Balaclava is a town near Sevastopol in Crimea. Finlandshette was born when someone in Norway knitted and sent such hats to Finnish soldiers during the

Winter War in 1939-1940. In 1999 Finland's ambassador to Norway urged the Norwegian Language Council to stop using the word since the hood is often associated with criminals and political activists who want to hide their identity. "Stop using the word 'Finlandshette.' It is burdensome for us Finns," he said.[30] An early example of political correctness in Scandinavia. It is not known if the Norwegians heeded the Finnish ambassador's plea. Probably not.

In one cellphone conversation intercepted by PST, Sumaira asks if she can also get a weapon. Knowing a happy wife makes a happy life, Vasquez asks her what kind of weapon she wants:

> We will find out when I'm there.
> No problem, I would at least give you a grenade or something in case something should happen. But it's extremely unlikely.
> I will learn to use it.
> And if the city is raided, if someone comes and rapes you or something, you just open the grenade, right? It's better than being raped and tortured.[31]

When asked directly by defense attorney Nils Christian Nordhus, Sumaira says that she never received a weapon when she came to Syria:

> I was so in love that I did not question what he said. I should have done that because what he said did not correspond at all with reality. I sound very naive. I also said I could not stand getting yelled at, but he didn't give a damn. He said we should have a nice house and stuff, but it was just a gray factory house when I got there.[32]

Sumaira also claims she never received information that Vasquez and the al-Nusra Front fought against anyone other than the Assad regime before she left.[33]

It's Not Like Norway

> You have to bring your black niqab. There are only black niqabs here. You will shock people if you bring that 'green thing.' You can't wander out. What are you going to do out in the city? It's not like Norway. You'll probably have to go to a building with a separate entrance when you get here. Wallah, I swear, it's so incredibly beautiful here. Words cannot describe it.[33]

Bastian is determined that Sumaira cannot bring anything but a black niqab. In the same conversation, Vasquez also talks about fighting in a Syrian city. NRK writes that it is not clear how Sumaira responded to what he said, which is odd, but not really. They have access to the intercepted conversations. She had to have responded to the atrocities Vasquez is talking about, whether positive or negative. Being highly suspicious of NRKs reporting, I think they are leaving it out on purpose. It wouldn't look suitable for their campaign to bring the ISIS woman back. As Billy Joel sang, "I may be wrong for all I know, but I may be right." Vazquez tells her in Norwegian:

> Vi omringet dem og slakta dem. Generalen sa han skulle ta alle kvinnelige muslimer som slaver. Vi kutta av huet hans.
> We surrounded them and slaughtered them. The general said he would take all female Muslims as slaves. We cut his head off.[34]

If my jihad boyfriend had told me that, I would have hit the road faster than a Wuhan bat out of hell.

The conversation continues between the lovebirds, and Vasquez tells Sumaira he will take her out into the woods to teach her how to use the AK47 and a grenade. She responds by laughing, according to NRK, and they write that Vasquez also laughs at her plans to start an orphanage. NRK seems genuinely disappointed she never got the chance to open up the orphanage. Sumaira wonders why he is laughing. "Because it's sick to think about. It's a good idea, but I do not know how we start. Like, what do I say to my leaders?" Sumaira helps Vasquez set up a fake Facebook profile with an al-Nusra flag as a profile picture. Next time, if Facebook allow me back on, I will use an ISIS flag as my profile picture, to avoid getting locked out. They end the conversation but talk the next day again. Vasquez describes in detail how he has helped bury dead fellow soldiers. "The bodies were absolutely beautiful; it was as if they were sleeping."[35]

On December 12, Vasquez tells Sumaira they have made significant progress in the battles against Assad. He doesn't think it's safe with a pregnant wife if NATO enters Syria. In the following conversation, which is also from December, Sumaira tells Vasquez that the USA has terrorist listed al-Nusra Front. Says the one who knew nothing about the terror organization before she left. And neither does Vasquez, the man who decapitates people's heads off and plants roadside bombs. He tells Sumaira he didn't know and asks Sumaira to find out more about the terror list designation. Sumaira calls him later and tells him it is because the al-Nusra Front is part of al-Qaeda. Vasquez responds with a laugh. "Like, it's the same as has been in the media before," says Sumaira.[36]

Postcards From Hell

The Police Security Service also has documentation that the woman bought clothes and equipment for Bastian Vasquez at XXL at Sandvika shopping center shortly before she went to Syria. Sandvika is 15 kilometers west of Oslo, in the municipality of Bærum. Around the same time, Sumaira also made a cash withdrawal of more than 10,000 kroner from Stovner center, located in the borough of Stovner, to the far northeast Oslo. Sumaira told the court, she sold assets and took out several credit loans to raise money for the trip to Syria. Because that's what victims of human trafficking and terrorism frequently do. At this point, she was under surveillance by PST. They were thus aware that Sumaira had plans to travel to Syria. The reason for the investigation was information that Vasquez was supposedly in Norway. Now, they believe the tip was wrong, and Vasquez was in Syria at the time. The following bank withdrawal Sumaira made is from Reyhanli, a town in Turkey. PST believes she left Norway on February 7, 2013.[37]

The Police Security Service also presented evidence in the court of conversations Vasquez had with a friend. On February 27, 2013, Vasquez calls the comrade in Norway and talks about life in Syria. He tells him how he helped taking over the airport in Idlib with tanks, planes, and helicopters. He boasts about being in ten big battles:

> Did you kill, or what? Har du drept, eller?
> Yes, you can safely say that, Vasquez answers and laughs.[38]

In the conversation, Vasquez also brags that he has captured tortured supporters of the president of Syria, Bashar al-Assad. He then says that he has married a woman from Europe without revealing her name. No word on the elaborate wedding on WhatsApp. On March 2, 2013, PST intercepted a call where Sumaira calls from Syria to Norway. At the other end is the oldest sister from Bærum, known from the bestselling Norwegian author Åsne Seierstad's book *Two sisters*. At first, I understood her to be Sumaira's older sister, but as I learn something new every day, I later discovered that Muslims frequently use sisters and brothers when referring to one another. The sisters, Leila and Ayan, of Somalian descent, in Seierstad's book, is a true story of their journey to the Islamic State and the father who tried to bring them home. The prosecution believes Sumaira encouraged Leila and Ayan to travel to Syria.[39] Leila and Ayan left Norway in October 2013, leaving their family devastated. As of May 2021, they have not returned and are under investigation and wanted by the Norwegian Police Security Service.

"It is decided now, we will come to you," says the big sister, who is Ayan. In the conversation, Sumaira tells Ayan she has been in contact with her father, and he was afraid that someone had kidnapped her. "Mom would like me to come back, but I do not think I will be allowed to come back here (to Syria), you understand?"[40] Sumaira denies that she contacted the sisters from Bærum to help them find the best way into Syria. She claims that Ayan had already decided to travel to Syria or Somalia:

> My journey had nothing to do with her. It was at the very beginning. I had not seen the reality and did not know what happened. It wasn't

until April when I found out that Bastian did not mind fighting against other groups.⁴¹

The prosecutors also presented Skype conversations where Ayan talks to a foreign warrior, a friend of Bastian Vasquez. In the discussion, the foreign warrior asks her if she can speak to Chile's wife. Shortly after, Ayan arrives in Syria.⁴² Chile is presumably Bastian Vasquez since his parents are Chilean. In later conversations, Sumaira talks positively about life in Syria to another friend in Norway:

What is it like to be there? *Kjempedeilig. Kjempedeilig.* It's awesome. It's awesome.
Isn't it dangerous? Last night, three bombs exploded right next to us. A rock hit my head. I was not afraid. What can I say? It was great fun.⁴³

Sumaira tells her friend she does not miss her family and that it's almost the same as living in Norway. Testifying in court during Sumaira's trial, the friend, suffering from amnesia, did not remember much of the conversation. She did, however, admit that her group of girlfriends considered many foreign fighters to be attractive husbands. So was Ted Bundy. Sumaira testified that she believed her friend wanted to travel to Syria, but they were not that close and did not have a lot of contact. The friend reportedly never traveled to Syria to join in the holy war.⁴⁴

The Police Security Service did not start an investigation against Sumaira until the autumn of 2018. Even though they already in 2012 revealed through surveillance that the Sumaira was in Syria. A former head of PST investigation explained in court that they did not have the capacity, and there were numerous challenges. In 2018, PST received funding from other police districts. It depended on the number of people who traveled to Syria from Norway and the investigative capacity. When asked by defense attorney Nordhus, he acknowledges that it would have been easier to obtain information about the case if PST had initiated an investigation earlier.⁴⁵

Hindsight is twenty-twenty, but in favor of law enforcement, especially those men and women in the streets keeping us safe, the challenges PST faced, I believe, were imported problems. Problems our peaceful country never had to deal with and was never prepared for. Ill-advised and uncontrolled mass immigration promoted by social justice warrior politicians. Islamic extremism and jihad had gone unchecked or not adequately dealt with for a long time and still are, as you will learn in later chapters. It is ultimately the people running the Kingdom of Norway responsible for its demise, and with great help from the mainstream propaganda media funded by the very government it protects.

Before leaving for Syria, the accused woman posted several posts on social media with jihadist content, writes NRK. It was, I imagine before

Mark Zuckerberg started controlling and censoring those not in line with Facebook's ideology. During the trial, Sumaira was asked about Facebook accounts that the prosecution believes she used to post before the demonstration in 2012. The protest in question was most likely against Norwegian forces in Afghanistan, covered in a later chapter. One account had the username *Umm Ar-Rabee*, who posted several messages with radical content. In one of the posts, she publishes a picture with the caption "Khalifah is coming."[46] Undoubtedly as in a global Caliphate. A government under a caliph, a spiritual leader of Islam who claims succession from Muhammad. The post also includes a mourning flag similar to the one ISIS used. Sumaira claims that ISIS did not exist at the time, and it is unclear if she meant during Muhammad's time or in 2012 when she was radicalized. Most historians agree ISIS was formed in 2003, other believe in the late 90's:

> ISIS did not exist at that time, and many in the milieu I was part of hoped for a caliphate. I have acknowledged that I was radical at the time.

She says she recognizes some of the posts, but not all, and some she wrote to get attention from Bastian Vasquez.[47]

Well, you did, Sumaira. You've made his bed, and now you have to lie in it.

CHAPTER 3
Do Not Return. Wait for Your Reward from Allah

Oslo District Court, March 3, 2021

ON MARCH 3, 2021, a French-speaking woman is the only voice heard in Oslo District Court. When she stops talking, the Norwegian interpreter relays the information to the Police Security Service investigator questioning the former ISIS woman. The scene unfolded on a video screen and was recorded in a French courtroom on January 6. The French woman has ditched her Muslim garb and wears 21st-century woman's clothing. Eyeglasses and a surgical mask obscure her face, and she tells the investigator she no longer considers herself a Muslim. After joining ISIS in Syria, she now lives a civilian family life with a job in France.[1]

She is a friend of Sumaira, and her testimony is part of day three of the accused ISIS woman's trial. Her name is not revealed, but we'll call her Rahila, meaning "one who travels" in Arabic. Rahila had converted to Islam and became active in the radical Muslim community in Oslo, NRK reports. Where she met Sumaira before the two traveled from Oslo to Syria in early 2013.[2] When the French woman speaks, it sounds sophisticated, passionate, and carefree. It is hard to believe the woman talking the language of love had joined ISIS in Syria.

Sumaira made most of the preparations for the trip, but Rahila got the impression Bastian Vasquez was planning the route. "Sumaira was determined to live in Syria for a long time. She wanted to be with her husband, the Norwegian foreign warrior," says the French woman. The two friends took a train to Sweden and flew on to Turkey. Bastian picked them up at the airport in a van and drove them across the border from Turkey to Syria. Rahila says Sumaira seemed content with life for the first few months, but Bastian had a terrible reputation even in the ISIS-controlled territory where they all lived:

> I knew many women who did not live in the same way as Sumaira and her husband. I did not live like them. In addition, I must say they had an awful reputation.
> What do you mean?
> People did not trust Bastian; he was a difficult person. He was like a five-year-old who wanted to play war.[3]

Rahila lived with Sumaira and Bastian in a house for two and a half months. After a short time in Syria, she had to get married to survive, but left the country and went back to France in August the same year. It would have been impossible to leave the country without the help of her husband:

> In Islam, a woman does not do anything without the consent of her husband.
> Did you talk to Sumaira about leaving Syria? No. And I did not trust her husband either.
> Did you trust Sumaira? It is difficult to trust a woman when the husband has such a big hold over her. She was not the same person in Syria as in Norway.[4]

Rahila believes Sumaira had had the opportunity to leave Syria at the beginning of her stay if she so wished. But Vasquez would never have let Sumaira go and would have seen it as treason:

> If I had known that it was as difficult for her as for me, I would have asked her to go home with me. Bastian was radicalized. He really believed that jihad was obligatory and that Islam should unite everyone.[5]

I Have Met Sisters Who Sacrificed Everything

> I nagged him to allow me to go back to Norway to give birth and then come back to him. He denied me going. I had not said I wouldn't return to Syria. But he understood my intent, so I was not allowed to go.[6]

Sumaira was pregnant with Bastian's child in the spring of 2014. She hoped to use her desire to give birth outside Syria as an excuse to leave the country, but he saw through her, she told the court. On May 26, 2014, a woman contacted her on the encrypted messaging service Telegram. The sender was the youngest of the two sisters from Bærum, Leila.[6]

Bærum, where the jihad sisters come from, is a borough in the Greater Oslo Region, bordering the west end of Oslo, Norway's priciest and most fashionable residential areas, with the highest income per capita in Norway. Growing up, we used to regard people from Bærum as snobs and said they were from *Blærum*. The word *blære*, meaning bladder, is also used in Norway as slang for pretentious or snobby. They would "invade" our little mountain town on ski vacations in their BMWs, high society attitudes, and the latest Lacoste fashion, thinking they were something else. But we were probably more in awe than anything else. Why couldn't we *bondeknøler*, hillbillies, be more like them? If someone told me back then, two young women from *Blærum* would join the most vicious terrorist organization in the world; I would have thought they were insane. How times have changed.

The younger sister, Leila, used a different name in the Telegram text and warned Sumaira against leaving Syria. She wrote that it was not sure that it would be as easy to return to Syria another time:

> I have met sisters who had sacrificed everything to come here. Are you just going to throw this invitation out the window? Many sisters would take your place with joy. DO NOT RETURN NO MATTER WHAT HAPPENS AND WAIT FOR YOUR REWARD FROM ALLAH ".[7]

Leila must not have known that etiquette concerning correspondence generally discourages the use of all caps when sending or posting messages. ALL CAPS are considered rude as if you are shouting and can be irritating and offensive to some people.

The prosecution revealed that Sumaira and Bastian Vasquez lived with Leila and Ayan in Syria. Sumaira met and befriended them through the controversial Muslim youth organization Islam Net. Sumaira was surprised by the message. She claims she has never told her former friend that she wanted to go to Norway. Hopefully, doctors will check her for early-onset dementia in Norway because she surely has difficulty remembering things for a young woman:

> When I talk to a person, it goes from one person to another. People talk. I do not remember sending a message to the sister in Bærum that I wanted to return to Norway. I was completely flabbergasted and lost the courage I had to get back to Norway.[8]

Defender Nils Christian Nordhus, continuing grasping at straws, now holding on to a hay bale, believes the Telegram message from Leila has evidential value. And the French woman, Rahila, sent from heaven, has provided essential travel descriptions that Sumaira made it clear that she wanted to go to Syria, and the purpose of the trip was only to be with her husband, Bastian.[9] Never mind, she admitted to being radicalized and wanted to fight a holy war. Attorney Nordhus is beyond thrilled about the new revelations:

> It is an important message for us. It shows that our client had decided to go home because of the situation down there. This text is documentation of that. And the French woman's testimony is one of several pieces of evidence that can shed light on whether our client has found herself in

a situation where she had no choice but to stay in Syria and continue participating in the home.[10]

The prosecution has said several times that it is of little legal importance if the woman at some point wanted to return to Norway, as she voluntarily chose to join her husband in Syria. Sumaira also told the court about the period after Bastian Vasquez died in 2015. She had by that time a son with Vasquez living in al-Shaddadi, a town in northeastern Syria.[11] The al-Nusra Front attacked the city in February 2013. Over one hundred Syrian Arab Army soldiers, dozens of petroleum workers, and forty al-Nusra fighters were killed. The city, besieged by ISIS, remained one of the last ISIS strongholds in the province.[12] And Sumaira was there of her own free will, *only* cooking and doing laundry, and producing future jihads; supporting all three terrorist husbands that made such atrocities possible.

Bastian notified Sumaira's parents of the birth of their son via Facebook. After Vasquez's death, Sumaira frequently contacted his father in Norway. How she was on Facebook, Telegram, and WhatsApp without an Internet connection is still an unsolved mystery. As she claimed in court on the first day and why she didn't know much about ISIS. Nevertheless, months passed by, and even though several people tried to help her, she got nowhere. She could not tell anyone that she wanted to leave. If you left the ISIS area, you were considered an apostate. "I had to get to the border because then I could be picked up. But the big problem was getting me out of town. I needed permission to get out."[13]

Sumaira eventually tried to get to Raqqa, a war-torn place where she had better chances of finding human traffickers. It is unknown where she met her second husband, an Egyptian sharia judge, but moving to Raqqa became a condition for marrying him. It was impossible to survive without a man, and the alternative was a so-called women's house. And marriage, for Sumaira, was a means of survival and getting out. She did not tell her family in Norway too much about what she was going through. There was not much they could do, and she did not want them to worry. Sumaira had a child with the Sharia judge, a girl born in 2016.[14]

Her second better half was a hardworking man keeping two jobs simultaneously, as a Sharia judge and a jihad warrior, fighting heroically in armed missions for ISIS. Sadly, he suffered a timely death in battle, and not long after, Sumaira searched for husband number three, whom she found in a friend of the sharia judge. Love is always closer than you think. He was also an Egyptian and associated with ISIS, although Sumaira denied his ISIS connection. He allegedly had an honest job selling yogurt and mobile phones.[15] What a business idea to think of for T-Mobile or AT&T. Join forces with Haagen-Dazs. Instead of laptop loungers at Starbucks, you'll have cellphone loungers at a yogurt store. The clever entrepreneur did help her leave ISIS territory, she has said.

By the time Sumaira arrived in Raqqa in 2016, ISIS had taken complete control of the Syrian city on the northeast bank of the Euphrates River. And the war was raging:

> We heard planes coming down, and we feared that there would be bombs destroying the house. You sat and waited to die, but then it did not happen. It is not so far up enough that you are at the border. You cannot just go to the border with a kid. You have to have a smuggler come in and pick you up. I pretended I wanted to visit family in Turkey and said they were sick. You cannot say that you want to leave because what they do is not right.[16]

During the battle of Raqqa in 2013, Islamist jihadist militants from al-Nusra Front, Ahrar al-Sham, the Free Syrian Army, and others overran the government loyalists and took control. They attacked the central square and pulled down the statue of the former president of Syria, Hafez al-Assad. The al-Qaeda-affiliated al-Nusra Front set up a sharia court at the sports center. In early June 2013, ISIS said that it was open to receive complaints at its Raqqa headquarters. It was undoubtedly where Sumaira's husband worked as a Sharia judge. Not the yogurt and cellphone entrepreneur, but the full-fledged jihad. ISIS took complete control of Raqqa by January 2014. They wasted no time and executed Alawites, a sect of Shia Islam, and suspected supporters of Bashar al-Assad in the city. Bashar is the current president of Syria and the son of former president Hafez al-Assad.[17]

ISIS destroyed the city's Shia mosques and Christian churches. They converted the Armenian Catholic Church of the Martyrs into an ISIS police headquarters, and an Islamic center tasked to recruit new fighters. Around ten percent of Raqqa's population were Christians, and most fled the city after ISIS took over. ISIS quickly went to work fortifying the town and its surroundings with bunkers and a tunnel network. By June 2017, Raqqa remained the only major Syrian city entirely under ISIL control and was, therefore, its effective center of operations. *Raqqa was a planning center for terrorist attacks against European cities with its large number of foreign fighters.*[18]

See what you supported, foreign fighters and ISIS brides. And let's not forget all those terrorist attacks worldwide around that time. How does one put that on a job resume after the war is over and travel home to their cash-cow welfare state adopted Western countries with their tail between their legs? Nations, who, despite all the horror welcome them with open arms? And what would an ISIS terrorist's job application letter look like?

> Dear Hiring Manager,

I am applying for the administrative assistant position at the newly opened Sharia law center at Oslo City Hall. I can assure you I am more than qualified to fill the position and hope you will consider me for an interview.

I am a member of Islam Net since 2011, and I joined the Prophet Ummah before I traveled to Syria to fight for ISIS and the holy war in 2013. I proudly joined ISIS in Raqqa, a center of operations for planning terrorist attacks against cities worldwide. It was the best time of my life.

We planned or inspired the Brussel bombings, the Iraqi soccer stadium bombings, The Real Madrid Club Fan bombing, the Orlando nightclub shooting, the Sana'a mosque bombings, the Ankara bombings, the Metro Jet Flight 9268, the Paris attacks, the Brussels bombing, the Iraqi soccer stadium bombings, the Nice truck attack, the Kabul bombing, the Berlin truck attack, the Istanbul nightclub shooting, the Sehwam suicide bombing, the Westminster attack, the Manchester Arena bombing, the Barcelona attack, and hundreds more.

In 2016 alone, we executed more than 11,072 terror attacks worldwide, only a little over 25,600 people died, and a mere 33,800 were injured. The most exciting endeavor in 2016 was the more than 15,500 kidnappings and hostages we kept.[19] To see the infidels and their suffering was priceless.

I am a people person, great at organizing, go above and beyond the call of duty in any job, and am friendly unless provoked. I hope you consider me for an interview. Depending on my schedule, I am sure you accommodate my five daily prayers now that Norwaystan is under Sharia Law. The Fajr at sunrise, the Dhur at noon, the Asr in the afternoon, and the Maghrib at sunset. And if I work overtime, the Isha, the night prayer. And if hired, I cannot share an office or sit next to a woman or an infidel drunkard Norwegian. And no pork in the cantina, please.

I look forward to hearing from you.

Did You Hear About the Yazidi Women?

It is unknown how long Sumaira stayed in Raqqa, but later she and her children were constantly moving and lived in a dozen places in the east and south of the country. While Sumaira and the children were on the run, her son became ill. She had contact with her father on WhatsApp and a human trafficker who said she had to get out of the ISIS-controlled areas:

> To get past the government forces, we had to hide. If you came with a smuggler, they can't know that you were from abroad. The only people I heard about who got out were the Syrians. The only way out was to pay smugglers. Or walking through the desert, I don't know how many hours,

> with children. It's not possible. Everyone moved in the same direction. We came to villages. We often lived in women's rooms with the children, and we had to seal bomb holes so it would not be too cold.[20]

Sumaira's last stop in ISIS-controlled areas was the city of Baghuz, close to the border with Iraq. She tried again to find a human trafficker without success. She should have gone to the U.S. border. The new administration is all about creating jobs, and human trafficker have never been busier. For a time, Sumaira lived in a cave covered with blankets. They had to be careful going outside because there were snipers in the area:

> In Baghuz, it was more like you saw more planes and bombing. You had to move very often, and you heard gunshots. There was no food either. You had to fight to get food. I thought the race was over, and I got nowhere. I had tried several ways, but it was always about the money.[21]

No worries now, ISIS woman. Money is no object anymore. The Norwegian state will take care of you and your children for the rest of your life.

Baghuz, another Syrian town under the control of ISIS, is located 278 kilometers from Raqqa. The city was captured from ISIS by the Syrian Democratic Forces, SDF, on January 23, 2019. ISIS was left completely besieged in the town of Al-Marashidah to the north. The next day ISIS launched a series of suicide attacks to break the siege and recaptured part of the town. The international coalition targeted the outskirts with air raids. Violent clashes ensued until March 23, 2019, when SDF forces, backed by the U.S., retook all of al-Baghuz Fawqani. The siege ended ISIS's territorial rule over Syria, deprived the group of its final capital, and removed *almost* all territory under their control.[22]

In late February 2019, Adnan Afrin, commander for the Syrian Democratic Forces, said they discovered mass graves in the area of Baghuz, and many of the bodies found were women. They believe dozens of bodies and many decapitated are Yazidi tribal people held captive by Islamic State militants. "They were slaughtered," Afrin told Reuters, adding that the number of bodies remains unclear. Reporter Lucia I. Suarez Sang of Fox News reports that the discovery comes as Yazidi tribal leaders called on the international community to do more to investigate the fate of thousands of women and children who are still missing. When jihadists surged across the border in Iraq in 2014, they forced Yazidi women and girls into sexual slavery. The Yazidis is a religious sect whose beliefs combine elements of ancient Middle Eastern religions. ISIS regards them as devil-worshippers.[23]

I reluctantly admit that I had not heard of the Yazidi people until I started doing research for *Sympathy for the Evil*. I wonder if I had, if the mainstream media in Norway and other countries had covered the genocide as frantically as they do ISIS "brides", and the homecoming of, and rehabilitation of foreign fighters. I searched *Aftenposten*, NRK, VG, TV2 and *Dagbladet*, Norway's largest newspapers. Most of the articles on the Yazidi people and women are a few years old. A few pieces are about Nobel Peace Prize winner Nadia Murad, a Yazidi victim of ISIS brutality. She won the prize along with Dennis Mukwege. A worthy Nobel Peace Prize for once. He is a Congolese gynecologist and Pentecostal pastor. Mr. Mukwege founded and worked in the Panzi Hospital in Bukavu, where he specializes in treating women who armed rebels have raped.[24]

You would think there would be pages upon pages about the genocide in Norwegian news if Nadia Murad won the Nobel Peace Prize that is chosen and presented in Norway. But there are no recent updates or outcry in the media. All told, the Norwegian mainstream media have written thousands of articles about foreign fighters, both women and men, who went to Syria. Often sympathetic and forgiving. And the politicians and media in Norway cheered on and fought fiercely to bring back an ISIS woman. A traitor that was indirectly or directly an accomplice in making sure the jihads carried out the atrocities against the Yazidi people and millions of others. Besides, Bastian Vasquez was heavily involved with the Yazidis, as described in the chapter about his life. And so did probably everyone else who joined ISIS, except Vasquez is on video admitting it.

The 2018 Nobel Peace Prize winner Nadia Murad, a member of the Yazidi community, survived the ISIS torture camp. She writes the horror faced by Yazidi's women, like her, in the book: *The Last Girl: My Story of Captivity, And My Fight Against the Islamic State*. The Peace Prize winner's book's description on Amazon is harrowing and a disturbing account of the Islamic State's brutality:

> Nadia Murad was born and raised in Kocho, in a small village of farmers and shepherds in northern Iraq. A member of the Yazidi community, she and her brothers and sisters lived a quiet life. Nadia had dreams of becoming a history teacher or opening her own beauty salon.
> On August 15, 2014, when Nadia was just twenty-one years old, this life ended. Islamic State militants massacred the people of her village, executing men who refused to convert to Islam and women too old to become sex slaves. Six of Nadia's brothers were killed, and her mother soon after, their bodies swept into mass graves. Nadia was taken to Mosul and forced, along with thousands of other Yazidi girls, into the ISIS slave trade.
> Nadia would be held captive by several militants and repeatedly raped and beaten. Finally, she managed a narrow escape through the streets of Mosul, finding shelter in the home of a Sunni Muslim family whose eldest son risked his own life to smuggle her to safety.

> Today, Nadia's story—as a witness to the Islamic State's brutality, a survivor of rape, a refugee, a Yazidi—has forced the world to pay attention to an ongoing genocide. It is a call to action, a testament to the human will to survive, and a love letter to a lost country, a fragile community, and a family torn apart by war.[25]

In early March 2019, Sumaira fled Baghuz and ran into Kurdish soldiers who drove them to the al-Hol camp in a large truck. Sumaira explains it was important not to talk to others in the encampment, especially not about ISIS. At the same time, there was a shortage of food and medicine. "It was tough in the beginning because no one was willing to break the rules. In the end, you had to cross borders to get things. I thought I was free after Baghuz. When I came to al-Hol, I understood that it was not so."[26]

According to Doctors Without Borders, security in the camp has been unacceptable for the past two years, writes NRK. There have been over 30 killings in 2021 and several fires just since the New Year. When the Norwegian authorities decided to take the woman and her two children out of the al-Hol camp, the son's health condition was decisive. The four-year-old has had a bodyweight on a par with an average Norwegian one-year-old, NRK repeats[27] for the thousandth time. Just in case their readers with short-term memory loss had forgotten why, and has already been noted is a whale of a fish tale.

NRK causally notes that the prosecution and the woman's defense counsel have confirmed that the court will not discuss the children's health.[28] Well, I'll be darned. I could have never imagined that would happen.

The al-Hol refugee camp is on the southern outskirts of the town of al-Hawl, a town in northern Syria, close to the Syria-Iraq border. It is controlled and guarded by the US-backed Syrian Democratic Forces, SDF, and holds refugees displaced from the ISIS "collapse." The camp's population has grown to more than 60,000 after the SDF took the last of the Islamic State's territory in Syria. The refugees are women and children from many countries, primarily Syria and Iraq. In September 2019, an estimated 20,000 women and 50,000 children stayed at the camp.[29] Remember the prosecutor in Oslo District Court:

> The mothers were invaluable supporters. Children needed to be born for recruitment to ensure the next generation of ISIS recruits when someone dropped out. It is the tasks at home and the role as a mother that assume criminal responsibility.

Women and girls told a female journalist in April 2019 to convert, urging her to recite the *shahada*, an Islamic oat:

> I bear witness that none deserves worship except God, and I bear witness that Muhammad is the messenger of God. If you became Muslim, covered

your body and face like us, and became a member of our religion, you would not be killed.[30]

Many of them prayed for the caliphate of ISIS to return. The women justified the genocide of Yazidis by ISIS and the taking of Yazidi sex slaves. An Iraqi woman said they deserved it: "If they don't convert to Islam and don't become Muslim like us and worship Allah, then they deserve it."[31]

BBC journalist Quentin Sommerville described the camp as "an overflowing vessel of anger and unanswered questions." Some women "cling to their hate-fueled ideology, others beg for a way out, a way home." Mr. Sommerville mentioned a Moroccan-Belgian woman, a former nurse who grabbed her niqab, saying: "This is my choice. In Belgium, I couldn't wear my niqab, and this is my choice. Every religion did something wrong, show us the good." The woman felt there was no need to apologize for the ISIS attack in Brussels in 2016 and blamed the West and its airstrikes on Baghuz for their dire conditions.[32]

Where Was Jack Dorsey?

The woman in the photo poses as if she is the Virgin Mary. She looks up toward the ceiling with dreamy eyes and a Mona Lisa-like smile, and her dark blue headscarf, known as a hijab, hides her hair, neck, and ears. Only the shape of her oval face is made visible. She holds a baby dressed in an oversized red down jacket in her arms, and the child is obscured by the camera facing toward the mother. It is February 2019, and she sits in a dreary room at the al-Hol camp while being interviewed by two *New York Times* reporters. The *Aftenposten* of the USA. The two correspondents had traveled to Syria to speak to Hoda Muthana, a young woman from Hoover, Alabama, and Kimberly Gwen Polman, a dual Canadian-U.S. citizen. Kimberly Gwen is forty-six years old and Caucasian.[33] She reminds me of someone I know. Kimberly wears a light brown hijab with brown and black flowers and a black robe. She looks down with arms folded over her stomach in the *New York Times* photo. As if she has deep regrets.

Hoda Muthana was born in 1994 in Hackensack New Jersey. Her father, Ahmed Ali Muthana, was a former Yemeni diplomat at the United Nations but it is disputed whether he was a diplomat at the time of her birth.[34] The Muthana family left New Jersey and settled in Hoover, Alabama, where Hoda attended high school and was first drawn to ISIS reading on Twitter and other social media posts. She tells the *New York Times* she grew up in a strict household, no partying, no boyfriends, and no cellphone.[35] Not unlike my childhood, no partying, no boyfriends, and no landline.

Her father gave her a phone as a graduation gift, and it soon became a gateway to the world of extreme Islam. In 2014, after instructions from an online contact on how to join the Islamic State, she boarded a flight to Turkey.

Before she left, she had enrolled in classes at the University of Alabama at Birmingham under the pretense she was studying business but instead cashed the tuition check from her parents to fund the trip. She told her parents she was going to an event in Atlanta, packed a book bag with her clothes, and headed straight to Birmingham airport for a flight to Istanbul.[36]

Hoda has, since arriving in Syria, married three times. Her first husband was an Australian jihadist who went by Abu Jihad al-Australi. The Australi was killed in Syria in March 2015. She then married a Tunisian fighter and gave birth to a son. Her second husband's name is unknown, but it may have been Abu Jihad al-Tunisi.ˊ He was unfortunately also killed, fighting in Mosul in 2017, by either a missile or an airstrike. I hate when that happens. Hoda lived in Raqqa when the war was raging and bombs fell over the city. She was nine months pregnant, and after giving birth to a son, she, like Sumaira, moved from house to house, and town to town, until she ended up in the al-Hol camp in early 2019. She married a third time but divorced not long after.[37]

Hoda Muthana used her Twitter account frequently to incite terror attacks against civilians in the United States and encourage others to support ISIS. When she first arrived at the caliphate, she posted a photo showing her gloved hands while holding her American passport, promising "Bonfire soon." She used the pseudonym Umm Jihad on Twitter, meaning "Mother of Jihad." When jihadists at Charlie Hebdo killed twelve people, she tweeted: "Hats off to the mujs in Paris." using an abbreviation of mujahedeen,[38] meaning guerrilla fighters in Islamic countries, especially those who are fighting against non-Muslim forces.

Her Twitter account is now suspended, but one wonders why she could tweet out so much vile hatred and incitement to terrorism for so long. Jack Dorsey must have been asleep at the wheel or trimming his beard at the time. Or maybe he was strolling the beaches of Hawaii, with his buddy and *once* one of my favorite actors.

"Ms. Muthana now describes herself as having been brainwashed by the same type of online Islamic State propaganda she later spewed as a jihadi," Rowan Scarborough with *The Washington Times* writes in March 2019. MEMRI, a research group that monitors jihadi social media, has assembled a detailed report on Hoda Muthana. The former Alabama resident embraced mass killings as a three-time Islamic State bride in Syria but now wants to return to America.[39] The research group has been tracking Ms. Muthana, 24 years old since she emerged in 2015 as a prominent cheerleader for the Islamic State on social media. She joined thousands of imported extremists who committed widespread atrocities in Syria and Iraq. MEMRI Executive Director Steven Stalinsky told The Washington Times:

> The most troubling aspect of her time in Syria was her becoming a high-profile advocate for ISIS, tweeting regularly from Syria in late 2014

> and 2015, urging Americans to join the jihad and 'wake up u cowards'. Many U.S. media outlets have published sympathetic images of her with her child since she issued her public repatriation request. And some news stories' first paragraphs describe her as an 'Alabama mother.'
> While ISIS physical caliphate has crumbled, it and its ideology are stronger than ever online. Hoda Muthana is not alone. There are hundreds of jihadis like her in the U.S. And thousands across the West who have all pledged allegiance to ISIS. Their use of social media has provided us with information about their true intentions. It would be a tragic mistake to think that they do not mean what they say.[40]

And we are all too familiar with that, where media outlets in Norway mirroring the press in the United States publishing sympathetic images and stories of the ISIS women and their children. Similarly, the *New York Times* has Hoda Muthana propped up as if she is the most innocent of young women. The NYT article also demonstrates that they desperately try to humanize the women who joined the caliphate in Syria, although they do report on some of the atrocities. I still struggle to understand why and what motivates journalists to do that when we know the unimaginable horror ISIS afflicted on innocent victims. Mr. Scarborough cites examples of Ms. Muthana's posts:

> There are sooo many Aussies and Brits here, but where are the Americans, wake up u cowards. Terrorize the kuffar at home.
> Men and women altogether. You have much to do while you live under our greatest enemy, enough of your sleeping! *Go on drive-bys and spill all of their blood, or rent a big truck and drive all over them. Veterans, Patriot, Memorial, etc. Day parades Kill them.*
> We have men (and women!) who love death as ardently as you love your lives! I was watching an American documentary on a battle in Afghanistan, and the Americans are such cowards. Crying and shaking on the battlefield and saying, 'our aim is to get everyone home where they belong.' While our men's aim on the battlefield is to reunite with our Lord. Our honor is in jihad, either victory or shahadah [martyrdom]. These men cry for their lives while we cry for our death shahadah![41]

Hoda has claimed that others hacked her Twitter account. Maybe Jack did it. However, in an interview with ABC News in February 2019, when they asked about a tweet in which she called for the murder of Americans at Veterans and Memorial Day parades, Muthana replied, "I can't even believe I thought of that."[42] I can.

How Do You Burn Your American Passport?

Hoda and Kimberly Gwen met in the final territory of the ISIS caliphate, less than six square miles. Even though they are generations apart, they became friends and bonded while struggling to survive. Hoda tells the *New York Times* they collected grass from crevices in the pavement, boiled it, and forced themselves to eat it. "Seeing a potato was like seeing a Lamborghini," she said.[43] A Vegan's dream and what my family thought I was doing the year I decided to be a vegan.

Kimberly Gwen Polman was born in 1972 and is a dual Canadian-U.S. citizen. Her mother is American, and her father is Canadian. She was raised a Reformed Mennonite, who sees themselves as faithful followers of Christ's and the New Testament teachings. She later converted to Islam and met Abu Ayman online, whom she later married without meeting. She had taken an interest in nursing, and Abu told her they needed nursing skills in the caliphate. No kidding. I early 2015, she told her family she was going to Austria for two weeks but instead traveled from Vancouver to Istanbul on her U.S. passport. Polman left three adult children in Canada when she traveled to Istanbul. She has said she grew disillusioned by ISIS in 2016 and tried to escape. She was allegedly captured and imprisoned in Raqqa, where she endured brutal interrogation and rape.[44] Kimberly Gwen tells the *New York Times* of her regrets:

> I don't have words for how much regret I have. How do you go from burning a passport to crying yourself to sleep because you have so much deep regret? How do you do that? How do you show people that?[45]

Both Kimberly Gwen and Hoda are evasive when asked about the brutality. The reporters remind them that by the time they arrived in the caliphate, ISIS terror was well documented. Unimaginable horrors including systematic rape and enslaving of Yazidi minorities, burning prisoners alive, and beheading of journalists. Seamus Hughes, deputy director of George Washington University Program on Extremism, is quoted by the NYT that there were thousands of legitimate reasons to question the sincerity of appeals like those of Ms. Muthana and Ms. Polman:

> The foreign women of the Islamic State, while often reduced to simplistic narratives about 'jihadi brides,' 'brainwashing' and 'online grooming,' aided and abetted many of these atrocities and in some cases directly perpetrated them.[46]

The *New York Times* conveniently doesn't mention President Obama's part in the story, only President Trumps' refusal to allow Hoda back in the USA. But in January 2016, the Obama Administration revoked Muthana's passport, stating that she was not a birthright citizen. Her father's termination of diplomatic status had not been officially documented until February 1995.

In 2018, President Trump instructed Secretary of State Mike Pompeo not to allow her back into the country. Pompeo press release read:

> Ms. Hoda Muthana is not a U.S. citizen and will not be admitted into the United States. She does not have any legal basis, valid U.S. passport, right to a passport, or visa to travel to the United States. We continue to strongly advise all U.S. citizens not to travel to Syria.[47]

Muthana's father, Ahmed Ali Muthana, filed an emergency lawsuit in February 2019, asking the federal government to affirm Muthana's citizenship and allow her to return to the United States. A federal judge ruled that she did not have American citizenship. In January 2021, the D.C. Circuit Court of Appeals upheld the decision of the District Court, ruling that Muthana is not a U.S. citizen.[48] In a handwritten note obtained by CNN, Hoda Muthana regretted everything, writes Rowan Scarborough. And why am I not surprised she sent it to CNN. NRK's and the rest of the Norwegian media's most reliable source:

> When I left to Syria, I was a naive, angry, and arrogant young woman. I thought that I understood my religious beliefs. During my years in Syria, I would see and experience a way of life and the terrible effects of war which changed me. Seeing bloodshed up close changed me. Motherhood changed me. Seeing friends, children, and the men I married dying changed me. Seeing how different a society could be compared to the beloved America I was born and raised into changed me. Being where I was and seeing the [people] around me scared me because I realized I didn't want to be a part of this. My beliefs weren't the same as theirs.[49]

She told NBC News in an interview: "I am a citizen, and those papers prove it, as I'm just as American as any blond-haired, blue-eyed girl, and I would like to stay in my country and do American things."[50] Most American girls do not join ISIS, burn their passport and declare death and destructions upon America, Hoda.

Two years after the *New York Times* interview, the two women are still held in the al-Hol refugee camp and facing an uphill battle over ever returning to the United States and Canada. Time will only tell, but I believe with the United States' new administration and America last policy, Hoda Muthana will soon return to the country she, like Sumaira, betrayed.

A Twisted Turn of Events

On November 19, 2020, James Bradley posted a photograph on one of his Instagram accounts depicting a man walking in the desert with a backpack and what prosecutors say they believe is a portion of the flag used by ISIS in the background. So, write reporters Carol Robinson, and Jeremy Gray, on al.com, in Alabama. In a twisted turn of events, James Bradly and his wife

Arwa Muthana of Hoover, Alabama, were arrested in early April 2021. The two prepared to board a cargo ship to go and fight for the terrorist group ISIS.[51] Incredibly, Arwa Muthana is the sister of Hoda Muthana, who has fought fiercely for a couple of years now, to be allowed back in the United States.

One would imagine all mainstream media in the United States would cover the astonishing news of Arwa Muthana's arrest. Considering her sister, Hoda Muthana, has been widely and often sympathetic covered in the media. The most infamous ISIS woman in the U.S., as Sumaira is for Norway and Shamima Begum for the U.K. But nothing surprises about today's press, and not one major news station has covered the arrest except for *Newsweek* and *New York Post*. I did a general Google search and searched on the New *York Times* website, which had so passionately written about Hoda's plea to return to the U.S. Not one word about her sister, unless Google suppressed it. Being the conspiracy theorist I am, I suspect the news of Hoda's sister would not bode well for Hoda's alleged regrets that she joined ISIS and her repeated pleas for redemption and return to the United States.

Arwa Muthana and her husband, James Bradley, a 20-year-old Bronx man, were arrested in Newark, New Jersey, the U.S. Department of Justice announced. James Bradley is also known as, believe it or not, Abdullah. The Manhattan federal court charged them with attempting and conspiring to provide material support to a designated foreign terrorist organization. Bradley was familiar with and knew where military recruits trained and planned attacks on the U.S. Military Academy at West Point or other universities in the area. They had planned to travel to Yemen by cargo ship and, fearing they were under law enforcement's radar, initiated plans with another person. However, the other person they were planning the journey with was an undercover officer. "Their plans to wage attacks against the United States have been thwarted," said U.S. Attorney Audrey Strauss.[52]

The Department of Justice informs that Bradley has desired to support ISIS overseas and has expressed violent extremist views since 2019. He also wanted to commit a terrorist attack in the United States. If he could not leave the U.S. because he might be on a terrorism watch list, he would do "something" in the United States instead. Like somebody did *something* on 9/11, I suppose. He told the undercover officer in January 2021 that he knew of a university in New York State where he saw Reserve Officer Training Corps (ROTC) cadets training. He could use his truck in an attack, and he and Arwa could take out all of the ROTC cadets.[53]

Your propaganda worked, Hoda Muthana. And your sister fell for it, or was she always radical? Didn't you tweet:

> Men and women altogether. You have much to do while you live under our greatest enemy, enough of your sleeping! Go on drive-bys and spill

all of their blood, or rent a big truck and drive all over them. Veterans, Patriot, Memorial, etc. Day parades Kill them.

Imagine what would have happened if James Bradley and Arwa Muthana didn't get arrested.

Bradley and Arwa Muthana married in a large Islamic ceremony in January 2021 and planned to travel to the United Kingdom and then Gambia, where Muthana could work as a teacher. Why not an orphanage? Bradley flew to Alabama to visit Arwa on March 6, and the next day they traveled by bus back to New York and made plans to travel to Asia or Africa. Bradley allegedly paid the undercover officer $1000 to help them get to Yemen. Officers arrested them as they walked the gangplank to board the cargo ship. Sometimes I wish we were back in the 1700s'. Arwa Muthana waived her Miranda rights after the arrest and admitted during an interview that she was willing to fight and kill Americans if it was for Allah. She had told the undercover officer that she wanted to travel to the Middle East so that she could fight for the sake of Allah.[54]

AL.com writes that a team of FBI agents arrived at the family's Hoover home on Pine Rock Lane the day of Arwa's arrest. In the same house wherein November 2014, her sister Hoda Muthana tricked her family into letting her go to Atlanta for a school field trip and instead boarded a plane to Turkey and then to Syria to meet with ISIS. FBI spokesman Paul Daymond would only say they were at the home Wednesday as part of a law enforcement action. The reporters from AL.com went to the house seeking comments, but no one answered the door.[55]

In a United States Department of Justice press release, the following explains the charges and maximum penalty:

> BRADLEY, 20, of the Bronx, New York, and MUTHANA, 29, of Hoover, Alabama, are charged with (1) one count of attempting to provide material support to a designated foreign terrorist organization, which carries a maximum sentence of 20 years in prison, and (2) one count of conspiring to provide material support to a designated foreign terrorist organization, which also carries a maximum sentence of 20 years in prison. The maximum potential sentences, in this case, are prescribed by Congress and are provided here for informational purposes only, as any sentencing of the defendants will be determined by a judge.[56]

Are you sure you want to come back to the United States, Hoda Muthana? The maximum potential sentence would be forty years, even though it's highly unlikely to be carried out, seeing how the U.S. is copying the socialist Europe kid glove treatment of criminals and terrorists. But even one year in prison, or the rest of your life in the al-Hol camp would not compare to a righteous, decent, and honest life living in the United States of America.

As with Sumaira, you've made your bed and now you have to lie in it. Had your sister and her husband been able to carry out attacks on Americans and veterans at Memorial Day parades, blood would have been on your hands. And by joining ISIS, blood *is* on your hands.

CHAPTER 4
The Filthy, Shameless Acts of Western Culture

May 19, 2013, Islam Net Conference, Oslo, Norway

| Allahu Akbar. Are you all radical extremists? |

FAHAD QURESHI RAISES his hand and looks out on the large crowd of mostly young, dark-haired men who have come to hear him preach about Islam and the Qur'an. He is the founder of Islam Net, the largest youth Muslim Organization in Norway, with local chapters in some of the largest cities in Norway; Oslo, Akershus, Tromsø, Bodø, and Trondheim. The same organization the now accused ISIS woman, Sumaira Ghafoor, had joined in 2012. She had told the prosecutor in Oslo District court that Islam Net did not send her to Syria. When she connected with the Prophet Ummah and then Bastian Vasquez, she became radicalized, she claims. Judging from Qureshi's words, Islam Net could very well have been her stepping stone to radicalism. *Aftenposten* had recently written that many Islam Net followers went to Syria, and in a typical liberal media manner, addresses the terrorists at *Syriafarere* or Syria travelers. There may have been some of those *Syriafarere* among the audience this spring day in Oslo, in 2013.

Fahad Qureshi speaks in English with a slight accent, and his demeanor is that of arrogance and contempt for those that call out their radical beliefs. He is tall and thin, clad in black from head to toe, except for a white and tan short-rounded skullcap, a *taqiyah,* often worn by Muslims for religious purposes. Islamic followers believe that Prophet Muhammed used such head covering and consider it commendable to emulate him.[1] Qureshi is a dark man, both in appearance and thoughts. He wears the typical Muhammed beard and mustache, and black, soulless eyes work the crowd who enthusiastically listens to and embraces every word he says.

On the podium, next to him, sit three men, all Middle Eastern and middle-aged, with skullcaps, Muslim garb, and Muhammed beards. They are as dark in appearance as Qureshi, with the same aura of arrogance. One would wonder what goes through their heads sitting on a podium in a hall in Oslo, Norway, listening to Fahad Qureshi's words, blasphemy if spoken by anyone else. What are their motives? Are they sinister? Do they dream of Sharia Law in Norway? One of them resembles Haitham al-Haddad, a controversial Islamic "scholar" based in England, but cannot be confirmed. They do not react to Qureshi's words with disapproval and seem to care less about their surroundings, occasionally nodding in agreement. They are on the same page as Fahad Qureshi, who speaks, and the audience listens:

> Every now and then, every time we have a conference, every time we invite a speaker, the media always comes with the same accusations: This speaker supports the death penalty for homosexuals, this speaker supports the death penalty for this crime or that crime, that he is homophobic, that he subjugates women. It's the same old stuff coming all of the time. We always try to tell them. I always try to tell them that it is not that speaker that we are inviting who has these 'extreme radical views,' as you say. These are general views that every Muslim actually has. Every Muslim believes in these things. Just because they are not telling you about it, or just because they are not out there in the media, doesn't mean that they don't believe in them. I will ask you, everyone in the room: How many of you are normal Muslims–not extremists, not radical–just normal Sunni Muslims? Please, raise your hands. Everybody, with the grace of God. Okay, take down your hands.[2]

Almost everyone in the crowd raises their hands, except for a couple of men sitting in the first row. The listeners are predominantly Middle Eastern young men, many clad in Muslim clothing and others wearing typical street clothes, such as hoodies, jeans, and sneakers. And heavy jackets, even though it is May in Norway. There look to be over 2000 people in the crowd, perhaps closer to 3000. Although a CNN or NRK journalist would have estimated the crowd at one hundred. Who knows?

> How many of you agree that men and women should sit separately? Please raise your hands. Everyone agrees, brothers as well as sisters. So, it's not just these 'radical' sheiks, then?[3]

He points to three men on the podium. Again, almost everyone, except for a few, raises their hands. In the first row, a young man who looks to be about fourteen years old sticks out from the crowd. He is wearing a skullcap and a white tunic with a yellow reflective vest. He eagerly raises his hand to every question Qureshi spews out without hesitation.

> Next question: How many of you agree that the punishments described in the Koran and the Sunna, whether it is death, whether it is stoning for adultery, whatever it is... If it is from Allah and His Messenger, that

> is the best punishment ever possible for humankind, and that is what we should apply in the world. Who agrees with that?[4]

Everyone visible in the video raises their hands. Everyone! "Allahu Akbar. Are you all radical extremists?" The crowd laughs.

> So, all of you are saying that you are common Muslims; you all go to different mosques in Norway. Or are you a specific sect, like the Islam Net sect, or anything like that? Are you like that? No. Are you like that? Please raise your hand if you are like that extreme Islam, that sect, or anything like that? No one, Allahu Akbar. How many of you go to the normal Sunni mosques in Norway? Please raise your hands. Allahu Akbar. What are the politicians going to say now? What is the media going to say now? That we are all extremists? That we are all radicals? That we all need to be deported from this country?[5]

The video posted on MEMRI.org, the Middle East Media Research Institute, on May 19, 2013, suddenly ends. In silence, with a heavy heart, I raise my hand in agreement with Fahad Qureshi's last three questions. And God help us all.

Islam Will Penetrate Every Corner of This World
Two years later, in June 2015, Furuset, Oslo, Norway.

The young woman in the picture is staring straight at me. Innocent blue eyes are gazing out from the black niqab covering her face. A purple burqa drapes her head and petite body. She wears black gloves on small hands hanging dutifully to the sides of her body. In the background are black-clad women from head to toe, reminding me of the doom I always feel when I see images of ravens. An ominous warning. The disturbing picture evokes a bottomless sadness in me for what has become of my homeland. And I get a deep disdain for the politicians in Norway who allowed this to happen to my country. And for the mainstream media that systematically suppresses information about the dark side of unchecked mass immigration and the danger of growing Islamization in this Nordic nation, now populated by a little more than five million people.

The only thing in the photo that would resemble a young woman in 21st century Norway is a pair of white sneakers with a thin black band, a little worn, sticking out from the burqa. And her blue eyes. Had the scene been in a Muslim country, the image would have been just as oppressive, although an everyday sight. However, this young woman poses for journalists from *Aftenposten* in front of a sports hall at Furuset in Oslo. She has just converted to Islam in Norway. A Scandinavian country advocating gender equality, caring about human rights, and the happiest and best country to live in.

The young woman's name is Silje, a typical Norwegian name, making her sight even more distressing. My sixteen-year-old niece in Norway, Silje, has the same blue eyes and a small framed body. Only two years younger than Silje from Oslo. How do I know it is not her? Would her mom and dad recognize her? What if it was her?

> The large sports hall is filled with people eagerly awaiting, and the silence is interrupted by chair legs scraping the floor and the rustling of floor-length tunics. Someone turns on the lights, and a group of young women leads a woman dressed in a niqab towards the middle of the hall at Furuset in Oslo. Eighteen-year-old Silje from Oslo turns towards the stage, towards a young man dressed in pink trousers, a blue shirt, and a dark blazer.
> Imran ibn Mansur from the United Kingdom calls himself Dawah-Man. He is one of the charismatic Islamic preachers who evokes palpitations, tears, smiles [*Aftenposten's* words], and even a little shyness because he is so direct. His preaching resonates with young people seeking meaning in life, forgiveness, belonging, and peace of mind. Now he accepts and welcomes Silje.
> "Do you want to make the creed?" he asks into the microphone. "Yes," Silje answers into her microphone in the middle of the room. "Oh, yeah! Is anyone forcing you?" "No."
> He only sees her eyes. Silje has already used the garment to hide her outer appearance for a few months. But now the moment has come. She will convert to Islam with hundreds of witnesses. She is at the peace conference of Norway's most prominent Muslim youth organization, Islam Net. Word for word, she repeats the Islamic creed after Dawah-Man. "There is no God but Allah, and Muhammad is his prophet." Dawah-Man shouts: "Takbir! (Allah is greatest!)". The hall answers: "Allahu Akbar!"
> The newly converted Muslim is embraced and almost lifted out of the hall by her girlfriends. They cry and hug her as they pass smiling guards wearing yellow reflective vests that say "Support dawah" on their backs. Dawah means to invite to Islam, and Silje has just accepted. A female voice whispers from the back of the hall reserved for women. "Now her sins are forgiven. It's like being born again. Isn't that great? It's so… oh my God!
> *Aftenposten, June 6, 2015.*[6]

Being Gay Is Like Having a Disease

Eight months earlier, in November 2014, Imran ibn Mansur, Dawah-man, the charismatic Islamic preachers as *Aftenposten* describes him, who converted Silje, was banned from the University of East London after saying being gay is like having a disease. He blamed "filthy Western culture for impulses which should be suppressed and claimed that homosexuality, sodomy, is an act that in the sharia, comes under the category of obscene, filthy, shameless acts."[7]

In 2018, the same charismatic preacher advised his YouTube Listeners to return to Muslim lands. He preaches that it is impossible to live in infidel countries except for da'wa purposes, as one might be influenced by evil and corruption. He warned that in the U.K., hijab-wearing girls get abortions, and children come home saying: "Mom, Dad, I believe in evolution."[8] Passages from his speech tell of a man who despises the unbelievers in his adopted country, and the only reason to live there is for da'wah. Dawah is the act of inviting or calling people to embrace Islam. For some groups within Islam like the Salafist and Jamaat-e-Islami, Dawah is a political activity. Their goal is to reverse what they perceive as the decline of Islam in the modern era. They do this through the systematic spread of Islamist ideology and ultimately allow to establish an Islamic state.[9] When listening to Dawah-man's rant, thoughts come to mind that *Aftenposten* reporters who called him a charismatic spiritual leader need a severe reality check:

> What's the ruling on living in an infidel country? Yeah, it's… Go to a Muslim country. It's not allowed. It's not permissible. Allah made hijrah, which is leaving the land of polytheism for the land of Islam. It's leaving a place of polytheism [the belief in or worship of more than one God], a place of heresy, a place of disbelief, and going to live among the Muslims. Allah made that obligatory upon this nation until the Day of Judgment is established.
> I'll tell you why – because a Muslim can't practice his religion easily in the lands of the infidels. Either they will limit him or stop him from practicing, or stop her from practicing – can't wear hijab, can't wear a niqab, can't do this, can't do that… Or what will they do? Their evil will influence you; their corruption will influence you, and that will influence you in a wrong way. How many Muslims have fallen into serious sins because of the infidels that they are around?[10]

In February 2020, Dawah-man discussed marriage with young men and boys on his YouTube channel. What would they do if somebody were to try to take their moms or sisters as girlfriends? One boy answered that he would want to kill the man. Dawah-man responded that's not allowed, and an Islamic court would have to deal with the issue. And the boy would have to move back home for this because there is no Islamic law in England. Yes, there is Dawah-man. They could also have four wives, he said, but advised against it. The only Allah's form of marriage matters, he proclaims. But it's only illegal to have more than one wife on the wedding registry, but it is *not* illegal to have multiple partners. "Because the infidels in the U.K. are so filthy that they don't care how many people they sleep with." He added that while some people say that getting married young may increase the chances of divorce, it is better to get married young and ultimately get divorced than to commit adultery at a young age.[11]

Adultery Is Forbidden and Punishable by Death

Silje is part of a new trend and a phenomenon in Norway, and many countries writes *Aftenposten,* the *New York Times* of Norway. And like its twin *once* a highly respected paper. Reading the newspaper article, you almost get the feeling it's a celebratory event rather than a grave social problem in a democratic country. Conservative Islam and Salafism among youth are gaining a stronghold in Europe supported by an influx from the Muslim states in the Middle East. Young people with and without a Muslim background acknowledge a more conservative interpretation of Islam than the first generation of Muslim immigrants practiced. Salafism is gaining ground in the Middle East, and Saudi Arabia spends millions of oil dollars on projects aimed at spreading conservative Islam. Since its start in 2008, Islam Net in Oslo, Norway, has been a success story about growth. The organization is constantly using new arenas to get its message across. It raises money for a Dawah center, is very active on social media, and has created several elaborate websites to spread Islam. They regularly arrange meetings with well-known Islamic scholars from abroad, but also the imam from the Somali Tawfiiq mosque in Oslo is a frequent guest.[12]

And *scholars*, as we know, is a broad term. Ask the Washington Post.

Journalists from *Aftenposten* meet Fahad Qureshi, the leader of Islam Net, after Silje's conversion ceremony. Two years have passed since he preached that all Muslims believe in the death penalty for homosexuals and stoning for adultery. He wears the same type skull cap but now sports a thin, black down jacket over his Muslim garb. It's still chilly in Norway. He smiles for *Aftenposten's* photographer, and although his appearance seems friendlier by putting on a facade, his thoughts and beliefs are just as dark.[13] Qureshi explains their interpretation of Islam. He tells *Aftenposten* they are practicing Muslims and do not like labels such as conservative or liberal. They make no sense to him. He believes the ideal society is the first three generations after the Prophet Muhammad, so-called Salafism, which refers to the orthodox ancestors as-salaf as-Salih.[14] And they are not for the faint of heart and do not awake a feeling that this is a religion of peace. In addition to the rules to live by, prayer, fasting, and almsgiving are part of everyday life among the Salafist Muslims:

> Women and men shall not shake hands.
> Avoid workplaces where alcohol and pork are served or sold.
> Men shall grow a beard.
> Women shall cover themselves.

> The man is obliged to support the woman.
> Girlfriends and boyfriends are problematic. Sex outside of marriage is forbidden.

The controversial hudud punishments, part of the sharia system, are seen as God's guidance:

> Homosexuality is forbidden and punishable by death.
> Apostasy, defection, and disloyalty from Islam are forbidden and punishable by death.
> Infidelity is forbidden and punishable by death.[15]

Fahad Qureshi is not enthusiastic about the media interest. He believes that asking questions about gender division or the hudud punishments will only create division. Like carrying out the hudud punishment, wouldn't? These are no topics that are suitable in the media, he says:

> It would be to change the religion, to change the Islamic value so that the sexes do not mingle. It is rooted in the Qur'an, and the teachings of the Prophet as understood for eternity. Islam does not need reform and cannot be changed. God's guidance is superior to human decisions.[16]

The same applies to the view of the controversial hudud punishments, he explains. But he emphasizes that neither he nor anyone else wants to introduce the death penalty for infidelity, homosexuality, or apostasy in Norway. Well, aren't you special Qureshi:

> The hudud punishment has zero significance in Norway. These are theoretical scenarios in a perfect Islamic state. We live in Norway, and the hudud sentence will not be *executed* here.

Nevertheless, Aftenposten writes that Qureshi will not distance himself from hudud punishments in Muslim countries.[17]

Norwegian Society Does Not Provide Inner Peace

Qureshi believes that there are more practicing Muslims in his generation of Norwegian Pakistanis. He is not shy about bashing Norway and the Norwegian society, the nonbelievers, sinners, and drunkards. One wonders why he doesn't pack his belonging and travel to the Middle East and preach to the faithful followers of Allah the way it was 1400 years ago. Many Norwegians would gladly pay his one-way ticket out of the country. I would, and I live in the USA. And, if inner peace and joy mean stoning women, homosexuals, and defectors of Islam, the always mostly peaceful Norwegians would rather live without it. And drink their Aquavit and Hansa in peace. Audacious Qureshi spews his anti-Norway views and *Aftenposten* lets him:

> The parent generation came here to work and earn money and was not very focused on religion. But when you have grown up here, you see how Norwegian society does not provide inner peace and joy. Instead, fashion pressure, drinking pressure, and pressure from other sides often make young people reflect a little. Then it is easier to return to Islam.[18]

Imagine if Hans Olsen said the same things in Saudi Arabia or any Muslim country? Rest in Peace Hans, but you had it coming. What in the world made him travel to the Middle East, we would wonder?

Ghulam Sarwar, the chairman of Oslo's largest mosques, Central Jamaat-e Ahl-e Sunnat, represents the first generation of immigrants from Pakistan. He acknowledges that Islam Net is more active on the Internet, where many young people are. "We fight in a more old-fashioned way. But we think it's better to learn about Islam from an imam standing in front of you than to watch a lecture online."[19] And rumor has it that some Norwegians think it's even better to learn about Islam from an Iman standing in front of you in a mosque in the Middle East, far, far away from Norway.

The showman-like speakers at the peace conference appeal to the crowd, and *Aftenposten* describes them as preachers with "glimmer in their eyes." Like religious evangelists, they speak loudly and enthusiastically about faith, doomsday, and hell. They insist that makeup, fashion, and modern youth culture are delusional, with a touch of humor *Aftenposten* has to add. One of this year's main attractions is British Haitham al-Haddad, and he asks why we should reform Islam. What do we need to change? That we pray five times a day? He doesn't wait for an answer and shouts that Islam means submitting to God. "The Qur'an is the revelation of God and cannot be changed or reformed."[20]

What *Aftenposten* doesn't disclose, it that Haitham al-Haddad is a controversial scholar born and raised in Saudi Arabia. With a glimmer in his eyes, the preacher sits on the boards of advisors for Islamic organizations in the United Kingdom, including the Islamic Sharia Council. Many of his views have been controversial, including remarks on Jews, homosexuality, Osama bin Laden, and female genital mutilation.[21] In February 2015, four months before he spoke in Oslo, the LGBTI Society at the University of Westminster started a Change.org petition to "Stop ANTI-GAY preacher Sheikh Haitham Al Haddad talking on campus." The controversial and homophobic speaker was to speak at the university days before Westminster welcomes LGBTI students from across the country. Al-Haddad's event was called "Who is Muhammed?" and put on by the Islamic Society. The sheik has written about the scourge of homosexuality, which he calls a criminal act. In an article called "Standing up against Homosexuality and LGBTs'," he wrote:

> In this vein, I commend the many Christian bishops and ministers who have come out in opposition to the current proposals to allow

> homosexuals to marry, and I support them in their endeavor to dissuade the government from including LGBTs in current marriage legislation. We also appreciate the brave stance of the Nobel Peace Prize winner and president of Liberia, Ellen Johnson Sirleaf, defending a law that criminalizes homosexual acts and determinedly standing for higher moral standards.[22]

Nobel Peace Prize? Norway, that's on you.

Sheikh Haitham Al Haddad has also made controversial comments against women and has spoken about the *proper* way to perform FGM, female genital mutilation. The UWSU society asks how it is possible to create a safe space for thousands of LGBTI students if an anti-gay preacher is allowed on campus a day before the University of Westminster welcomes National Student Pride.[23]

I wish I had an answer for them, and then I ask. How is it possible that an anti-Semitic and homophobic Islamic sheik that supports killing the LGBTI community, female genital mutilation, stoning, wife-beating, Osama bin Laden, and death to those defectors of Islam is allowed to preach hate and indoctrinate youths in Norway? Some would say freedom of speech, but why then, was Alan Dershowitz banned from speaking at three universities in Norway?

In 2011, a Norwegian pro-Israeli group invited the Harvard law professor to speak at three major universities in Norway about international law as applied to the Israeli-Palestinian conflict. The dean of the law faculty at Bergen University said he would be honored to have Mr. Dershowitz present a lecture on the O.J. Simpson case, as long as he would promise not to mention Israel. An administrator at the Trondheim school said that Israel was too controversial. The University of Oslo simply said "no" without offering an excuse. In a Wall Street Journal opinion about the boycott, he writes that only once has he been denied lecturing at universities in a country. The other country was Apartheid South Africa. However, the Harvard law professor did thankfully deliver three lectures to packed auditoriums at the invitation of student groups. He received continuous applause both before and after the talks.[24]

As universities in Norway jump at the chance to have lecturers from elsewhere, the treatment of the Harvard law professor is disgraceful. Controversial historian and social activist Ilan Pappe, who teaches at Oxford, had recently lectured at the Norwegian University of Science and Technology, NTNU, in Trondheim. A man Mr. Dershowitz calls a demonizer of Israel. Mr. Pappe has argued that Zionism is more dangerous than Islamic militancy and has called for an international boycott of Israeli academics. I hope you now join the Taliban in Afghanistan, Mr. Pappe. And a colleague of Mr. Dershowitz at Harvard, Stephen Walt, who is the co-author of the not so pro-Israel book *The Israel Lobby*, was also welcomed to speak at NTNU.[25]

I am embarrassed that the brilliant professor Alan Dershowitz was treated disrespectfully by the universities' elites. And when witnessing the vile rhetoric allowed from others in all corners of Norway, it becomes even more shameful. Islam Net is not a university, but it is an organization in Norway allowing hate speech and radical indoctrination of young people. And so do radical mosques receiving funding from the government. Thank you to the student groups who had the graciousness to invite Professor Dershowitz and that he got to speak to a packed auditorium.

Receiving Welfare From the Kufar is Un-Islamic

In the sports hall at Furuset, Haitham al-Haddad, with a glimmer in his eye and a stone in his heart, preaches to the young crowd that it is the first three generations after the Prophet Muhammad is the best of Islam. Many of the worshippers find it challenging to live as they did at that time in the Middle East 1400 years ago, but they try. The sheik ends the sermon with a foreboding we should all take to heart:

> Islam vil trenge inn i hvert et hus og hvert et hjørne av denne verden.
> Islam will penetrate every house and every corner of this world.[26]

After Silje converted to Islam, her friends from Islam Net embrace her and think they are more than friends since she became a Muslim. They are like sisters, they proclaim.

Silje's name is fictitious *Aftenposten* writes. The 18-year-old fears harassment if her identity becomes known. Right after Dawah-Man had accepted her creed, she tells *Aftenposten* she feels great about becoming a Muslim. Before the conversion, she acquired knowledge about Islam through Islam Net and *finnveien.no.* Find the Road. One of the Islam Net's various subgroups in the Islamic network:

> It feels good! I was a little nervous about saying something wrong in the microphone when I stood there. But now, it feels as if the void, what was missing, has been filled.[27]

Aftenposten spoke to her a few months after the conversion, and she feels even happier because she has had time to become more familiar with Islam. "Islam has answers to everything in the Qur'an and the hadiths. I feel heard and seen by God, even as I cannot see and hear him." She wants to live like the Prophet's women, which involves wearing the niqab. She hopes to study and find work because it is un-Islamic to receive financial support when working for money is an option.[28]

If it is un-Islamic to receive financial aid, why do 56 percent of social assistance payments go to immigrants, including Muslims? The population of immigrants in Norway is allegedly at 18 percent, increasing exponentially year after year. And 56 percent of social services costs go to 18 percent of the immigrant population in Norway! In January 2019, *Statistisk Sentralbyrå*, Statistics Norway, reports that in 2017, immigrants receive 56 percent of social assistance payments for the entire country. The welfare recipients are strongly dominated by those with a country background from Africa and Asia.[29] That was four years ago; what are the numbers today?

How many men and women in the streets of Norway are aware of these numbers? Statistics that are usually suppressed by the mainstream media, where lying by omission is an Olympic sport. Not just by the press, though. Government-run Statistics Norway is known to church up, hide, and manipulate numbers to show the advantage of immigration. Politicians and the press constantly proclaim the benefit of mass immigration and multiculturalism, a colossal lie and an enormous betrayal to the four million Norwegians and the country they hold dear. They are imprinting it in their minds so that few dare to speak out. And those who do are labeled racists, right-wing extremists, xenophobic, and God knows what else. They pay a tremendous amount of taxes and live in the most expensive country in the world. Their hard-earned money goes to support a never-ending and increasing immigration bill that nobody asked them if they wanted to fund, and an extreme ideology allowed to flourish in their land. Injustice toward good people at its highest level.

Silje has not given much thought to the fact that in *hudud* punishments, apostasy, defection, and disloyalty are forbidden and punishable by death and happily declares:

> We are in Norway. It does not happen here." Her friend and now sister chimes in; "She is not someone who changes her mind. [30]

It is now 2021 and it is six years since Silje converted. I often think of that young woman or girl; who could have been my niece in my home country. She must be around twenty-five years old now. Put on display as a young girl by one of the largest and at one time most respected newspapers in Norway, *Aftenposten*. They are introducing Islam Net and the radical Iman's with a glimmer in their eyes to the Norwegian people, making it sound like a celebratory event. Normalizing insanity and an ideology that does not belong in Norway. What if any of the journalists had taken her aside and said, "Hey Silje, there are other answers in life. Do you need to talk to anyone? Are you okay? Can we help? Do you think the stoning gays, women, and apostasies is okay, and wearing a garb all your life only showing your beautiful blue eyes?" Or was she just part of the story, a sensational headline, and a pawn? I get the feeling she was. A pawn used by activists disguised as journalists who embrace and show understanding and love for everyone else's dogmatic beliefs and culture, but their own. And Silje was just a story.

I was eighteen once and thought I knew everything, but at the same time, I was so unsure of myself and did not know anything about life. Yet, I trusted everyone else and thought they had the answers. I hope Silje found her answers, and I pray it was not wearing a niqab reading the Qur'an and the Hadith and supporting the hudud punishments.

I hope you're okay, Silje. I really do.

CHAPTER 5
The Road to Syria Was Paved with Bad Intentions

Oslo, Norway, June 2014

> "Are you saying that the Norwegian Police Security Service is to blame for Bastian Vasquez's radicalization?"
> The radicalization happened after the arrest and harassment by the Norwegian press. Before that, Bastian Vasquez was an ordinary Norwegian boy with a Chilean background. He sat in the boys' room and made what he perceived as a humorous but provocative critical film.
> Then he was hung out as a terrorist in the Norwegian media, and after that, he has become a different person, but I do not want to blame anyone in that context. And he was indicted, not arrested. He traveled to Syria because he had been remanded in custody here in Norway and harassed by PST and the Norwegian media. He wanted to leave Norway and thus traveled to Syria.[1]

Bastian Vazquez's attorney John Christian Elden spoke to journalists at NRK in June 2014. In Norway, the news had just broken that Sumaira's husband, Bastian Vasquez, is the spokesperson of a fifteen-minute ISIS propaganda video released on LiveLeak boasting about killing Iraqi soldiers and blowing up a police station.[2] However, the video Attorney Elden talks about is another video made by Bastian Vasquez in Norway two years earlier, in 2012, and investigated by PST as a possible incitement to terrorism. The video was a promotion for a demonstration in Oslo the following Friday, January 20, 2012. Vasquez had posted on the Facebook group "Demonstration: Norwegian forces out of Afghanistan."[3] Along with hate speech by members of the group. And most likely, when Sumaira posted her inflammatory comments on Facebook mentioned during her trial.

> Brothers who speak must shake the dirty, infidel pork eaters and turn their Storting (The Parliament) into their little thing. Insha Allah. Over

800 participants. This will be bigger, better, and more dangerous for kufar than the caricature demonstration in 2010
MUSLIMS is organizing the celebration, intended for Muslims, and against Norway's participation in the occupation of Afghanistan and massacres of Muslims.
Americans, including civilians, should be killed by Muslims anywhere in the world.[4]

The video Vasquez made for the demonstration starts with dramatic music and pictures of suffering Afghan children. Armed Norwegian soldiers roll across the screen. An image of then Prime Minister Jens Stoltenberg appears with the words "Oh Allah destroy them." The following picture is of Crown Prince Haakon Magnus greeting Norwegian soldiers with the text "Oh Allah destroy them and let it be painful." Photos of coffins of fallen Norwegian soldiers' flashes on the screen. Below a picture of a soldier's funeral is: "Truly, the victory comes from Allah! That's what's coming!" The video ends with the sound of a powerful explosion and a white car in flames adorned with a Norwegian flag. A text flashes on the screen urging Muslims to attend the rally.[5]

Bastian Vasquez may have been an ordinary Norwegian boy a long time ago. Nevertheless, radicalization came long before he made the dreadful video threatening the prime minister of Norway, Crown Prince Haakon Magnus, Norwegian soldiers, and all Americans. In reality, Attorney Elden, he was most likely radicalized four years before he posted the awful video. And we can probably thank radical mosques, Islam Net, and the Prophet Ummah for his radicalization, not the Norwegian Police Security Service.

Once Upon a Time, There Was a Cross and a Picture of Jesus

It's a cold November night in Skien, Norway, somewhere around 2006 or 2007. Four young boys have just finished "An Evening Full of Beats and Rhymes" at *Et Annet Sted*, Another Place, a youth club in downtown Skien. It had been a long time since such a happening had occurred in the historic town in southeastern Norway, and the boys from neighboring Gulset were ecstatic. They had arranged the event and performed hip-hop in front of an audience for the first time. *Et Annet Sted* was a youth club run by the town, where young people hang out on a Saturday night instead of around the streets.[6]

Bastian Vasquez had formed the group Gull-Z with three other boys from Gulset, and they used nicknames such as Ghost and Blaiz. Bastian's was Busty. They would mix hip hop with lyrics in Norwegian, English, Spanish and African. They thought hip-hop had value in today's society and helped integrate young people. They made songs about everything from poverty, how the future would turn out, and their fantasies. Friends have said Basti was the one who introduced them to the *kool* hip-hop artists, and they would put on a beat and rap over it. He was the one that wore the cool gangster clothes, saggy trousers, the most fantastic Nike shoes, hoodies with brands, the most excellent caps. New era stuff.[7]

Growing up, they were a loose gang of four or five that loved hanging out and doing things and dreamed of becoming famous. Their names remembered. Bastian always had to show off and prove himself to friends. Once, he lit four giant firecrackers and threw them in a hallway just before people entered. He got in considerable trouble for it, a friend remembers.[8]

In 2006 Bastian started at Service and Transport at Skien Videregående Skole, at the high school's campus in Brekkeby. He was an energetic student annoying the teachers getting reprimanded and yelled at. Around tenth grade, something changed. Bastian became a rebel and bought even baggier pants. He quit the soccer game he loved since he was a little kid and started hanging out with boys who were two-three years older. "Then he'd come back and told us what he did. They smoked weed," a friend said. The father later told NRK that it did not help to give him a good upbringing. The older boys Bastian hung out with were in a destructive environment.[9]

Bastian Vasquez, of Chilian descent, grew up in one of the oldest cities in Norway. Archeological excavations have shown settlements from the Viking times. His mother and father came to Norway in 1988 from Chile, escaping the oppressive Augusto Pinochet dictatorship and arriving in Norway with two sons, six and seven years old, from a faraway land. Immigration to Norway from Chile began after a military coup in Chile on September 11, 1973. Many political refugees came for several years after that and picked up again after the mid-1980s. On average, there were over 900 a year from 1986 to 1991, increasing in 1988, the year Vasquez's parents arrived. Chile suffered a dire economic crisis and an authoritarian military regime with an ever-increasing and stronger opposition.[10] Statistics from 2015 estimates that about 5000 Chilian immigrants live in Norway. Chilean immigrants have a far more dispersed settlement pattern than other refugee groups. A large proportion of Chileans have started families with Norwegians or people from other countries. In general, unemployment is lower than among other immigrants, and there is less of a difference between women and men in this field than what is usual among refugees.[11] Immigrants that have, by all accounts, done very well for themselves in Norway.

Skien, 13,596 kilometers from Chile, is a historical town in the southeastern part of Norway and a center of seafaring, timber exports, and early industrialization. The city lies by Skienselva, a river at the Telemark canal's first lock, and runs through the town Porsgrunn before it meanders into the Frierfjorden. In the early 1100s, as Christianity was taking hold in Norway, a convent settled in Skien, and the nuns were known as successful entrepreneurs.[12] Before Christianity, the early Norwegians practiced Norse Paganism and the indigenous Sámi people Shamanism. History won't repeat itself with any luck and let another religion take a stronghold. Norwegians do not wish to go back to 600 AD.

Skien was the birthplace of playwright Henrik Ibsen, and many of his famous dramas are reminiscent of early 19th-century Skien. Henrik Ibsen recalled his home, Skien, as the city of sawblades and waterfalls.[13] The old form of the name Skien, Skiða, is derived from the Old Norse word skiða meaning straight plank, and the word ski. Skien's coat of arms comes from the oldest known seal of the city, dating back to 1609. The seal shows two skis and a Christian cross with a small star in the middle and two meadow buttercups on each side, and many believe the cross symbolizes the Holy Cross church in Skien. The petite star may be a symbol of St. Mary as the second medieval church of Skien was devoted to her.[14] A perfect sign of Norway's more than thousand years of Christian tradition, since Olav Tryggvason, a Viking king of Norway, the son of King Harald Fairhair. King Olav Tryggvason was instrumental in efforts to Christianize Norway.

The Vasquez family from Chile made a good life for themselves in Norway. Bastian's father got a job as an engineer, and his mother is a department manager. They were involved in folk dances and fundraisers, and the father coached youth soccer. Bastian came to the world in 1990. A childhood friend remembers a necklace with a cross and a picture of Jesus on the wall, but the family rarely discussed politics and religion.[15]

When in Norway, Don't Do as The Northmen Do

Outside of the state church, the largest religious community in Telemark is Muslim, with twelve congregations. Five Muslim congregations are located in Skien, where the membership has tripled in eight years due to immigration. Emina, a board member for the Telemark Islamic Association, founded in 1993, is happy and says they have become more visible around the city. "It is positive to be seen and have a fixed framework around Koran school and language training for the little ones." Before 1993, they had to gather for prayer at each other's homes. There are five Muslim denominations in Skien; two are Shia Muslims and the others Sunni:

> Language is the main reason why we are divided. They have the most members with a Somali background and use their language in education. We use Arabic.[16]

There is no call for prayer YET coming from the mosques, but Emina is okay with that because they know the time of day to pray. But adds, proving the phrase, "When in Rome, do as the Romans Do," has fallen out of fashion long ago: "I think it's nice to hear prayers when I walk the streets at home in Tunisia. It would have been nice to have had it in Skien as well." God forbid that will happen, but in my broken heart, I know it will. In a country that boasts about women's equality, the mosque has two separate entrances for women and men. But members think it is a good solution:

> We are proud of our entrance. People present it as a problem without it being one. We can have men and women in the same room, and there are both women and men on the board. The women have a balcony in the mosque, which is a good solution. After all, we have the best view."[17]

As of 2018, Telemark has 33 Christian congregations outside the state church and 12 registered Muslim congregations. Almost nine thousand members total, and nearly four thousand, belong to the Muslim faith. Muslim members have more than tripled in eight years. The Christian congregations have lost three hundred members since 2010, a trend that seems to be happening all over Europe. The Telemark Islamic Association, to which Emina belongs, receives public support. In Norway, a registered religion member outside the state church qualifies for approximately 1,100 Norwegian kroner yearly.[18] And there are now more than two hundred mosques in Norway.

In December 2020, Hege Storhaug at Human Rights Service, HRS, writes; *Like mange moskeer, i Norge som i Frankrike,* "Norway has as many mosques as France." The Norwegian population was 5.37 million at the beginning of 2020, writes Ms. Storhaug. HRS has counted around 220 mosques in Norway. Concluding that there is one mosque in our country per 24,398 people, and almost identical to France. France officially houses 2,623 mosques. The French population is over 66.6 million people per 2016 figures, which amounts to one mosque per 25,467 people. Ms. Storhaug asks:

> Should this be a cause for concern? Maybe, all the time, Islam in Western Europe has the same face. It is primarily about the Brotherhood, Salafism, and the extreme Maududi ideology. The latter a man who is a forerunner of both the Taliban and al-Qaeda.[19]

There is no overview of the number of mosques in our neighboring country, Sweden, writes Storhaug. [Because Sweden, for some odd reason, likes to keep stuff like that in the dark. Meanwhile the country is going to hell in a handbasket]. In Denmark, a survey back in 2018 revealed that the country had 170 mosques, compared to 115 in 2006. The Danish population is 5.7 million people, counting one mosque per 33,500 inhabitants.[20]

Why worry so much, Hege Storhaug? You must understand this is about multiculturalism. The U.N., our politicians, and George want us to be a big happy family, living in perfect harmony. They surely know what's best for us. At least *I* try to be tolerant, as I am crying in my beer.

Mosques are being built and increasing in record numbers as Islam continues to penetrate every corner of the Norwegian society, like the preacher at Islam Net with a glimmer in his eyes, said. In 2019, an estimated 180 million kroner of taxpayers' monies went to Islamic congregations around Norway. And that's just for the registered members. Hard-earned taxpayers' monies to run Koran schools, teach in Arabic and other Middle Eastern and African languages, and conducting a dogma that discriminates against women, gays, and the kuffar. And if that isn't enough, Muslim congregations get state and local assistance in other areas, too, costing taxpayers millions.

In 2019, online *Document* wrote that the government is giving the controversial congregation *Det Islamske Kultursenter*, The Islamic Cultural Center, more than 700,000 kroner to buy and convert a more than 100-year-old Baptist church in Stavanger into a mosque.[21] Let me repeat. The Norwegian government is funding a controversial Islamic center to convert a more than 100-year-old Baptist church into a mosque. In a country with a Christian tradition of more than a thousand years. In a country that regained national independence from Denmark in 1814, and the Norwegian Constitution recognized the Lutheran church as the state church.

It is heartbreaking for me to read what goes on in my beloved homeland. I can feel my countrymen and women's pain, who are in the midst of the insanity. Those who see the writing on the wall. A woman named Hanne comments on *Document's* article. She is dramatic, but if we think of what's going on in Sweden, and that Norway always lags a few years behind our neighbors, she may not be far from the truth:

> I think it's time we say this now. Goodbye to our dear country. Thank you, Norway, for all you did for us and for all the joy you gave us. It is with great sorrow what we now witness. Churches are disappearing, and we are invaded by someone that do not wish us well unless we change course and worship our new master and people who speak another language.

A person by the alias Norvegia answers Hanne: "The future undeniably looks bleak for what was once a peaceful Norway."

Reporter Øyvind Thuestad writes that we are facing the somewhat paradoxical situation that the politicians gave the Islamic Cultural Center almost one million kroner to purchase mosques. But at the same time, they are investigating the same Muslim congregation that runs the very controversial SFO, a daycare facility for schoolchildren. A daycare operation where Muslim children spend days and nights and sleep over several nights a week. Some politicians are now critical that the religious community allows children to spend the night in the mosques and request to investigate them. Nevertheless, with support from the government and the Ministry of Children and Family Affairs, they give the Turkish religious community money to convert Christian worship houses into mosques. Minister Kjell Inge Ropstad from the Christian Democratic Party does not think it matters what the premise was before.[22]

In other words, unless I am lost in translation, a politician in the Norwegian Christian Democratic Party does not care that a 100-year-old

Baptist church is turned into a mosque. They even have the word democracy in their name and there is nothing democratic about Islam. Is there any wonder Norwegians like Hanne say goodbye to the Norway she loves and once had? Although it has been known for years that Islamic religious communities such as the Islamic Cultural Center keep children overnight in Koranic schools disguised as daycare facilities, the abhorrent practice has not received national attention before now. And as with all justified criticism of the Islamization of Norway, it will be forgotten and nothing will come out of it. Because nobody tells Muslims what to do but Muhammad.

I Don't Want to Judge Those Who Join ISIS. For Me Islam Is Peace

On a winter day in Skien, journalists from the local newspaper *Varden* and the *Morgenbladet* visit the Telemark Islamic Mosque, where rumor had it that Bastian converted. The reporters were working on a story about Vasquez and how a boy from Gulset became an ISIS terrorist. They had conducted numerous interviews with people who knew him, many friends and acquaintances, some narrated in the following pages. Investigative journalism at its finest and the primary source for Bastian Vasquez's story herein. And now they wanted to talk to the Iman in the mosque Bastian frequented.[23]

The mosque, a white residential house, was once located in the center of Skien and now moved to the city's outskirts. Most people who go there are Somalis. They meet a man with a henna-colored beard at the door, who refers them to the headmaster and Iman Abdirashid, a young man in a black sports jacket. He tells them he came to Norway in 1996 and went to a Koranic school near Mogadishu. He has been an Iman for two years and does not know Bastian Vasquez. He believes it is Vasquez's own choice that he traveled to Syria. He does not know who the Prophet Ummah is, and when asked about ISIS, he does not want to judge others. "I am not interested in judging others. I do not have enough knowledge. I do not want to say that something is wrong and something else is right." What a surprise. The journalists point out that sources believe Vasquez became radicalized in his mosque:[24]

> No one can influence or radicalize others here. I lead the prayer, no one else can take the podium, and I am, therefore, a hundred percent sure that Vasquez did not radicalize with us. For me, Islam is peace.[25]

But he does not denounce ISIS or anyone who traveled to Syria to join the terror organization.

Have You Heard of The Zeitgeist Movie?

In 2007, Peter Joseph, an American musician, filmmaker, author, and activist, performed in New York City over a 6-night period. The performance was a vaudevillian-style multi-media event using recorded music, live instruments, and video. He named it *Zeitgeist*, meaning intellectual, spiritual, and cultural awareness. His goal was to explore what makes us who we are, how we relate, what we are doing, and what we should be doing if we wish to live in a peaceful, humane, sustainable, and healthy global society. After the performance in New York, Joseph shelved the project until a friend suggested "tossing it up" on what was known as Google Video at the time. The video unexpectedly went viral, as we say today, and had over 50 million views within six months. *Zeitgeist,* the stage event, had become *Zeitgeist: The Movie.* Peter Joseph made two follow-ups. The entire series was watched over 500 million times as of 2020, with tens of thousands of uploads in dozens of languages. Some considered it as the most-watched Internet movie in history. The enormous publicity inspired The Zeitgeist Movement, founded by Joseph, to spread new social reform ideas, an economic and sustainability movement unrelated to the film's content.[26]

The original 2007 *Zeitgeist* movie consists of three parts presenting many conspiracy theories. Part one, influenced by the work of Acharya S, claims that the Christian religion derives from other faiths and traditions, astronomical assertions, and myths. Jesus, the movie claims, is a literary and astrological hybrid developed by political forces and opportunists.[27]

Part two alleges that the September 11 attacks were either orchestrated or allowed to happen by elements within the United States government. To generate mass fear, justify the War on Terror, provide an excuse for limiting civil liberties, and produce economic gain. It declares the U.S. government had advanced knowledge of the attacks, and the military deliberately allowed the planes to reach their targets. The World Trade Center buildings underwent a controlled demolition.[28]

Part three states that a small collaboration of international bankers controls the Federal Reserve System to create global disasters to enrich themselves. Three wars involving the United States during the twentieth century were part of this alleged plan. The sinking of the *RMS Lusitania,* the attack on Pearl Harbor, and the Gulf of Tonkin Incident. The wars encouraged conflict and forced the U.S. government to borrow money, thereby increasing the profits of the international bankers. The film also claims that the Federal Income Tax is illegal and a secret agreement to merge the United States, Canada, and Mexico into a North American Union. A step toward the creation of a single world government. The film speculates that every human could be implanted with an RFID chip under a government to monitor individual activity and suppress dissent.[29]

Bastian and his friends were absolutely obsessed with *The Zeitgeist* movie. A friend recalls how they would talk about it for hours, speculating, arguing, and disagreeing:

> Have you heard of a Zeitgeist movie? You have to watch it on YouTube. We saw it. It deals with 9/11 and that the U.S. government was involved in planning the plane crash. We were pretty convinced of that. We talked about it for hours. It becomes double standards, we thought, with Western values. They are good, but only on the surface. And there are a lot of weird things going on. One lives for money in the western world, and money is one's, own God. There were discussions. We speculated, argued, disagreed, and then started talking, and it led from one thing to the other.[30]

Another friend says Bastian started hanging out with Muslims, not so radical, but he may have started to think a little differently, maybe influenced by cannabis:

> Like all the stoners, talk about conspiracies, the United States, and 9/11. It didn't seem like he had thought that much through it. Many people who have been doing drugs will look for an alternative reality, a new start.[31]

Morgenbladet spoke to a source from one of the mosques Vasquez attended. He believed Bastian converted to Islam in 2009. He had started to hang out a lot with people from the Muslim community, Somalians, Syrians, Palestinians:

> It was about Bastian and a half Latin American friend, let's call him Tom. They hung out with us and saw how we were. They were part of that culture, even though they were Catholics. We invited them to the mosque. There was a lot of arguing, discussions about which religion was the right one and such if Jesus existed.
> They weren't actual Christians, but they believed in a god, the God in the Bible. But there was a lot back and forth. Then I remember that Tom suddenly converted. Bastian probably looked up to him. Tom was fun. Everyone wanted to hang out with Tom. Tom was one step ahead of Bastian all the time, and we would instead go home to Tom than to Bastian.[32]

Bastian stopped smoking hashish after the conversion and returned to school in 2009. He picked up the same program, Service and Transport, at Skien Videregående Skole. The school Vasquez dropped out of two years earlier. Teachers observe him as calmer, and he does the work he is supposed to do. This time he graduated. A convert and a native Norwegian, who had taken the name Yousef, met Vasquez a few times around 2009 and 2010 in Vestfold County, bordering Skien. They were together at many events and mosques in the cities of Larvik and Tønsberg:

I think I met him in mosques in Larvik and Tønsberg. There was talk of common Islamic themes, nothing radical. He was conservative but not radical. Some in these mosques have been radical and given leeway. The leaders there do not care who uses the mosque. If you supported al-Qaeda, it was like, 'Okay, I don't, but that's your business.' Some cars from Porsgrunn and Skien often came to these events, and I believe Bastian did.[33]

Yousef remembers how Bastian wanted to do everything right within Islam:

I remember that Bastian wanted to do absolutely everything right. How he ate, greeted, what he said before he went to the bathroom. His whole life was about Islam, trying to make amends for something. As if he had done a lot of stupid things and wanted to make up for it. We were just talking about Islam. He was a bit conservative but may not have known it himself.
He was searching and insecure. He wore a robe, beanie and grew a long beard. In the mosque, he was against music. He thought it was un-Islamic. Details were important to him. Not to eat with the left hand, always go to the bathroom with the left foot first. The manner of speaking was critical. One should say 'salam aleikum,' not 'hello.'[34]

It's autumn 2010, in Skien. In a class photo from the second year of Service and Transport, Vasquez is smiling and wearing a Palestinian scarf and a cap. Facial hair is visible on his chin. He starts changing a couple of months into the semester. In the coming months, he lets the beard grow. He wears Muslim clothes, robes, trousers, and a beanie hat. He starts isolating himself at school, greets others politely, and spends every spare hour in the mosque. People started talking about him, and classmates got nervous because of the new clothes. A friend is worried:

Basti said he wanted to wear Muslim clothes, not clothes that the infidels had made. I tried to talk to him about it. You have to stop it, I said; we're not in the Middle East now; that's piss. But he said that we were Muslims and had to wear such clothes. He would not relate to girls, then either. Sometimes he would cover his eyes. It was a whole comical thing, lots of mocking. 'Damn, I can't look at the girls.' When we drank, he was just there, did not drink himself. He was a good student, though.[35]

Another friend said Bastian tried to convert other people:

Basti read a lot of hadith. It tells the story of the Prophet Muhammad. There is a lot of sickness in the hadiths, things Mohammad did at that time. There, Basti sat and read. I was at his house once, and he showed

> me some pages, what I should read. I was shocked that he was so into it. He said he had tried to get his parents to convert.[36]

Bastian had many friends, and they were all concerned about his sudden change:

> He came to us once, then he had a lot of beard, looked completely different. Bastian had taken another leap about how money and all that rules the world, and doomsday is not far away. It was a bit like he was trying to put fear in us.[37]

In January 2010, at the University Square on a cold winter day in Oslo, Mohyeldeen Mohammad reads aloud from a small note. "When will the Norwegian authorities understand the seriousness? Maybe not until it's too late? Perhaps not before September 11 or June 7 happen on Norwegian soil?" Bastian Vasquez was there and was now ideologically embraced by his friends from Larvik, Mohyeldeen Mohammad, and Arfan Bhatti. Friends think it was after the demonstration that Bastian started hanging out with them. He was in the phase where he began to get rid of the old life, and there was no turning back.[38]

In January 2011, Bastian was suddenly gone from school. A friend said it looked like he was fine, then gone. He deleted Facebook and the whole package. It seems like he abruptly changed his environment. Then Bastian appears back on Facebook, but now under Muhammed Jundullah, "God's soldier." He has updated his political ideology as sharia law and Krav Maga as a favorite sport. Around the same time, The Islamic University of Medina, in Saudi Arabia, accepts Bastian as a student. Mohyeldeen Mohammed was admitted at the same time, but is later deported from Saudi Arabia.[39]

A friend of Bastian says that he got hostile towards everyone except his friends. He liked to be better than others. Noisy. In November 2011, he suddenly appeared in soccer photos on Facebook. At Old Trafford, the home ground of Manchester United. He's there with the family sporting a long beard, smiling calmly. His father stands by his side and looks lackluster. His big brother says they tried desperately to talk to Bastian and get him away from religion. They never understood what drove him and why did he suddenly convert. It spiraled through the mosque; he got new eating habits, stopped eating pork, started praying everywhere at specific times. Stopped everything he had done before and concentrated on religion. They watch in despair of his downfall, and his face getting sterner as if he was angry all the time.[40]

The Point of No Return

On an ordinary January morning in 2012, Norwegians wake up to the breaking news that the prime minister and the royal family have received terror threats online and a man is in custody. And soon, Bastian Vasquez's name is known and forever a household name in Norway. After he posted the video, the police had searched his bedroom and seized his computer. Incarcerated, he tells the police he did not want to threaten anyone but show what is happening in Afghanistan. He tells them he is engaged and expecting a child. He has asked police to call Arfan Bhatti, his friend from the Prophet Ummah. Bhatti tells him to take it easy and contact his attorney for life, John Christian Elden.[41]

The police release Vasquez from custody, and his family realizes how grave the situation has become. The father has said Bastian was sad after the arrest, but he chose to move to Oslo after a short period at home. Sources say that he moved in a collective with others who later became members of the Prophet Ummah and would practice the religion 24 hours a day. Sometime before that, Bastian has met a 17-year-old Norwegian Somali girl. In March 2012, the Norwegian Somali girlfriend, now fiancé, contacted a crisis center. It had happened once before because of violence and threats. Now the charge is threats against her and threats to take the child she had with Bastian. He denies all allegations but cannot see her or the child. A friend says he just got angrier and sadder, given up on life; he wanted to die as soon as possible:

> His dream was to die before turning forty. He wanted to die for the sake of Allah. He said that I would not be forty. I think he was anxious. And probably depressed too. He was giving up on life. He did not get what he wanted in Norway. He had no license, no car, no apartment, no job. He was mad at Norway. All unbelievers.[42]

On September 19, 2012, Vasquez stood by Arfan Bhatti's side during a demonstration at the United States Embassy in Oslo. Bhatti is now leading the notorious Prophet Ummah. Unconfirmed sources assume Bastian went to Syria shortly after, on October 3, 2012. Others say it was later, but everyone knows he never returned. His brother found out about the trip via a friend and got angry. Then sad. The good memories of his little brother come back when he goes to bed at night. Then he is afraid that something will happen to him. In January 2013, a picture on Facebook showed one of the Prophet Ummah leaders Mohyeldeen Mohammad holding the Islamist flag in what looks like Syria. The person next to him is said to be Vasquez. Bastian wears a beard, a hat, and a military jacket. He holds an AK-47, looking up at his comrade with admiration in his eyes as he points the weapon towards the sky.[43]

The Yazidi People Worship Lucifer

A year and a half later, on June 29, 2014, LiveLeak published a promotional video for the Islamic State from the ruins of a border station between Iraq and Syria. An ISIS-controlled region. The 24-year-old Norwegian Bastian Vasquez of a Chilean family that adored him, proudly strolls around in a worn-out grayish-blue cap, grayish-blue Muslim tunic with thin stripes, combat boots, and military pants. He has long scruffy facial hair, a mustache, and hair is covering most of his face. Around his body hangs a weapon, maybe the AK47 Bastian bragged to Sumaira about. He defiantly hoists the black ISIS flag, laughs at the camera, and poses with captured burned-out cars. "As you can see right now, we're at the border of Iraq and al-Sham," says Bastian Alexis Vasquez.[44] Once a young boy with dreams, he wanted his name to be known. In a desolate, war-torn country far from the Nordic land, he left to join Earth's most heinous terrorist organization. He speaks perfect English with a hard-to-detect accent. The only thing resembling a Scandinavian pronunciation is the deep breaths between words:

> We're going to break other borders also, but we start with this one. Let's walk across the border. We shall break the border to Iraq, Jordan, Lebanon, Libya, all the countries. This is the first border of many that we will destroy.[45]

He stands in front of vehicles belonging to the Iraqi army, destroyed beyond recognition. "We killed most of them, some of them ran off, and we took a lot of prisoners." In a later clip, the 24-year-old opens a heavy-armed door, and terrified prisoners of war, with unimaginable fear in their eyes, are being scolded and berated by Vasquez:

> See here. Prisoners. This is just some of the hundreds of prisoners that we have. Most of them are Shia and Yazidi. Those people who raise their hands right now are Yazidi people. They worship Lucifer; they say he was thrown out of Janna (paradise), and they worship him, he says with disdain, lips curling. These people used to patrol the border between Iraq and al-Sham. Look at these idiots. They claim to be Sunni Muslims but have nothing with Sunni Islam to do.[46]

The following video sequence shows Vasquez at a border police station and proudly proclaims ISIS is blowing it up. "Right now, they are setting up the cables and the explosives, so we take a look inside." He meets frightening-looking militias preparing to blow up the border station. Some of the terrorists wear the Palestinian keffiyeh headdresses, balaclavas, and army fatigue clothes. Are some of the uniforms from American soldiers? They carry automatic weapons and what looks like suicide vests. Or perhaps they are storage for ammunition. "The brothers also blow up the other buildings belonging to the Iraqi government." Then, Vasquez smiles, looking at the building from afar, sitting on top of what looks like a police car with lights. "This is the police station. They are going to blow it now. Al shama, beautiful?"[47]

Bastian laughs as the entire building blows up, and we will never know if the Shia and Yazidi prisoners were in the building. The video is only three minutes of the fifteen-minute-long video posted on LiveLeak. It is hard to shake the images of the prisoners of war and think this is the man that Sumaira, on trial in Oslo District Court, supported. The next day, friends and family around Norway watch with shock, sadness, and anger as the media releases the video. Comments of outrage and loss:

> I was empty of thoughts and words.
> I felt so sorry for the people in the video. I know that if he punishes them, he will punish them severely. He was always the weak one.
> The one I saw in the video was Bastian on the tough.
> He is probably proud of what he is doing. That he has status, when he thought it was going well for him, he was like that. I saw a Bastian who thought it was nice to be on T.V. and wanted to point out that 'here we have control.'
> Why he traveled to Syria? Jihad. I understood that he could finally gain power, gain status, freedom, gain leadership over someone. Finally, he could be the one he always dreamed of.
> I will never see that video again, said the father to NRK. To me, it does not look like my son. The body is there, but it seems that the soul and the spirit belong to another.[48]

Vasquez had, by then, a leadership role in ISIS. The following year, in 2015, unconfirmed sources report that he died in an explosion at a factory producing explosives. His family is devastated, and Bastian Vasquez's father told NRK:

> I distinguish between two people. It was my son, Bastian. And it was the radicalized person who called himself Sheik Mohammed. It was a total transformation, and he became a completely different person with a lot of hatred and violence. I did not recognize my son Bastian.[49]

I can't stop thinking of Bastian Vasquez's childhood friend's memory of a necklace with a cross and a picture of Jesus on the wall in Bastian's childhood home in Skien. And I can't stop thinking about his family despair over his downfall. What would have happened to Bastian if there were no mosques in Norway and radical Muslims to preach their dogma and indoctrinate young, impressionable minds?

You have every reason to be worried, Hege Storhaug.

CHAPTER 6
Bureaucracy Is the Art of Making the Possible Impossible

Somewhere in the United States, March 2017

It was early morning in March 2017, and with a cup of coffee in hand, I quickly scanned through the daily news in Norway, a habit I had started years ago. Living in the United States, I have a profound interest in what goes on in my home country and the United States, and thanks to the Internet, I can get daily news updates. To the annoyance of friends and family, I sometimes inform those in Norway who do not share my news addiction of what is going on in their own country. "Say, did you hear about the Swede…"

I was just about to sign off and prepare for work when a headline from one of Norway's largest tabloids caught my eye. *American man (24) must leave Norway*. A picture accompanied the article, and I saw a handsome young man with dark hair and blue-green eyes and a woman with blond hair and beautiful blue eyes. The caption under the picture said Eric had to travel to the United States on Thursday after being denied family reunification in Norway. I started reading the article, and soon tears were falling. I imagined their pain, remembering what I had gone through myself, and I could almost see sadness and despair in their eyes. Ten years ago, I had been up against the bureaucracy of The Norwegian Directorate of Immigration, or UDI. And although I had put it all behind me by now, it was upsetting to see someone like Eric, a young American man, being stonewalled and rejected by immigration officials in his Norwegian mother's home country.

It was on this day, I first learned of Eric and Heidi's story. And since then, I have taken a more than average interest in their plight and felt an affinity for them that I have to this day. Even though we have never met.

Reading the story that morning, I learned it was seven months since Eric had opened the letter from UDI and found out his application for immigration and a residence permit was denied. And a national Norwegian mainstream tabloid had finally agreed to publish their story. Had they not,

I would have never known about Eric and Heidi. "*The Daily News*" writes that UDI rejected Eric's application for family immigration and ordered him to return to the United States on the following Monday. But winter storms ravaged the east coast of the United States, and Eric's plane was canceled and scheduled to depart in a couple of days as soon as the storms subsided. The journalist sums up the story since the family decided to move to Norway and tells of UDI rejecting Eric's application for family immigration because Heidi was an American citizen when he was born.

Since receiving the rejection letter in September 2016, Heidi has hired an attorney to appeal UDI's decision. She wasn't a terrorist, so she was destined to pay for her counsel. The family attorney also argued that Heidi was unaware that she lost her Norwegian citizenship when becoming a U.S. citizen in 1991. They should not blame Eric for this. "Had I known that I lost the Norwegian, I would never have said yes to American citizenship," Heidi tells the *Daily News*. In the request for a reversal of UDI's decision, the attorney argues that there are strong human considerations, and Eric has a special connection to Norway indeed:

> Eric's immediate family, his mother, and brother have been granted a residence permit in Norway. Considering the time, he has lived here, it indicates that Eric has strong connections to Norway. As my client Eric sees it, he has no connection to the United States anymore. His father, and his last relative in the U.S., passed away in 2013. If Eric has to return to the United States, his opportunities for regular contact with the family will be impossible, including maintaining the relationship with his Norwegian girlfriend and cohabitant.

Furthermore, the attorney notes that Eric is well-integrated into the country and has no family or network in the USA. She also believes that the Norwegian authorities must emphasize that the 24-year-old has ADHD, which will make it difficult for him to get an education or a job in the USA. A reversal of the decision was sent to the Immigration Appeals Board, UNE, by the attorney. And not surprisingly, it was rejected. UNE writes that Eric is an adult who spent his entire upbringing in the USA. It, therefore, cannot be unreasonable that he is not granted a residence permit with his mother and brother:

> That the complainant has resigned from his job in the United States and has no place to live on return does not warrant another evaluation of the application.

If there ever was an example of insensitive bureaucratic language, the above statement takes the cake. The callousness of the language used by UNE is inexcusable. It is unforgivable in a country often voted the happiest on earth, priding itself on solidarity, understanding, and diversity. The journalist at the

Daily News was able to contact the section leader for UNE, and her bureaucratic rhetoric is no better than the correspondence from the immigration officials:

> There are strict requirements for obtaining a residence permit due to a strong human or special connection to Norway, and it happens only in exceptional cases. The complainant's claim must be so unique that the same situation will not apply to many others. The fact that someone has a close family in Norway is evident in many applications and is therefore very rarely given decisive weight.

The journalist also spoke to the family's attorney, and she says this case is not all black and white, and UDI and UNE use the connection to the USA for all it's worth. The attorney stresses that they must consider family connections. She points out that UNE has not made a *Forholdsmessighetsvurdering* in the case. A "proportionality assessment" in English, and the translation doesn't make it more comprehensible. The Norwegian language has many words with numerous letters. Still, only the government can develop a bureaucratic word that is 27 letters long to confuse the "commoners" they want to intimidate ever further.

UNE uses the assessment to accurately picture complex cases, cases where two or more legitimate rights collide. A decision will lead to one right prevailing over the other. This type of review should, in principle, take place in cases involving deportation. UNE uses the assessment to weigh the seriousness of the deportation case against the person's connection to Norway.

The attorney feels that Eric is entitled to a review even if his case is not deportation. In answering the request for a review, the section leader bureaucrat from UNE does what bureaucrats do best; refers to laws of the Norwegian Immigration Act. Rules they so blindly adhere to, especially when dealing with native Norwegians, it seems. And according to section 70, UNE has NO obligation to conduct a proportionality assessment because Eric is not deported from Norway. The following is their reasoning:

> When a person is deported from Norway, it means that the person must leave the country. That person will also lose the opportunity to return to the country, either for a period or forever. The complainant (Eric) has not been deported. He has had his application for a residence permit rejected. He can travel to Norway as a visa-free citizen if he so wishes. He can also apply for a residence permit on a new basis, such as a student or studies or work-related.

Visa-free means three months maximum, basically a tourist visa, and for Eric, that would mean three months in Norway and three months in the USA. And as long as it takes for UDI to get their finger out and process his application. A walk in the park, according to UNE. The bureaucrats conclude with a language only a bureaucrat can understand. The gobbledygook reads:

> When an application for a residence permit is rejected, it is not considered whether the refusal is disproportionate. However, an assessment is made as to whether there are strong human considerations or a special connection to Norway, which dictates that a residence permit be granted, even if the permit's conditions are not met.

The *Daily News* writes that Eric must leave Norway and return to the United States because of UNE's decision. Heidi tells the reporter she feels the decision is unfair. They followed advice from the consulate to establish residency in Norway. She and Robert have finally received their residence permit. She had bought a house, and they have settled down in the country. Heidi has even guaranteed living expenses for Eric until he gets his residence permit. She feels it is unfair and destructive to her family and that they are torn apart.

Hijack a Plane to Norway Eric. You'll Be Fine

It is difficult for me to accept UDI and UNE's decision-making in Eric's case, and my number one question to the bureaucrats would be: What in the world constitutes a special connection to Norway if Eric's case doesn't? What does Eric need to do to allow him to stay in Norway? Besides joining ISIS or al-Qaeda, should he pretend he is an Iranian, hijack a plane from the United States (Iraq), make it land on Norwegian soil, and demand residency? Not only will Norway take him in, but he may even get a job at NRK. The state-owned, taxpayer-funded newspaper and television station. This is not irony, folks. That, as insane as its sounds, is a true story.

Or should he form two terror organizations on Norwegian soil, like Iraqi Mulla Krekar, and claim for decades, along with his tax-appointed attorney, they cannot deport him for fear of the death penalty and torture. Or how about joining the Popular Front for the Liberation of Palestine, hijack a Lufthansa flight, and murder the pilot. Like Souhaila Andrawes, who did just that, together with the PFLP in 1977. They are all harbored and protected in Norway by the government, along with many others, but they could not leave room for Eric. An upstanding young American citizen with an ethnic Norwegian mother.

The tangled hijacking story, spanning over decades, is too long to include in this book but deserves mention. In 2002, the *Guardian* reported an uproar erupted in Norway after its immigration directorate UDI defied the government and granted political asylum to two Iranians who hijacked a flight and forced it to divert to Oslo, Norway, in 1993. The justice minister at the time had said that the two men, Mansour Mohammadi Injeh, 37, and his brother Farhad, 29, would never be granted leave to stay in Norway. Nine years later, the immigration directorate has gone against this and the wishes of the current center-right government. They could not send the brothers back to Iran, UDI concluded, because they would face the death penalty. This claim was disputed by the Iranian government and by the Norwegian embassy in Tehran. Many politicians, from all parties, believe that Norway's legendary generosity towards refugees fleeing persecution is being abused, writes the Guardian.[1]

At the time, Erna Solberg, Norway's current prime minister, told *Aftenposten*. "We can't accept that Norway becomes a safe haven for hijackers. The signal we send is that we are more liberal in relation to crime than others."[2] Apparently, Ms. Solberg now, twenty years later, thinks Norway should be a haven for ISIS terrorists and other foreign criminals because it is a question of morals according to her, as you will find out later. Like many other Norwegian politicians, she has changed her political position through the years and makes decisions whichever way the globalists wind blows. Guardian writes:

> The violent nature of the men's crime, threatening to detonate hand grenades and a homemade bomb aboard an Aeroflot plane bound from Azerbaijan to the Russian city of Perm, shocked many Norwegians at the time and is still embedded in the national consciousness. However, the government cannot overrule the immigration directorate. It must wait until the case comes up for review next year.[3]

Pilots in Norway were alarmed by the decision. "This is bad for everyone who flies," said Sigurd Løkholm of the country's pilot's union. "For all, we know the next hijacking with Norway as a destination may already be on the drawing board."[4] The brothers from Iraq have continued making news since they hijacked their way into Norway. In 2002, reports surfaced that NRK hired Mansour Injeh as a sound technician. A desirable job, I imagine lots of Norwegians would love to have. I remember in an interview with Mansour he stated, "I do not work with dynamite," and "What else should an asylum seeker or refugee do, sitting at home?"[5] So hilariously funny, I forgot to laugh.

In 2008, Mansour's brother, Farhad, was sentenced to six years in prison for drug smuggling. He was arrested with five Eastern Europeans, linked with the smuggling of 4.9 kilos of methamphetamine.[6] Isn't that special. In 2019, one of the brothers sued the state in Oslo District Court, claiming he is entitled to a residence permit on humanitarian grounds in Norway. He has had a temporary residence permit since 2002 because he risks the death penalty on return to Iran.[7]

I intend on writing more about the two brothers in my next book about Norway's Immigration experiment gone awry. It's a twisted story. The decision to give them political asylum was based on a blatant lie from certain government officials. Just as it was when bringing the ISIS woman back because her child was allegedly sick. Politicians and bureaucrats are constantly deceiving the Norwegians, and I cannot bear to watch it from across the ocean and see my home country go to *helvete*. That's why I have to put it down on paper and pray that the insanity we are witness to will some day end.

It's a Burden for Norway's Relationship With USA

Two weeks before Heidi and Eric's interview with the *Daily News*, Heidi's brother, Leif, had written an open letter to Sylvi Listhaug from the conservative Progress Party and Minister of Immigration at the time. Leif, a former police officer, has been involved in Heidi and Eric's fight for his nephew to stay in Norway since the day Eric received the rejection letter from UDI.

"He is full of enthusiasm. He wants to work and manage on his own. He has no criminal record," assures Eric's uncle. Leif has a long police career behind him. Both in Nordmøre and Vestfold, he worked in the border and immigration section before retiring a few years ago. Leif knows quite a bit about "the system" and thinks it is incomprehensible that Eric cannot settle in Norway. He is reasonably confident that if the Directorate of Immigration and the Immigration Appeals Board check their archives, they will find countless cases where residence and work permits are granted on a much weaker basis than in Eric's case. Frighteningly many, he believes.

He thinks the handling of Eric's case is shoddy and that they have found an easy target to "push around." A victim without a tax-payer-funded attorney. The slow case processing is also unfathomable, and Leif characterizes it as shameful. He has the same perception of local and central politicians who see the other way and do not dare get involved in Eric's cause. Leif has been a local politician for the Labor Party for several years, but the party dues are now put on hold. He has visited the party's headquarters several times and received promises to discuss Eric's case. But then there's silence. He tells the local newspaper:

> I perceive politicians I have contacted to be interested in their gimmicks of self-promotion rather than respect us as voters, serve our interests, and protect our rights and justice.

The same local newspaper he spoke to published Leif's letter to Sylvi Listhaug regarding UDI and UNE's handling of Eric's immigration case:

> Norway does not have room for my 24-year-old nephew from the USA. He has lived with the rest of the family in my hometown in Møre and Romsdal since August 2015. My little sister traveled to the USA in 1982 as a 20-year-old to work as an au pair. There she married and eventually had two sons. The eldest was born before my sister became a United States citizen. The youngest boy, who is now 24 years old, who I, in

this letter, refer to as my nephew, was born after my sister had become a United States citizen. After she became a widow a few years ago, both my little sister and her children were determined to travel to Norway and continue their lives there. They had no family left in the USA, while in Norway, they had many family members.

The consulate in New York wished my little sister, the Norwegian American, and her children the best of luck and helped them comfortably burn all bridges. With the expectation that relocation was permitted, they came to Norway in 2015. There they did what the consulate had advised, and among other things, found employment. They are self-sufficient.

My little sister and her sons bought a house in Norway and have not cost the country a single penny per date. In Norway, however, the Directorate of Immigration quickly and brutally broke all their hope and dreams. After an intense battle with a self-paid attorney against the UDI's attempts to refuse a residence permit for her for almost two years, she, and her oldest son, finally received a temporary residence permit. She then most graciously accepted her affiliation with Norway.

My nephew, however, has received no mercy from the UDI. He is by a letter and a clause born of an American citizen, and UDI refuses to use discretion and reason in his case. My nephew has an intense desire to work, has established a relationship with a Norwegian girl, is full of enthusiasm for everything Norwegian, and wants to contribute to our society, which UDI considers irrelevant. My nephew was diagnosed with ADHD diagnosis as a child and had no higher education. Many others with the same diagnoses do not adapt well to long and demanding schooling.

He is also without funds and is dependent on the network he has in Norway, which no longer exists in the United States. The young man's mother is willing to guarantee to be his financial sponsor in Norway, until he gets a residence permit, which is also irrelevant to UNE.

The Immigration Appeals board demands that he return to the United States with a deadline of one week. Even though he has no network in the USA, but ALL his immediate family is in Norway. His mother, grandmother, aunts, uncles, cousins, and many others. Even though he has a Norwegian girlfriend and cohabitant, UDI and UNE interpret that his connection to the USA is greater than to Norway.

Decisions made by UNE become further erroneous when looking at human considerations and consequences for my nephew and his mother. Another critical point is that my sister, during the preparations for the return to Norway, received confirmation from the National Register as late as 2014 that she was still a Norwegian citizen. Later, in July 2014, however, the authorities swiftly deleted her citizenship from the

> population register. UNE has not considered this aspect, which is of absolute importance for granting a residence permit for my nephew.
> My nephew's connection to Norway and vital human considerations must be considered. And decisions made by the Norwegian consulate in the USA and unresolved issues regarding the mother's citizenship to Norway at my nephew's birth should justify a decision in his favor.
> UDI states that 15,580 people received family reunification in Norway in 2016. I dare to claim that many of those positive reunification decisions are less justified than my nephew's. Based on my previous work experience from the police immigration administration, I have a definite impression that the UDI and UNE in my nephew's case have not shown the same reasonable judgment as in many others. I request that the Ministry use its ability to govern to instruct UNE to change its decision in this matter.
> This case has another side that I allow myself to draw attention to. In this respect, Norway's relations and cooperation with the United States are interesting to see from a larger perspective. Historical, cultural, national interests, whether it is security policy or economics. *It is a burden for Norway's relationship with the United States when a young American man with a strong affiliation with Norway is denied a residence permit.*
> *At the same time, it is expected and taken for granted that American soldiers are brought here and demanded that they sacrifice their lives for our security and freedom.* Our closest friends in the world, among many things, constitute our most significant security guarantee. Perhaps we should favor Americans, and the requirements for a residence permit should be similar to our agreement with our Nordic neighbors. I am assisting my sister and nephew in this matter to the best of my ability and have additional information in the case that may further shed light on the issue in my nephew's favor.

It Is as Sad as The Pouring Rain

> The decision is incomprehensible. I refuse to accept that my mother and brother are allowed to stay while I have to return to the United States. Unfortunately, I will have to leave in a week, but I will continue the fight in the United States.

A local newspaper interviews Eric after a weekend with unbearable anxiety. A few days earlier, he had received the bad news from his mom that he is not allowed to stay in Norway with his mother and brother. The UNE rejected the request to reverse the decision to refuse Eric a residency permit and postpone the deadline for returning to the USA. On the same day, the police notified Eric to return to the United States.

Over the weekend, the attorney had worked against the clock to obtain the decision by UNE, so they could prepare for Eric's departure and buy airline tickets if necessary. UNE would not give any information over the phone, and a letter was sent in the mail on Friday along with an e-mail link sent to the attorney. She experienced technical problems and could not open the link. UNE would not help her open the link nor send the decision by e-mail. "Bureaucracy is the art of making the possible impossible," said Javier Pascual, and is seemingly a newly adopted motto at UNE. On Monday, she called for I.T. assistance, and even they could not open the link from UNE. Astoundingly, late Monday afternoon, she got UNE to tell her the outcome over the phone. They would not tell her the reason for the rejection, only that the decision was unfavorable.

On Monday afternoon, she had to call Heidi with the bad news. "I honestly know very little, and the little I know I heard on the phone today. We have to wait for a letter posted before the weekend before we can get the reasons for the rejection," the attorney tells the local newspaper. As far as she has understood, UNE has also not extended the departure deadline by a few days, so he has time to book the necessary airline tickets. "I still expect them to be lenient at this point since the refusal came on the same day as the departure deadline expired." She felt for the family and told the reporter that Monday was a sad and dark day for everyone involved in the case.

When the journalist spoke to a shattered Heidi a little later, she was waiting to take a ferry home to tell her son the bad news. She was disappointed, tired, and crying. Uncle Leif told the newspaper a little later that it would probably be impossible to get Eric tickets and travel that same evening. And it will undoubtedly cost tens of thousands in addition to what the family has already spent on legal aid. He can't believe what is happening as he is shaking his head talking to the reporter:

> I do not know, but maybe now Heidi must consider moving back to the United States. It's very distressing. They have sold everything they owned in the United States and bought a house. Heidi and her eldest son Robert got residence permits while Eric is not allowed to stay.

Leif says he has tried to contact many politicians but without getting a response. He has also tried to get in touch with Sylvi Listhaug. After he wrote the letter to Listhaug, he wrote on her Facebook page that his mother, Eric's grandmother, is distraught that Norway does not have room for her American-born grandson. Leif, who has fought a hard fight for Eric, is devastated and pours his thoughts out on Eric's Facebook support page:

> Today, politicians and the UDI and UNE have managed to make me feel like a second-class citizen in my own country. UNE has decided to deny my nephew Eric a residence permit, regardless of my opinions about justice and reasonableness and many people I have talked to. That there

are human considerations, they refuse to admit. It is incomprehensible that NO politicians, not even within our county, step forward and dare to help. It is shameful. That the boy is more 'Norwegian' than many real Norwegians I know and that he has a Norwegian girlfriend, and they live together does not matter.

It also doesn't matter that he has been living in Norway since August 2015 and has never asked or cost the Norwegian society a single penny. All he has is the only desire to be in Norway with his girlfriend and family, working and living everyday life and enjoying healthy hobbies like fishing and outdoor life that he loves so much. All these factors make it extra sad for me when such a final decision is that Eric is not welcome in Norway. Then my thoughts go to the 15,580 people who were granted family reunification in Norway in 2017. And I dare to claim and cannot help wondering if any of those granted residence permits are less justified to call Norway home than Eric is.

During Eric's case, I have contacted politicians, both in the Parliament and the government. Before the election, they spoke to you using words with promises to join the fight preventing the perceived injustice of refusing Eric a stay. They failed to keep promises but are still rude enough to develop their lofty ideas and demand applause in votes and elections. *It is as sad as the pouring rain and the low cloud cover in the morning hours today to register how these politicians make themselves inaccessible.*

My trust in politicians and their handiworks is wearing thin to the breaking point. At the same time, my confidence in the ruling politicians, the Parliament and several departments, party organizations, the UDI and UNI, has suffered severe setbacks. I wish humility will knock on the door of these men and women in power and institutions and correct their lofty egocentric self-image.

Tuesday, Eric will be sitting on a plane back to the USA. He will probably be wondering, without getting any answers; Why does he have to go back to where he has no family network, job, and place to live? And his only family and his girlfriend are left back in Norway. He is probably also wondering how in the world is he going to make it when he gets back. And he is probably thinking; with all the people supporting him getting residency in Norway, there must be some faults with the democratic systems laws and legislation. Are UDI and UNI something uber national that is above the democracy?

And while Eric is sitting on the plane with his thoughts, and the plane is getting closer to the USA, Norwegian politicians are not getting involved and do not care because they are busy cooking up their porridge of talk. In this porridge they are cooking up, they are busy blaming others for their wrongdoings. The bag of porridge of the things they need to do is still sitting unopened in the cabinet.

> I give the Norwegian immigration officials treatment of Eric's case the grade 'not passed.' At the same time, I present our politicians, who make our laws and ensure that the regulations work in practice as intended, the same grade. NOT PASSED.
> If politicians don't have time to see if the regulations work as intended in this and similar cases because they are busy bringing home foreign fighters and their wives (who are no longer allowed to keep their heads down in Syria), that's not an excuse for me.

I can almost feel Leif's outrage, disbelief, and emotion. You are in a state of disbelief when you discover that what should be a minor problem, an American citizenship, would cause the government of your home country to stonewall and deny a young, amazing man like Eric residency in Norway. And on top of that, native Norwegians, and many of us who live abroad, witness the bending over backward and catering to those who arrive in Norway with outstretched hands; it becomes more outrageous. And when the Norwegian government risks national security and the welfare of its citizens bringing home foreign fighters and harboring terrorists, as I write in these pages, Eric's story becomes that much more shameful.

CHAPTER 7
When Norwegian Journalists Become Social Justice Activists

Al-Hol refugee camp, March 12, 2019

> The niqab-clad woman with the rectangle eyeglasses is crying a river. She shakes her head and rubs her eyes vigorously with her red nail polish-painted fingers, producing more tears that quickly disappear down the heavy Muslim garb she is wearing. The ISIS woman speaks fluent Norwegian with a slight accent and pleads for help in a quivering voice: Jeg vet ikke hva jeg skal si. Jeg vet ikke. Det vet jeg virkelig ikke. Jeg vil virkelig tilbake til familien min. Det er det eneste jeg ber om.
> I do not know what to say. I don't know. I really don't know. I want to return to my family. That's the only thing I ask for.[1]

AN IMAGE OF a crying woman in need would typically evoke empathy and sadness in me. But for the life of me, I cannot produce that state of mind looking at the women in the video posted on NRK's website with the headline *Jeg angrer. Vær SÅ snill og hjelp oss.* "I'm sorry. Please be SO kind and help us" The Norwegian ISIS woman begs the authorities in Norway to bring the children, and her, home to Norway, writes NRK.[2] And then I feel guilty that I have such feelings. So, I think of Eric and Heidi, and I say to myself, "to hell with NRK, to hell with the ISIS woman, and to hell with the Norwegian government."

It's March 12, 2019, and the social justice warrior activists from NRK have just begun their mission to get the Norwegian ISIS woman and her two children home to Norway. Her name is Sumaira Ghafoor, and she is the same woman facing charges of joining a terrorist organization in Oslo District Court in March 2021. Almost two years to the day when NRK is now interviewing her at the al-Hol camp in Syria.

Sumaira has ditched the crocodile tears in the following short video segment. She seems defiant, feels victimized, shows no significant regrets or any impression that she thinks she put herself in the dire situation she is in now. She does, however, admit she has ruined her parents. And that's sad. But it is essential all about her:

> My life under ISIS. Locked in a house and only allowed one thing. And it's washing clothes and cooking.
> Do you support ISIS? asks the female journalist.
> I have never supported ISIS and will not do so.
> What punishment do you feel you deserve after being part of ISIS?
> I've already had enough punishment, six years without the family. That's enough.
> What has been your punishment?
> I have not been with them. I have missed six years of my brother's upbringing. Six years that I've ruined my mom. She has become ill, and my father the same. And I lived in longing for my family. It is enough.[3]

Journalists from NRK are at the al-Hol refugee camp. Also called the al-Hawl refugee camp, named after the town of al-Hawl in northern Syria, close to the Syria-Iraq border. The reporters focus on Sumaira's children, a two-year-old daughter and her four-year-old step-brother, whose father is Bastian Vasquez. They have seen things no children should see, they write.

Well, at least they can still see and are not like little Ulrik, the little blue-eyed, blond-haired 4-year-old Norwegian boy who was denied experimental treatment from the Norwegian government just recently. The only remedy available that may give hope that he will not lose his eyesight. But the only treatment available for little Ulrik. It was too expensive, too risky, and not an approved medical procedure. And when asked by the Progress Party leader Sylvi Listhaug, Prime Minister Solberg said there was nothing they could do to change the regulations.

So instead, ethnic Norwegian Ulrik may lose his eyesight, and NRK is worried about children born into an ISIS caliphate by a quisling mother. It is clear where their priorities are. Ulrik is only one of many Norwegians set aside for more important and pressing things the globalists and multiculturalists have on their minds. NRK, whose funding comes from the very government and politicians it protects, didn't give Ulrik the time of day. Only two news outlets in Norway did. Liberal TV2 broke the news,[4] and the online conservative *Resett* followed up. But time and empathy for an ISIS woman in Syria they have. And they will for the next two years and beyond.

> They could have had it so much better, stopped seeing hunger every single day, watching all that shooting, all that bombing, and fires…

Sumaira lays it on to NRK. And the activists kick the drama up a notch, writing that the children were born and raised in the caliphate of the brutal terrorist group ISIS by a mother who says she regrets it all. Now she wants to go home, and the children are sitting with bare feet on a black mattress. In silence, they eat dry biscuits and drink water, they write.[5]

Dry biscuits and water? Bare feet? State-owned NRK rakes in six milliard Norwegian kroner from the government and taxpayers every year, almost one billion U.S. dollars. And the reporters could not bring adequate food to Sumaira's children when visiting her in the camp? Or socks and shoes? Conspiracy theorists would call out the liberal media and say they are trying to pull at one's heartstring scheme. And we all know it wouldn't be the same if the activists told their readers, the children sat in silence enjoying Peppe's pizza and a Coca-Cola, admiring their new Nike baby sneakers and H&M socks.

She Swears They Did Not Keep Yazidi Slaves

The woman left Norway six years ago, writes NRK. She escaped from a marriage the family had planned. Instead, she chose the Norwegian foreign warrior Bastian Vasquez, already known for his extreme attitude. And so was Sumaira, but NRK churches up her story the best they can. She went to Turkey to meet Bastian and claims that he took her to Syria against her will. She was only a mother and a housewife in the terrorist group ISIS, information that NRK does not have the opportunity to control they write,[6] which I assume means fact check.

Oh yes, you do NRK, but you won't dig deeper and act like real investigative journalists unless it fits your agenda. No matter what she did, Sumaira was an accomplice. She knowingly, voluntarily, and intentionally assisted Bastian Vasquez in committing atrocious crimes and did not stop him. "Because I loved him, I closed my eyes and did what he said. That's the mistake I made."[7] She claims that none of her husbands or she had Yazidis as slaves when asked by a journalist. NRK does not press her further on the subject. Her husband Bastian Vasquez kept Yazidi prisoners and bragged about beheadings and killings. And even though the tabloid VG published Vasquez's ISIS propaganda video online, I have not seen any mainstream media mention the prisoners he kept and killed.

She made that happen somehow; brutal facts NRK do not wish to check.

As in the case of Jennifer W., whose court proceeding began in March 2020 in Frankfurt, her last name is not disclosed, following German privacy law. We got to protect them, terrorists, because their lives matter too. The 27-year-old woman reportedly let a Yazidi child die of thirst in 2015. Jennifer W. left Germany for Iraq in August 2014 after joining ISIS. She shared a household with her husband, ISIS jihadist Taha al-J. In the summer of 2015, Taha al-J bought a Yazidi woman and her five-year-old daughter taken captive by ISIS. No, you did not read that wrong. They purchased the Yazidi woman as a slave. The couple kept the Yazidi woman and her daughter imprisoned as slaves and exposed them to inhuman living conditions. They were forced to convert to Islam and severely beaten regularly. To punish the five-year-old, she was chained outdoors in scorching heat, which led to her death. Jennifer W. witnessed her husband's acts and did not take any steps to prevent the child's death.[8]

Or the case against Omaima Abdi, a German-Tunisian, which came to the attention of authorities after Lebanese journalist Jenan Moussa gained access to her phone. A real investigative journalist. Abdi had thousands of ISIS-related files and photos on the phone. She taught her children the ideologies of ISIS. In some of the photographs, her children are holding weapons and dressed as jihads. She was married to Dennis Cuspert, one of Germany's most notorious ISIS jihadists. They kept a 13-year-old Yazidi girl as a slave. Omaima Abdi, a mother of three, returned to Germany in 2016 and worked as an event manager in Hamburg for three years before being arrested in September 2019. Omaima's explanation was the same old song and dance as Sumaira. She was just a housewife and a mother. But in reality, as investigators discovered, she was as radical as they come. Pari Ibrahim, executive director of the Free Yazidi Foundation, said in 2019:

> ISIS women were fully complicit in the torture of Yazidi women and the enabling of their rape by ISIS fighters. These 'women of the caliphate' are therefore far from innocent.[9]

I Will Take Off the Niqab When I'm In Norway

Sumaira and her children have been at the al-Hol camp for a week when NRK is there. The Syrian Democratic Forces, SDF, took control of the family and evacuated them to the internment camp from the ISIS enclave in Baghuz. Now the family lives in a tent with ten other families. NRK notes that the two-year-old girl keeps going to the bathroom. She does not make it in time and soils her white trousers. "They both have diarrhea and go to the toilet all the time. First one, then the other." Sumaira tells NRK her four-year-old son has a chronic lung disease. The disease is called cystic fibrosis, later labeled by some Norwegians as mystic fibrosis, and requires advanced treatment. NRK asks the only hardball question they can muster. "Are you responsible for putting your children in this situation?" "Yes, that's why I want to do something about it and send them somewhere where they can be safe."[10]

The journalists are not permitted to film or take pictures inside the camp, but they do anyway. There are plenty of empathetic photos of the children adorning the news story online at NRK. A French ISIS woman sticks a note in a reporter's hand. "Can you call mom and say I'm here?"[11] In the camp, most ISIS women still wear the niqab with the loose black garment burqa that covers from head to toe. The niqab is the veil with a small opening for the eyes, their window to Islam's narrow-minded world. Sumaira tells NRK that those who do not wear the niqab in the camp get reprimanded:

> What are you going to do with the niqab if you come home?
> I will take it off because I do not feel like going with it. I've been wearing it long enough. I want to be free again the way I was before.[12]

Sumaira's evasive language, spoken by many, would translate to, "Attorney Nordhus says it will help me in court to dress as a Western woman." NRK allows Sumaira to ask for help from the Norwegian authorities, and the activists have just begun their job as mediators and cheerleaders for the woman's return to Norway:

> I want to say to them: I regret that I trusted the person I trusted and made a mistake. I want to make things right, so if it's possible, please help me. I want to make my children's future a little better.[13]

Both Prime Minister Erna Solberg and the Minister of Justice have stated several times that it is not relevant to help the Norwegian children or the women out of the detention camp, writes NRK. "Come to a Norwegian foreign services station, and we will assist," has been the message from Norway.[14]

She Was Almost Left Behind

A little over five months later, on August 23, 2019, NRK reports that the ISIS woman will not give up her children to Norwegian authorities. Her eldest son is seriously ill, a mantra NRK will repeat time and time for months. The Kurdish self-government authorities have refused to separate mother and child but have recently been open to allow it if a child is seriously ill. But there is only one problem, says NRK. In a letter to the woman's attorney, the Ministry of Foreign Affairs has clarified that they can only assist the children's return to Norway, not the ISIS woman. The Norwegian government has said NO. They will only help the children back to Norway, and the mother must stay behind. That means the woman and the two children remain in al-Hol indefinitely,[15] cries the activists at NRK.

"She Was Almost Left Behind: An ISIS Woman Dramatic Escape to Norwaystan" comes to mind. While writing *Sympathy for the Evil,* I am also working on a possible Academy Award-winning movie or television series script. To my understanding, Hollywood, the wokest of the woke, wants diversity in all films. The story tells of a niqab-wrapped ISIS woman's dramatic homecoming to the Scandinavian country once utopia and now under Sharia law? Mosques have replaced all the beautiful ancient churches, and social justice warrior politicians fight tooth and nail to get the traitor back so they can support her to the end of times. On taxpayer's money paid for by the few native Norwegians left in Norway.

85

The rest of the Vikings took their red, white, and blue flags and moved to Greenland, now owned by the United States after President Trump bought it from Denmark. He got a good deal for the vast land, the clever businessman he is. And Trump is now their president and Governor Ron DeSantis of Florida his part-time vice president. Floridians won't let him go completely; DeSantis has to govern Florida too. The most competent governor, the land of the free, has seen in years, no matter what the Democrats and media will tell you. I have the ability to see the future, as the Vanir gods in Vanaheim. And Governor Ron DeSantis will be president someday, loved by both the left and the right. *Some* on the left, I should add, for those others, there is no cure. His accomplishments are second to none. He's a Yale, Harvard, and Naval Justice school graduate, a U.S. Navy JAG Officer, assigned to SEAL team one, and an assistant U.S. attorney. And absolutely no scandals, like smoking crack or painting $500,000 pathetic work of art. Trivial shames if you're on the left. Except he had the nerve to take his mask off to drink a beer at a ballgame. And the left reamed him for it. "She Was Almost Left Behind," will soon be coming to a theater near you. Or Netflix, if they will allow it. They may, since they had no problems releasing the French film *Cuties*, sexualizing young girls. There are not boundaries today, so a controversial film about an ISIS woman's escape and the Islamization of Norway should pass Netflix's standards with flying colors.

The ISIS woman has consulted with her attorney, Nils Christian Nordhus, and she has concluded that she does not want to send the children to Norway alone, despite her son's illness. Nordhus informs NRK, "After an evaluation, she has assessed the situation and believes it will expose the children to trauma and stress they simply will not tolerate." However, Attorney Nordhus does not rule out that the woman will evaluate the case differently in the future due to the problematic situation her four-year-old son is in. The Norwegian authorities are responsible and cannot let the boy pay with his life. She wants to travel with her two children to Norway, and they have an opportunity to save this boy's life, says the audacious attorney:

> It is the mother's evaluation, and then the Norwegian government can agree or disagree with it, but they cannot let the mother's decisions lead to the boy simply having to pay with his life. The Norwegian authorities must take responsibility for the situation. They cannot push through such an implementation method in a position that could lead to her boy having to pay with his life.[16]

For Heaven's sake, since when does a jihad-joining "Norwegian" woman get the right to evaluate her case and determine she has any right to return to a country she betrayed to join ISIS? Only in Norway does a traitor and terrorist have more rights than a regular citizen. And as soon as she puts her niqab-hijab-and-burka-wrapped body back on Norwegian soil, the government will support her for the rest of her life. And who pays for her attorney? I understand the right to an attorney, but incidentally, every radical Islamist and criminal portrayed in this book has acquired high-profile Norwegian counsels. How? And why were Heidi and Eric not afforded the right to free legal aid? Heidi spent an excessive amount of money on attorneys.

Even if Sharia forbids it because it is from the unbelievers, many of the radical Islamists were on welfare. And if they worked to make a living, although highly unlikely, none of them would afford the astronomical fees attorneys charge in Norway. And conveniently, because of laws and attorney-client privilege, it is almost impossible to find numbers, who pays for, and how much money Norway spends on defending foreign nationals, including terrorists. The politicians and authorities go to great lengths to keep the numbers in the dark.

In March 2020, the online conservative newspaper *Resett* wrote about Najmuddin Faraj Ahmad, 63, an Iraqi known as Mulla Krekar, mentioned earlier. Norway has been "trying" to get rid of Krekar for years, and luckily the knight in shining armor Italy came to the rescue when sentencing him to 12 years in prison for plotting terrorism. Krekar was extradited to Italy in February 2020. He landed his jihad ass on Norwegian soil in 1993 and was cancer to the Norwegian society for 27 years, treated as a loving and misunderstood grandpa by some. He formed two terror organizations, most likely on welfare in Norway. The Ansar al-Islam, a known affiliate of the al-Qaeda network; and Rawti Shax, an ISIS-linked network.

A few years ago, the conservative Progress Party estimated the total cost in the Krekar case had cost Norwegian taxpayers at least 20 million Norwegian kroner, writes *Resett*. Including around three million in free legal aid, five million for interpreting services, four million for the police, prosecutors, courts, and twelve man-years in various ministries. Eight years later, the cost of Mulla Krekar more than likely has multiplied. However, still, there is no public information on how much he has cost Norwegian society, except for estimated numbers. Krekar's wife and family still live in Oslo. Whether they are moving from Norway is uncertain, writes *Resett*.[17] Why should they? I'll bet my family in Norway's hard-earned taxpayers' dollar they are well cared for by the Norwegian state.

A man named Peder commented on a story online about Islam in Norway recently:

> How much have supporters of the violent ideology Islam cost Norwegian taxpayers in the last ten years? Housing, welfare payments, health services, interpreting services, special education, support for Muslim denominations, support for Islamic associations, the judiciary, imprisonment, etc. What could We and the Norwegian society get for all the billions? Improved conditions for the disabled. Better conditions for the elderly.

> Better offers for young people in business. Medicines for the seriously ill who today do not receive the best treatment. Personal assistant hours for the disabled so they can live a dignified life. Relief for parents with seriously ill children. Lower tolls, etc., etc.

An enormous cost both for society and native Norwegians, all in the name of multiculturalism and political correctness.

In early August 2019, NRK reported that the family in the al-Hol camp had received a dramatic message. And always one step ahead in their activism, they reproduce the boy's health information with the consent of the child's mother. It's a handwritten, detailed, long-drawn-out and thorough medical record from the field hospital in al-Hol, dated August 22, 2019:

> Patient treated for CF. We cannot perform that in our hospital. Please help with a referral.[18]

Desperate times call for desperate measures, so Attorney Nordhus has produced an expert statement written by a professor and a psychologist specialist. The experts report that it is both unwise and risky to separate mother and child in a crisis. Children can develop a high degree of anxiety, insecurity, become apathetic, emotionally unstable, and refuse to eat. Since World War II, the professional advice has been that children have not evacuated alone during war, especially not small children.[19]

Everyone involved seems to have horse's blinders on and forgets that this woman joined ISIS and Jabhat al-Nusra! She is not some innocent war-torn mother in the 1940's World War II, evacuating because someone else put her in such a predicament. My grandfather fought in Milorg, the Norwegian military organization and resistance movement against the Nazis. As the old saying goes, he would be rolling in his grave if he knew what the country, he risked his life for has become.

And, if they allow this woman to come back to Norway, she may be taking the place of a true mother in crisis from a worn-torn country. Maybe even from our dear neighbors, Sweden, in a few years from now. A country that was once an actual utopia, now on the brink of destruction. I know firsthand because I grew up with a Swedish grandfather. And I grew up with Sweden as our neighbors and when the Nordic country was Heaven. We Norwegians adored Sweden, and we told silly jokes about them and they probably told the same jokes about us. But we loved our Swedish brothers and sisters, and we still do.

It's not funny anymore. And it is heartbreaking to watch.

Cystic Fibrosis or Mystic Fibrosis
NRK: Fears for the four-year-old Norwegian Boys Life

What's could be causing the dramatic headline at NRK in early August 2019? The little boy who just a week earlier weighed 12 kilos has lost 0,3 kilos and now weighs 11.7 kilos, less than an average Norwegian one-year-old, writes NRK. The child has lost what amounts to a little over half a pound, and Attorney Nordhus and the staff at NRK are panic-stricken. Attorney Nordhus has sent a letter to the Ministry of Foreign Affairs, warning that the health condition of the woman's child is critical.[20]

The boy's mother is Pakistani, and the father, Bastian, is Chilean. Although the boy is underweight, children from those countries are typically smaller than Norwegian children. And the average height of a Norwegian male is almost 6 feet, compared to 5.6 feet in Pakistan and 5.7 in Chile. But they are just numbers that mean nothing in the scheme of things, especially for the activists at NRK.

The 4-year-old boy was, according to the mother, assessed by a doctor in Raqqa, Syria, in 2017 when he was one year old. Raqqa was under ISIS control at the time. So, did a jihad doctor examine him? NRK has seen the assessment, where the doctor writes that the child *probably* has cystic fibrosis.[21] Oh Lord, either you have cystic fibrosis, or you don't. Nordhus diligently continues his hunt to prove the little boy is deadly sick and has contacted a professor who has written a doctorate on Cystic Fibrosis and treated patients for many years. The doctor has not seen the boy but wrote an expert statement about the child, sent to the Ministry of Foreign Affairs.[22] Remote diagnoses became popular during the Trump presidency and are now widely used and accepted. Although, curiously, now in 2021, the practice has almost died out. At least in the mainstream media.

The professor fears for the boy's life writes NRK. He determines he is severely underweight, which can, of course, be due to many factors, he notes. Still, *if* he has Cystic Fibrosis, treatment is needed immediately, he concludes. The disease will develop faster in the al-Hol camp than in Norway, and the lifespan will most likely be lower in the refugee camp. The conditions in al-Hol are equivalent to not receiving treatment. He emphasizes that he has not examined the child and therefore does not know if he has the diagnosis.[23]

Oh, Lord…

On September 20th, 2019, almost six weeks after the four-year-old was on his deathbed according to Attorney Nordhus, NRK reports *Syk fireåring Mister vekt: Regjeringen endrer ikke politikk.* "Sick four-year-old is losing weight. The government is not changing its policy." NRK has spoken to the attorney, and he tells them the boy now weighs 11 kilos. He has lost one and a half pounds in six weeks. The reporter asks the attorney if the mother has considered asking for assistance from the Norwegian authorities to pick up the children, without her, to Norway?[24] The Academy Award-winning attorney and part-time Hallmark movie actor has studied his lines well:

> We presented new information related to the boy's health condition to the Ministry of Foreign Affairs. His health condition is serious, and he is in danger of dying shortly. There is no time to ask for assistance from the Norwegian authorities to pick up the children and not the mother. The situation is that the boy is dying now and that the authorities must intervene. He is in a persistent miserable state of health. He has lost weight from 12 to 11 kilos. We cannot deal with bureaucracy, and it must be done now and not next week.[25]

The high-strung Attorney Nordhus cannot deal with the bureaucracy *he* is part of. The bureaucracy that is most likely responsible for those substantial figures trickling into his bank account while defending a traitor. And why don't the attorney mention other side effects of the alleged cystic fibrosis diagnosis to make his plea more hilariously dramatic than what it already is? He has access to the child's health records and wants to plead his case, but losing weight is the only symptom he can come up with. Two months have passed, and he has lost one kilo or a little over two pounds, and he is in danger of dying shortly?

And what if the burqa-clad mother withheld food from the child to save herself and her sorry a…? Or suffers from imagined Munchausen syndrome by proxy? Or what if Attorney Nordhus suffers from Munchausen? Questions I would ask if anyone cared to know my opinion. But nobody in the Norwegian mainstream media cares what I think. All those letters I wrote to them and they never answered me. Dang.

Losing weight and breathing problems are not the only side effects of Cystic Fibrosis. People with the disease have a higher-than-normal salt level in their sweat, and parents can often taste the salt when they kiss their children. Thick and sticky mucus clogs the tubes that carry air in and out of the lungs, causing a persistent cough and wheezing. In addition, repeated lung infections, inflamed nasal passages, a stuffy nose, and recurrent sinusitis. And lo and behold, Cystic Fibrosis is a white people's disease. According to the Mayo Clinic, Cystic Fibrosis is an inherited disorder, it runs in families, so family history is a risk factor. Although CF occurs in all races, the clinic concludes, it's most common in white people of Northern European ancestry.[26] Inspector Jacques Clouseau would have been proud of me for following in the footsteps of his masterful and competent detective work.

And speaking of Northern European ancestry. Ancestry.com did my DNA, and I am 76% Norwegian, 25% Swedish, and 2% from the British Isles. It is incredible how close they got to my heritage. My grandfather, as I mentioned, was 100% Swedish, and Ancestry.com has me down to a quarter Swede. But does it matter? Not the way many politicians and Norway's current prime minister is carrying on, it seems. ISIS women matter more than ethnic Norwegians. At the Munich conference, she sat right next to that smooth-talking Canadian prime minister, woke as heck, except for the black face. She smugly said that if you believe in Western ideas, then everybody is equal. I assume in the concept of globalism. She said, and I will never forget it; and Eric, Heidi, and others, are living proof she meant every word she said:

> You don't have any special rights because your parents have been living here forever.

Since I'm playing private investigator Clouseau, what's puzzling is that NRK has met the ISIS woman several times at the al-Hol camp. The last time was august, one month before they report the child is allegedly dying. Why did none of the journalists mention their observation and the boy's condition? Just the audacious attorney's exaggerated claim the boy is on his deathbed. "His health condition is serious, and he is in danger of dying shortly," they write. Like an annoying parrot, they repeat it time and time again. I may have already said that. He has allegedly been sick since 2017 when he was one year old. Was the kid couching up thick mucus in the journalist's face? Was he wheezing? Did they not wonder why a boy with Chilean and Pakistani parents had a white people of Northern European ancestry disease? And wouldn't this be considered cultural appropriation? Adopting, or practically stealing a white people's disease. I'm so offended, let me go on Twitter and tell the world.

In the meantime, Attorney Nordhus had met with State Secretary Audun Halvorsen with the Ministry of Foreign Affairs and presented the new information related to the boy. Mr. Halvorsen informs that they have worked to facilitate medical follow-up for the boy in al-Hol based on a request from their mother and the reports of concern they have received. But the mother has rejected the health services offered so far. The Foreign Service will still try to facilitate medical follow-up of the boy, but all possible assistance requires the mother's consent.[27]

That U.S. politician who said it's all about the Benjamin's was utterly wrong.

It is mind-boggling to read how the politicians, the Foreign Services, and other governmental agencies went to great lengths to please the ISIS terrorist woman. The disgraceful jihad woman rejected everything they offered, and she would not give consent to anything they suggested to help the boy save his life. What the ISIS woman wants, the ISIS woman gets, and I cannot help comparing Eric and Heidi's case to this absolute fiasco.

The Green Party Forgot the Carbon Footprints

In June 2019, NRK reported that the children in al-Hol are a problematic issue for the government. Later given the award for Understatement of the Year. At their national convention that summer, the Christian Democratic party decided that children should not separate from their mothers. "It is time for everyone to come home," said Kjell Ingolf Ropstad, the party leader. Prime Minister Erna Solberg gave Mr. Ropstad a clear answer that bringing the ISIS mothers home is not the government policy so far. It is not something they plan on doing right now. The Progress Party also disagrees with the Christian Democrats. Party leader Siv Jensen says they have agreed to bring the orphaned Norwegian children home. Still, she does not think the Norwegian government will help Norwegian adult female ISIS fighters, even if they have children.[28]

On September 26, 2019, the Norwegian Green Party asked (demanded) the government to bring the ISIS woman and her two children to Norway. Une Bastholm announces they want an urgent vote in Parliament, and the Liberal Party and Red Party supported the proposition. One week later, the Parliament voted down the proposal from the Green Party.[29] Perhaps the rest of the liberals recognized the ecological damage such an undertaking would cause.

Did the activists from the Green Party not realize the amount of carbon footprints it would take to charter a plane and fly down to the al-Hol refugee camp? And then fly back to Norway? With stop-overs in multiple cities adding to the pollution. I am no engineer, but does it not take more fuel to land a plane and take off? And not to mention the staggering amount of waste generated from just one flight. Debris from food trays, bottles, single-use cutlery, soda pop, corn pop, wait…that was a bad dude…, plastic packaging from snacks, liquor bottles, Wuhan virus masks, diapers, Depends, you name it. Tons of trash that don't just disappear into thin air unless you're in the Twilight Zone.

And, did they think of the CO_2 emitted when they drove the ISIS woman through deserts and across borders with gas-powered trucks? I reckon they have no Tesla's down there. The cars that run on batteries made possible by child labor in Congo. But who cares about that as long as we can show those climate deniers, we are environmentally correct? Right? And how do you bicycle through a desert if they chose that mode of transport? The Green party wants everyone in Norway on a bicycle and has proposed a ban on all new petrol and diesel cars in Oslo by 2030. The party leader in Oslo has said that petrol and diesel cars must be banned throughout the Norwegian capital by 2030. "We want there to be a zero-emission zone in the entire city." Good luck with that.

So, they can show the world and Greta how environmentally correct they are. Or perhaps they fear the school dropout will cast a spell on them, but how dare they think that way. Meanwhile, China is building new coal-fired power plants faster than Jeff Bezos rocket ship.

The Green Party is often in the news lately, and some daring Norwegians have labeled them spewing their propaganda like religious fanatics. Presumably with a glimmer in their eyes. They are promoting radical party politics that would make AOC proud, perhaps even green with envy. And for the millions the ISIS woman's rescue operation will cost, they could probably buy bicycles for all the five million inhabitants of Norway. Maybe even two bikes each!

But as we will learn, there are no limits to how far the politicians and the media in Norway will go to rescue an ISIS woman and downplay and show leniency towards radical Islam. And Sumaira Ghafoor is only one of many.

CHAPTER 8
The Formation of the Prophet Ummah

University Square, Oslo, Norway, February 2010

> When will the Norwegian authorities understand the seriousness? Maybe not until it's too late? If this is allowed to continue, it will eventually be too late. Then we will have a September 11 and a June 7 on Norwegian soil. This is not a threat. But a warning!"[1]

MOHYELDEEN MOHAMMAD, A spokesperson for the Volunteers group, *De Frivillige*, reads aloud from a small note in a city center in Oslo, Norway. A center surrounded by three large buildings of the Faculty of Law at the University of Oslo. Nearly three thousand Muslims were gathered at the University Square on a winter day in February 2010. The large crowd is mostly shadowy men clad in black Muslim garb, and women and children stand in the back where they belong, according to the Qur'an. Earlier, the protesters laid down on the university square and prayed towards Mecca, shouting Allahu Akbar. They demand an apology from the Norwegian daily tabloid *Dagbladet* Later, the large crowd carried hundreds of black and white printed placards with wooden handles as they march down to *Havnelageret*, *Dagbladet's* headquarters. "Today, we gather to show disgust at the Norwegian media's caricatures as part of the war against Islam," says a representative for the protest.[2]

The demonstration was professionally planned, as is always when Muslims must rally their latest grievances in Norway, and they are always well organized in their quest for who knows what. If only Norwegians were so vocal and protested more. There are no tacky, handwritten, misspelled, quickly put-together posters when the Muslims protest. The grievance of the week, printed in the Norwegian language spoken by the nonbelievers. The well-made signs read:

> Freedom of speech is not to offend other religions. PST and *Dagbladet* create hatred. Stop publishing the caricatures. Yes, to the blasphemy

> clause. New Holocaust against Muslims. The media should take moral responsibility. *Dagbladet* and PST split the nation in two.[3]

Change the wording and put in words from the Qur'an and Islam's rhetoric and ideology, one would get proof they can dish it out, but they can't take it. They make a sport of offending other religions, and freedom of speech only belongs to them. They create hatred with their hateful and discriminatory ideology. They should stop preaching radical Islam in Norway. Yes, to the blasphemy clause. Jews, women, gays, and infidels will rejoice. You are prejudice against Norwegians, nonbelievers, and sinners. Muslims preaching the Qur'an should take moral responsibility. Radical Islam is splitting the Norwegian nation in two.

Ten days earlier, *Dagbladet* had published a screenshot of a website with a caricature of Muhammad on the front page. With the headline, *Islamhets hos hysj-politiet*; "Islam hate campaign at the hush police." *Dagbladet* reports that somebody at the Norwegian Police Security Service posted the caricature on their Facebook page. The image surprisingly provoked strong reactions from many Muslims. Several shop owners refused to sell *Dagbladet* on that day.[4]

Being that the tabloid was voted the Worst Voice in Norway in 2020 by *Natt & Dag*, that may not have been such a bad thing. I would react strongly against *Dagbladet*, the scandalmongers getting the secret "hush" police in trouble if I were PST. On Saturday, February 6, and the following Monday, hundreds of taxi drivers protested the caricature by rallying and illegally parking taxis in central Oslo. When I was young, and we crazy drunkard Norwegians needed a designated driver on a Saturday night, Erik and Hans drove the taxis in Norway. And buses too. Sadly, not anymore.

Speaking of bus drivers. Meanwhile, in Sweden, as I write, conservative online *Fria Tider* reports in early August 2021, a 20-year-old man was charged after attacking a bus driver in Malmö and demanding to know if the driver was Muslim. The incident took place in November 2020, and the bus had reached the final stop, but the 20-year-old requested to continue anyway. In anger, the man started pushing the buttons on the bus dashboard and asked if the bus driver was Muslim. He physically attacked the driver, pulled on his tie, calling him "fucking black" or *jävla svarta* in Swedish. The thug got angrier when he found out the driver was a Christian. The bus driver told the police:

> He got even angrier when I said I was a Christian and shouted that he would hurt my family and my children and fuck them all. He said that he is not afraid of the police.[5]

Daily life in utopian Scandinavia these days, Michael Moore.

The day after the cartoon demonstration in Oslo, editor-in-chief Lars Helle from *Dagbladet* and Imam Mehboob-ur-Rehman met in a fruitless dialogue meeting. Mr. Helle declared that *Dagbladet* refuses to apologize for the front page. A week later, Arfan Bhatti announced a demonstration at the University Square. And a few hours later, Mohyeldeen Mohammad, a friend of Bhatti, told the protesters that Norway might have another September 11 on Norwegian soil.[6]

The Norwegian convert Yousef, who had met Bastian Vasquez in mosques in Tønsberg and Larvik a year earlier, was at the demonstration and saw Bastian there. He believes that his friend had by then ideologically embraced Mohyeldeen Mohammad and Arfan Bhatti from Larvik. The group became more active not long after, and eventually, the Prophet Ummah emerged on the Norwegian scene. Notorious jihadists praising Islamic terrorism and recruited many to fight for ISIS in Syria and Iraq while on Norwegian soil. The same group, the ISIS woman Sumaira Ghafoor joined and where she met Bastian Vasquez.

Profeten Ummah or the Prophet Ummah was a Salafi-jihadist Islamist group based in Oslo, Norway.[7] Salafi jihadism or jihadist-Salafism is a religious-political ideology based on the Sunni sect of Islamism. Their followers seek a global caliphate, advocate for physical jihadism, and the concepts of Salafi believed to be the actual teachings of Islam. The September 11, 2001 attacks against the United States by al-Qaeda is the most infamous jihadist-Salafist attack.[8]

It is unknown if the group is still active in 2021, but many leaders are still in Norway walking amongst the nonbelievers. And so are many foreign fighters that returned and, unfortunately, never prosecuted. Prophet Ummah was inspired by the al-Qaeda ideologue and leader Anwar al-Awlaki. They later pledged support for ISIS, and austere religious scholar Abu Bakr al-Baghdadi, their leader since 2010.[9] Notorious members and leaders of Prophet Ummah, are well known to many Norwegians, as the group from its emergence received extensive coverage in the press. Critics have noted the media give the extremist an arena to spread their message of terror, or as they say in Norway, they gave them a *mikrofonstativ*. A microphone stand to spew their ideology and hatred. In the following few chapters, we may prove the critics right.

Ubaydullah Hussain is considered the founding member and original leader of the group. Arfan Qadeer Bhatti was a leading figure with a rap sheet as long as a bad year. And Mohyeldeen Mohammad, who threatened a 9/11 on Norwegian soil, was another infamous group member. Bastian Vasquez, the Chilean Norwegian we now know so well, and his wife Sumaira joined the Prophet Ummah and not long after traveled to Syria. Other members were Egzon Avdyli, a Kosovan, and Algerian Omar Cheblal,[10] two career criminals allowed to flourish on Norwegian soil. Cheblal, for instance, spent ten years in prison in Morocco for trafficking arms for the terrorist group GIA before moving to Norway. But he was still allowed residency in generous

Norway. I don't mean to beat a dead horse, I love animals, but learning who the Norwegian authorities allow into Norway, I cannot help think of Eric and Heidi and the disgraceful and heartless treatment they got from Heidi's homeland.

The Persecution Against Norwegian Muslims Must End

Arslan Ubaydullah Maroof Hussain was born in 1985 into a Pakistani family in Bjerke, Oslo, a borough of Groruddalen, a suburb in the northeastern part of Oslo. A district not long ago inhabited primarily by native Norwegians from the working class and lower-middle-class, now populated mainly by Somalis and Pakistanis. Today, eight out of ten who live in Groruddalen are non-ethnic Norwegians, perhaps more. Immigrants heavily settle Bjerke and Groruddalen, and Groruddalen is a stark example of the rapid change in the Norwegian population and a dire warning for future Norway. Estimates by some predict the little over four million ethnic Norwegians will be in the minority som time in the future, but more on that in my next book.

Ubaydullah Hussain played ice hockey and soccer with *Hasle-Løren, IL*, a club team with a rich history of Norwegian hockey. He was also a soccer and futsal referee, overseeing matches in Norway and elsewhere, including the Norway Cup.[11] Futsal is a type of soccer played indoors on a small court, with five players for each team instead of eleven, the soccer we all know.

Ubaydullah's coaching career ended abruptly after the Norwegian Soccer Association found out about his extreme attitudes on social media. Someone had reported him to the referee committee, and he was summoned to a meeting and later dismissed. Ubaydullah idolized British militant Islamist Omar Bakri Muhammad. A Syrian Islamist militant leader born in Aleppo, Syria. In 1999, before email became popular, at the tender young age of 14, he sent a letter to Omar Bakri and received a reply.[12] Ubaydullah proves later that he is fond of writing, often keeping the news media and others abreast of what he is up to via email. He also uses his penmanship to incite terror and is with the help of Facebook and Twitter able to spread his message. And luckily both platforms have eased up on the rules for supporters of terror organizations, which is good news for Taliban, al-Qaeda and ISIS. Conservatives with an opinion need not apply. What would we do without them?

In 2016 *Dagbladet* published a story about Ubaydullah extreme change: *Ekstremistens forvandling; fra fotball til ekstremist.* "The transformation of an extremist; from soccer to radicalism."[13] It is important for the Norwegian mainstream media who so diligently promote multiculturalism to constantly remind us that even jihad extremists once were destined for success. They must have been a victim of their circumstances, I imagine. Both the media and the jihadists.

Friends and family described Hussain as friendly, polite, well-integrated, and destined for success. And then he turned into a young man that became a radical Islamist within a short period of six months. He made new friends, changed radically, got new opinions, got rid of his Western clothes, and grew a beard. His new friends were Mohyeldeen Mohammad and Arfan Bhatti. And they were, along with Ubaydullah, later central in establishing the Prophet Ummah. His friends and family find the change incomprehensible, the hatred and extremism, and tried to talk to him:

> He was like all other young Norwegian men. Trained and ran around in soccer clothes. Polite and friendly, and now we see him on T.V. as a monster, a man who threatens and behaves like a silly extremist. We hope that Ubaydullah will once again become Arslan and come to his senses. And that this will not be more than a harsh lesson for him.[14]

The silly extremist Ubaydullah was arrested in October 2012, charged with making threats against two journalists, hate speech on Facebook against Jews, and harassing an author for her sexual orientation. He was convicted in February 2014 and sentenced to a 120-day prison term, although he was released immediately due to the time he had already spent in custody. The 27-year-old claims that the threats against the Jewish were irony because he and his comrades-in-arms at Prophet Ummah felt hung out and accused of enrolling in a hunting course to gain legal access to weapons. Some of his friends explain the threats against the Jews as a strong need to make an impact. While his new friends have traveled to Syria to fight with al-Qaeda, and others have previously been arrested and questioned by the Police Security Service, stay-at-home Ubaydullah Hussain had to do something to gain status in the environment. "The humiliation was probably significant when it was not the secret police who arrested him, but local police officers from the city station at Stovner in Oslo," said one of the Islamist's former friends.[15]

Hussain later praised numerous terror attacks online, including the In Amenas hostage crisis, the Boston Marathon bombing, the Murder of Lee Rigby, the Westgate shopping mall attack, and the November 2015 Paris attacks, commenting that the West should expect more attacks. In July 2014, he faced multiple counts of inciting and encouraging others to commit murder and acts of terrorism for remarks following the Boston Marathon bombing and the machete killing in London in 2013 and other terrorist attacks.[16]

The threats in question were between January and November, almost a year. One would wonder where were Mark Zuckerberg, Jack Dorsey, and all others responsible for monitoring the repulsive content on the Internet that is allowed to flourish. I am still trying to figure out how it is so easy to monitor and remove conservative content on Facebook, Twitter, and YouTube. Still, terrorists, child pornography, and other horrendous videos, images, and rhetoric, Big Bad Tech seem to have a problem battling. And now the Taliban. You give the Taliban a *mikrofonstativ*? Really, Jack? Maybe it is true what they say about your beard.

Bill, Mark, Jack, Larry, Sergey, Jawed, Chad, Steve, and all of you have had decades to fix the insanity that occurs on the Internet. What is taking you so long? Now you spend all your energy removing conservative thoughts that you disagree with and Hunter's laptop story from hell. It's deplorable, and dare I say, so are all of you. If a presidential candidate can say that about half of the American voters, I have no regrets saying it about you. I reckon you will take a break this weekend from censuring freedom-loving amazing Americans and mingle with the elites at the biggest birthday bash an ex-president has ever flaunted. Have fun while you bask in each other's glories. Don't forget to wear masks. Oh, that's right. You're a sophisticated vaccinated crowd.

In May 2013, Ubaydullah posted a link to an article about the murder of Lee Rigby, a British soldier, who was brutally slaughtered on an open street in London by two terrorists, Michael Adebolajo and Michael Adebowale. They ran him down with a car, then used knives and a cleaver to stab and hack him to death. Wait for it: Right after the slaughter the media and politicians most likely proclaimed it had nothing to do with Islam, the religion of peace, and that the two Michaels were lone wolfs. Then in solidarity, they all visited the mosques around London where the two probably got radicalized. Ubaydullah's response was:

> Good news from England. A terrorist pig from the British military slaughtered our brave brothers while shouting Allahu Akbar. May Allah accept their action and intention and humble enemies of Islam in the worst possible way.[17]

After the Boston Marathon bombing in April 2013, in which three people were killed, and at least 144 people were injured, he echoed his views:

> To hell with Boston, and may Allah destroy america!! Our prayers and tears go to our loved ones in Afghanistan, Mali, Syria, Iraq, Myanmar, Yemen, Pakistan, Chechnya, Somaliam Bosnia, and to all the Muslim Ummah!" In addition, he posted pictures of the two terrorists and wrote: "REAL LIONS!!! May Allah reward them! Amiin!"[18]

When Islamist terrorists raided the Statoil plant in In Amenas, Algeria, in January 2013 and killed 40 hostages, including five Statoil employees, Ubaydullah Hussain made the following statement:

> May Allah reward our brothers with the greatest and best Paradise and drive enemies of Islam out of our land and eradicate them."[19]

Incredibly I find out, a Somali living in Norway, Hassan Abdi Dhuhlow, participated in the terrorist attack on the shopping center in Westgate in Nairobi in 2013, where 67 were killed and 175 injured. After the attack, online *ABC Nyheter* posted the headline: "Terror widow is behind the terrorist attack in Nairobi." Ubaydullah responded, "May Allah give her high rank in Jannah!"[20]

As I research information for *Sympathy for the Evil*, I unfortunately, come across more and more shocking details on radical Islam in Norway. I did not realize a Somali living in Norway was one of the planners and perpetrators of the Westgate terror attacks.[21] He was also a member of Prophet Ummah, I find out. It is almost too implausible to believe, and Norwegian authorities have received widespread criticism of the handling of radical extremist Hassan Abdi Dhuhlow. But seeing how they have handled other radicals; I am not surprised. And it pains me to acknowledge it.

After numerous threats online, Ubaydullah was the first person in Norway charged with indirect incitement to terrorism and multiple counts of encouraging others to commit murder.

In October 2014, *Aftenposten* reported Ubaydullah Hussain was found not guilty. "That these statements by many can be perceived as highly offensive, can nevertheless not have an impact on freedom of expression," said the district court judge.[22] Sometimes, I get lost in translation, but from what I understand, the court believed the accused has remained within the limits of freedom of expression. And the threats concerned terrorist acts already committed, and he has therefore not called for the implementation of new terrorist acts.

Aftenposten writes that the verdict in Oslo District Court is most likely appealed, probably to the Supreme Court, to set a precedent. If, in the end, it ends up with an acquittal, the Police Security Service will, according to *Aftenposten's* understanding, consider promoting a proposal to tighten the legislation. In other countries, they note, it is a criminal offense to pay homage to terror, in English described as glorification.[23]

Ubaydullah, as cocky as they come, celebrates the acquittal. It's a slap in the face for the Norwegian Policy Security Service, he boasts. "I will celebrate this under *id* tomorrow."[24] Id or *Id-al-Fitr* is a Muslim holiday that now NRK, the state-funded channel in *formerly* Lutheran Evangelical Norway, celebrates with pride. Not during Pride month, of course, which is also heavily promoted. Not that there is anything wrong with that. But NRK goes through great length, forcing down their viewers' throats how great Islam is and at the same time undermining Norway's Christian tradition. When NRK first started the all-embracing programming of the Muslim holiday, the state-owned channel received hundreds of complaints. But as with any such resistance coming from their underlings, NRK continues their Islam propaganda, and there is nothing the Norwegians that pay the NRK license fee can do. Those who complain are often called out for being Islamophobic, racist, and right-wing extremists, slanderous words I believe I may have mentioned in previous chapters. But unfortunately, the left has no imagination and cannot think of other bigoted words, because that's what they are, against those on the right that have concerns for the future of their country.

I like to get off the topic of Ubaydullah Hussain for a moment and share a complaint letter sent to NRK last year after the Id festivities. It was posted on HRS and written by a female freelance journalist and photographer. I will not mention her name, as I do not want her to face repercussions. But she, like many others in Norway, reacted strongly to NRK's excessive coverage of the end of the fasting month of Ramadan. It's not just about the coverage of a Muslim holiday, but about excluding Christian programs and banning Christian traditions and programs on NRK, we all grew up watching.

I chose to recite the letter in its entirety. I can feel the woman's frustrations and helplessness and the feeling of despair of what is happening to the country we all love. I have translated it to the best of my abilities, as with everything else in this book. It sums up what many Norwegians are going through, including myself. We who see the writing on the wall. I happen to love that saying from the Bible and why I use it so often. The writing of the wall is from the Book of Daniel *5:30–31*: *That very night Belshazzar the Chaldean (Babylonian) king was killed, and Darius the Mede received the kingdom.* It is a foreboding story of doom. Mission bible class sums it up:

> Almost twenty years after the death of Nebuchadnezzar, Belshazzar (the acting ruler) held a drunken feast. To add excitement to the party, he called for the golden goblets that had been taken from the temple in Jerusalem many years before. The revelers praised their false gods and used the holy temple objects to drink wine from. A human hand appeared from nowhere and wrote on the wall. None of the king's court could interpret the writing so Daniel was brought to the feast. Daniel interpreted the writing to mean that Belshazzar and the kingdom would fall. That very night, Darius, king of the Medes, killed Belshazzar and took over Babylon.[25]

The Norwegian female journalist and photographer has seen the writing on the wall. Following is her letter to NRK.

Discrimination, Whitewash, Polarization, and Missionary Work[26]

> For decades, NRK, as a state channel, has been the glue of our society and the most important information channel for the Norwegian community. Those days are over. We now see a collapse of journalism regarding some of the most important areas NRK is covering. I, with this, complain that NRK engages in discrimination, whitewashing, polarization, and missionary work, which affects the country's Christians and the population in general. NRK has for years and progressively discriminated

against Christians in favor of non-Norwegian, reactionary and totalitarian religions without roots in Norway. To name a few:
In 2010, NRK removed the *fedrelandssalmen* [the patriotic hymn or the hymn of the fatherland], which has been played on the radio every Sunday since the 1920s. NRK was eventually pressured to take it back.
In 2013, NRK banned newscasters wearing the cross as jewelry but has since almost daily promoted the hijab, the foremost symbol of Islamism, which millions of the world's women are suffering under.
In 2015, NRK wanted to include Muslim morning worship. One more attempt to remove another piece of Christianity.
And now, in 2020, Islam is in full swing. From morning to night, NRK advertises, preaches, and paints a rose-colored picture about the religion that has for 1400 years oppressed and persecuted Christians and other dissidents. In 2020, 260 million Christians were persecuted, many of them massacred by Islamists. Ongoing tragedies that are bordering on genocide, something that NRK never mentions.
As I write this, there are at least three different, rose-colored programs about Islam on NRK.no. This week, Islam has been in full swing; Muslims talk about Islam, eat Islamic food, everything is just Islamic delight while waiting for Palestinian Rima Iraqi rounding it all off with a live Islam show on Sunday, May 24. NRK's unveiling of hijab users such as Iman Meskini, Iraqi Faten, and Somali Rawdah Mohamed as 'role' models in Norway was just a prelude. All this while *Kristi himmelfartsdag* [Ascension Day, celebrates when Jesus ascended to heaven], one of the most important days in Christianity, was totally canceled by NRK. Altogether canceled like Christian Easter celebration, Christian Christmas celebration, and probably, Christian Pentecost celebration coming up next week.
When have we seen NRK invite Christian celebrities to talk about Christianity? When have we heard Christian artists, Christian comedy shows, or seen Christians cook food and talk about Christianity? Or a large-scale, festive live broadcast with Christians in different roles and on both sides of the microphone? When have we heard Christians and Christianity praised without opposition? When have we seen Christians entitled to NRK's most important jobs, such as Afghan Yama Wolasmal and Rima Iraki, have been?
I quote Iraki AFTER she got a substitute job at NRK and posted Facebook in August 2013: 'Look here, Muslim Facebook friends! Do you want to show others how you and your family celebrate Eid? *Dagsrevyen* wants to visit today. Send me a message in your inbox if this is something you would like to be a part of. I guarantee it will be a happy one.'
Then and there, her career should have been over. Instead, she was promoted to a permanent job and news anchor and host of a large-scale,

> Islamic live broadcast. Because as a journalist, you do not guarantee entertainment programs for your own group only. Guaranteed entertainment for their group, and definitely the opposite for Norwegians who do not like where it's ending. By the way, how many programs has NRK made about the Christian fast, now or in recent times?
> Of course, NRK must cover Islam. The most urgent should be the countless negative consequences and costs of Islamic immigration, such as increased crime, honor killings, parallel societies, social security fraud, etc. NRK does the opposite; cover-up whitewashes and paints a rose-colored picture. It was rounded off with all the rosy programs NRK has produced this week. Programming that undoubtedly leads to increased polarization in a previously harmonious society.
> NRK not only breaks customs and etiquette but also the Norwegian press code of ethics, the *Vær Varsom Plakaten*, about fair news coverage, open debate, and neglect of a critical spotlight on the consequences of immigration. [Section 1.4. It is the right (obligation) of the press to carry information on what goes on in society and to uncover and disclose matters, which ought to be subjected to criticism. It is a press obligation to shed critical light on how media themselves exercise their role.]
> NRK also violates Article 2 of the Constitution: 'Our values will remain our Christian and humanistic heritage.' Norway's values are thus not Islam. On the contrary. Norway has a thousand-year-old Christian cultural heritage, and there are over four million members in Christian congregations. NRK discriminates against all of them, plus our Christian cultural heritage, favoring a religion that came here as a guest a few years ago. After not being invited, by the way.
> I have favored a shared, advertising-free public channel all these years, but not anymore. I also protest that I am forced to pay for NRK's operation, as it is not in my or the nation's interest. On the contrary, in more and more areas. Christians and other non-Muslims must soon be exempted from paying the NRK license in our tax bill.[27]

She's got a point, every word she writes, and that I wholeheartedly agree with. And I feel her pain deep in my heart.

Getting back to Ubaydullah Hussain, he tells an Aftenposten reporter he does not regret anything:

> Do you regret any of what you have said? I do not regret anything, and now I have the support of the court.
> Does Norway's support for the fight against ISIS mean that we can expect terror here as well? I have no answer to that. But Norway is among the most active countries waging war in Muslim countries.[28]

In June 2015, after the appeal by the prosecution, Hussain was found not guilty. His attorney John Christian Elden, his fierce defender, tells NRK, "freedom of expression is so vital in Norway that one has the opportunity to express unpopular opinions." He says the Storting (Parliament) and human rights set the framework for what should be punishable and says so far, they have not wanted to punish unpopular opinions.[29] Sorry, Attorney Elden, but freedom of expression was thrown out with the bathwater in Norway long ago, as it was in the freest country in the world, the United States of America. Especially if you don't conform to the leftist crowd.

And did the attorney read what Hussain wrote? Unpopular opinions? Inciting death and destruction on innocent people. Hailing horrible, unimaginable terror attacks. My husband tells me of one of his coworkers that has the same answer almost every time he says, "how's it going"?

| You know, the world is going to hell in a handbasket. |

At one time, an optimistic person, I wholeheartedly second that. But maybe hell is not so bad compared to this world. At least it's not cold in the winter. NRK cites an email Ubaydullah sent them after the acquittal:

> I thank Allah for the acquittal and hope to put this case behind me. After spending countless resources in this case, I hope that their persecution, harassment, and intimidation propaganda against Norwegian Muslims may soon end.[30]

Unfortunately, Allah didn't hear Ubaydullah's prayers. The Norwegians were continuing their persecution, harassment, and intimidation propaganda against Norwegian Muslims. Or one could say it was the other way around. But let's take a break from Ubaydullah for a moment to look at the second prominent member of Prophet Ummah.

You Dirty Pig, May Allah Burn You in Jahannam

Mohyeldeen Mohammad was in every way a man that got away scot-free for too long. A central figure in the Prophet Ummah, he has made numerous threats and controversial statements through the years. His resume includes recruiting "Norwegian" jihads for ISIS and other terrorist organizations, being arrested and released on weapons charges, deported from Saudi Arabia and Tunisia, and fighting a holy war with ISIS in Syria. Never serving considerable time in prison and the straw that finally broke the camel's back he should have sat on was a threat against Abid Raja, a parliamentary member of the Norwegian Liberal Party, and surprise: A Muslim.

Mohyeldeen Mohammad was born in 1986 in Manchester, England, in an Iraqi family, although other sources claim they came straight from Iraq to Norway. His family migrated to Norway in 1989, settling in Larvik, a town on the Eastern coast of Norway[31] with an idyllic coastal scene close to mountains and forests. Explorer and Ethnographer Thor Heyerdahl, of Kon-Tiki fame, was born in Larvik. A true Norwegian hero from a bygone era.

In September 2006, Mohyeldeen legally changed his name to Giovanni, which means God is Gracious.[32] He must have grown tired of being Italian and reverted to his original name in January 2007, only three months later.

Not much is known about Mohammad's upbringing. But he did study Islamic Sharia law at the Islamic University of Madinah in Saudi Arabia in September 2009, and if his birthdate is correct, he was 23 years old then. At the same time, Bastian Vasquez had attended the university. Mohyeldeen was expelled a few months later for being politically active but appealed the verdict and continued studying at the university. In 2011, returning from a trip to Norway, he was detained by Saudi authorities in Medina and later deported. According to Saudi police, his arrest came from Norwegian sources, although the charges were unclear. He returned to Norway on September 12, 2011,[33] as he seems preoccupied with causing a stir around the anniversary of 9/11.

His attorney John Christian Elden astonishingly said Mohammad suffered from nerves around the 9/11 anniversary, which was the reason for the arrest. And he most definitely wasn't mourning the victims, say I. The attorney also blames the Norwegian authorities for the arrest. Because nobody is responsible for their own actions anymore. Attorney Elden tells Aftenposten:

> I understand that nerves associated with the 10th anniversary of the 9/11 attacks in the United States were the cause of the arrest in Saudi Arabia. The problem started when he was in the country after the Norwegian authorities sent information about him. So now they have to straighten things out.[34]

Mohyeldeen Mohammad first became publicly known in Norway in February 2010 when he spoke in front of 3000 Muslims at the university square threatening his adoptive country that a 9/11 can happen on Norwegian soil. Being instrumental in forming the Prophet Ummah with other jihadists, he traveled to Syria in 2012. The following year Mohyeldeen got media publicity when posting a series of photographs online, posing alongside armed jihadists. One month later, he posted a video on YouTube, armed with automatic weapons warning Norwegian authorities against spreading lies. In February 2009, when the daily *Klassekampen* in February 2009 questioned him about the stoning of a person in Somalia, he said: "As far as I know, the person was gay; that was the punishment he deserved."[35]

The remarks caused outrage. The Norwegian National Association for Lesbian and Gay Liberation filed a complaint with the police and called it; "probably the most extreme we have heard in this country for many years." "Death to the Jews" and "slaughter the Jews" at the Oslo riots were pretty bad, too, in my opinion. But perhaps it didn't make the breaking news. Later that year, Mohammad posted on Facebook that infidels should be decapitated, and he also honored Osama bin Laden and other extreme Islamists. He praised the beheading of American journalist James Foley, and after the death of four Norwegian soldiers in Afghanistan, Mohyeldeen posted the message:

> Allahu Akbar! Norwegian terrorists killed in Afghanistan! Alhamdulillah, praised be Allah, we must celebrate!

In September 2011, the day before 9/11, Mohammad had published a video on YouTube titled "Jihad Norge," where he fires an air rifle and shouts Allahu Akbar.[36] In 2012, Mohyeldeen Mohammad blamed Norwegian authorities for ruing his studies and his life. Eighteen months after he was deported from Saudi Arabia, he traveled to Tunisia. Two days before New Year's Eve, Mohyeldeen was arrested when he landed at Tunis International Airport. They questioned him for four hours and *even* kept him imprisoned overnight. The next day, he was thrown out of the country where he intended to establish himself, but they accused him of planning to take part in a riot and coup. After the interrogation, he was deported back to Rome on December 30, 2011, where he must have traveled from. Mohyeldeen Muhammad told Norway's ABC News:

> Now I want to sue the responsible authorities behind this stigma, and unfair persecution that has ruined my studies, robbed me of my freedom, and put my life in danger by these detentions and arrests. [37]

In May 2013, a day before Norway's Constitution Day, heavily armed security police arrested Mohammad for carrying a gun. After being fined and released on the condition, he signed a written promise to stay away from Oslo's capital during the constitution day celebrations on May 17.[38] "Only in America" we often say." And only in Norway does a jihad get the old chalkboard punishment. A more appropriate sentence would have been writing a hundred times "I will not bring my gun to Oslo during the 17th May celebrations?" While sitting on a plane for a one-way trip back to Iraq.

The final straw happened in September 2016, when Mohammad sent the following threatening, but mostly peaceful, ˜ text messages to the Liberal Party representative Abid Raja:

> You dirty pig, may Allah burn you in Jahannam (hell) your disobedient kafir dog. You are a disgrace to Pakis and Muslims, do not call yourself a Muslim, for Wallahi, you have NOTHING to do with Islam, dirty traitor!!! You really are a ZERO and a dirty murtad kafir! May Allah give you incurable disease, anxiety, tribulation, poverty, a painful and pitiful life before death, and let you rot in Jahannam forever and ever !!![39]

Finally, Mohammad had gone a bridge too far. After years of terrorizing everybody except for his mother and brothers, it was threats against a fellow Muslim and a politician from the liberal party that got him a prison sentence.

He did not regret his threats and posted a video on YouTube, showing a man who clearly has an anger problem:

> First, I sent that dog, Abid Raja, the messages because this infidel traitor has mocked Islam and Muslims for a long time. And lately, these days, he has mocked the hijab and the niqab. In order to make clear who this Abid Raja is, my respected fellow siblings in Islam must know for sure that this Abid Raja is not a Muslim.
> He is a murtad kafir who has performed the actions of kafir for a long time. Without the 'vegetable sellers' of Iman's that we have here in Norway, having done anything about this case. This Abid Raja gets disgusted. He gets nauseous when he sees our siblings in hijab or niqab. Well, Abid, we Muslims get really disgusted every time you open your ugly, dirty mouth. May Allah make you mute and deaf … Allah.[40]

The maximum penalty for threats against members of the Storting is ten years' imprisonment. An appropriate sentence, I believe, but I have seen murderers get less. In 2019, the Supreme Court sentenced Mohyeldeen Mohammad to two years and six months in prison.[41]

But unfortunately, that was not the last the Norwegians had heard of Mohyeldeen Mohammad. But first we must get to know Arfan Bhatti.

I Live for Islam and Hate Norwegian Values

In August 2002, *Dagbladet* interviewed Arfan Qadeer Bhatti, one of the founders and leading figures in the Prophet Ummah. Dagbladet's headline was: *Jeg lever for Islam, og hater norske verdier*. "I live for Islam and hate Norwegian values." The journalist calls him *en virkelig versting*, negative labels directed at a radical Muslim rarely seen in the liberal news media today. V*ersting* translates to "the worst" in English. Arfan Bhatti was in every way a man that got away with murder, or almost intentional murder. In other words, he's a bad apple, practically rotten to the core. Feared by the police and an idol for other hardcore criminals, the 25-year-old has just spent 263 days in prison. Without a charge, indictment, and sentence, he whines and demands compensation and redress. "We Muslims are oppressed," says Bhatti.[42] Tell me something we don't know.

"It is not so strange that the police want to arrest you and lock you up. You are a criminal. One of the very worst criminals in Norway," informs the journalist.

> No, I'm not a criminal now. I've been a criminal. I have indeed committed many crimes, brutal violence, and other things. But remember: I have never attacked innocent people. Those I have been in conflict with or have done something to are people who themselves have skeletons in their closets.[43]

The man who testified against Arfan Qadeer Bhatti in 1998 was later found dead in Sweden, notes *Dagbladet*. Bhatti shrugs. That's not his problem. Snitches have no high star among criminals, and nobody dares to snitch on Bhatti anymore.

> I now live for Islam! I have a lot of Sympathy for my Muslim brothers. Jews, Hindus, and Americans have always oppressed us Muslims.[44]

The 25-year-old, born in Norway and unfortunately a Norwegian citizen, has only contempt left for the values in Norwegian society:

> In Norway, you have homos in top positions, even in the government. Gays can adopt children! You protect pedophiles and rapists in prisons. You call Norway a Christian society of values. How can Norwegians call these values? At Ila National Prison, the correctional service protects pedophiles and murderers who have murdered and abused young children. What kind of society do you want? I have a hell of a lot of hatred in my head. I'm so livid that tears start to flow, just thinking about the Norwegian authorities.[45]

"You say you have found peace and want to live for Islam. Are you going to do that in Norway?" ponders the journalist. "When I was on the run, I got married in Pakistan. My thoughts are with my Muslim brothers who are fighting Hindus, Jews, and Americans who oppress my people." "Last autumn, Osama bin Laden and his terrorists killed several thousand people in New York. Are these the Muslim extremists you support today?" "How many hundreds of thousands have not the Jews, Hindus and Americans killed?" answers Arfan Qadeer Bhatti.[46]

The 25-year-old who feels oppressed and hates everything Norway stands for was only fifteen when he stabbed a shop owner at Bislett in Oslo in 1992. Rumor has it that it was an assignment from others. Bhatti went behind the counter in the store and hit the man in the head with a glass soda bottle. Then he stabbed the owner several times in the chest and stomach with a kitchen knife.[47] For this heinous crime, he served seven months in prison in 1994.

Arfan Qadeer Bhatti was born on August 9, 1977, and raised in Norway with parents of Pakistani origin, the youngest of four siblings. As a young man, he spent time in child welfare institutions. He went to primary schools in Oslo but spent several years in Pakistan.[48] At 13, Bhatti was the youngest member of the notorious criminal gang Young Guns in Oslo, also known as a Pakistani criminal fraternity. The first members of Young Guns were all between 10 and 12 years old when they came to Oslo from Pakistan in the late 1980s. Young Guns became known for the Romsås murder in 1988, called "Norway's first gang murder." The fine "youths" in Young Guns committed aggravated violence, extortion, threats, abduction, and robbery through the years. They had several conflicts with other gangs, including Pakistani Killers, Filipino Outsiders, and the Rebels.[49]

No wonder the politicians and the mainstream media in Norway are so Gung-ho on a multicultural Norway; it adds such diversity to this tiny Nordic nation-state. And it's not just the exotic cuisine. And a homogenous country; talking the same language, sharing the same kind of ethnicity, cultural values, history, and religion; is *so* yesterday.

In 1997, three years after Bhatti stabbed the shop owner, he spent ninety days in prison for threats and illegal firearms use. Two years later, he shot a man in the arm and held a weapon against his temple. The Court of Appeal believed that the act was close to intentional attempted murder. Not hitting the brachial artery must have been a deciding factor. In 1999, Bhatti was sentenced by the Supreme Court to three and a half years in prison for extortion, bodily harm, and serious threats.[50] In connection with the trial, the forensic psychiatrist stated that Bhatti had "inadequately developed mental abilities." Later diagnoses found "dissocial personality disorder." Other court documents note that a psychiatrist thinks he is friendly and a great talker and has expressed that he has broken with his past and become an adult.[51]

Two years later, Bhatti gets prison leave, and to the surprise and shock of almost nobody, he did not return to Ila Prison after his holiday had ended. Sources said he went to Pakistan. It's hard for me not to comment here. Travel ban? Take away passport? Ankle monitor? Or what about the obvious, issue no prison leave until the sentence is done? He was later arrested at the *Baronen og Baronessen* nightclub in Oslo with a loaded pistol and sentenced to detention in the district court.[52]

As Norway does not have life sentences, the maximum civil penalty is 21 years, detention in the Norwegian judicial system is a criminal law passed in 2001. Offenders considered sane by a court can be sentenced to confinement if there is a great danger that the offender may repeat the crime or be considered a danger to society. Renewal of the detention every five years can, in theory, result in actual life imprisonment.[53]

However, Bhatti avoided confinement on appeal and was again a free man. The Supreme Court emphasized that if Bhatti commits new acts of violence, he will face detention.[54] In other words, if he went out and blew up embassies, killed another snitch, and dumped him in Sweden, or if he does something close to intentional attempted murder.

At that time, Bhatti has been assessed three times by experts, all of whom concluded that he has a dissocial personality disorder, with a high risk of reoffending. Later, a statement of expertise from 2007 concluded that "Bhatti's prognosis is very gloomy and very difficult, almost impossible to treat." Furthermore, it states that:

> Bhatti lacks a sense of responsibility and respect for social norms and obligations. He has shown an inability to feel guilt or be influenced by experience, including punishment. By committing new criminal acts, he has shown gross indifference to the feelings of others and a lack of sense of responsibility, including the family who has constantly cared for him and his spouse and children. He is immature and apathetic, with little ability to withstand risky situations.[55]

A shorter and more accurate diagnosis would have been; He's a radical Islamic terrorist. In the early 2000s, Bhatti lived in Pakistan and may have sought religion there, in a way many believed was extreme *Aftenposten* reports, always speaking of radical Muslims with soft tones.[56]

In February 2012, *Dagbladet* interviewed Arfan Qadeer Bhatti where he answers questions about his relationship to terrorism, religion, and Norwegian society. "Are you working on Norway becoming an Islamic nation?" asks the journalist:

> We want Norway to one day to become an Islamic nation and be governed by Sharia law. And it is our convincing belief that the whole earth will one day be ruled by Sharia. It is an Islamic obligation for every Muslim to fight to elevate Allah's words and laws everywhere.
> Do you understand that Norwegians think you are threatening and abusing freedom of expression?
> People can think about what they want. I warned but did not threaten. If someone believes that some people abuse the freedom of expression, just remove the part where freedom of expression is protected in the Constitution. It is a paradox that those who are passionate about freedom of expression are the same ones who shout at the opinion police when they hear or see something they dislike.[57]

When asked if he was willing to commit or encourage terrorist acts to achieve what he believed in, Bhatti replied: "What terrorist acts are, depends on the eye that sees." The police security service believes Arfan Qadeer Bhatti is one of Norway's most dangerous men, writes *Dagbladet*.[58]

On September 17, 2006, at around 02:30 Sunday morning, shots were fired with an automatic weapon at the Oslo Synagogue at St. Hanshaugen. At least 11 bullets hit the synagogue, some around the Star of David. Shortly after the shooting, witnesses saw a man dressed in dark clothes running from the scene and a small, red car with two people leaving the area.[59]

But Bhatti, You See, Has A Personality Disorder

In September 2007, Arfan Qadeer Bhatti was arrested along with three other men charged with grievous bodily harm for the shooting at the Oslo Synagogue at St. Hanshaugen. A few days later, the charge was extended to all defendants for entering into a terrorist alliance to plan attacks on the U.S. and Israeli embassies in Oslo. The attack against the synagogue was later upgraded to a terrorist act according to section 147 (2) of the Criminal Code.⁶⁰

Bhatti was also charged in connection with two murder attempts related to extortion and debt collection. In one of the incidents, shots were fired at a man's home in Bærum while he was home with his wife and two children. Several of them went through the walls, but no one was physically injured. Prosecutors believe Bhatti had others responsible for the shooting on the night of January 31, 2006. Bhatti, however, admitted to having shot at another home. The residence of one of the tops of the controversial pyramid company T5PC on the night of August 1, 2006. But he has argued he thought the house was empty when the shots fell and had therefore not admitted guilt for attempted murder.⁶¹

Arfan Bhatti was arraigned in Oslo District Court in March 2008. On his first day of the trial, the man who hates Norwegian values, and wants an Islamic state in the country, wore a traditional wool Norwegian sweater, a *Lusekofte*. An important cultural symbol, knitted by Norwegian women in bygone days, for the people of the cold north. My mom knitted one for my husband, and he loves it. Blue and white with an elk motive and snowflakes. Snowflakes from the sky that is, not millennials and liberals. You can't get more Norwegian than that. In several pictures and videos of the trial, Bhatti is seen smiling and waving to the press and his jihad friends as if he is the second coming of Allah. Arfan Bhatti and his colleagues at Prophet Ummah receive enormous press coverage from the mainstream media and is precisely what they are looking for.

During the trial, Norwegian-Pakistani and Labor politician Aslam Ahsan and attorney Abid Q. Raja warned that terror accused Arfan Bhatti is about to achieve hero status with some immigrant youths. Young people who have dropped out of the education system and who are in danger of becoming criminals. Mr. Raja is the same man Mohyeldeen Mohammad threatened and went to prison for a few years later. "The majority of young people turn their back on Bhatti, but among the weaker youths, there is a certain proportion who look up to him," says Mr. Ahsan to *Dagsavisen*. He believes that the young people, through countless press releases, get the impression of Bhatti as someone who lives an exciting life where power and honor are central. The indictment for the shooting at the Jewish synagogue in Oslo and the relationship with a high-profile TV2 reporter strengthened Bhatti's status with the outsiders. "Access to weapons and the conquest of women is seen as cool," said Ahsan. Attorney Abid Q. Raja confirms that some immigrant youths idolize Bhatti. "It is a well-known fact that these young people do not idealize taxi drivers, bus drivers, doctors or lawyers," he said.⁶²

One day under questioning in court, Bhatti explains the shooting at Asker, a suburb of Oslo, one summer night in August 2006. He admits to shooting at the home but insists it was only to frighten, and as the conscious extortionist he is, he did a thorough survey around the neighborhood to make sure no one was in the house. Then Bhatti came back, at about two o'clock in the middle of the night, and peppered the house with 17 shots from a machine gun. Nothing was indicating that people lived in the house.

| It was utterly dark, and in the windows, I could not see a single person.[63] |

Never mind, it was in the middle of the night. But then again, he's not the sharpest jihad in the tool shed.

"Did you ring the doorbell?" District Court Judge Kim Heger wants to know. "No, it didn't seem appropriate if suddenly a stranger stood on the stairs in the middle of the night." "But it was appropriate to shoot at the house?" "As I said, it was a terrible act, and I regret it. I have been bothered by this since I learned that it was an old mother who was sleeping there." The 'old mother' was a 76-year-old lady sleeping and the mother of an executive of T5PC, a controversial Norwegian multi-level marketing company that went bankrupt in 2004. Seventeen bullets went into the home in several places and could have had fatal consequences:

| I was going to scare N.N. by shooting at his house. I would scare him into paying back the debt he had to another person. I could not have known people who lived in the house. He lived most of the year in Spain.[64] |

The prosecution did not doubt that Arfan Bhatti is a terrorist. In the closing proceedings, public prosecutor Kristian Nicolaisen stated that Arfan Q. Bhatti was planning actual terrorist acts against both the Israeli and the American embassies in Oslo and firing shots at the synagogue Mosaic faith community at St. Hanshaugen in Oslo. They requested ten years of detention, with a minimum term of six years for Bhatti. "Ordinary prison sentences are not sufficient to protect society against Bhatti," said the prosecutor. In addition, forensic psychiatrists paint a bleak picture of his future. Nicolaisen listed several crimes that Bhatti has been convicted of in recent years.[65]

As early as 2003, the Supreme Court had considered detention for Bhatti. But then he got another chance since it looked like he was about to straighten himself out.[66] And probably to the surprise of the court phycologists and experts believing Bhatti's trumped-up tales of redemption, it did not work out that way. They should have thought about that when he stabbed a shop owner when he was only 15 and received less than a year in a high-end prison. His devoted attorney Elden believes there is no basis for sentencing Bhatti to custody.

The prosecutor recounted what Bhatti did the summer before the synagogue was shot at with automatic weapons. Since February 2006, Bhatti had been hunting for heavy weapons, such as grenades and anti-tank missiles. When German police stopped Bhatti in June 2006, he had several handwritten notes in the car with pictures of the heavy weapons. As well as a photo of a dead Palestinian girl. "I may have needed weapons since I was going to the Middle East. In such a country, it can quickly happen that you need weapons to protect women and children, and yourself," Bhatti explained. In a conversation with someone in Pakistan later that summer, Bhatti asks if the contact knows anyone who can get heavy weapons in Europe. In addition, the prosecutor listed several conversations that veggie loving Bhatti has had about acquiring handguns and rifles:

> There is talk of 'Anne Grete,' which is without a doubt an AG3 rifle. There is talk of potatoes and onions, but there are few potatoes in this case. These are undoubtedly grenades.[67]

Moreover, the prosecutor did not doubt that Bhatti was involved in the shooting at the synagogue. Eyewitnesses said they saw Arfan Bhatti in a red car near the scene, where he picked up a person unknown to the police. The person was allegedly carrying a machine gun. But Bhatti claims he had little to do with the shooting at the synagogue in Oslo that September night. He was sitting in a park smoking cannabis:

> A friend and I drove to Torshovdalen. There we smoked a joint, talked about family problems, and relaxed. It was not at all unusual for me to drive around and meet people in the middle of the night.[68]

The comrade Bhatti brought to the park was the 29-year-old co-accused man, accused of having fired or contributed to the shots fired at the synagogue. No one else was involved. "In that case, there must have been an invisible man,"[69] the terror accused and part-time comedian explained in court.

According to Bhatti, after the two had solved family problems smoking hashish in Torshovparken, they drove to Stensparken at St. Hanshaugen. There they smoke another joint and got rather stoned. As Bhatti put it, his friend became hungry and crazy, hangry, they call it in the United States. And from Stensparken, the trip went to Torggata for kebabs, now a Norwegian national dish. ̄ It was almost half-past three at night. "It might not have been a good idea to drive a car, but I was not so stoned," Bhatti ponders. "Did you see any commotion," district court judge Kim Heger wants to know? "No, we did not see anything special," Bhatti replied.[70]

During the period when the shooting took place, Arfan Bhatti was under continuous surveillance by the police. Still, he managed to sneak out that night without the police noticing. He used a red car, which belonged to his brother-in-law when he drove out that night. His car, a Mercedes that was under surveillance by the police, was left at home. "The kids, or my nieces, had lost the car key. That's why I borrowed my brother-in-law's car," he explained. The prosecution believes Bhatti drove a red car that night and that he picked up a person outside the synagogue after the shooting. A newspaper delivery man had seen the car at the spot. The prosecutor said:

> There are many red cars in Oslo. But how many red cars pick up people outside the synagogue in the middle of the night. And how many red cars have drivers who have previously expressed a desire to attack the synagogue? Then the amount is reduced to one man, Bhatti.[71]

Bhatti told the court about his connection with a profiled TV2 reporter, with whom he is said to have had a relationship. In court, it emerged that he had discussed a trip to the Middle East with her, a journey where he intended to fight against Israel. Bhatti booked flights but canceled at the last minute. The 30-year-old explained that he had doubted whether it was right to travel, consulted with the Norwegian TV2 reporter, and several others in Germany, and decided to stay at home. "It would not serve my cause or my family. It could end in my death," he said.[72] Thank the lord, because that would have been a tragedy.

The Police Security Service believes it has evidence that Bhatti planned terrorist acts against the U.S. and Israeli embassies in a conversation with a 28-year-old on August 8, 2006. Bhatti's defense attorney, John Christian Elden, always going above and beyond the call of duty, said in court that Bhatti's actions do not provide grounds for accusing him of terrorism:

> They talk in a closed room and express frustration over what is happening in Israel and Palestine, as many others do. This is not a terrorist case, and there is no legal coverage for the indictment.[73]

In February 2009, Arfan Bhatti was sentenced by the Oslo District Court to detention for up to eight years, with a minimum term of four years. He was convicted of conspiracy in the shootings at the synagogue. The court characterizes this as gross damage and not as an act of terrorism or a terror warning. He was acquitted of plotting terrorism against the Jewish synagogue in Oslo or against the American or Israeli embassies. The court found him guilty of complicity in an assassination attempt on a financier in Bærum but acquitted him on robbery charges. He was also cleared of attempted murder against the "old woman" sleeping in Bærum. The two other co-defendants in the much-discussed trial were acquitted on all counts.[74]

After the verdict, TV2 reported that the U.S. ambassador to Norway was very surprised and disappointed that Arfan Bhatti was acquitted of having planned terrorist attacks. The embassy is grateful that the prosecution went forward with the case, but in the end, they were disappointed that there was no conviction in the accusations of terrorism. The ambassador had hoped that Bhatti would have been convicted of planning terror against the Jewish synagogue, the U.S. embassy, and the Israeli embassy. He believed Norwegian legislation must change to get terrorists convicted. The attacks on the Jewish synagogue and plans to attack the U.S. embassy show that Arfan Bhatti is a terrorist. "Those actions form a pattern that I think it is important to identify as it is, namely terrorism," he tells TV2. "But Bhatti, you see, has been diagnosed with personality disorder," says the reporter. The ambassador's answer is spot-on:

> I'm not a doctor. But by definition, anyone who carries out a terrorist attack is crazy. Therefore, it does not make any difference whether you are healthy or not. If he is not healthy, it is still the actions that define his behavior. Shooting with automatic rifles at innocent civilians and actions against embassies and diplomats is very serious.[75]

And here lies the problem. The American ambassador is right, in my opinion. And the journalist has been indoctrinated into the socialist mindset that if you have a personality disorder that anybody can also fake, you are not responsible for your actions. Faking sickness for an ulterior motive is, by the way, quite common. As in criminal malingering. Especially in crime where perpetrators fake illness so they can be found incompetent to stand trial. More on that in my next book. And it's troubling how a reporter is so quick to defend a person that hates everything that Norway stands for and is willing to kill for it. Bhatti has committed severe crimes since he was 15 years old. It is time to face the facts, Norway. Not everyone can be rehabilitated, and at one point, you need to Viking Up and put your foot down.

In my next book, *They Had a Name. The Bloody Failure of Norway's Immigration Experiment,* I will write about what I call Norway's reckless immigration experiment starting around the late 1970s. I will reveal the government plans to open the flood gates and indoctrinate Norwegians into thinking this was the best for this small country with a little over four million inhabitants. The project involved media and education campaigns focusing on the positive side of large-scale immigration and practically bury the opposing side. It may not have been a sinister plan at the outstart, perhaps one to prevent problems and outcry, but it was an insidious plan, nonetheless. One that kept many Norwegians in the dark. In the defense of the authorities, they probably had no idea what can of worms they opened at the time. But they do now, fifty years later, and still carry on.

In fact, media and schools were instructed not to focus on anything negative, even if it occurred, which is a practice apparently alive and well today. And the reason, I believe, the mainstream media is lying by omission at every turn. Even the horrendous daily happenings in neighboring Sweden are suppressed, except on alternative conservative media. *They Had a Name* will be a tribute to those Norwegians that have been brutally murdered by immigrants, both illegal and legal, through the years. The murdered get hardly a mention in the media after the horrendous acts have blown over. A pattern I notice is that many murderers plead insanity and may spend a couple of years in psychiatric care before being released on the streets. Never classified as terror attacks and often excused because the accused come from war-torn countries and have trauma. And, the media and politicians are often more focused on rehabilitation of the perpetrators, the root cause of their anger, than the murdered and their families. And Arfan Bhatti is no victim. Lock him up, and if I were the warden, I would have thrown away the key. So yes, American ambassador to Norway. You were right about Arfan Bhatti.

The Israeli ambassador to Norway was also disappointed that the shots fired at the synagogue were considered gross vandalism and not characterized as terrorism. And Bhatti was also not convicted of planning terror against the Israeli embassy in Oslo, something the prosecution believed he had done. "The entire Jewish community felt threatened by what happened to the synagogue," the ambassador said. And she wonders if the embassy had been subjected to terrorism if Bhatti had not been arrested and detained. *Aftenposten* writes that in the intercepted conversations the Police Security Service had of Bhatti, he wanted to cut off the head of the Israeli ambassador:

> When I heard this, I immediately called my son-in-law in Israel and asked him to protect my daughter against reading newspapers or watching T.V. The statement shocked me. Daily life was greatly affected by the shooting, and it is to this day.[76]

Arfan Bhatti was already out of prison in 2012, not even serving three years. Initial reports by news outlets were that he had traveled to fight in Syria with other "Norwegian" Jihadists. But soon, other sources reported him being in Pakistan hanging out with the Taliban and eventually imprisoned in Northern Pakistan from January 2013 to August 2014. But according to his attorney, Bhatti's was ultimately acquitted of having had contacts with the Taliban.[77]

Aftenposten wrote in 2012 that Bhatti was in Syria and probably participated in weapons training and resistance against the Assad regime. While in Pakistan, Bhatti's family in Norway asked the Ministry of Foreign Affairs for help in finding him, but Bhatti did not want help from Norway. "According to Sharia law, I cannot receive help from the infidels," said Bhatti, the jihad who collected welfare in Norway for years, told TV2. Previously, he told the Norwegian media that he would not return to live in Norway because he believes that Islam does not allow Muslims to settle in the land of the unbeliviers.[78]

If we were only so lucky.

Still, he returned to Norway, the land of the midnight sun and the infidels. He was released from prison in Pakistan in August 2014 and returned to Norway in January 2015, but only after they lifted a flight ban against him. It is not known who had a flight ban on him, but I guarantee it was not Norway. Back in Norway, he was detained and charged with two domestic violence cases against his ex-wife and children. But already in March, the globe trotter Bhatti was spotted in Greece, where he was bringing personal belongings to his colleague at Prophet Ummah, Omar Cheblal.[79] The same man who ranted for ten minutes in Arabic in front of stunned reporters in Oslo, the most bizarre press conference in recent memory, covered in a later chapter. Cheblal was deported from Norway but never sent out because authorities feared he would face capital punishment or torture. But God must have answered many Norwegians prayers as he miraculously traveled to Greece on his own accord. Bhatti, at the time, had been sentenced to ten months in prison for domestic violence against his children. Something about reading the Qur'an.

He had also been charged with violence against his ex-wife and lost a custody case. The two eldest children had told the judge that their father was violent towards them and their mother. The ex-wife and the children fled to a crisis center and then moved to a home at an undisclosed address. According to the court, the wife has said that Bhatti has expressed a desire for jihad.[80]

Bhatti appealed the verdict, and not even a month after he returned to Norway from Greece, *Nettavisen* reports that he has traveled to the Middle East. The newspaper had received information about the trip from people in Bhatti's circle of friends. The anonymous tipster told *Nettavisen* he left the country and is not expected to return until a few weeks later. He needed a place to disconnect from it all, according to the friend. "Wasn't a holiday in Greece enough," asks the reporter. "He visited a friend in Greece that he hasn't seen in a long time. But the place he is visiting now is the only place he can find peace without worrying that PST is persecuting him." Arfan Bhatti's attorney, John Christian Elden, confirms that Bhatti has left Norway. "Bhatti and his 80-something mother are on a pilgrimage to Mecca. He has received a visa and traveled by plane in the usual way," says the attorney. Bhatti did not receive a travel ban, and this will be his second trip abroad in less than one month, writes *Nettavisen*. The Police Security Service does not want to comment on the case. "We do not comment on individual cases," said the information adviser at PST. And they do not wish to comment whether they know where Bhatti is.[81]

Although Bhatti went on a pilgrimage to Mecca for a chance to wipe clean his past sins, deepen his faith and start anew before Allah, the man can't win for losing. About two months later, in June 2015, *Dagbladet* reports that authorities detained the well-known Islamist Arfan Bhatti at the border of Turkey:

> I was going on holiday to Turkey but was refused entry by the Turkish border police. I do not have a travel or exit ban and do not understand why I was not allowed to enter. I hope the Norwegian Ministry of Foreign Affairs will follow up on this case and contact the Turkish authorities to clarify why a Norwegian citizen was denied entry.[82]

Bhatti claimed he had booked a hotel in the coastal city of Izmir in Turkey, which is the country's second-largest port city after Istanbul. The entry ban document for Bhatti checks off as a "danger to national security." It is currently unclear what that means, writes *Dagbladet,* who had access to the document.[83] I guess I have to spoon-feed the obvious to *Dagbladet*. It means that he is a danger to national security.

Bhatti did not want to comment on the interrogations and about connections to the Taliban and his role in the Islamist milieu in Norway.[84]

It is unfathomable that Arfan Bhatti was not given a travel or exit ban and could globetrot around the world. Especially considering that only a couple of months before he went to Greece, a trial in Oslo District Court went underway, where evidence confirmed that Bhatti was involved in possible terror planning. On February 23, 2015, the trial in Oslo District Court was the first of its kind in Norway, as three men had returned from Syria and were accused of joining ISIS. The defendants were a 30-year-old family father with a Somali background who lives in Oslo, and two brothers, 25 and 28 years old.[85] Egzon Avdyli, an Albanian and a member of Prophet Ummah, is their brother. All four are in NRK's world, Norwegians, as they make a point of writing when reporting from the trial.

The Somalian and the two Albanians, now miraculously Norwegians, swore allegiance to ISIS in May 2014 and stayed in Syria until January 2014. The prosecution believed they have violated section 147 (d) of the Penal Code by participating in a terrorist organization and they had plans to return to Syria. During the trial, the prosecution presented evidence of lists found during the investigation. The "hit lists" contained names of key Norwegian politicians, employees in the Ministry of Defense, and officers in the Armed Forces. They also found pictures of employees in the Police Security Service, bomb recipes, and manuals for close combat and weapons training. Minor stuff. The Police Security Service linked the papers to the 37-year-old convicted Islamist Arfan Bhatti. They questioned him about the discovery three weeks ago but are not said to have opened an investigation against him.[86]

Bhatti's defense attorney, John Christian Elden, confirms that Bhatti spoke to the Police Security Service and answered all the questions asked as the straightforward guy he is. "PST had made some findings that they wanted him to explain. Bhatti appeared in a short interrogation and answered all questions that investigators asked," said Elden, who was also present during the interrogation. For some unexplained reason, they did not confront him about photos of Police Security Service employees, but Mr. Forthright Bhatti said that the list of names was his. And as usual, Attorney Elden is always by his side defending his client's innocence:

> As for these so-called manuals for weapons training and bombs, we talk about openly available books and sources online. It's within Bhatti's field of interest and probably something you could find in the office of a researcher who works in the same area.[87]

I wish I were making this stuff up.

CHAPTER 9
I Swear by Allah I Didn't Know He Was a Terrorist

On October 8, 2019, NRK reported that The Norwegian Police Security Service formally charged Sumaira Ghafoor with participating in a terrorist organization. The penalty of imprisonment is a maximum of six years.[1] Other foreign fighters' returning to Norway have received around four years in prison for violating the same penal code. Four years to join the most violent terror organizations on Earth, in prison resembling a four-star motel?

Certain crimes deserve strict sentences, and joining a terrorist organization is one of them. They support an organization responsible for organized and widespread terrorism, targeting civilians, children, and women, with kidnappings, slavery, beheadings, torture, and execution. They deserve no empathy and forgiveness, or twenty psychiatrists trying to understand what made them do what they did. As in, finding the root cause, a term often heard in the news in the USA these days. And most of all, they do NOT deserve Norwegian politicians bending over backward at their every beck and call.

If I were the mother of Maren Ueland from Norway or Louisa Vesterager Jespersen from Denmark, I would want to ask Sumaira if she would have cooked and cleaned for the jihadists that brutally raped and beheaded the beautiful Scandinavian hikers. Two young women full of life and a future in front of them. They were brutally taken away by those how loved them in the High Atlas Mountains in the summer of 2018. During the same year, Sumaira was allegedly only a housewife for the Islamic State of Iraq and the Levant. The same terror organization the barbarians swore allegiance to in a video released on Internet while decapitating Louisa Jespersen. Shouting "enemies of Allah and "revenge for our brothers in Hajin."[2]

All but three of the terrorists said they supported the Islamic State during the trial, although ISIS has never claimed responsibility for the murders. The prosecution said the three killers of the women were bloodthirsty monsters, pointing out that an autopsy found 23 injuries on Louisa Jespersen's decapitated body and seven on that of Maren Ueland. Ejjoud, an underground imam, had confessed at a previous hearing to beheading one of the women. Younes Ouaziyad, a 27-year-old carpenter, admitted to beheading the other woman. Rachid Afatti, 33, had videoed the murders on his mobile phone. Helle Pedersen, the mother of Louisa from Denmark, called for the suspected jihadist killers to face the death penalty as their trial neared its end. Her attorney read a letter from her in court in Sale, near Morocco's capital, Rabat. She said, among other things:

> The most just thing would be to give these beasts the death penalty they deserve, and I ask that of you. My life was destroyed the moment that two policemen came to my door on December 17 to announce my daughter's death.[3]

I don't know how sentiments in Denmark are about the death penalty but try to say to a Norwegian on the left that someone deserves the death penalty; you are likely to be flogged. As I almost was when I once said to a couple of my friends that Anders Behring Breivik, the terrorist that murdered 77 innocent people in Norway, deserved nothing but. Among a host of accusations towards me, they also managed to say they were glad to live in a country where even ABB had rights. And boy, does he have rights, living in his three-room cell. Would they have said the same if their sons or daughters were killed? I agree with Helle Pedersen one hundred percent, and I cannot imagine how it must be for the parents and family of Maren and Louisa and what the two young women went through in the last minutes of their lives. May they rest in peace.

It's Eerily Quiet on The News Front

For some odd reason, it has been uncannily quiet in the news about Sumaira's four-year-old son after Attorney Nordhus's dramatic performance almost three weeks ago. Granted, the first season of *She was almost left behind* had ended, but still. Did the boy miraculously heal? If he did, why isn't NRK writing about it? He was in danger of dying within days. What happened to him? Now, the second season of the award-winning series is all about his mother, the ISIS woman.

And then, out of the blue, on October 9, Attorney Nordhus tells NRK that Sumaira has taken the dramatic step by asking to be arrested immediately by the Norwegian police. He will submit a claim to the Oslo District Court and says they should meet her wish. And if they do, he reckons Sumaira and her children will be taken out of Syria as soon as possible:

> She wants to try out all possibilities. Therefore, she took this dramatic step by asking to be arrested immediately. It will to a greater extent, also oblige the prosecution to take action. They are investigating a serious criminal

> case. We expect that they will resolve this matter and will meet her wish to be arrested. We ask the court to meet a mother's understandable needs and desire to save her children's lives and her own life. She is also ready to help solve the criminal case and prepared for prosecution in Norway.[4]

Of course, they should meet her wish so she can put her ISIS-loving foot on Norwegian soil and keep twisting the Norwegian government, politicians, the media, and attorney Nordhus around her little finger.

In late October 2019, NRK reports they have access to details from Sumaira's indictment. She is charged with participation in two terrorist organizations, Jabhat al-Nusra and ISIS, from June 2013 to the spring of 2019. The Police Security Service believes the woman participated in the terrorist organizations by marrying a person affiliated with the organizations, establish herself in the area with her spouse and other persons who were under the command of the organizations.[5]

NRK doing investigative journalism only when it suits their agenda uncovered an e-mail that shows that Sumaira wanted to get out of Syria in 2015. Sumaira then contacted the Norwegian attorney Bjørn Nærum, who sent an e-mail to the Norwegian embassy in Turkey in May. Attorney Nordhus tells NRK it is illogical that PST has chosen to target her for participation after 2015.

> I have been contacted by a young woman who is staying in troubled areas in northern Syria with her five-month-old child. She and the child are in a difficult and uncertain situation. She very much wants to go home to Norway.

The attorney and the embassy exchange show how the Foreign Service tried to assist the woman and the child. The embassy could get the woman across the border into Turkey when she is at the border itself, but Sumaira never reached the Turkish border.[6]

If Sumaira is returned to Norway and stands trial, she will be the first woman in the Nordic country to be charged with actively participating in a terrorist organization. However, a year and a half earlier, in January 2018, another woman had stood trial for joining ISIS. Also, a first in Norway, but the difference was she never made it to Syria. Although she did not get to be part of the holy war she desired, it was her intention, and therefore punishable by the Norwegian court of law. New laws recently put in place that is, because of jihad allowed to flourish on Norwegian soil.

But, let's go back in time for a moment.

A Ship Worthy of The Last Voyage to Valhalla

In 1874, a young archaeologist named Anders Lorange traveled from Bergen to Nordfjordeid to investigate a large burial mound at *Myklebustgarden*. The farm housed several mounds, but Mr. Lorange had his eye on the largest, thirty meters in diameter and four meters high.[7] Excavating the site, the archeologist from Bergen found charred remains of a ship and large quantities of boat nails, shield dents, and broken weapons. It was the largest Viking ship found in Norway. He uncovered a large enameled bronze vessel with burnt bone remains of a man around 30 to 35-years old. The bronze vessel was of Irish origin and originally belonged to a church or monastery. It is one of the finest examples of Irish enamel art from the period and is probably loot from a Viking voyage to Ireland. My sincere apologies Ireland.

In the coal layer in *Rundehogjen*, the mound's name, Anders Lorange found 44 *skjoldbuler*, shield bosses, indicating the ship may have had up to 22 shields on each side. The burial field at the farm Myklebust is from the Iron Age, from somewhere around 600-1000. Nordfjordeid was at the time the center of power and trade in Nordfjord. There is reason to believe that the man buried in the ship is King Audbjørn of Fjordane, who fell in the battle of Solskjel in 870. King Audbjørn is mentioned in the Snorre saga.[8]

Over a thousand years later, the *Myklebust* ship has risen from its ashes only a few meters from Eidsfjorden, where the ship first sailed. In 2019, a near copy of the vessel was launched and displayed at Sagastad, western Norway's new information center about the Viking Age. The Sagastad center proudly announces you can experience the 30-meter long *Myklebust* ship and learn about mystery and rituals, great voyages in fantastic vessels, and Norway's proud cultural history:

> There were many different ways to bury a person in Viking times, but mounded ship graves were something that only the wealthiest and most powerful got. The objects in the grave are also evidence of this. The dead man had a complete set of weapons, jewelry, game pieces, and most beautiful of all was a Celtic bronze vessel that housed the burnt bone remains. All this indicates that the buried man was a rich man, one who was central to society. Probably a Viking king. The Myklebust ship is a royal ship, a ship worthy of the last voyage to Valhalla.[9]

The burial mound in Nordfjordeid contained traces of a proud past for the ship and the buried king and his people. A proud history of Norway that must not be forgotten and deserves to come to light. Now, more than ever.

Almost 140 years after Anders Lorange discovered the *Myklebust* Viking ship, a young mother of five settled in Nordfjordeid, in the small town not far from the Viking burial site. Growing up in Somalia, she now lived in a faraway land surrounded by majestic mountains, blue glaciers, lush valleys, and deep lakes. A place with some of the most scenic and beautiful nature

Norway has to offer. Raqiya Ahmed Hussein was 26 years old when she first came to Norway. She had spent eight years of Koranic schooling in Somalia, married very young, and had five children. After a few years, she divorced her husband, remarried, and traveled to Norway in 2013 in search of a better future for herself.[10]

The alleged plan was to get the children and husband to Norway eventually. She was granted a temporary residence permit with refugee status in Norway. And after arriving in Nordfjordeid, she was given housing by the municipal refugee service and most likely a generous monthly income. Norway spends an enormous number of taxpayers and oil fund money on asylum seekers, immigration, and integration. And not to mention other generous public assistance "refugees" are entitled to. Aid and personal attention that native Norwegians could only dream of. Supposedly, she sent money back to Somalia every month so her family could eventually join her in Norway.

What the refugee service at Nordfjordeid didn't know, was that the Raqiya Hussain was an ISIS sympathizer when she settled in the small town on the North Sea and was preparing to travel to Syria to join in her holy war. She planned her atrocities in a land inhabited by Vikings over a thousand years ago who, from the middle of the 7th to late 11th centuries, spread Norse culture to foreign lands. A people that rated, pirated, traded, brought home slaves, and settled throughout Europe. A people that was also highly skilled craftsmen, boat builders, explorers, and believers of Norse mythology. A pretty awesome bunch in that regard. But those were medieval times. Some of the barbarisms of the Norsemen are factual but may have been exaggerated and pale in comparison to today's ISIS and its brutality. For the simple reason that we are not in medieval times. Beheadings and executions of innocent civilians, genocide, slavery and systematic rape, human rights abuses, ethnic cleansing, war crimes, and destruction of cultural heritage sites. Most Norwegians, one would imagine, are proud of their heritage and unique history, and some may choose to suppress the Vikings' brutal reputation. It is therefore bewildering that an ideology as barbaric as ISIS was allowed to flourish on Norwegian soil. And that the radical teachings within Islam Net and in some mosques around the country are allowed. In the 21st century democratic Norway.

When a representative for the town of Nordfjordeid was asked by TV2 how public funds supported a person who is an ISIS member, he said they did not know at the time that she supported ISIS. And nothing was indicating she was when settling in the town.[11] *Norges Røst*, Norway's Voice, is an alias used by a person who frequently comments on the conservative online newspaper *Document*. He or she always finds the right words; it seems, that often resonates with our thinking in a clear and decisive language. And does not rant like some of us when commenting online or in books. I am not personally guilty of that, but I know some others that are. *Norges Røst* says:

The councilor in Nordfjord municipality stated that he did not know her background. I believe him in that. He could not have known. What we all now know, however, is that many hundreds and perhaps even thousands of those who settle in Norway each year are bearers of radical and jihadist attitudes. Our politicians know this and welcome them and ask us all to submit to their policies. And even though few of them are willing to carry out personal terror, at least in the prevailing situation. What do we say about these politicians? We, who are critical of these new settlement policies, are accused of spreading fear or polarizing. At worst, they accuse us of being hateful. I have no words to describe how I feel.[12]

Kill The Old Woman Elizabet, The Jews, and The Footballers

In the autumn of 2017, Raqiya Hussain left Nordfjord and visited several European countries before arriving in Vienna. She received help from two people with lodging, a plane ticket, and possibly a passport in another name. No matter where these people are, they always seem to find like-minded radicals. It is almost as if there are these sleeper terror cells placed all around the world. And the trouble is; they are not asleep.

On November 1, airport police arrested Raqiya when she tried to fly from Vienna to Istanbul in Turkey. She had 50,000 kroner and a fake passport on her. Probably money given to her by the Norwegian government as an alleged asylum seeker. The poem "The Snake" comes to mind. Police believe she was on her way to Syria. She applied for asylum in Austria and while staying in an asylum reception center. Shortly afterward, she traveled to Italy, was arrested and imprisoned, and deported to Norway on December 5, 2017. The Police Security Service detained the woman at Oslo Airport Gardermoen. She was placed in custody as the Court of Appeal believed she would try to leave the country if released. Later in Oslo District Court, she explained that her Norwegian travel documents had expired and that she could not wait for new ones when she learned that her son in Somalia had become seriously ill. He was to undergo surgery in a hospital in Ethiopia. That would be a likely story if it were true. She was charged with attempted participation in a terrorist organization. PST believed the woman was on her way to Syria to meet the foreign fighter she is said to have had a relationship with.[13]

The foreign fighter Raqiya Hussain had a relationship with was 38-year-old Aweys Shikhey, born in Somalia. A Dutch citizen, he dreamed of taking part in violent jihad after moving to Tottenham in North London. The British-based *Jewish News* writes that he harbored chilling fantasies of killing former prime minister David Cameron and the "old woman Elizabeth." And he wanted to shoot Jewish people and launch an AK47 attack at White Hart Lane, then-home to Tottenham Hotspur football club. Shikhey worked as a delivery driver and kept up an aura of hard-working respectability, sending money to his families abroad. He raised money for his trip to ISIS territory by applying for several loans and securing £10,000 from Barclays for a "wedding." The jihad chatted with a fellow Somali, Abdirahman Hassan, who lived in Kenya, and they discussed committing atrocities in the UK.[14] In 2017, he allegedly fell in love with the Somalian ISIS sympathizer, Raqiya Hussain, from Nordfjord in Norway. Later investigations in England revealed that Aweys Shikhey sent several messages to Raqiya Hussain. In the texts, the man refers to the woman as his fiancé.

See what monsters you have created European "leaders"? In Norway, England, Sweden, Denmark, and most countries in our once awesome continent. Are you happy now? Angela? Are *you* happy?

Shikhey was arrested at the Stansted airport in May 2017 before boarding a flight to Istanbul. Investigators found chats on Threema and Telegram, both encrypted messaging apps, revealing terrorist plans with Hassan. Shikhey told Hassan three or five people were needed to carry out a bloody attack, and they needed to find AK47s and other automatic weapons. In 2018, Shikhey was found guilty of preparing terrorist acts and sentenced to eight years in prison. Judge Martin Edmunds, who presided over the trial at Old Bailey, told the defendant words increasingly echoed by judges in the last two decades throughout the Western world:

> In traveling, you were abandoning your two families, one in Holland and one in Kenya, behind. On the surface, you appeared to be a hard-working man, regularly sending money to your families. But under the surface, you were progressively radicalized. During your conversations with Abdirahman Hassan in Kenya, you had discussions about the murder of David Cameron and Her Majesty the Queen and about committing atrocities against football fans and members of the Jewish community in the Tottenham area. These conversations, although chilling, dangerous, and testament to your increasing radicalization, were, in my judgment, more in the nature of fantasy than conspiracy. I am not sentencing you, indeed cannot sentence you, on this charge, for threatened acts of terrorism in this country. Given the scope of your ambition, including your fantasies about the commission of very grave terrorist acts in the UK, and your hatred for those who do not share your views, I have no hesitation in finding you to be dangerous within the meaning of the Criminal Justice Act 2003.[15]

Sound words by the judge, but I do not agree with his sentiment that they were just fantasies. Has he not seen the carnage across the world caused by ISIS sympathizers?

Shortly before airport police in England arrested Shikhey, he had sent a message to Raqiya Hussain in Norway:

> Raqiya, you know that I love you, do not be upset because the enemy of God is waiting for us at the airport. I want you to give a pleasant farewell, and let's hope that we will be those who share happiness in the world after death. I do not want you to worry, and this is my voice also. I will call you before traveling and when I arrive at the airport. Also, I will give the mobile to the man; God will. Be strong, pray for me, and I will do the same.[16]

Raqiya Hussain's Recipe for Disaster

Investigators in Norway found a bomb recipe on Raqiya Hussain's phone, as well as step-by-step instructions on how to make explosives in your kitchen. In her home in Nordfjordeid, I suppose. In the country that had so generously taken her in and given her a life she only could dream of in Somalia. A screenshot from her phone shows that she has filled out an ISIS immigration form, where they gave her the Arabic surname *Oum Seyfullah Aomaliya*, The Mother of God's Sword.[17] I was unaware ISIS had an immigration department. Hopefully they are more forgiving than the Norwegian immigration authorities are to native Norwegians.

The man who prepared the application was a foreign fighter for ISIS in Syria. Information from the form gave the impression the plan was for Hussain to marry the ISIS fighter, most likely her jihad beau in England. On January 14, 2018, the woman appeared in Oslo District Court. The first time a woman has been charged with terrorism in Norway using new terror laws. Unlike Sumaira, she never made it to Syria but is still accused of participation in ISIS from June 2016 to November 2017. Raqiya Hussain explained herself with the help of an interpreter in court and believed the case is based on a misunderstanding. How is that for integration Norway, a failed project you spend millions on? Give them everything they need and want, but ask for nothing in return, not even making them learn the native language of the kafirs.

The indictment states that Raqiya Hussain had contact with several persons associated with ISIS in Syria, Great Britain, and Sudan and participated in open and closed forums on the Internet that published propaganda for ISIS. She developed and spread ISIS propaganda by proofreading propaganda text and sharing violent jihadist content to an ISIS sympathizer. Hussain also helped create fictitious user accounts on various social media.[18]

The Somalian woman also provided financial support to ISIS. She sent money to several foreign fighters, including Aweys Shikhay in the UK and a Somali-Norwegian who has still not returned to Norway. Phew. She claimed the $847 transferred to Shikhay was her paying back an initial sum of $3,500 he had sent her when proposing to her:

> I said that I was a married woman and that I could not marry him. I had still spent his money but said I did not know he would marry me. I transferred the rest of the money in two rounds. I am a married woman, and it is not permissible for someone who has been married before to marry another man. They slandered me for being accused of contacting several foreign men with whom I have no relationship.
>
> I swear by Allah that I did not know he was a terrorist. I also had no opportunity to find out.[19]

UDI's Judgment Is Incomprehensible

In March 2021, three years after the woman's arrest, Julie Dahle, a journalist for Human Rights Service, HRS, covered Raqiya Hussain's release from Trandum Immigration Detention Centre. The convicted terrorist woman from Somalia who poses a security risk is released. Human Rights Service, is co-founded by Hege Storage, author of several books, including *Islam, den 11. Landeplage,* a bestseller in Scandinavia. The book's English version is *Islam: Europe Invaded, America warned.* Highly recommended, but not for the faint of heart. Excellent written, very personal, and a totally and utterly depressing subject. But necessary to understand radical Islam. She knows. The only way I could get through it was to read one chapter at a time while drinking myself into a stupor.

Hege Storhaug is known for her factual criticism of Islam and advocates for human rights for Muslim women and girls. She is not some fly-by-night bigot hiding in the dark corners of the Internet.

HRS's mission is to promote equality between people regardless of ethnic, national, or religious affiliation, gender equality, religious freedom, freedom of speech, and loyalty to the welfare state and the nation-state.[20] All reasons to be outspoken about Islam. Ms. Storhaug and her highly competent investigative journalists at HRS are also not a right-wing white supremacy racist "blog," as portrayed by many. Or dare I say all on the left in Norway. Including politicians and mainstream media. Their hatred is real, and they fight dirty. The smear campaign against HRS that has been going on for years and still ongoing is inconceivable, and George Orwell's haunting words ring true and are disturbingly accurate. "The further a society drifts from the truth, the more it will hate those that speak it." The quote *has* been credited to Orwell but disputed by some. If he didn't say it, who did? Nevertheless, it fits, especially in today's world.

Among those who have praised Storhaug and HRS's work is Ayaan Hirsi Ali, in an article as a fellow of the American Enterprise Institute. She wrote that while most non-governmental organizations in Europe are embarrassingly silent on human rights for Muslim women and girls, "there is one in

Norway that pays attention. Human Rights Service, run by a brave, determined woman, Hege Storhaug."[21]

In 2007 Hege Storhaug was assaulted outside her home and beaten unconscious with blows to the head by an unknown assailant. She did not go public with the story until 2010. She initially wanted to keep it private for fear it could scare like-minded activists but changed her mind after an attack against Danish cartoonist Kurt Vestergaard.[22]

The mother of five from Somalia was sentenced in March 2019 to two years and nine months in prison, writes Ms. Dahle. The former resident of Nordfjordeid was released from prison in August 2020 and detained at Trandum National Police Immigration Detention Centre before planned deportation out of Norway. She is considered by the authorities a threat to fundamental national interests and poses a future security risk.[22]

But even though the Norwegian Directorate of Immigration decided to deport and permanently ban Raqiya Hussain from Norway, the same UDI consider it a violation of human rights to return her to Somalia forcibly. She may be in real danger of being subjected to the death penalty, torture, or other inhuman or degrading treatment or punishment upon return to her home country. The woman is now released, writes Dahle. And the logic behind the release is they can't detain the ISIS woman as long as she can't return to Somalia. Police Attorney Marianne Aune explains:

> The police assessed that there was no basis for keeping her interned, pending possible alternative return countries at release. However, she will be returned to Somalia as soon as the return protection ceases.[23]

But there is no word on when that will be and will most likely never happen.

HRS had previously questioned Raqiya's relationship with terror convicted Aweys Shikhey and suggest there may be more to it that they met online while she was in Norway and he in England. Could they have been married with children before "shopping" for residence permits in several countries? And what about the five children the woman allegedly has? Ms. Dahle writes:

> The ISIS woman is supposedly a mother of five, but why do we not know where the five children are. According to NRK, the woman was granted refugee status in Norway in 2013. But previous information, which the woman herself is said to have given PST, says her children are not in Norway. And where these children remain an open question.[24]

After Aweys Shikhey's arrest and during the trial, the Somali with a Dutch passport living in England said he had a wife and children in Kenya. In addition, the Somalian Casanova had a wife and five children in the Netherlands and was also in love with the woman in Norway. At the time,

HRS asked perhaps it could be the same woman in question, at least in the Netherlands and Norway. It is not an unknown phenomenon that Somali's "shop" for residence permits in various European countries.[25]

In other words, was Raqiya's Hussain his wife all along?

"So, we ask again; where are the kids? If it violates human rights to return the woman forcibly, then we must be able to ask what human rights her children have?" Ms. Dahle finds UDI's judgment in the woman's deportation case incomprehensible and questions how they have concluded that they cannot deport the still dangerous woman back to Somalia. She has lost her refugee status, so why does she have a right to protection? Moreover, the police consider her dangerous and believed she posed a terrorist threat upon release. But police now agree with UDI's decision, and the terrorist threat the woman poses to Norwegian society must give way for human rights reasons.[26]

It is unknown what investigations the UDI may have conducted to conclude that it is dangerous for the women in Somalia. HRS has previously mentioned factors that make the assessments further disturbing. Somalia is *not* considered hazardous by the Somalis themselves. Once they have Norwegian citizenship and are protected from being forcibly returned, many go on holiday to Somalia on what they describe as an annual consolation trip to their homeland.[27]

Another equally serious matter is the UDI's employees. Last week, HRS reported that the UDI does not require Norwegian citizenship when hiring caseworkers in asylum cases. Instead, they have a set of rules which stipulates that UDI employees can, in principle, have the exact national, ethnic, or clan origin as the foreigners they process the cases for. As a result, confidence in a Directorate of Immigration that appears to promote the interests of convicted terrorist interests over Norway's interests can quickly fade.[28]

The story of Norwegian authorities handling Raqiya Hussain's case becomes even more provocative when Dahle writes that instead of detention and a forced return to Somalia, Raqiya Hussain now lives in a public housing apartment in Oslo. Since she is technically deported and has lost her asylum status, she cannot work and support herself. The state, therefore, must fund her and take care of her and make sure she is taken care of in the best possible way. In Julie's words:

> The citizens of Oslo can thus live with the certainty that they share the city streets with a convicted terrorist, considered a dangerous woman, which they also finance.[29]

Police attorney Marianne Aune confirms to NRK that the woman now lives in a public housing residence in Oslo and receives close follow-up, including a private mentor:

> The officials must cooperate, and the goal is prevention and making sure the woman is cared for in the best possible way.³⁰

I wish I were writing fiction, and sometimes I think I am and I will wake up from this nightmare someday.

"In other words, making sure a person who wants death and depravity over the rest of is doing well," writes Ms. Dahle. It is not just an absurd situation but contrary to any sense of justice. No "refugee" who joins terrorist organizations like ISIS should stay in Norway. They should be returned by force, regardless of circumstances. The logic should be simple, and UDI can use its assessment criteria. The terrorist woman is allowed to stay in Norway, as free as any law-abiding citizen, because UDI concluded she faces a real danger of being subjected to the death penalty, torture, or other inhuman or degrading treatment or punishment upon return to the home country:

> When people themselves pose a real danger of subjecting others to a death sentence, torture, or other inhuman or degrading treatment or punishment: They should not be protected.³¹

CHAPTER 10
Michael Moore's Norwegian Fairy Tale

When the Norwegian immigration authorities ordered Eric out of Norway, the reaction from family and friends was of disbelief and shock. A close friend of the family found a handwritten note in her eight-year-old sons' bedroom. A farewell letter to Eric, the young boy, had come to love and adore. He feels so sad and cannot understand why Eric is not allowed to live in Norway. He wants to help him but doesn't know what to do.

> Eric,
> I feel so sad, and it is so senseless you have to leave. I do not understand why you can't live here. I want to help you so much, but I don't know what to do. I am So fond of you. We are good buddies. You are *kool*. Please come back.
> Love from your buddy

His mom is heartbroken and writes:

> How in the world am I supposed to explain to a brokenhearted eight-year-old boy what an unfair and heartless world we live in? How is he supposed to understand why Eric must leave us? How are we supposed to explain this to him when we grown-ups are sitting here ourselves, powerless and with so many questions? Questions that have until now given us inexplicable and heartless answers. My heart bleeds for my son, and my heart bleeds for Eric. Two boys with an incredibly strong bond that both mean the world to me.

To picture this little boy writing a letter to Eric, I think of my brother much younger than myself. He was only ten years old when he first met my American husband. And I think my brother thought my husband was *kool* like the eight-year-old thought of Eric. As in all American kool with his good looks, cheerful attitude, dressed in a suit jacket and jeans. I remember when my little brother first met Kevin and him snickering and whispering to me, "he is wearing a suit jacket with his jeans." A casual fashion statement back in the day that had not reached Norway yet. I hope the little eight-year-old Norwegian boy gets to spend time with his American buddy Eric. And they get to be buddies forever like my little brother and my husband are.

Why Is the Media Silent?

After reading about Eric and Heidi in the *Daily News* in March 2017, I was sad and angry, and for the first time, realized other Norwegians had faced stonewalling treatment from Norwegian immigration officials. For years I thought I was the only one that had lost my citizenship without knowing and had berated myself for being so ignorant. Looking at letters and e-mails I had written to the Norwegian Directorate of Immigration, I sounded timid and excused myself for taking up their time. I remember the one and only time I had been able to talk to them on the phone after waiting hours on hold. I was so nervous and afraid I would say the wrong thing. They held my destiny in their hands, I thought. I felt I had disowned my country, pledging allegiance to another flag, and I deserved the backlash and rejection. What if they banned me from Norway forever? I would be stateless, or lost in space, maybe. Out there with the bad guy from the Austin Powers movies and electric car maker Elon Musk. I also thought my case was unique because of my stupidity and that surely every Norwegian wishing to come back to their country after living abroad would be welcomed with open arms.

Why shouldn't they? Norway welcomes people from all over the world who have no connection to Norway and are given special treatments and handouts that native Norwegians could only dream of. And they harbor terrorists and criminals and give them preferential treatment over their own who has a will to work and contribute to their country. Why wouldn't the government then give a few native Norwegian a chance to make a new life in their home country instead of making it almost impossible to do so?

A day after reading Eric and Heidi's story, I began searching all the nationwide newspapers in Norway to see if they had covered their story. When I saw the headline and the picture of Heidi and Eric, my first thought was how unusual it was to see a mainstream Norwegian daily cover an immigration story where the people were Norwegian Americans and white. Immigration stories I had seen extensively covered in the media before often involved people that disobeyed laws, committed crimes, and made it to Norway on false premises, and dare I say, most often from MENA countries. But the media and politicians had their backs, nonetheless, covering cases extensively for days, maybe weeks, even months, sometimes years. I wouldn't be surprised if it went on for centuries. The media would call in expert opinions, politicians, court-appointed attorneys, and immigration officials to discuss the case, often pleading for those affected. Both on television and in the papers, the news coverage would be what Eric and Heidi could only dream of. Their family attorney had said to the journalist in the *Daily News* that had covered their story that Eric and Heidi's case *is* special. It certainly was, and I expected all the papers to write about it as they would other immigration stories.

I searched the state-owned channel NRK, tax-subsidized media such as *VG, Aftenposten,* TV2, *Dagbladet,* and *Nettavisen* and found no mention of Eric and Heidi. I did a general Google search, and the only information that came up was the article I had just read and a public Facebook page in support of Eric. Maybe it's too early, I thought. But deep inside, I knew that their case would not be covered. I had at the time started to see the bias propaganda that is now mainstream media in Norway and probably most of Scandinavia and Europe. I watch helplessly and with deep concern the destructive policies made by politicians in European and Scandinavian countries, including Norway. Policies and ill-advised decisions that drive once prosperous, unique, independent countries with their own culture, languages, and traditions on the brink of suicide. Eric and Heidi did not fit into the Norwegian mainstream media's far-left-socialistic-globalist-ideology plan they wanted to relay to my countrymen and women. Receiving tax write-offs and funds from the far-left socialistic Norwegian government, they are no longer journalists covering the news but activists spewing their propaganda and indoctrinating their readers and listeners with one story after another.

A couple of days later, I checked again, and still, no other newspaper had covered the case. I then decided to send an e-mail with an attachment of Eric and Heidi's article to all the large newspapers' tip hotlines. I got no response and found no coverage of Eric and Heidi's story. A week later, I re-sent the e-mail to the tip hotlines, and again no answer and no coverage. I later found out that the family and friends involved in Eric's case had repeatedly contacted the media, immigration officials, and politicians to plead Eric's case since they received the letter of denial from UNE and UDI. All they got was silence and stonewalling. And it took an ISIS jihad bride a couple of phone calls, and she had a taxpaid state attorney on the case and a taxpaid delegation rescuing her from the al-Hol camp in Syria. A risky operation costing millions. Not only that. She had the majority in government on her side, who were willing to risk a dissent from the conservative Progress Party. Probably wishful thinking from the left, or maybe it was the game plan from the leftists all along. And although she had joined the most notorious terrorist organizations on Earth, the media pleaded her case, portrayed her as a niqab-clad-victim of her circumstances, and were instrumental in her return to Norway.

Good Morning Norway Left Them Out in the Cold

A few days after UNE's disastrous and callous decision and delivery of the news that he cannot stay in Norway, Eric is on a plane back to the USA, with Sonja at his side. His Norwegian girlfriend wanted to travel with him to support him on his first weeks away from Norway. The day before departing for the USA, they made a desperate attempt and visited TV2's headquarters in Oslo.

They hoped to get media attention about the unfairness they were experiencing because of the immigration official's treatment of Eric. I can almost picture them going there. Discouraged, nervous, and not knowing what to expect. But I also imagine they must have been excited and hopeful their story could be featured on the popular daily program *Good Morning Norway*. TV2 is one of the largest news stations in Norway, and Eric and Sonja's immigration case would fit right in with the type of human-interest stories they would cover on the morning program.

The young couple hoped that a feature on *Good Morning Norway* could perhaps get some responsible politicians to jump on the bandwagon. As had happened in other cases receiving media attention where politicians have acted and even changed laws. Maybe the politicians would have noticed the unreasonableness of the law or wondered why UDI would make it so difficult for a son of a native-born Norwegian mother who would have made an outstanding contribution to the society in Norway. Perhaps they would have wondered why the Norwegian mother becoming an American citizen 24 years ago would prevent a young American man who was otherwise a perfect applicant with no criminal background and obeyed all the requirements set forth by UDI. Shamefully, TV2 did not find room for Eric's story. They pretty much left them out in the cold, so to speak.

And after being rejected by the news channel, Uncle Leif said he had searched TV2 online and found many examples of how big an impact breaking news stories have on a case. In Eric's story, there had also been countless inquires to Prime Minister Solberg and many of here ministries, but there has been zero engagement in his case so far. Leif notes that he found many hits on Maria Amelie's case on TV2's online webpage. Headlines such as:

> Government leaders discuss Amelie's solution: The three red-green party leaders Jens Stoltenberg, Kristin Halvorsen, and Liv Signe Navarsete, were discussing all possible ways to prevent Maria Amelie from leaving Norway.

Most Norwegians know Amelie's story because she received widespread media attention, as so many others have. The politicians found a solution for Amelie, who could come back to Norway and establish a life after a short period of being deported. Leif believes if there is a will, there should be a solution. And they are all waiting for a good answer for Eric.

The integrity of Eric and his family is second to none. Shame on the government in Norway for what they did to them.

Maria Amelie. The Illegal Norwegian

In 2019, NRKs headline is: *Maria Amelie - kvinnen som nesten ødela en regjering.* "Maria Amelie, the woman who almost broke up the government." When Maria Amelie emerged as a paperless refugee, as NRK labels her, she became a media favorite and was named Norwegian of the Year in 2010. The conflict in 2011 almost split the red-green government in two.[1]

Maria Amelie lived as an illegal immigrant in Norway between 2002 and 2011. She was born in 1985 in the city of Vladikavkaz in North Caucasus, Russia. Maria Amelie's parents took their daughter with them when they fled the Caucasus area to Finland in 2000. After being turned down for asylum there, they traveled to Norway in 2002 and applied for asylum. Norwegian immigration authorities turned down the application, and the Immigration Appeals Board also turned down an appeal in 2003. She and her family then filed a lawsuit, but the Oslo District Court agreed with UNE's decision. After the verdict, Maria Amelie and her family went into hiding. In 2010, Maria Amelie published *Ulovlig Norsk, Illegal Norwegian*, about living as an undocumented refugee (illegal alien) in Norway. In December, the weekly magazine *Ny Tid* named her the 2010 "Norwegian of the Year".[2] Because honoring dishonest lawbreakers is the new normal.

It all started when Maria Amelie published a book about her life as an undocumented refugee in 2010 and received enormous sympathy and attention, writes NRK. When she was arrested after a lecture in January 2011, it provoked strong reactions, not least because it happened on the steps of the Nansen School in Lillehammer. It was the beginning of the Nansen year, in honor of polar explorer Fridtjof Nansen, who received the Nobel Peace Prize for his relief work for, among others, Russian refugees. "If you really were to put immigration policy on the agenda so that many have sympathy with those who must be deported, then you should proceed in precisely this way," said The Socialist Left party leader Kristin Halvorsen.[3]

Pål Lønseth was the State Secretary in the Ministry of Justice and became the Labor Party's external face. Today he looks back on the arrest as a crisis, and from a political communication point of view, it was a disaster. The Socialist Left party wanted a more liberal refugee policy and invested great prestige in Maria Amelie's case. The Labor Party did not want to change course and thought the law had to be the same for everyone and stood almost alone when they criticized Maria Amelie for having stayed in the country illegally. The political war within the government was underway. It was a battle no one could lose. "We are in government until we get what we want, and in this case, it is about Maria Amelie being allowed to stay," said the Social Left politician Heikki Holmås.[4] There's no denying the leftists know their priorities and at times act like three-year-old's not getting what they want.

Marie Amelie had become a media favorite and appeared to be a perfect "refugee." She spoke fluent Norwegian and had taken a master's degree at NTNU in Trondheim. In addition, she had been active in student life and cultural life. Although orders were issued to Maria and her parents to deport the country, the police did not actively look for them. In 2011, many Norwegians, in light of the Maria Amelie case, participated in demonstrations for undocumented refugees. After the arrest of Maria Amelie, there were frantic crisis meetings until late at night in the red-green government. No other emergency or important issues were going on in Norway at the time, I suppose. While politicians in the government parties were in intense meetings, the main character was in shock at the Trandum asylum reception center at Gardermoen. "I have not talked about it before. I thought about finding something sharp and hurting myself so that I could be taken away from Trandum," said Maria Amelie.[5]

In the end, the Social Left and the Labor Party politicians managed to agree. Maria Amelie was sent back to Russia, but new laws allowed her to return to Norway quickly. The political "horse-trading" was about changing the rules so that working immigrants with offers of permanent jobs in Norway could get a quick shortcut into the country. In April 2011, Maria Amelie returned to Norway after having been granted a work permit. The Labor Party's Pål Lønseth today doesn't have great feelings about the conclusion of the case. "Here was someone who had tremendous resources, which was to have an impact that people with smaller resources had not received," Lønseth believes today. During the eight years that have passed, around ten people have been granted residence through the new law that has been called "Lex Amelie." Eric certainly could have fit under the Lex Amelie rule. Maria Amelie still lives in Norway and has worked as a technology journalist and an author. Her parents chose to return to Russia after living for many years, partly in hiding. Now they have settled in another country.[6]

In January 2011, NRK wrote that financier Trygve Hegnar believes the Norwegian media has run an uncritical journalism campaign for undocumented Maria Amelie. Trygve Hegnar is a Norwegian businessman, investor, and chief editor of *Kapital* and *Finansavisen*, founded by Hegnar in 1971 and 1992. "Microphone stand for Maria Amelie" is the headline.[7] *Mikrofonstativ* previously mentioned is a term used in Norway when the media gives people a platform to advance their cause, whatever that may be. Jihad Mulla Krekar, Sumaira Ghafoor, the Prophet Ummah, and many others come to mind.

By that time, five-hundred-and-forty-seven articles, editorials, and comments had been written in Norwegian print newspapers about Maria Amelie. In addition, the case has also dominated online newspapers, radio, and television. NRK online had written sixty-three articles about the issue.[8] In comparison, Eric and Heidi got one piece in a nationwide newspaper.

The editor-in-chief of *Kapital* reacted to the enormous volume and wrote an editorial opinion in *Finansavisen* yesterday reports NRK:

> It must be allowed to say that the law should be the same for all immigrants and asylum seekers. We cannot reward those who cheat the system. All articles, editorial opinions, and comments have gone in the same direction. Maria Amelie's sympathizers have been given an unreasonable amount of news coverage. The media is helping to create a ripple effect. They all interview the same people. Those who writhe in pain and stand there with torches. Jan Erik Vold, Anders Heger and others.[9]

Neither *Dagbladet* nor NRK will take self-criticism for their coverage of the case, writes the magazine *Journalisten*. Editor-in-chief of *Dagbladet*, Lars Helle, rejects that the newspaper is a helpful tool for the support apparatus around Maria Amelie. But he thinks Trygve Hegnar raises an important debate. "I hope the media can have a thorough discussion about the coverage in retrospect. But I think *Dagbladet* has been on the safe side. We have shed light on this matter from many angles," says Helle. His journalistic position is that this is a burning issue that falls within the media's responsibility to cover social problems. News editor Stein Bjøntegård in NRK states that he does not feel affected by Hegnar's criticism. He says NRK aims to provide balanced coverage and has allowed various sources to comment on the case. "Both the Immigration Appeals Board, the Police Immigration Unit, and the government have had to justify their positions in a thorough manner," he says to the trade magazine *Journalisten*.[10]

Precisely NRK. They certainly have. In Maria Amelia's case, and many others, but not in Eric and Heidi's. And if ever there was an example of an oxymoron, NRK and balanced coverage is.

Trygve Hegnar also reacts to the media using the name Maria Amelie. "It's fake, and I think the media could use her real name. I also think they could track down her parents in Norway and find out about the conditions where she comes from." *Dagbladet's* editor-in-chief Lars Helle claims that the newspaper has looked for her parents and shed light on conditions in Russia. NRK has done the same. Terje Angelshaug, senior lecturer in journalism and former reading Ombudsman in *Bergens Tidende*, refers to the *Vær Varsom* poster. The Code of Ethics of the Norwegian Press. He believes the press has taken the point of view in Maria Amelie case based on the obligation and mission the media has:

> It is the task of the press to protect individuals and groups against injustices or neglect committed by public authorities and institutions, private enterprises, or others.[11]

I have yet to experience that anyone in the Norwegian media takes self-criticism if called out on biased news coverage. Of course, it has happened, but only after the backlash is so significant that they have no choice. And it is always halfheartedly. As when NRK published a racists Jewish cartoon and got hundreds of complaints. But they did not really apologize, instead removed the offensive article and cartoon. Fourteen days later, mind you. Or the time an NRK reporter went on a racist tirade against the Jewish people, and said among other accusations, that he wished the Covid vaccine didn't work in Israel. Trivial stuff, ˜ all on public radio. He was not charged with hate speech like the 72-year-old Norwegian woman who called a controversial Somalian activist a corrupt cockroach. And NRK still employs him because he didn't go on a racist rant against the Muslims. And that Somalian activist gets away with being on stage and shouting "fuck you Sylvi Listhaug, fuck you police and fuck democracy." The 72-year-old Norwegian woman was sentenced to fourteen days in prison. Whether or not she spent time in prison is uncertain, but the hate speech law in Norway, seems to apply to light skinned Norwegians only. Actually, it *does* only apply to white people, us oppressors. Yes, CRT has reached Norway too. America, we always loved your music and the movies, but CRT? Not so much.

And that the media believes their reporting is balanced and fair is satire. Or perhaps sad because they most certainly live in Lalaland, detached from any reality in real life, existing in their own dogmatic world. The Norwegian mainstream media consistently cherry-picks what they want to cover, 365 days a year, 24/7, even in the dead of winter when the cherry season is over. They have an agenda, and their self-imposed watchdog role only goes as far as their activism and what they want the Norwegian people to know. And when someone like Trygve Hegnar, a man with common sense, calls them out, they always have the answer. Maria Amelie's case almost divided the government, and the ISIS woman Sumaira Ghafoor caused a dissent from the Progress Party. That would not have been possible had it not been for the media's relentless and almost frenzied coverage and cheerleading in mainstream media of both cases. And countless other immigrant cases have been reversed because of media attention. But I have yet to see an ethnic Norwegian struggling with UDI receive widespread media attention. And that is Gods honest truth.

And when speaking of fair and balanced news, I have here from the United States for five years been witness to a witch hunt of enormous proportions against President Trump, the Republican party, and the president's nearly eighty million supporters. The bias 24/7 media coverage in the Norwegian mainstream media has been painful to witness and caused many difficult conversations with friends and family in my home country. And sleepless nights. When trying to defend something outrageous written about the political situation or coronavirus pandemic in the USA, it fell on deaf ears. The media had told them, so it must be true.

It was then I realized that the years of propaganda and indoctrination of my countrymen and women had worked, and it was an eye-opening and disturbing revelation. And my family has always loved the USA, and it bothered me that the press had created an animosity toward America I had never experienced before. The media would consistently use sources from the *New York Times, Washington Post,* CNN, and other left-wing news in the U.S. and add their own USA-expert opinions, at times more biased than the source, if that's even possible. I read that this has been going on in left-wing media in many European countries, and I don't like it. One day you may need the United States to come to rescue you again in Europe, so stop your anti-Americanism. Update: As the previous sentence was written before the Afghanistan catastrophe, an update is necessary. I believe America will rise again, and soon have leadership that will put America back on the world stage as global leaders. Leaders that put America first, then the world. I must believe that, because if America falls, as I see it, there is no hope.

And now, with a new president in office, there is an eerie silence about the politics in the USA. Politics that resemble far-left progressive socialism, the type of government the Norwegian media and practically all countries in Europe promote. If there is coverage, however, the new administration is almost always put in a positive light. To repeat, balanced coverage is not in your job description mainstream media Norway, but lying by omission is. And it's all your fault, that I started smoking again. Now I have to go on *yet* another five-year plan like John Candy in Uncle Buck telling his snooty and uptight sister-in-law:

> Hey, I stopped smoking cigarettes. Isn't that something? I'm on to cigars now. I'm on to a five-year plan. I eliminated cigarettes; then I go to cigars, then I go to pipes, then I go to chewing tobacco, then I'm on to that nicotine gum.[12]

It's a struggle out there, that's for sure.

Blatant Lies, Cover-Ups, and Half-Truths

As soon as Eric and Sonja left for the United States, Heidi and the family attorney contacted the Civil Ombudsman for help. The Norwegian Parliament appoints the Ombudsman to safeguard the rights of individual citizens in their dealings with the public administration. The Ombudsman investigates complaints from citizens who believe they have suffered an injustice or an error in the public administration. The word Ombudsman, also used in the United States, was borrowed from Swedish, meaning representative and derived from the Old Norse words *umboth (*commission) and *mathr (*man*).* Sweden was the first country to appoint an independent official known as an ombudsman to investigate complaints against government officials and agencies. Those Vikings really had it together.

The Ombudsman office accepts Eric's case and informs that it will take six to eight weeks to process. The bureaucratic mill churns slowly in Norway, except when they decide to remove you from the population register. Heidi is hopeful and sending out positive energy. I admire Heidi for the way she is handling herself throughout the entire process. With such integrity and never lashing out at the bureaucrats or politicians. I was, in a way, like her. I appeared calm, collect and stoic on the outside, but I felt helpless and afraid on the inside. A basket case in plain English. Now, years later, I am just bitter on the inside and angry on the outside. Perhaps somebody might find that evident in my writing. Going up against the bureaucracy that is UDI and UNI is not for the faint of heart. And if you lose, it tends to leave lasting resentment.

In early June 2017, Heidi received bad news from her attorney. The Civil Ombudsman has agreed with UNE and UDI's decision to deny Eric a residence permit. Heidi writes from the United States; where she visits Eric for two weeks before they both return to Norway. The anxious mom has clung to the hope that the Ombudsman would see the injustice in the case but no such luck. She is determined to keep fighting, and when they get back to Norway, they hope for a personal meeting with the UNE case manager. While in the U.S., Heidi had been in contact with a local newspaper from her hometown. She is corresponding with a journalist via e-mail. After being deported, Heidi writes that Eric's situation had been problematic, and she is worried about her son. He had not gotten a job in the United States because of the short stay and has no permanent place to live. "I only get odd jobs of short duration since I am only there for ninety days," Erik had told the newspaper earlier.

Heidi has supported him by sending money, so he has enough to survive on. He sometimes sleeps at a friend's house and sometimes in a car. Eric is frustrated, has lost his courage, and is stressed about his future if not allowed to stay in Norway. Despite strongly disagreeing with the authorities, he has followed their directives and returned to the United States. She tells the journalist about the bad news from the Ombudsman and that they said the rules on family immigration are strict and tightened in recent years. After reviewing the case, the Ombudsman concluded that the UNE's decision appears to be within the framework of law, regulation, and current practice. They have found no circumstances that offer enough reason to examine the case further.

It is unbelievable that not ONE person, governmental institution, or politician that Heidi and others reached out to said the words: "This is a special case. Heidi is Norwegian. We would love for Eric to make a life for him and his family in Norway. He would be a great addition to our country. Let me look into the case, contact so and so, and perhaps we can find a solution." It can be done, I know, as we have seen it in other immigration cases. It is also incredible that the mainstream nationwide media, who deem themselves the protector of individuals against injustices or neglect, could not give Eric and Heidi the time of day. There are no words to describe how I feel about the unfairness of Eric's case handling compared to those who want to hurt Norway.

After the bad news from the Ombudsman, Heidi's attorney advised that they may have to resort to a possible court trial of Eric's case. Meanwhile, the attorney has sent a request to UNE for a committee meeting with a caseworker.

As the Ombudsman had said that the rules of family immigration are strict and tightened in recent years, a little detective work shows a different story. The online newspaper *Nettavisen* reports that 15,580 people were granted residency in Norway through family reunification in 2016.[13] The same year, Eric received the rejection letter from UDI. Also, keep in mind Norway is a country of only five million people. Yearly mass immigration on steroids, to use another term frequently heard in the U.S. media these days.

The figures are from the Norwegian Directorate of Immigration. That's 20 percent more than in 2015 and will affect 2017 as well. In addition, 3,460 asylum seekers came to Norway from over 100 countries. And the majority were from Eritrea, 586, Syria, 529, and Afghanistan, 373. Also, nearly 12,500 asylum seekers were granted asylum in Norway in 2016, including 7,414 from Syria, 1,635 from Eritrea, and 1,195 from Afghanistan.[14]

In 2017, the year Eric was ousted from Norway, *Nettavisen* writes that 14,432 people were granted residence in Norway through family reunification, according to recent statistics from the UDI. The largest group reunited with their family in 2017 were family members of a refugee. These make up 4,703 people, of which 2,687 came from Syria and 997 from Eritrea. In addition, 3,546 asylum seekers came to Norway in 2017.[15]

As with any legible and concerning questions about the ill-advised mass immigration to Norway, the media, officials, and politicians' resort to blatant lies, cover-ups, and half-truths to shut people up. This is precisely what the Ombudsman did when telling Heidi that family immigration rules are strict and tightened in recent years. And even if it were true, I dare to say that most sensible Norwegians would have rather had 15,000 men or women like Eric than some of the people granted residency of Norway.

The United States Is All About Me, Me, Me

In June 2017, Eric arrived home after his first three months of forced stay in the U.S. His family meets him at Gardermoen Airport with tears of joy, and Heidi celebrates his homecoming and is elated. Sonja, Eric, and everyone meets again. They wait anxiously to hear from UNE if they grant them a committee meeting in July or August. A friend shares a video of Michael Moore titled "Norway is unbelievable for Americans." The friend suggests starting a campaign to hire a philosopher for UDI and UNI oversights:

> They seem to make morally reprehensible decisions, crush dreams, and split up families. I think this idea would fix this problem for good.

What did Eric's friend mean about hiring a philosopher for UDI and UNI oversights? I got curious and found Michael Moore's video online after some intensive investigative work. The answer came clear after watching the famous movie producer's five-minute fairy tale video of Norway. In the video, Moore talks to an audience, and a woman is seated next to him. He tells a story of Norway that he says would be too unbelievable for Americans and why he did not include it in his movie *Sicko*. He did not think the American public watching the movie would believe it, he says.[15]

Is there any wonder many Americans, most on the left, pitch socialism and use the Nordic models as examples? Those who want to turn the greatest country on Earth, The United States of America, into a socialistic, maybe even a communistic land. God help us all. There is a reason the Americans, your countrymen, and women would not believe you, Michael Moore, because it is not true. They are imagined and promoted as an ideal socialist globalist society by both the left in the USA, Norway, Scandinavia, and most of Europe. It is far from perfect and far from exceptional. And that ideal society painted by liberals is falling apart little by little because of the damaging policies put in place by politicians, officials, and elites, without regard to what their men and women in the street burdened by such policies think.

Talking to the audience, Michael Moore is as excited as a kid in a candy store and sort of endearing in a way because he genuinely believes what he is promoting about Norway:

> There is no way they are going to believe they run their prison system like this. I also interviewed someone from the oil industry. You know the government owns the oil, and they lease the oil rights to Shell or Exon or whatever. They don't let Exon or Shell own the natural resources that belong to Norway. The Norway state oil company rule is that they must hire a philosopher. The philosopher is employed to make sure the state oil company does the right thing, for the planet, for the people of Norway, and just the larger sort of global thing a philosopher would be thinking about. He or she has a very important say in how the oil is supposed to be used, how the money is used, and how the Earth is treated. It's very cool. And just to remember. These people were Vikings. They were one of the most vicious killers in history. They were awful. I am just saying things can get better. Over a period of a thousand years.[16]

Michael Moore chuckles and seems to be having the time of his life. And by the way, Mr. Moore, the Vikings that you call the most brutal and vicious killers in history got their act together one thousand years ago. There are people on this Earth *today* that are far worse than the Vikings. You should know that.

I am confident the Vikings could not have orchestrated a September 11th or any of the horrendous terror attacks the world has experienced in recent decades. Vicious and awful does not even come close in describing their acts and their ideology.

And how about if the Norwegian government hired a philosopher to make sure that the immigration authorities do the right thing for Norway and the people of Norway? And for Eric and Heidi. How about if they had a philosopher looking at how the bureaucrats treat people who do nothing but follow the rules they enact and would do anything to be a good citizen of Norway? And how about if they had that philosopher look at the big picture, and in Moore's words, the sort of things a philosopher would be thinking about? And how about if the Norwegian government asked the philosopher to give them a picture of how Norway will look in the future if uncontrolled mass immigration continues. A helpless little country of four point two million people when I grew up there. How about that, Norway? You care about how Exon and Shell use your oil and treats the Earth. How about you start watching how you treat native Norwegian and your country Norway?

Michael Moore continues marveling about the utopia that is Norway, and the woman seated next to him asks him: "As long as we are in Norway, was there really a video of Norwegian prison workers singing "We are the world?" And Michael Moore exited beyond words says:

> Yes, yes. I know. It was, and this kills me. I know I have a sense of humor to come up with this idea, but seriously that would take a sense of humor and drugs to come up with that idea. And I don't do drugs, so that I would be limited. But people are going to think we did it as a joke. But it's true. When they opened this prison, they decided to do this video for new prisoners. And the orientation talks from the warden when he greets all new prisoners is: 'We don't have the death penalty. We don't have life in prison, and that means that someday you are walking out of here, and there is a possibility you can be my neighbor on my street. Therefore, I am highly motivated for you to have a good life. Because I want you to be a good neighbor if it turns out that way.[17]

The woman next to Moore then comments that to get the idea that prisons are for rehabilitation rather than revenge is a concept that needs more discussion. Moore continues:

> And their whole prison philosophy is driven by how we can make them good neighbors. We won't even admit it's revenge here (USA). That word rarely gets used. Even a right-wing politician will rarely come out and say, 'our prisons are used for revenge.' We need to be honest with ourselves, and as Americans, we have a few things that need to be fixed. It is we versus me. We are all about me-me-me. Pull yourselves up by your

> bootstraps. You got your problem. I got my problems. You take care of yourselves. I take care of myself. And over there in Norway and Canada, and half the third world it is; we are all in this boat together, and we are going to sink or swim together. And they see it in their self-interest. They have a safer society, a better society, to make sure that the cracks that people can fall through are closed as much as possible. And they see that that is something that is for the greater good. And they operate with a sense of WE not ME, and it's amazing to witness. It's not that they are better than us. They believe they are going to have a longer life, and they do. They have a longer life expectancy than we do. They are going to have less crime, less murder."[18]

Sorry, Michael Moore. Crime is on the rise in utopian Nordic nations. Neighboring Sweden, similar to Norway's government and society, and an actual dreamland when I grew up, has topped worldwide rape statistics for years. And you know that. Didn't you send a letter to the Swedish government about the lack of penalties for rapists in Sweden, a crime that only increases year after year? You even wrote: "Sweden has the HIGHEST per capita number of reported rapes in Europe." Didn't it also have something to do with Sweden going after Julian Assange on sexual assault charges? I applaud you for writing the letter, but then don't tell the Americans that the Nordic countries will have less crime and less murder. And unexpectedly, the enormous increase in rapes coincides with an influx of young men from MENA countries. But it probably doesn't have anything to do with that. Or, was I not supposed to say that out loud?

And he was speaking of less murder. In May 2021, a report came out that Sweden tops Europe in fatal shootings. In less than a decade, Sweden has overtaken Italy and Eastern European countries to have the highest number of deadly shootings in Europe, primarily due to criminal gangs. And nobody wants to talk about where the criminal gangs come from, but most of them aren't ethnic Swedes. If any at all. See above paragraph. My grandfather, born in Sweden, would be devasted to see what is happening to his home country. "The rate in Sweden ranks very high in relation to other European countries, at approximately four deaths per million inhabitants per year. The average for Europe is approximately 1.6 deaths per million inhabitants," the report said.[19]

Crime is on the rise in Norway also, which always lag ten years behind Sweden. We used to say that as a joke many years ago before Norway got rich in oil. We were like the car rental company in the U.S., always number two, and it Hertz. Sweden had Abba, Bjørn Borg, Volvo, IKEA, Swedish meatballs, Ingrid Bergman, the Swedish chef, all world known. All we were known for were crushing the winter Olympics and Jarlsberg cheese. I'm kidding, and of course, Norway, we're more than that. And so were you Sweden. But it's not a joke anymore. Now we lag behind Sweden on something we would never have imagined. And if allowed to continue, we are well on our way toward "Swedish conditions." A shattered society that was once a utopia destroyed because of delusional politicians' pursuit of globalism and multiculturalism.

Michael Moore continues brainwashing his audience and Americans about his imaginary utopia:

> They will have fewer social problems by constructing their society by the concept of WE. And you are not alone. There is something there for you. If the shit hits the fan in your life, you don't have to hit the fan. We're going to take the fan away. We're going to put a guard over the fan. Something will be there so that you have a chance. And they don't think that's a weak thing. They have the attitude that that's actually a strong thing. It's a sense of strength to be able to forgive.[20]

The video ends with a clip of the prison guards in Norway singing "We Are The World." And it is very well made by the prison staff, and I commend them for it. These are real people in the video, and it's not about bashing my countrymen and women, the regular men and women in the streets of Norway. It is about badmouthing the despicable government and the propaganda media. And Michael Moore, sort of.

I have not seen the movie *Sicko*, and I commend Michael Moore for making a movie highlighting a problem with the health care system in the United States. It needs some fixing, just like any healthcare system in any country, including Norway, Canada, and most definitely the third world. And I never thought of the United States as a more me-me-me country than Canada, any European, or any third-world country. When the shit hits the fan, to use Michael Moore's analogy, I find that most Americans ban together and help those in need, are generous, and among the most welcoming people in the world.

Michael Moore's ideas are bias and one-sided, and his portrayal of Norway and that it's a we-we-we attitude does not ring through to me. His notion that the Norwegian government operates with a sense of WE is highly incorrect. We don't need to go further than Erics and Heidi's story for proof of that. But I also see the struggle many in my family face in Norway at various points in their lives. And the bureaucracy and indifference they face when trying to go through the system. The ideal system Moore preaches about is not so perfect. Ask those who have been victims of crimes or murder by those good neighbors the warden hoped to get next door.

Ask Marianne's family, the 52-year-old woman brutally murdered by a Somalian on the streets of Norway this past summer of love, and ignored by the media and the politicians because the BLM movement and alleged systematic racism in the United States was covered 24/7. The Somalian was previously charged with aggravated battery but received no jail time, and now a Norwegian woman is dead. He got more publicity than her because he had not gotten the psychiatric help he needed. He stabbed three women, two were wounded, and Marianne succumbed to her injuries. I will never forget Marianne, her murder and the senseless ignorance from the media and politicians. It is also interesting to note that Norway's prison population consists of 35% foreigners, who comprise 18% of Norway's population. Not too much written about the in mainstream media, though. It just doesn't sound good.

My family went through a horrendous experience when my brother-in-law died at the hands of doctors and staff in a Norwegian hospital. He was a man of honesty, integrity, hardworking and loved by everyone. He worked his entire life never using the system, and when he needed them the most, they failed him, and it killed him. Numerous medical mistakes caused his death. Imagine that Bernie Sanders and AOC, promoters of the Nordic healthcare model. You both have no idea what you are talking about. And you are lying to the American people, just like Michael Moore. In the aftermath of his death, his wife encountered so much indifference trying to handle affairs. Most paper-pushers must follow senseless establishment rules and regulations. Even though many public servants have empathy and want to help, they have to follow a bureaucracy without compassion and concern for many who need help. Innocent people who have done everything to be good citizens get put on the back burner in favor of many who do not deserve it. Does that sound like we-we-we?

So, no, Michael Moore. Stop your preaching about Norway, or any country except for the USA, as an unbelievable Shangri-La. And stop bashing your own country, the great United States of America, and start loving it.

A notion that is even more important in 2021 where the left has indoctrinated half of America to hate their country. You have, I believe, been part of that indoctrination Mr. Moore. And if the third world is so great and they are all about WE, why are they all trying to come to America, Norway, and other European countries? Or why don't all those people thrashing their country and burning the American flag on U.S. soil move to another country they hate it so much. And why don't you move to any of those countries Michael Moore? If the United States is all about ME, why are people from all over the world dying to come here? And in 2021, they *are* dying, crossing the wide-open border. And now after the Afghanistan triumphant withdrawal thousands are coming to America, even bringing child brides and polygamous families and who knows what else. To the most selfish country in the world if we should believe Michael Moore. Taking them in with open arms.

Being an immigrant to this country, I wish I could tell those Americans who hate this country. They have no idea how good they have it. Is there any country on Earth where you can go to fifty sovereign states and see incredible sites and meet amazing people that all share common values such as freedom, liberty, self-government, individualism, diversity, and unity? Because that to me is America, no matter what those on the left will say. America *is* the shining city upon a hill, quoted by so many politicians, and it is heartbreaking to witness those within our country trying to tear that city down. Stop brainwashing Americans that the grass is greener overseas on the socialistic side, Michael Moore because it isn't. And keep fighting for this country so it can continue to be that shining city on the hill. Please!

In April 2015, a fourteen-year-old young man wrote an opinion to *Aftenposten's* Si;D about Norwegian prisons. His name is Jon, and he is wise beyond his years. He believes that money spent on prisons in Norway is money thrown out the window:

> In today's Norway, we spend almost more money on prison than old folk's homes. The conditions in prisons are so good, and it may seem more tempting to stay in jail for a couple of years for some. And better than to struggle through a dreary life on the outside. It is almost as if one is rewarded for committing criminal acts.
>
> At the same time, money that can go to a newer and better Norway is thrown out the window. I believe that we must reduce spending on prisons so that those who deserve punishment get their punishment. And those who have given so much to our country really get to live in good conditions throughout their life.[21]

A fourteen-year-old boy with more common sense than all the politicians in the Norwegian *Storting* combined: And Michel Moore, Bernie Sanders, and AOC.

CHAPTER 11
Beating Up Jews Awakened Youths Politically

The Embassy of Israel, Oslo, December 2008

Although the Prophet Ummah emerged on the Norwegian scene sometime in 2011, many group members took part in another demonstration three years earlier. Forgotten by many who may wish it went away, never to see the light of day, the infamous Oslo riots against the Gaza War were by many considered the worst anti-Jewish event in Norway since World War II.

On December 29, 2008, about 1,000 anti-Israel protesters moved towards the Israeli Embassy in Parkveien, in Norway's capital Oslo to protest the Gaza War. The Socialist Left Party, the Red Party, Red Youth, Socialist Youth, and the Norwegian Peoples Aid were the organizations behind the protests against the war in Gaza.[1] I recently came across the term Islamo-leftism, considered a derogatory term by the far right to attack the far left. Islamo-leftism explains the political alliance between Islamists and leftists. Judging from the Oslo riots' alliance, there may be some truth there. I may be wrong, but not really.

The peaceful demonstration was soon broken by left-wing autonomous Blitz activists, the Antifa of Norway, and many "young boys," as the media would say, and primarily Muslim youths. The mob began throwing Molotov cocktails and stones at the Embassy and the police, shouting Allahu Akbar, striking several police officers. The thugs siphoned gasoline from nearby cars, set fire to trash bins hurled at police. Police responded by firing tear gas and eventually detained nine youths. Four were arrested, including two asylum seekers.[2]

Protesters aren't what they used to be and must have taken a break for the "Christmas" holiday, to spend quality time with their families, collecting presents and loot all at the same time. A new year and a new beginning, and the riots continued on January 4, 2009. A coalition of Islamo-leftists, the Palestine Committee of Norway, the Red Party, and left-wing Blitz had arranged an anti-Israel demonstration outside the Norwegian parliament building and later moved towards the Israeli Embassy. The march grew violent, and around 200 protesters, including Hezbollah supporters, began throwing stones and shooting fireworks against the police.[3]

Take Him. He's a Jew, a F***ing Jew

On January 8, *Med Israel for Fred,* With Israel for Peace, and other pro-Israel groups had arranged a peaceful rally outside the Norwegian parliament building. Two hundred police officers deployed in anticipation of protests soon had their hands full as anti-Israel activists started throwing rocks at the peaceful demonstrators. The conservative Progress Party leader Siv Jensen scheduled to give a pro-Israel speech, had to leave the podium. Rioters attacked a bus that tried to evacuate pro-Israeli demonstrators from the area, including many elderlies. A Jewish man was struck and injured by the mob who shouted, "take him, he's a Jew, fucking Jew," and "Allahu Akbar." Many overheard protesters chanting in Arabic "death to the Jews, killing the Jews," and "slaughter the Jews." The riots resulted in forty smashed shop windows, and several cars and buses were damaged, including fifteen police cars. At least six people were reported injured, including five police officers, one mutilated in the face by an iron rod. Police found secret stashes of Molotov cocktails, club weapons, and knives throughout Oslo. Of the thirty-seven, primarily young men with an immigrant background, detained by the police, only nine faced violence against police charges.[4]

A day later, an Islamo-leftist alliance of several organizations, plus the Islamic Association and other pro-Palestine and Muslim groups, arranged new anti-Israel demonstrations. As is typical for left-wingers and even some Democrats, autonomous Blitz stated they supported the violent riots. Peaceful in their twisted minds.

The last day of the demonstrations, January 10, would be the most violent. Destructive riots soon erupted as protesters hurled fireworks and rocks at the police and the Israeli Embassy. Objects struck police officers, and at least two people were injured. As the riots spread throughout Oslo, the mob left violence and destruction in their path. A false rumor spread by text message that all McDonald's earnings that day would support Israel, and subsequently, the mob destroyed five McDonald's restaurants. Some of the "older and wiser youths" told younger rioters to hunt for Jews. One group severely beat a shop owner accused of being Jewish. Rioter smashed a window and attacked The Oslo Freemasonry Lodge hosting a children's party with 300 people, nearly causing a fire.[5]

The police arrested 194 protesters during the January 8 and 10 riots and stated they would investigate all the detained. Most of them would receive fines of 9,000 Norwegian kroner, around $1,300, they said. In the end, the police prosecuted only ten rioters, and less than that were convicted. They were mirroring how authorities handled the Antifa and BLM riots, a warning that far-left "democratic" socialism and enabling criminals are not the answer America. The Oslo Trade Association called the small number of prosecutions by the police unacceptable and deeply worrying. Police investigators saw alarming similarities in the *modus operandi* of earlier riots in Paris and the Middle East. In the aftermath, Islamic leaders, in cooperation with Norwegian education authorities, initiated dialogue meetings with the youths in mosques, using the Qur'an to reach out to "children" who had participated in the riots.[6]

The same failed tactic was used to reach out to pyromaniacs with the bestseller *Pyromania for Dummies*. Tariq Ramadan later visited Oslo and held speeches in the Rabita Mosque, a role model sure to reform the angry youths. A controversial Swiss Muslim academic, philosopher, accused rapist, banned from the U.S. a couple of times, and writer.

Scanning through mainstream media from those five days in Oslo, there are no dialogue meetings with the riot victims. Not surprisingly, those affected by the riots and the damages did not get much press. However, there are many conversations about those wayward youths that caused so much pain and suffering. The thugs that the Norwegian education authorities, Islamic leaders, politicians, and media treat with kid gloves. And those dialogue meetings, and which people with feet planted firmly on the ground could have guessed, amounted to nothing. At least for the Norwegian Salafi-jihadist group, the Prophet Ummah, and the Norwegian jihadists who fought in the Syrian Civil War.

In the aftermath of the horrendous anti-Jewish Oslo riots, some noted the insurrections were a significant shared experience for many of them and the seed planted for the future Prophet Ummah to emerge.[7]

Fiery But Mostly Peaceful Protests

Forskning.no, an online forum offering news concerning Norwegian and international research, posted an article in January 2013 titled *Opptøyene i Oslo vekket unge muslimer politisk.* "The riots in Oslo awakened young Muslims politically."[8] Reading the article and observing the downplay of the violent riots in Oslo in 2008-09 is reminiscing of left-wing news media in the USA. CNN first comes to mind and its coverage of the 2020 riots in the United States. Riots still going on in 2021, but the media is too busy covering the insurrection and disastrous pullout in Afghanistan. Wait for it: That was a success. I meant the insurrection on January 6th.

Molotov cocktails in the air are a rare sight in Oslo, the author of Forskning.no states, a few of them were "thrown into the air" when thousands demonstrated against Israel's attack on Gaza.[9] Failing to mention that the mob threw Molotov cocktails and stones at the Israeli Embassy and the police and shouting Allahu Akbar, striking several police officers.

Referring to extracts from the Forskning.no article, the demonstrations in Oslo were *mostly peaceful*, but things got out of hand at times. Several windows were smashed during the worst of it, and some of those who had gathered in separate, pro-Israel demonstrations were attacked, they write.[10] Who can forget the CNN reporter standing in front of a building engulfed in flames during violent riots in Kenosha, Wisconsin? And CNN's ridiculous caption that read: "Fiery but Mostly Peaceful Protests After Police Shooting."

The brawl in Oslo, as Forskning.no call it, received a lot of media attention, and several organizations and prominent people in Oslo's minority environment strongly opposed the use of violence. But "fortunately," the episodes of violence and the strong reactions were a political wake-up call for many minority youths. Researchers at the University of Bergen conducted interviews in Oslo's mosques in the time before the demonstrations, while they were taking place, and afterward. Carefully planned, another words. Many saw the invasion of Gaza as an attack on the global Muslim community, and many young Muslims went out in the cold winter in Norway to express solidarity with the Palestinians and anger against Israel and their allies.[11]

Many had not demonstrated before, the author notes. [But many had prior convictions.] They went from having an unarticulated frustration around their situation to being drawn into collective arenas *where they could discuss, formulate and publicly express a form of criticism of power.* The Gaza demonstrations led to mobilization and commitment, and allowed minority youth to be visible and have a say in the debate, says one researcher. The researchers asked those of the young people who had participated in the violent demonstrations to evaluate their actions afterward. Most of those who had thrown stones at the police said they regretted it later, while others said they only did it for fun and had no regrets.[12] Apparently, a good time was had by all.

So, to get rid of unarticulated frustration and have an opportunity to be visible and a say in the debate, go out on a cold winter day in Oslo, Norway, and beat innocent Jews. While you are at it, injure police, hurl Molotov Cocktails and rocks at the Israeli Embassy, destroy five McDonalds, and wreak havoc and destruction. The thugs may have had a political wake-up call, more like a radical wake-up call depending on the eyes that see, but the authorities and most of the media in Norway need to wake up and smell the damned coffee.

Anyone seeing the similarities of what is going on in the United States these days? This type of leadership is what the left wants. Wake up America.

A few weeks after the demonstration, Hans Rustad at *Document* writes that one of the things that left a lasting imprint during the Gaza demonstration in Oslo on January 8 last year was the attacks on older people from *Sørlandet* (south of Norway).[13] Mr. Rustad is the founder and editor-in-chief of *Document*, a leading online, conservative, independent, and nationwide media house for news, political analysis, and commentary. A critical media voice sorely needed in Norway.

Document reports of a man who had sustained permanent injuries during the riot, and state-owned NRK was not interested in filming him when they heard who had injured him. In Jon Gunnar's own words:

> I was exposed to violence twice during the riots. First, I was beaten with the pole of an Israeli flag that the anti-Semites had taken, and I fell on the street. Just after I got back on my feet, a new gang came and hit me with sticks - on my hand, thigh, and back so that I fell again, and cut myself and bled in my right hand. But I did not know then that I had broken my left wrist in four places.

Later, he also experienced those three fingers on his hand withered away, and he had to undergo an operation. After a few months, he got the feeling back in his fingers but notices that it has become more difficult to play guitar, for example. In addition, Jon Gunnar still has pain in his hand in some positions. He is bothered by the media's position on Israel.[14]

> What irritates me is that Norwegian media try to hide the truth about Israel and anti-Semitism. They present cases to benefit Israel's enemies, and Israel is viewed as a terrorist empire. When I returned to the bus after being subjected to acts of violence bleeding from the hand, NRK aimed its camera at me, and the reporter asked what had happened. "The Palestine Committee attacked me!" I exclaimed. They quickly turned the camera off.[15]

Sadly, Jon Gunnar died in October 2011, at the age of 64. *SMA Senter for Antisemittisme*, Center for Antisemitism, wrote the following about Jon Gunnar:

> Jon Gunnar was an important SMA partner, a very determined and brave person who was never afraid to stand for the truth. He was a true Bible-believing Christian and a faithful friend of the Jewish people. Whether it was against Blitz or the Muslim demonstrations, he was present and on Israel's side. He was a great man and will be deeply missed. We remember him when he bravely opposed the supporters of the Palestine Committee. They attacked him in the violent riots in Oslo on January 8, 2009, and injured him because he carried an Israeli flag. Thank you, Jon Gunnar. On behalf of SMA and the Jews, he strengthened and encouraged them to fight on for life. We would also like to thank his wife Ruth and the family for supporting Israel and SMA together with Jon Gunnar. May God bless them and give them comfort and strength in the great sorrow they experience. Jon Gunnar is with God now, and he is in good hands. We light peace over Jon Gunnar's memory.[16]

The ISIS Leader and Austere Religious Scholar
Prophet Ummah idolized the al-Qaeda ideologue and leader Anwar al-Awlaki. They later pledged support for ISIS, and Abu Bakr al-Baghdadi, their leader since 2010. We must not overlook their atrociousness and that the dogma they preach is alive and well and can strike at any time. And the ISIS foreign fighters, women and men, many European countries are hellbent on reforming and giving laughable sentences to, including Norway, most likely still embrace their barbaric ideology. And mainstream media in Norway have rarely dug deep and reported ISIS slaughters. They are too busy sugarcoating Islam, the Qur'an, and radical Muslims.

Notorious ISIS leader Al-Baghdadi was born in 1971 in the city of Samarra, Iraq, northwest of Baghdad. His family was Sunni Muslim members of a tribe, claiming descendance from the Prophet Muhammad. They named the newborn Ibrahim bin 'Awad bin Ibrahim al-Badri ar-Radawi al-Husseini as-Samara'I, so people could easily remember his name. Al-Baghdadi allegedly showed signs of radicalization early on in life and had joined an extreme branch of the Sunni dissident group, the Muslim Brotherhood, as a youth.[17]

While visiting a friend in Fallujah sometime in 2004, U.S. forces in Iraq captured and imprisoned al-Baghdadi at Camp Bucca, a notorious prison known for generating Sunni jihadists. There he met and bonded with future ISIS fighters. It is unclear why they let him see the light of day, but al-Baghdadi rose in the terrorist ranks after leaving Camp Bucca, fueled by his ideological and religious leadership. He earned a Ph.D. in Islamic Studies and was known for his dogmatic approach to Islam.[18] The Ph.D. earned him a distinction at the time of his death by the *Washington Post* as an austere religious scholar. And today, in the news, as I am writing, I read the *New York Times* labeled Osama bin Laden as a devoted family man. What in the world is wrong with these people?

Al-Baghdadi first joined the Iraqi group al-Qaeda in Iraq. Abu Musab al-Zarqawi, a Jordanian, had founded the group. Al-Zarqawi had pledged allegiance to Osama bin Laden after the U.S. invasion in Iraq in 2005. The group carried out suicide bombings, fought U.S. and Iraqi government troops, and enforced a strict interpretation of Sharia law, including beheadings. U.S. forces killed Al-Zarqawi in 2006, and for four years, several leaders took a turn as heads of al-Qaeda in Iraq.[19]

When al-Baghdadi took over in 2010, he cut the group's connection to al-Qaeda and renamed the group Islamic State in Iraq. The group desired to create a single Sunni regime that ruled over the entire Arab world. Al-Baghdadi and his men had greater ambitions and renamed the organizations two years later to ISIS, the Islamic State of Iraq, and Greater Syria. Under al-Baghdadi's leadership, the Islamic State took over territory in Syria and Iraq. The group did so by enforcing Sharia law, collecting taxes in Mosul, and capturing oil fields and refineries in Syria. It created a government in the town of Raqqa, in Syria, where Sumaira lived for a time. The regime included courts, schools, and bus services.[20]

Al-Baghdadi believed that Muslims must follow Allah, and all non-Muslims are the slaves of Muslims. Democracy at its finest. One of his four wives captured in 2019 told interrogators that women and girls were sex slaves for ISIS militants. And Kayla Mueller, the American aid worker, and human rights activist from Prescott, Arizona, was raped and tortured before her death by al-Baghdadi. [21]

ISIS rule, under al-Baghdadi, spread quickly throughout Iraq and Syria, focusing on creating an Islamic state and implement sharia law. The terrorist group took control of Falluja, Mosul, and Tikrit in Iraq in 2014 and declared itself a caliphate. A caliphate is ruled by a leader known as a caliph, historically known as Muhammad's successor. In 2014, they attacked a northern town in Iraq that was home to the Yazidis, a minority religious group. They killed hundreds, primarily men and women too old for sex slaves. ISIS sold Yazidi women into slavery, forced them to convert to Islam, and tens of thousands of Yazidis fled from their homes.[22] Bastian Vasquez ISIS propaganda video was released in 2014, and we can't forget the terrified prisoners taunted by Vasquez. The Yazidis, he said, worshipped Lucifer and boasted they were only a few of the hundreds of Yazidis they had captured.

ISIS has released numerous videos of brutal executions, and a video posted on YouTube in August 2014 was one of the first publicized acts of ISIS violence. The bloody execution and beheading of U.S. journalist James Foley sent shockwaves worldwide. Not long after, the beheading of U.S. journalist Steven Sotloff was uploaded. And in the following months, ISIS posted a series of gruesome videos showing the beheadings of kidnapped journalists and international aid workers. Jordanian military pilot Moath al-Kasasbeh was burned alive in a cage in February 2015. Also, in 2015, a video showing militants beheading twenty-one Egyptian Christians on a beach in Libya. and men believed to be gay thrown off buildings in Syria.[23]

ISIS has claimed responsibility for hundreds of terrorist attacks in the Middle East and worldwide. On Western soil, innocent women, children, and men in cities worldwide are killed in unimaginable bloodbaths forever etched in our minds. Paris, San Bernardino, Brussel, Pulse Nightclub, Nice on the French Rivera, a Christmas market in Berlin, and Manchester Arena in England, to name a few. And the world watched as ISIS militants destroyed ancient ruins, monuments, and historical artifacts throughout Iraq, Syria, and Libya. They demolished Iraq's Mosul Museum, the Mosul Public Library, and many churches, temples, mosques, and shrines. Worship of cultural monuments, statues, and shrines is forbidden and believed idolatrous. However, it did not stop them from selling and profiting off many artifacts. Much of ISIS's money has come from seizing control of banks, oil refineries, and other assets in the territories it occupied. Kidnapping ransoms, taxes, extortion, stolen artifacts, donations, looting, and support from foreign fighters added to their loot. It is known as the wealthiest terrorist organization globally, believed to have made $2 billion in 2014 alone.[24]

Early Sunday morning, on October 27, 2019, President Donald Trump announced the death of what he described as the world's number-one terrorist leader.[25] The austere religious scholar Al-Baghdadi had killed himself and three children by detonating a suicide vest during the Barisha raid in Syria's Idlib Province. The military operation was named Operation Kayla Mueller, after the American aid worker raped, tortured, and murdered by al-Baghdadi. After receiving Islamic funeral rites and being buried at sea, ISIS named Abu Ibrahim al-Hashimi al-Qurashi, the new leader.[26]

U.S. forces had searched for al-Baghdadi for more than five years. He reportedly developed an elaborate effort to avoid capture. Al-Baghdadi avoided cellphones and kept his face concealed from all but a chosen few. Hence the nicknames the Invisible Sheikh and the Ghost. He frequently changed his travel plans, delaying his capture, Trump said. His death was a crucial victory against the embattled terrorist group. The man who was the head of a worldwide caliphate, a single Sunni regime to rule over the entire Arab world, was dead. A brutal man whose ideology led the group to take over enormous territories, mainly in Iraq and Syria, the size of Great Britain. And building an international terrorist organization that drew recruits from the Middle East, Europe, and North America, inspiring terrorist attacks worldwide.[27] And recruiting terrorists from once peaceful countries in Northern Europe.

In 2019, the Norwegian Police Security services provided an update of the status of around 100 people with Norwegian connections who had traveled to Syria and Iraq to join extreme Islamist groups, including ISIS.

Sixty foreign fighters are Norwegian citizens, and the rest are connected to Norway in other ways, including family and work. Simultaneously, debates are raging about what will happen to the "Norwegian" foreign fighters when they return. PST confirmed to NRK 40 were killed, 40 had returned to Norway or traveled to another country, and 20 are still alive. They had earlier believed around 30 foreign fighters with Norwegian connections had survived the civil war in Syria, but several have not given signs of life for a long time and are believed dead. Of the 20 fighters still alive, PST believes just under half are women. At least 11 women with Norwegian connections have gone to Syria, and two have allegedly died. They emphasize that the figures are not entirely accurate because it is difficult to confirm the information from these areas.[28]

In 2018, NRK reported that in 2015 ten foreign fighters were convicted of joining ISIS, and four are already released. They happily announce the government has presented an action plan against radicalization and extremism. One measure is to help extremists find a place in society again. They offer a so-called mentoring scheme, where the terrorist convicts converse with a qualified person.[29] Admirable measures, but these guys are terrorists, for crying out loud, and something Norway or any peaceful country should never have had to deal with had they not imported the problem in the first place.

All Possible Reasons to Have a Watchful Eye

Thomas Hegghammer, a terrorist researcher for the Norwegian Defense Research Establishment (FFI), has estimated at least 2,000 extreme Islamists live in Europe today who have been foreign fighters or served a terrorist sentence. If only a small proportion continues with their activities, it can pose a significant terrorist threat, writes the FFI researcher. Former foreign fighters have been central to several terrorist attacks in Europe. The alleged mastermind of the Paris terror in 2015 had been a foreigner in Syria. The same was true of the man who attacked a Jewish Museum in Belgium.[30]

The Police Security Service chief Benedicte Bjørnland does not answer directly whether there is reason to believe that the terrorist threat increases in Norway as a result of the releases, writes NRK:

> Some findings from research on terror convicts in Europe show that people with foreign war experience and involvement in extreme Islamist activity also carry out new terrorist plots. People will get a second chance, but if they carry out an activity that we believe is dangerous for the nation of Norway, we must monitor them.[31]

"Is this something PST is worried about? asks the NRK reporter. "There is every possible reason to have a watchful eye on people who have served terror-related sentences," said the PST chief.[32]

People will get a second chance, says the PST chief. Did the people murdered by ISIS and other terrorist groups get a second chance? How many chances should these people get, I would ask? Mulla Krekar, members of the Prophet Ummah, Sumaira Ghafoor and Raqiya Hussain got too many chances. So have many repeat offenders within the Norwegian penal system. Isn't it time you played tough and started giving those who support terror and murder, maim, and hurt innocent people the harsh punishment they deserve? Watching the Norwegian penal system from afar, it seems the rights and lives of hardcore terrorists and criminals are more important than law-abiding citizens. And how well are the terror convicts monitored? When they can carry out terrorist attacks on Norwegian soil, it will be too late anyway. But at least they had a second chance.

The Happiest Countries in The World

Every year the list of the happiest countries in the world is released, and the Scandinavian countries are proud to be in the top ten. Another list they may not be so proud of is which European countries have produced the most ISIS fighters per capita? It is disheartening to find out that Denmark, Sweden, Norway, and Finland were in the top ten, reported by CBS News in 2016. According to the International Centre for the Study of Radicalization and Political Violence (ICSR) at Kings College London, about a fifth of all foreign fighters in Iraq and Syria come from Western Europe. Europe's largest countries have technically produced the most fighters estimating that France saw 1200 people traveling to Sunni militant groups in Iraq and Syria. The United Kingdom and Germany each contributed somewhere between 500 and 600 people. Larger populations, more significant numbers of fighters, writes the author of the article.[33] Well, I'll be darned.

But if one looks at the countries that produce the most ISIS fighters per capita, the smaller countries, including the happiest countries, are in the top ten. Belgium, at the time, had more citizens fighting in Iraq and Syria per capita than any other European country, with 40 for every one million people. The second country topping the list is Denmark with 27 fighters for every million people, and Sweden with 19.[34] Keep in mind this was 2016 and not absolute numbers. They are way higher in 2021. Are these figures indicative of more significant problems, asks the author of the article?

Could it indicate treating criminals with kid gloves and believing it is good in everyone is not working, I ask? Or could it have anything to do with providing taxpayer-funded attorneys, monthly social services payouts, or unlimited unemployment benefits? Or how about a platform in the media, allowing extreme Islam rhetoric in radical mosques and Muslim organizations, unchecked and unsustainable immigration, laughable sentences for serious crimes, and five-star prison accommodations?

The top ten per capita is France with 18, Austria 17, the Netherlands 14.5, Finland 13, Norway 12, the United Kingdom 9.5, Germany 7.5. Then follows Ireland with 7, Switzerland 5, Spain 2, and Italy 1.5.[35] The numbers may not seem significant, but they are atrocious considering the carnage just one foreign fighter caused, like Bastian Vasquez. Take notice that Eastern European countries that have experienced little immigration and small Muslim populations have contributed relatively few foreign fighters.

The Soufan Group, a global intelligence and security consultancy headquartered in New York, in a publication titled "Hotbed for Recruitment," wrote the following about Norway and Belgium:

> In a year, eight young men left the Lisleby district of Fredrikstad in Norway to go to Syria. Lisle is an area with a population of around 6,000, so the proportion of recruits is exceptional. If replicated across the United

States population, this would mean 413,400 Americans had joined the Islamic State. This cluster appears to have flowed from the influence of a single, charismatic individual.

The district of Molenbeek in Brussels, the hometown of many members of the Islamic State cell that attacked Paris in November 2015, is another example of a concentrated area where a cluster can develop. Belgium's Interior Minister Jan Jambon said in November 2015 that the majority of Belgian foreign fighters came from Brussels, in particular Molenbeek.[36]

I reckon those dialogue meetings with some of the young wayward youths back in 2009 didn't work, did they Norway?

CHAPTER 12
The World Needs Another Osama bin Laden

American Embassy, Oslo Norway, September 2012

> The world needs a new Osama bin Laden. We love Osama. Obama, Obama, we love Osama. We love Osama. We damned you, your leaders, and your deeds. If we get arrested, we will still say that we sacrifice ourselves, our families, and our money for the sake of the Prophet. We damned you. No honorable person will not offer himself for, and will not sacrifice himself, for the Prophet. Both young, old, children, and women thirst for revenge, thirst for revenge.
> The crowd shouts Allahu Akbar.[1]

Ubaydullah Hussain stands in front of the American Embassy in Morgedalsvegen, Oslo, Norway, on a cloudy September day in 2012. His head is wrapped tight in a keffiyeh, a Palestinian headscarf, and he's wearing a dark green tunic. His sideburns intersect with his long scruffy black beard, symbolizing that he is a devout Muslim man emulating the Prophet Muhammad. Around him are angry intimidating men, all radical Muslims just like him.

Next to Ubaydullah Hussain stands Arfan Bhatti, his friend and colleague from Prophet Ummah.[2] Fresh out of prison, serving only a couple of years after charges of attempted murder, extortion, firing against the Oslo Synagogue, and planning attacks on the American and Israeli embassies. Norway, hellbent on rehabilitation, even for the worst offenders, allows Bhatti to stand in front of the American Embassy in Oslo and spew hatred along with 150 others.

They have come to protest the release of the *Innocence of Muslims*, an anti-Islamic two-part short film uploaded on YouTube in July 2012. In September of that year, the *Innocence of Muslims* appeared on YouTube again. This time with anti-Islamic content dubbed, without the actors' knowledge. The footage sparked outrage among the Muslims, and demonstrations and violent protests broke out on September 11, leading to hundreds of injuries and over 50 deaths. Imagine if Christians acted like that every time someone blasphemed or slandered our religion. Fatwas were calling for the harm of the actors, and Pakistani government minister Ghulam Ahmad Bilour offered a bounty for killing the producer. The film has sparked debates about freedom of speech and Internet censorship.³

Just think of that. A fatwa from a Pakistani government minister. That would be similar if for example a speaker of the house would call out a bounty and fatwa against a former president. Just an example how crazy politics in a non-democratic country is. I am talking Pakistan here.

Some hold black Islamic flags, defiantly waving them in the air. No red, white, and blue Norwegian flags for miles. And one man has a sign that reads: "The Prophet was sent as a mercy to mankind. We won't let you mistreat the mercy of God." Looking closer at the video, the man holding the sign looks like Bastian Vasquez, and now I am sure it is him. He is wearing a white Muslim headscarf, a white tunic, and a black suit jacket. He has a full beard and looks deadly serious. A far cry from his debut with his band Gull-Z in Skien just five years earlier. He does, however, look more clean-cut than in the ISIS propaganda video released on LiveLeak three years later.

Next to him stands Arfan Bhatti wearing black skullcap, gray tunic and trousers, a blue sports jacket, and a long scruffy black beard. He carries a huge sport backpack-type bag on his back, and one would wonder what's in it. Weapons Bhatti was looking for all over Europe to shoot at the embassy? He looks as miserable as can be. As the Prophet Ummah has just emerged on the Norwegian media scene, the VG journalist notes that they demonstrated with Arfan Bhatti, already infamous in Norway. He asks Ubaydullah if Bhatti is part of their group.⁴ Ubaydullah has no comment and goes into a rant about the oppression of Muslims worldwide.

As one U.S. politician from Mogadishu, notorious for disrespecting the country that so generously took her in and gave her shelter, stated it's all about the Benjamin's baby. "It's all about the Muslims" would have been more appropriate. At least in this case, I must add.

A group kneels in the middle of the road, right on the tram tracks. Because they can. They bow down, placing their faces on the ground, and prays towards Mecca. Allahu Akbar. Those two words still give me chills. It was Muhammed Atta who said "Shout 'Allahu Akbar,' because this strikes fear in the hearts of the nonbelievers."

Loudspeakers play Arabic music as Ubaydullah Hussain continues his incensed speech claiming, "The Prophet Muhammad is the dearest of us Muslims." Ubaydullah says the film from the USA is a betrayal from the western world, and the world needs another Osama bin Laden. Punishment for mocking Islam is death, he proclaims and rants about the cartoons in

Jyllands-Posten, Denmark, and the French magazine *Charlie Hebdo* which just printed cartoons of Muhammad.[5]

NRK spoke to Muslim youths, as young as 14, at the demonstration against *The Innocence of Muslims*. "They want to support their Prophet, and they hate the United States," is the headline. The reporter asks 16-year-old Ismail why he is at the protest?

> I want to support my Prophet and show my opposition to the United States, which I hate. It is hurtful that someone is making a film about the Prophet Muhammad. But this thing with Osama bin Laden is a bit exaggerated, I think. I just want peace.

Another 16-year-old tells NRK that the man who made the film about Muhammad should pay with his life:

> The United States should kill him, and then the world is spared a number of problems. Showing a film with a character who is supposed to be Muhammad is like taking a picture of Jesus and pooping on it.

16-year-old Ahin says to NRK that Norway should support showing opposition to the film. "We want to support our brother." "Do you also support what is said about Osama bin Laden?" "I do not think they mean anything by that," he says, referring to the majority of protesters who shouted, "Obama, Obama, we love Osama."[6]

NRK meets up with Ubaydullah Hussain after his menacing rants and asks him if he is happy with the attendance at the rally:

> Allah is pleased. It is not attendance that is most important, but the message.
> Why do you give so much support to Osama bin Laden? He is the most learned Muslim who has stood up for Islam.[7]

Politicians Are Silent About Oslo Jihadist Center

A month after the demonstration at the American Embassy, *Aftenposten* reported that Arfan Bhatti and Mohyeldeen Mohammad are in Syria. Acting as a work-from-home secretary and spokesperson for the group, Ubaydullah Hussain wrote in an email to the newspaper that the Prophet Ummah had nothing to do with recruiting them:

> Those who have traveled are brave brothers who only want to protect the Muslim civilian population in Syria. The Prophet's Ummah has not recruited any of these brothers but contributed with their help and support. When they travel for such a beautiful cause, it is our duty as believing Muslims to help them with whatever they want.[8]

Norwegian authorities, at the time, reported that many "Norwegians" have traveled to Syria. Between twenty and thirty are on their way there to join various groups fighting against Assad, writes *Aftenposten*. They fear young Norwegian radical Muslims will receive training, combat experience and make international contacts that will allow them to plan terrorist acts in Norway. And weapons training, which is challenging to achieve in Norway.[9]

But the challenge of weapons training may soon change now that Fahad Qureshi, the founder of Islam Net, and spewer of a hateful ideology, has purchased Norway's largest shooting range, *Oslo Skytesenter*. They plan to establish an activity center for minority youth. It has created reactions from many in Norway and suspicions that the money comes from abroad, which may be illegal. When remembering Fahad Qureshi's speech in front of hundreds, many of them impressionable youths, about stoning and the death penalty for gays, deserters of Islam, women, and adulterers, one would wonder what type of activity center Islam Net is planning. And that he is allowed to go forward with the planned center is outrageous, but not surprising in today's Norway, that bows to radical Islamists at every turn.

On May 1, 2021, online *Resett* reports early risers observed a large banner hanging outside the premises of the Oslo Skytesenter (Oslo Rifle Range) at Haugenstua. In the early hours of Sunday morning, someone had placed it there to protest Islam Net's plans for the activity center. It depicted the logo of Islam Net and the words Oslo Jihadist Center. The banner was hung there by the group SIAN, *Stopp islamiseringen av Norge*,[10] or "Stop Islamisation of Norway." On Wokepedia SIAN is depicted as part of a series on Islamophobia. A small group that gets more condemnation and hate from the politicians and media on the left than Islam Net and all radical Iman's preaching extremism in mosques around Norway combined. SIAN uses controversial methods such as tearing out pages of the Qur'an, on occasions, to prove a point. Desperate times calls for desperate measures. But their aim is to hold peaceful rallies, educating the people of Norway about Islam, the Qur'an, and preventing the Islamization of Norway. With the methods they use, they have received nationwide attention, and that I believe, is their goal. I would like to know what the hysterical haters of SIAN would say in ten years from now if the madness is allowed to continue and Norway is like Sweden is today.

People are up in arms about the SIAN's treatment of the Qur'an and their message to stop the Islamization of Norway, but when the Bible, or Norwegian, Israeli, and American flags burn, it's freedom of speech and protesting a good cause. So is chasing Jews around Oslo and threaten death and destruction on them, so youths can be awakened politically. And burning old wooden churches. Islam is, after all, so much more peaceful than Christianity. The hundreds, sometimes thousands of protesters that show up at SIAN's demonstrations, both Norwegians Islamo-leftists and Muslims, have been violent and SIAN members have been brutally attacked. But the media and politicians condemn those Norwegians risking their life for their country not to turn into the Middle East.

I summarized and translated the information page about SIAN from their webpage Sian.no. One of the most detested organizations in Norway. Compare the following to Fahad Qureshi's hateful speech from chapter four about all Muslims believing in the death penalty for homosexuals and others:

> SIAN's goal is to work toward, stop and reverse the Islamization of Norway. Our purpose is to distribute information about what Islam stands for and what consequences Islamization will have. SIAN also wants to cooperate with democratic forces in other countries that have the same purpose in mind. Islam is a threat to our peace and freedom. Not only in Norway, but all over the world, unrest accompanies Islam. Since September 11, 2001, Muslim terrorists have carried out more than 38,000 deadly attacks worldwide. Islam is a complete political system of social governance (dominance), disguised as a religion. SIAN is not affiliated with any political party, and the members belong to the entire party spectrum from the Social Left to the Progress Party (*SV til FRP*). SIAN is fully funded through the membership fees and donations from private individuals. SIAN distances itself from racism and all other political ideas that run counter to democratic and humanist ideals. Islam is not a race. SIAN is also not against Muslims as human beings, but instead Islam as a religious-political ideology. Muslims are the first victims of Islam.

The twentieth anniversary of September 11, 2001 is coming up in five days and there's a small group in Norway who didn't forget that day. And neither did millions of others. We can't let our guards down. That's why 9/11 happened.

The leader of SIAN confirmed to *Resett* they were responsible for the banner. "Islam Net confirms with the property purchase that they want to shield their young people from being influenced by dirty unbelieving young people. We did it to focus on what the good Muslims are doing to our country." They wrote the following on their website about Islam Net and having learned more about Islam Net than I care to know, I wholeheartedly agree:

> Jihad means any effort to advance the cause of Islam. Islam Net has primarily encouraged verbal jihad. After the purchase of Oslo "Jihadsenter," they have adopted the tactics of the brotherhood, where they try to pump the dirty infidels full of sweet and sly lies, half-truths, derailments, and other distraction techniques. This fork-tongue (*ormtunge*) attempt does not change that Islam Net is a fundamentalist Muhammadan sect.[11]

When the purchase of the shooting range became known in the media in early 2021, some politicians had the obligatory concern and outrage. Now that the investment is final, there is silence, except for a couple of politicians on the right. Jon Helgheim, of the Progress Party and quoted many times in this book, is one of the few politicians who speak out. He and other Progress Party politicians have proposed new legislation preventing such activities and said to *Avisa Oslo:*

> I don't know if it was the case that they just wanted to say that they were against the plans of Islam Net. It was almost unanimous from the far right to the far left, and then it went completely silent. The Storting asks the government to present a bill that gives the municipalities the legal authority to intervene and stop activities and leisure activities aimed at children and young people; Activities that inhibit integration.[12]

Mr. Helgheim told the newspaper that the proposed bill would stop the type of activities Islam Net are planning in Groruddalen:

> I imagine that Islam Net's plans in Groruddalen are now an excellent example that such a legal authority can go in and stop or limit. A radical group with a history that speaks for everything but integration. A group with a view of women and Norwegian laws is not compatible with ordinary democratic principles of freedom. That they promote and offer to recruit children and youth goes against our goal of integration.[13]

I feel for the Progress Party and the politicians who go against the stream in Norway and dare to speak out. However, they are few and far between. No matter what they propose, even though the recommendations are often practical and best for the country and the Norwegians, they are bound to face criticism and stonewalling from their colleagues in government and the mainstream media. A hateful organization like Islam Net, which practices indoctrination, hates Norwegian values, and supports the Hudud punishment, should not run an activity center in Norway. Above all, at Norway's largest shooting range. If a white supremacist group bought the shooting center and had plans for an activity center disguised as hateful ideology indoctrination, the politicians would have been up in arms and passed laws to stop it. And rightfully so. And the media would have a field day for weeks, months, even years, proving they were right all along. That those right-wing extremists are alive and well in Norway and the country's biggest national security problem, which is a blatant lie. The same old story is playing out in the USA today. Now some Democrats even compare Trump supporters to the Taliban. Have they no shame?

The Jihads in Syria Are Good Norwegians

Aftenposten continues its story on the Syria travelers and has spoken to a source that describes the adventurers as extreme, young Muslims and untrained military idealists, recruited by several leaders in the radical Muslim community in Norway. Some of the older leaders involved in recruiting young people are also well known to the Police Security Service, which follows several of them closely, writes *Aftenposten*.¹⁴ Apparently, not followed closely enough because the recruitment was allowed to continue. For me, it is inconceivable that these older "leaders" are permitted to carry on their activities and not deported to whichever country they came from. And if they were born by first-generation immigrants send them back to the country, they received radical Qur'an schooling from. A practice in Norway that is allowed to continue. A little googling reveals many headlines of Muslim parents living in Norway and sending their children to their home countries to Qur'an schools in fear of them becoming too Norwegian and indoctrinate them with Islam ideology. Reports of torture and abuse for not knowing the Qur'an well enough have also surfaced. But we're not supposed to talk about that either. Nevertheless, more on that in my next book; uncovering the madness, one book at a time.

A source who wished to remain anonymous tells *Aftenposten*, "These young people have no impact at all on the situation in Syria, but the situation in Syria will have an enormous impact on them."¹⁵ Say that to the Yazidis and Iraqis captured by Bastian Vasquez and most likely other "Norwegians" that traveled to Syria. He boasted to Sumaira that he was in ten big battles and helped chop a general's head off. Not too much of an impact, unless you're Yazidi people in mass grave or that headless general.

In its threat assessment for 2012, PST writes that members of extreme Islamist networks in Norway are more operational than before. The developments in Syria are of great concern because they fear what may happen when they return. The recruits reportedly have large sums of Norwegian money collected in their luggage and receive help from go-betweens in Ankara, Turkey, to enter Syria for resistance warfare with groups associated with al-Qaeda's ideology. The Turkey to Aleppo Syria route is the easiest since the border is primarily open and controlled by resistance forces. Some have gone through Lebanon but considered it difficult since Hezbollah supports Assad and controls the border. Many fundraising campaigns had collected money for women and children in Syria. Fundraising campaigns that most likely helped fund trips for the foreign fighters, perhaps all of it, as they declared large sums of cash at customs before departing.¹⁶

And nobody questioned the large sums of money carried by these recruited young men already known to authorities? Or did they have a dialog meeting with them serving pizza and Coca-Cola before they left, making them promise not to get in trouble down in Syria? That must be a thing going on in Scandinavia, as I see many comments on social media mocking this practice. Instead of the punishment the young lawbreakers deserve, they have dialog meetings and pizza. Sweden, apparently, is notorious for this socialistic experiment, but I bet Norway is no better. Please don't quote me on that, but

I wouldn't be surprised. And now that type of kid glove treatment of criminals has reached American shores. At least it would give Pizza Hut and Woka Cola more business and Michael Moore gets exactly what he wished for.

Aftenposten spoke to John Christian Elden, the high-profile attorney who defended Bastian Vasquez's making the video threatening the crown prince and the prime minister in 2010. He must have a monopoly on defending terrorists and can confirm Bhatti and Mohammad is abroad:

> I can confirm that Mohyeldeen Mohammad is in Syria. Bhatti is abroad, without me giving you details where he is. None of them must report to me, and I assume that they, as good Norwegians, do not break Norwegian law.[17]

Perhaps someone should remind Attorney Elden what the definition of a good Norwegian is. Arfan Bhatti and Mohyeldeen Mohammad are as far from great Norwegians as they come. And they certainly do not need attorneys like Mr. Elden.

One Must Remember That Norway Is at War

On October 17, 2012, jihad recruiter Ubaydullah Hussain proudly boasts to NRK that a dozen members of the Prophet Ummah are now in Syria fighting a holy war. And there are others ready to go:

> I do not know the exact number, but a dozen members from the Prophet's Ummah. They are there to protect and defend the civilian population, and many are on their way. They have been motivated by these brothers who are out in the field.[18]

Hussain denies that Norwegian Muslims go to Syria to receive terrorist training but says all Muslims must protect Muslims during attacks. He allegedly does not know if they have joined al-Qaeda-related organizations and questions Norway's foreign policy. He has a lot of time on his hand to ponder such a plight:

> Strangely, Norway focuses on Muslims traveling from Norway to protect the civilian population instead of focusing on Assad's regime, torturing and killing tens of thousands of women, men, and children.[19]

The Prophet Ummahs members are not concerned with what the Police Security Service and the Norwegian authorities think about Norwegian Muslims going to conflict areas. Simply because the nonbeliever's laws are human-made, and Muslims follow Allah's law. And when confronted with the news that PST fears the jihadist can be inspired to commit terrorism in Norway after being in Syria, smartass Ubaydullah is okay with that and believes an attack is legitimate because of Norway's warfare against the Muslim world.[20]

Well, Ubaydullah Hussain, you know us Viking warriors, all four million of us, can take down 1.8 billion Muslims without a problem. Just like we took down the Swedes in the old tale, "Fifty Swedes ran through the woods, chased by one Norwegian."

Ubaydullah, well prepared as always with his declarations to the Norwegian media:

> Even if the human-made Norwegian law says otherwise, we will follow God's directions. On a general basis, one must remember that Norway is at war. Norway has been at war, against Iraq, against Afghanistan and involved in arms and bomb sales to countries such as Israel and the United States. So, I will not be surprised if there is an attack in Norway. I have said that before as well, but I do not say that the specific people who are now in Syria will participate in an attack in Norway.[21]

On October 12, NRK reported a young Norwegian man killed fighting for the Syrian city Aleppo. Well, their headline says *Norsk mann drept i Syria*, "Norwegian man killed in Syria," but casually notes at the bottom of the article that he has a background from Algeria but grew up in Norway. According to mainstream media, growing up in Norway and becoming a Norwegian can mean he came to Norway a year ago or yesterday. The Norwegian, with a background from Algeria, had joined the rebels against government forces in a fight that had lasted for weeks. With persistent recruiters like Ubaydullah, his great desire in life was to fight for Allah and protect Muslims.

A person that knew the Algerian describes him as quite religious. "I think he left last month; he had a feeling he wanted to do something for Syria. The man's younger brother is still in Syria and has no plans to return to Norway.[22] Presumably, his background is also Algerian. Hussain has previously confirmed that the 21-year-old is part of Prophet Ummah but says conflicting reports about whether he is dead. The man's family has confirmed his death, but maybe Allah told Ubaydullah that he is still alive, hanging out with 72 virgins. Or was it a 72-year-old virgin? I can't keep track.

Ubaydullah and members of The Prophet's Ummah are incredibly proud of the young brother's courage. Along with others in the radical Islamist milieu, they hail him as a martyr. And since Ubaydullah is only a jihad recruiter and let others risk their lives in a holy war, he has time to concoct another email to the media, this time NRK:

> We are incredibly proud of the young brother's love for Islam and his courage and hope, if Allah wills, that this brother's Martyrdom will motivate and guide more Muslims.[23]

These Pigs Belong to An Occupying Power

A few days after shooting off brotherly love emails to *Aftenposten* and NRK, Ubaydullah Hussain goes on a racist and menacing rant on Facebook, delivering death threats against the Jewish people in Norway:

> I'll give them protection, inshallah [if Allah wills it], as soon as I have taken the hunters test and get an AK47. These pigs belong to an occupying power, Israel. Also, they have occupied our mosque, Al-Aqsa. Ya Allah, get the dirty Jews out of our mosque and give us every opportunity to pray salah in masjid Al-Aqsa before our death. Amiin!!! They are the mothers of our prophets!!! Who Kills Prophets??? Prophet Muhammad, may peace be with him, gave us orders to protect three places. Mecca, Medinah and Masjid Al-Aqs.[24]

The Oslo police district is investigating the Facebook post, and PST is assessing the situation on an ongoing basis. As audacious as ever, Ubaydullah Hussain tells NRK he will neither deny nor confirm that it was a threat:

> It's an open comment, and it must be up to each individual to speculate on what is meant by that comment. I will neither deny nor confirm that it is a threat. As long as a group, religion, or people is in physical war with Islam, they are our enemies. Any group or country at war with another party must expect a response back.[25]

Yeah, right, tough guy Ubaydullah. That little community of around 1500 of our friends from Israel that live in Norway is at physical war with Islam and are your enemies? You are appalling, and so are those Islamo-leftists that condemn, boycott, protest, and discriminate against the Jewish people in Norway.

Ubaydullah's threat was a response to the Jewish congregation in Norway asking for police protection amid what they perceived as threatening situations. He writes that he has already acquired an AK47 and mentions Arfan Bhatti's conviction of shooting at the synagogue in Oslo in 2006:

> It is a pity that the brother who shot at the synagogue in 2005 or 2006 did not hit anyone![26]

Dagbladet has spoken to a source close to Hussain who tries to explain the Facebook posts as Hussain's deliberate attempt to provoke the Norwegian society. What is the reason for this rather unusual desire is unknown, writes *Dagbladet*, but it may give status in the *small* Islamist extremist community?[27] The liberal tabloid makes a point of noting the *small* Islamist extremist community. To counter *Dagbladet's* claim, I would use Arfan Bhatti's answer in an interview with *Aftenposten*. They asked if he was willing to commit or encourage terrorist acts on Norwegian soil to achieve what he believed in. "What terrorist acts are, depends on the eye that sees," said the radical Islamist.

And *Dagbladet*, what constitutes a small Islamist extremist community, depends on the eye that sees.

Ubaydullah tells NRK the Jews should not take on the role of the victim and does not rule out a new attack on the synagogue in Oslo:

> It is a way of reacting when the Jews go out and say they feel threatened by Muslims or other groups because I do not see that the Jews should take on the role of victim. They are part of an occupying force. They are part of an occupying power, Israel. As long as a group, religion, or people is in physical war with Islam, they are our enemies. Any group or country that is at war with another party must expect a response back.[28]

A few days earlier, it had come to light that several Islamists have attended hunting courses over the past year to take the hunting test, a legal entrance to acquire up to six weapons legally. The Police Security Service can prove they know the identity of several of those who have taken the hunter test. The Norwegian Hunters' and Fishermen's Association and the multicultural outdoor organization Wild-X confirms the news, and the leader for Wild-X became anxious and alerted the authorities:

> I can confirm that we have had participants who have expressed extreme views on hunter test courses for the hunting test. They seemed more concerned with getting weapons than being out in the woods and fields. With a passed hunting test, you will be able to have up to six weapons registered in your name. Rifles and shotguns that are in the wrong hands are dangerous.[29]

I was going to quote the NRA here, but you get the picture.

The Islamists in question come from North and West African countries affiliated with the Prophet's Ummah, now under surveillance by PST. And NRK reports that a man associated with Ansar al-Sunna, a group that appeared In Norway earlier this year, has attended a hunting course. Ansar al-Sunna attracted attention when it demanded that the district Grønland, on the east side of Oslo beleaguered by immigrants, becomes a separate state and that Norwegians should pay taxes to Muslims. The group is also under investigation for sending threats to several top Norwegian politicians, including Jens Stoltenberg, Jonas Gahr Støre, and Espen Barh Eide.[30] All happening in the small Islamist extremist community in Norway, *Dagbladet*. And why the f*** are they allowed to stay? I ask the question thinking of how easy it was for authorities to deny Eric residency in Norway.

Ubaydullah Hussain, never at a loss for words, argues that the hunter test allows any person with Norwegian citizenship without a rap sheet. It's a private matter, and if anyone in Prophet Ummah has taken the hunters' test, it's up to them.[31]

Perhaps it's time Norwegian authorities stop handing out Norwegian citizenship like it's free candy on Halloween.

The Most Bizarre Press Conference in Norway

Prophet Ummah members Egzon Avdyli, Omar Cheblal, and an unnamed person sit at a conference table surrounded by reporters from the largest newspapers in Norway. The radical group has called for a press conference in early November 2012 to call out the media and the persecution against them. They intend on clarifying what they call misinformation about Prophet Ummah. Omar Cheblal, a balding heavy-set man with glasses and a salt and pepper beard, starts the press conference with a ten-minute rant in Arabic. Evidently, for the international media, that's not present.[32]

Cheblal came to Norway sometime around 2005. Before coming to Norway, he had ties to Islamists in his native Algeria. But no worries, folks, as soon as he set foot in Norway, he became a Norwegian, a good one too if we should believe attorney Elden. Convicted of arms smuggling for Islamist groups in the home country in 1994, Cheblal received 15 years in prison for selling weapons to the GIA. This Islamist group emerged in Algeria in the 1990s. Cheblal served ten years in jail in Morocco for selling and smuggling weapons to the GIA. Pardoned in 2004, the following year, Cheblal was in place in Norway. And only God knows why they let him in. Around 2012, Cheblal was deported from Norway because authorities deemed him a threat to national security. Still, in a statement in VG earlier in 2012, the authorities feared he would face torture in his home country and postponed the deportation.[33] Reckless decision-making among officials in Norway knows no boundary, so instead of being waterboarded in Albania, he spews hatred in Arabic in front of speechless and stunned reporters in Oslo, Norway.

Omar Cheblal informs the media that Muslims worldwide must demonstrate against the Norwegian witch-hunting:

> In Norway, a powerful lobby has emerged that strongly influences police intelligence, the media, and politicians. They want to restrict freedom of expression and exploit the free press that is not free. We are shocked at how many institutions and authorities' pressure and harass us. It is no longer permitted in Norway to demonstrate or speak out. Only in Tahrir Square in Egypt can one act and speak freely without being denied. Norway is a dictatorial democracy like Egypt's former president Hosni Mubarak. He said he was a democrat, but everyone knew that he was a dictator. If the Norwegian media and others do not stop persecuting us, we will ask Muslims through our channels to demonstrate outside Norwegian embassies abroad to end racism against Muslims.[34]

After the Norwegian reporters got a quick ten-minute lesson in Arabic

101, Egzon Avdyli continues the press conference in Norwegian. Egzon is either born in former Yugoslavia or Albania, as sources online differ. But we know that as soon as he set foot in Norway, no matter what age, he miraculously became a Norwegian, at least according to the media. Only when you are an American born to an ethnic Norwegian will you never be Norwegian, no matter how much you love the country.

Egzon Avdyli is the new spokesperson for the Prophet Ummah after the recent arrest of Ubaydullah Hussain for threatening two journalists via email and the Facebook death threats against the Jewish community in Oslo. Avdyli says they have nothing to hide, and it's the Norwegian foreign policy and mockery and attacks on Islam in Norway that radicalize Muslims. He repeated several times that the group would put the freedom of expression to the test but would not say anything more about what it means:

> Recently, we have seen that the media, led by the police, the PST, and the politicians, have actively talked about the terrorist threat never being higher in Norway than it is now. They base this on the fact that some Muslims have left this country we live in for Syria. And the fear is that they will receive weapons training and join al-Qaeda, which makes them come back here to carry out an attack. At the same time, they are also claiming facts that so-called Islamists have only become more numerous. This witch hunt that has taken place in recent weeks, started by PST, is based on nothing but a lie. The authorities, and the PST, have been unanimous in the fight to stop the radical Muslims or Islamists. But we ask them from what? What is it they want to prevent them from doing? Are they committing any crimes? Something criminal? Anything criminal? Muslims who have taken or signed up for a hunting course is suspected of having sinister intentions after completing the course, even though the participants have denied this. They accuse others of taking the lead in al-Qaida by doing humanitarian work or donating money to those in need in Syria. I wonder why PST or the police have not contacted us. Not a single phone call. Suppose we are such a significant threat to the Norwegian people. Why have you not got in touch with us? We're wondering.[35]

Avdyli continues ranting and accuses the authorities and the media of attacking their values and freedom of speech, which is hilarious in itself:

> In a democratic society like Norway, where they say that freedom of expression is so highly valued, why is it okay for you to attack our values, like the Prophet Muhammad, or speak condescendingly about Sharia? Either the law is the same for everyone, or you must add a new section in the Constitution which states: 'If you are a Muslim, you are not allowed to comment on this.' Then we can agree, but do not come here and claim

Sympathy For The Evil

> that freedom of speech applies to everyone. When someone chooses to put it to the test, it becomes a circus, as it has been in recent weeks.³⁶

The press conference ends with questions from the journalists. With a chip on their shoulders, the jihads refused to answer practically every question and did not attempt to clarify whether the Prophet Ummah distances itself from violence and terror. Reporters asked Egzon Avdyli's about his relationship to the Norwegian Constitution and what they wanted to be changed:

> We accept the law of Allah. If you think your Constitution is better than God's laws, prove it, then we will disprove it.
> Do you support al-Qaeda? We are not here to discuss al-Qaeda or anything else. Here we are talking about what we stand for in Norway. It's not a question of whether we are compatible with al-Qaida or not. That has not been the topic at all.
> What do you stand for? We stand for Islam.
> Are you a member of any organization affiliated with al-Qaeda or others in Syria? It depends on what you mean by al-Qaeda. Suppose you talk about those who pray five times a day because we know most likely that al-Qaeda prays five times a day. They fast during Ramadan, and we fast during Ramadan. They do hajj (pilgrimage); we do hajj. They pray toward Kaaba in Mecca. We pray toward Kaaba in Mecca. If that's what you mean, we share, I am saying, a lot with al-Qaeda. All Muslims do. But if we are part of al-Qaeda, I do not think we would have been sitting at this table today.
> You have a leader, Ubaydullah Hussain, who has no comment when asked if he would notify authorities if he knows of any plans for an attack on Norwegian soil? You have to discuss that with his lawyer or with him. I'm not here to talk about my opinions… you have to speak with his lawyer.³⁷

In April 2014, a year and a half after the off-the-wall press conference, *Aftenposten* reports that a Norwegian Islamist is killed in Syria. That Norwegian Islamist is Albanian Egzon Avdyli, the press conference lead spokesperson. As far as *Aftenposten* knows, he stayed in Syria for more than three months. Avdyli is said to have fallen in battle, and according to *Aftenposten's* sources, he was shot and died from the injuries he suffered. He was very active on social media under the pseudonym Abu Ibraheem writes *Aftenposten*. Avdyli posted on an extreme Islamists YouTube channel and his network in the U.K. In the video, the 25-year-old describes the West as infidel cowards and accuses them of having bombed innocent civilians in many Muslim countries. Avdyli said that Muslims born and raised in the West had had enough secularism, democracy, and what the man describes as false freedom. Egzon Avdyli, who asked what laws they have broken at the press conference, was convicted in 2007 of violence, in 2008 for theft, and in 2009 for more violence, threats, and embezzlement. In 2009, he was convicted of robbery in the district court but later acquitted in the court of appeal.[38]

In December 2015, Omar Cheblal made headlines in VG, and the deported terrorist Cheblal is still a Norwegian-Algerian to the tabloid, but now he is also an ISIS fighter. *Norsk-algerisk IS-kriger: Det er en drøm som går i oppfyllelse.* Omar Cheblal, who once gave Norwegian journalists a lesson in Arabic, has had his dream come true fighting with ISIS in Syria, and it's a gift from Allah. For several years the 49-year-old was a spokesman for the Prophet Ummah, writes VG. The picture accompanying the article shows a proud Omar posing with an automatic weapon in front of the terrorist organization flag ISIS, the Islamic State in Iraq, three years after the press conference.[39]

Sadly, not long after, in January 2016, NRK reports that the Norwegian-Algerian Omar Cheblal is dead. After informing their readers, who have probably already started on the five stages of grief, lasting for about five seconds; NRK adds that after finally being expelled from Norway because he was considered a threat to national security, he sued officials in Norway. With the help of his Norwegian attorney, he filed a lawsuit against the Ministry of Justice and the Directorate of Immigration to have the deportation decision reversed. The suit was rejected by the Oslo District Court in May last year. His attorney filed an appeal in June:

> The appeal case was up in May this year. He took it very hard that he was not allowed to return to Norway after the district court proceedings.[40]

Inexplicable, the jihad that was already a terrorist by the time he came to Norway in 2004 had obtained a Norwegian attorney to fight his way back to the land that considered him a threat to national security. And the activists at NRK have to make a point about his attorney being worried about the ISIS fighter and his feelings. Not one word about the atrocities the organization he fought for afflicted on millions of innocent people. May he not rest in peace, and the media wake up.

The Armchair Jihad on Unemployment

After one of the most bizarre press conferences in recent Norwegian history, the outspoken, in your face, Prophet Ummah, that couldn't go a day without seeking attention, have seemed to disappear into thin air. No email updates to media from secretary Ubaydullah, no death threats on Facebook, no testing the freedom of speech as they had promised, and no Muslims worldwide demonstrating the witch-hunt against the Prophet Ummah and Norway's war on Islam.

On February 2, 2013, three months after the press conference, TV2 reported significant internal strife between the members of Prophet Ummah. And there is mainly growing frustration with the leader Ubaydullah Hussain.[41]

Many in the radical group do not like that Hussain receives unemployment benefits from the infidel Norwegian tax dollars. As they would say here in Good Ol' America, "You can't make this stuff up." Some member believes that receiving public funds from the nonbelievers, is forbidden according to Sharia. One of the few Sharia laws radical Muslims most definitely and most defiantly do not follow.

The armchair jihad, Ubaydullah, who recruits others to fight his holy war, received 19,260 Norwegian kroner a month from NAV, the Norwegian Labour and Welfare Administration. Around $2500. The benefits are based on a 37.5-hour work week and calculated from report cards submitted by the unemployed. Ubaydullah receives *dagpenger* or daily money of 963 kroner. More than the average payout of 750 kroner.[42] It pays to be a terrorist recruiter in Norway.

Hussain has previously criticized those who pay taxes to Norway. He believes Norway is an infidel state unless he, himself, can milk it for all it's worth. On a few occasions, the 27-year-old has spoken in mosques in Oslo, where he has lashed out at the Norwegian state for having to pay taxes. "You pay taxes to these authorities, used on the war against Islam."[43]

TV2 has reached out to Hussain, but the chatterbox must have lost all speaking ability and has no comment. Hussain, who has previously stated that tax money goes to Norway's war against Islam, will not comment on his NAV benefit to TV2. Later he emails TV2 and claims there is no internal strife:

> We have no division in the Prophet Ummah. On the contrary. We thank Allah that He has gathered us under the same organization. I continue to function as a leader and do so for as long as Allah wishes.[44]

Another reason for the strife is the disappearance of Arfan Bhatti. He has been reported missing by his family in Pakistan since January 8. In recent months, several other leaders have also laid low, including Bastian Vasquez in Syria and Mohyeldeen Mohammed. Since returning to Norway from Syria earlier this year, Mohyeldeen has not said anything publicly. Ubaydullah's recent secret marriage to a Kurdish woman has also caused conflict within the group. The woman's father and six brothers are furious with Ubaydullah Hussain. And TV2 wants to know if Hussain gets help from the Norwegian police to stay hidden from the family of the woman he married:

> As the leader of an organization, I take precautions regardless of individual situations. And no, I do not receive assistance from the police.[45]

Not surprisingly, Ubaydullah Hussain is not the only one in the Prophet Ummah to receive unemployment benefits. Arfan Bhatti, who now has gone missing in Syria, used the infidel Norwegian state's coffers. Last November, TV2 reports that Arfan Bhatti, an outspoken critic of the Norwegian tax laws, receives money from NAV. It is not as much as Hussain, 9,400 kroner a month, but he is still taking money from the unbelievers. Bhatti has long accused Norwegian Muslim organizations of milking the treasury. He told *Dagbladet* not long before he traveled to Syria: "In reality, they represent themselves to satisfy you, infidels, to suck more money out of the Norwegian state."[46]

Wahab Butt, another Prophet Ummah member, is also a recipient of the kafir money. The 27-year-old, convicted many times, receives 15,420 kroner monthly. But Butt's attorney, probably also paid by taxpayers' cash, thinks it is excellent for his butthead client to receive financial support from NAV. "My client is an ordinary Norwegian citizen like you and me, and NAV assesses whether he is entitled to support or not."[47] Not sure what they teach in law school in Norway, but most ordinary Norwegians do not join ISIS.

Nettavisen writes that the news of Ubaydullah has made former Progress Party leader Carl I. Hagen see red. He wrote on Facebook after TV2 broke the news:

> TV 2 reports that one of the leaders in the Prophet's Ummah receives more than NOK 19,000 from NAV per month. It is more than a minimum pensioner receives after years of paying (into the system) as far as I know. This is either a crazy regulation or crazy handling from NAV.[48]

Nettavisen has spoken to the former Progress Party icon:

> It is a mockery of the Norwegian people, minimum pensioners, and others who suffer and struggle with NAV applications. A man who spends most of his time fighting against Norway and Norwegian values receives the support of such a nature. If he is unemployed, I take it for granted that he regularly meets NAV and is available for incidental work, picking up rubbish in the city, or the like.[49]

I remember Carl I. Hagen from growing up in Norway. He is an icon in Norwegian politics and spoke out when nobody dared. He warned of short-sighted immigration policies, catering to immigrants and giving them preferential treatment over native Norwegian. Something the government has been doing this since they opened the country to mass immigration. And they never stopped. The anarchist Blitz gang, who we remember from the Anti-Jewish Oslo riots, wasted many rotten tomatoes and eggs on Carl I. Hagen back in the day. A revolting crowd, reminiscent of the Antifa reigning in the streets of America these days.

NRK interviewed Hagen in 2012. From the end of the '80s until well into the 90's it would get out of control when he spoke to the people writes NRK. On May 1, 1997, Mr. Hagen held a May 1st speech in Oslo. Several police officers protected Hagen with shields when the Blitz gang served the politician eggs and tomatoes:

> It was not so bad. At least it was not dangerous. It got worse when they started throwing rocks. It was not pleasant and completely unacceptable, said the former chairman.[50]

The *Blitzerne*, as some call them, were highly provoked and offended that Carl I. Hagen was allowed to even give a speech on May 1. Obviously, the first generation of the eternally offended. Hagen himself says that he would have taken the young people seriously if they had followed the democratic rules of the game:

> It was completely hopeless. They should have fought the opponents with argumentation and point of view. Had they done that, I would have taken them more seriously.[51]

He tells NRK that he would look over his shoulder a few extra times while he was out among people if something happened. But he adds that the Blitzers have been one of his best friends in politics and labels dem *nyttige idioter*, or useful idiots:

> Yes, there is no one else who has given me more sympathy than they have. In that sense, they have actually been helpful to me. Useful idiots.[52]

He believes they should have received more training in behavior and how to keep calm and order. When NRK spoke to him, Blitz had their 30th anniversary on May 1.

> Exactly, they have an anniversary, yes. I've not seen much of them lately, and that's fine.[53]

The Blitz gang, an autonomous youth house founded in 1982, started out occupying and squatting in a building in downtown Oslo. When evicted, they moved to Skippergata and agreed with the City of Oslo to maintain the place for a symbolic rent. The city council tried to put the Blitz house up for sale in 2020, led by the conservative party, but the activists responded with protests and battered the entrance of the Oslo City Hall, stopping the sale. They host political meetings, run a feminist radio station, a vegan café, and practice sessions for musicians.[54] I didn't need Wikipedia to figure that on out. And all great undertakings if they weren't so malicious against those they don't agree with.

They became notorious for their involvement in often violent protests. During the visits of the British prime minister Margaret Thatcher in 1986 and U.S. Secretary of Defense Caspar Weinberger in 1987, the demonstrations turned into street battles between Blitz sympathizers and the police. They obstructed legal meetings of right-wing political parties such as the Progress Party, the minor Fatherland Party, and the Democrats. Neo-Nazis bombed the Blitz house in 1990 and 1994. The black metal band Mayhem's bassist Varg Vikernes allegedly planned to blow up the Blitz House and had stockpiled 150 kg of explosives and 3,000 rounds of ammunition at the time of his arrest for the murder of bandmate Euronymous in 1993.[55]

As previously written, Blitz openly supported and took part in the 2008–09 Oslo Anti-Israel riots. One of their main activisms is fighting against racism, but apparently, the Jewish people don't count. I vividly remember the Blitz controversy growing up have no respect for their methods and their viewpoint. Every time I see Antifa on the news here in the United States, I think of them.

As early as 1977, Carl I. Hagen saw what uncontrolled immigration was doing to Sweden and England and already then warned of "Swedish conditions." If politicians and authorities had listened to Mr. Hagen, instead of labeling him as a bigot and racist at every turn, Norway would not be in the irreversible predicament it is today. When Donald Trump ran for president of the United States, Mr. Hagen endorsed him, and called him a man of the people. He compared him to Ronald Reagan. Indeed, he is a man of the people, and so are you, Carl I. Hagen. It is September 24, 2021, and God do we miss President Trump.

CHAPTER 13
Sometimes A Government Has to Make Moral Decisions

After NRK reported that the Norwegian Police Security Service charged Sumaira with participating in a terrorist organization, it's quiet for three weeks in the mainstream media about the ISIS woman. On October 31, 2019, NRK reports the Borgarting Court of Appeal rejected her request to be arrested and extradited to Norway. Attorney Nordhus is considering taking the case to the Supreme Court. Because jihad attorneys in Norway always go above and beyond the call of duty when defending terrorists. The newspaper only has a brief mention of the decision and no word on the boy's condition. The four-year-old was on his deathbed three weeks earlier.

Then a strange thing happens. NRK and other media outlets that have taken a profound interest in and cheered on the return of the ISIS woman and the sick boy are utterly silent for two and half months. I know they have generous vacation leave in Norway, but they couldn't have all gone on vacation at the same time. Or were they all down at the al-Hol camp holding the ISIS woman's hand until Norway caved in? I am not trying to start conspiracy theories here, but NRK has relentlessly reported on the ISIS woman and her sick child for a year. According to the attorney, politicians, and the news media, a child could die any day. And not only do we not hear from NRK about the case for weeks, but astonishingly the breaking news headline on January 14, 2020, is: *Norge henter tilbake IS-siktet mor og to barn fra Syria.*

Norway Brings Back ISIS Accused Mother

I picture many Norwegians choking on their coffee reading the morning news and the headlines from NRK and the rest of the mainstream media. And I bet a few choice words uttered on this cold January morning weren't, "Thank heavens! She is finally home." It was probably more like; *faen I helvete, hva er det norske myndigheter tenker ... jævla politikere ... verden står ikke til påsken ...*

NRK, self-proclaimed cheerleaders for Muslims and Islam, have been silent about the ISIS woman for over two and a half months. But on January 14, 2020, they report that Norway is bringing the accused ISIS woman and her two children from Syria. Prime Minister Solberg and her comrades have taken a 180-degree turn, and they have secretly planned to rescue this exemplary citizen since October 2019. Around the same time, Eric and Sonja were ousted from Norway because the American-born to a Norwegian had no special connection to Norway.

By the way, Prime Minister Solberg and colleagues? Anything else going on in Norway worth fighting for? Any deaths in hospitals lately from medical errors because of health care cutbacks? The kind of horrible death my brother-in-law suffered. The man who was like a brother to me. Any elder abuse or neglect in nursing homes? Any children being unnecessarily taking away by Child Services these days? Any 4-year-old ethnic Norwegians boys denied medical treatment? Any Norwegians killed on the streets by violent migrants you so eagerly bring in to Norway? The last one being 52-year-old Marianne, who was stabbed to death on the streets of Norway by a Somalian and got no attention in the mainstream media. During *the summer of love*, when the streets of America raged with violent, deadly protests and reported on 24/7 in Norwegian news for months. Except the media told us the demonstrations were peaceful and systematic racism in America was rampant. It was a tragedy that happened thousands of miles from Norway, but they couldn't give Marianne the time of day. Update: Another Marianne was killed just as I published this book. In late September 2021. Marianne, 59 years old and her 29-year-old colleague was stabbed in a meeting with the Libyan refugee at the NAV welfare office they worked at in Bergen. Marianne died. The media claimed the man had no prior convictions, but two young women came forward and said he had threatened them with a knife a few years earlier. No charges were filed. They are working feverishly to declare him insane, as with most of the perpetrators are, when killing Norwegians.

Have any young American men like Eric, who would have made such an outstanding contribution to your country and loved Norway above all, been denied residency and thrown out of Norway lately? Instead, you allow men who killed Norwegians like Marianne, 54 years old; Heikki, 24 years old; Håvard 18 years old; Marie 17 years old; Linn 32 years old; Eilif 85 years old; Margaret 19 years old; Arve 53 years old, Einar 35 years old and Ann-Mari 32 years old. Those are only a few killed by either illegal or legal immigrants. They were murdered in cold blood and then forgotten. These innocent Norwegians get no yearly memorials, no statutes, no politicians speaking out, and no outrage in the mainstream media. They are just forgotten as if they never existed.

And how are things going with vaccinating the Norwegian people for the Wuhan virus? Is the government content about giving almost one million vaccines away to Africa when only a fraction of Norwegians was vaccinated? Those obedient Norwegians who pay enormous taxes so you can take care of everyone in the world but them, like my 78-year-old mother that still hadn't gotten her vaccine in late March. It is now the end of June, and she is finally vaccinated. Still, only a few others in my family are because you prioritized Africa and the immigrant communities in Oslo. The migrant community that is highly overrepresented on statistics of infected, and politicians and media used excuses of living in close quarters and language barriers. But then, inconveniently, a report from the National Institute of Public Health came out proving that close quarters had nothing to do with it. And ethnic Norwegian living on top of one another were less likely to become infected. You know, those racist, right-wing extremist Norwegians.

But we are not supposed to talk about that. You are too busy bringing home ISIS fighters anyway then to worry about your country and the Norwegians.

The government had so far refused to bring back the accused ISIS women, writes NRK. Still, Prime Minister Solberg and her administration have now changed course, and the woman and her two children were escorted across the border between Syria and Iraq by Norwegian authorities. Thus, she is the first woman to be actively brought back to Norway after being in an ISIS-controlled area. NRK has to repeat for the hundredth time that the boy is seriously sick. They note, "In August, the boy weighed 12 kilos, the same as an average Norwegian one-year-old. According to a Syrian doctor, the boy *probably* has the serious disease cystic fibrosis, *"but other doctors have not confirmed the diagnosis."*

The woman accused of terrorism has not been willing to send her son back to Norway without her. The ISIS woman told NRK last year:

> They have been through a lot in a short time. Are they going to lose their mother on top of it all? It will be tough for the kids, and it will destroy my son.[1]

Cry me a river. As if a Jihad mother who joined two notorious terror organizations wouldn't destroy the son when he finds out. In October, the security situation in the area worsened after Turkey started a military operation in northern Syria. A central source in the Kurdish self-governing authorities in northeastern Syria told NRK. "We have negotiated with the Norwegian authorities for some time to pick up the family on humanitarian grounds."[2]

Siv Jensen, leader of the often-scorned conservative Progress Party, addressed the ISIS woman directly after a previous news report about the family on *Dagsrevyen*, NRK's evening news:

> I want to say to her: I have no sympathy with you. I do not think we should lift a single finger to get you back.³

Since then, the Liberal Party and the Christian Democratic Party have worked diligently to change the policy on bringing the ISIS woman home. In an email to NRK, Liberal Party leader Trine Skei Grande writes that she is happy and relieved and that the innocent and vulnerable children are on their way back to Norway:

> The Liberal Party in government has been working intensely on this for a long time. Children should not be punished for their parents' misdeeds, no matter how horrible they may be.⁴

And Norwegians shouldn't be punished by having terrorists living in their neighborhoods. And they shouldn't have to pay for the homecoming of ISIS women.

When the government decided to bring the ISIS woman back in October, Foreign Minister Ine Eriksen Søreide held a meeting conveniently shielded from the public. The Labor Party leader Jonas Gahr Støre said that there was probably a majority in the Storting to return the ISIS women:

> If this is what it takes for a child to come home, that the mother accompanies him, we all are for it, provided there are measures taken in Norway. I think it is an attitude that has the parliamentary majority with it.⁵

How about you ask the Norwegian people, Jonas Gahr Støre? Is there a Norwegian folk's majority bringing a traitor home? I'll answer my question because, being a politician, you will beat around the bush about the asinine decision. No! There isn't a folk majority in Norway for bringing the ISIS woman home. In February 2020, Sentio surveyed readers for the online *Nettavisen and o*nly one in four Norwegians, twenty-five percent, agreed to bring ISIS women and children to Norway. Thirty-one percent answered no, and twenty-nine percent believed only the children should be picked up. So, if not taken the children into account, sixty percent of Norwegians are against bringing ISIS women back to Norway. And fifteen percent didn't know.⁶ Of course, the answers vary across party line, but in liberal Norway, the numbers are significant and shows that the issue of bringing a traitor home pulls a people's sense of justice.

Nettavisen, once fair and balanced, now quite left-oriented, has a random survey within the article, which they often do about various issues. They ask, "Should Norway assist ISIS women that want to come home to Norway."⁷ Almost 16,000 people have allegedly answered the survey. The answers are the exact opposite of the Sentio survey. Exactly sixty percent answered YES. Thirty-eight percent said NO, and one percent don't know. That doesn't even add up to one hundred percent. The conspiracy theorist in me kicks in, and I guarantee the numbers are "fudged." As I said, the survey is the exact opposite of a professional survey done by Sentio and probably not the opinions they wanted to hear from the Norwegians. *Nettavisen's* numbers may not be physically altered, but the leftists may have banded together, making sure they all participated and gave a resounding YES to bringing an ISIS woman back. Maybe it was all those journalists and politicians cheering on the homecoming of Sumaira. I know. I just don't trust these people.

The Progressive Party's immigration policy spokesman, Jon Helgheim, is not surprised by the population's skepticism and says to *Nettavisen*:

> We have seen several surveys on this topic recently, showing that the skepticism about bringing back the ISIS women is great. All the polls show that the Progressive Party's voters are very united and agree on our party line in this matter.
> For the Progressive Party, it is entirely unthinkable to spend a lot of time and resources on bringing potentially dangerous people to the country just because their ISIS affiliation has given them a lot of media attention. Many families struggle all around us, who have never done anything wrong, but never get any help from the Norwegian authorities. To spend resources on helping ISIS women rather than helping others, I think people react to it. It sends completely wrong signals that ISIS members get help more readily than law-abiding citizens.[8]

Nettavisen also presented a survey by Sentio, which showed that the Progress Party received tremendous support from its voters for the government exit because of the ISIS woman. Eighty-four percent thought it was right of the party to leave the government and only three percent voted no. Thirteen percent didn't know.[9]

I Don't Want a Norwegian Boy Dying on My Watch

| But it's okay that a Norwegian boy goes blind on her watch. |

On January 17, Prime Minister Solberg is a guest on *Debatten*, an NRK debate program. She had already informed NRK that she would not risk a sick Norwegian five-year-old dying on her watch. The ISIS woman and her two children are allegedly on their way home to Norway, but their arrival has been a well-kept secret until now. Prime Minister Solberg explains:

> PST and the police have the best control of the situation, and as far as I understand, they will arrive tomorrow. But what is important is that they return and that this child, *who is believed to be ill*, can receive treatment in Norway.[10]

The government's primary wish was to pick up the children alone, but the mother refused to send them away. The prime minister believes it is essential that people face prosecution in the country where the alleged crime happened.

Still, in the end, this became a humanitarian situation the government had to solve.[11]

So, what an ISIS woman wants, an ISIS woman gets. And notice the rhetoric is changing. It went from the boy probably having Mystic Fibrosis, then he's on his deathbed, to the boy is believed to be ill. Next, we will see headlines in Norway, "Miracles do happen. Boy healed from Mystic Fibrosis." And it's all about a humanitarian situation, a word the Norwegian politicians love to throw around.

NRK notes that bringing the family home has caused turmoil in the government. Siv Jensen, the Progress Party leader, has called for an emergency meeting with party members to prepare a list of demands the party will deliver to Prime Minister Solberg. If they cannot meet their needs, the government's cooperation with the Progress Party may be over.[12] The prime minister then suddenly forgets her role as the leader of a country and transforms into a preacher speaking of morality, humanitarian aspects, and making important choices. As if the Progress Party does not know the difference between right and wrong or good and bad behavior.

> First of all, this is a decision we made some time ago. It has been an operation that has taken a long time, simply because it has been difficult in those areas. Sometimes as a government, one has to make some moral, important choices. We have done that. And for the majority of the government, consideration for the child was the most important thing. Of course, I will relate to what the Progress Party says and think about the case. Still, sometimes the majority in government must make important decisions that have significant humanitarian aspects.[13]

The moral dilemma here is that most of the politicians my fellow Norwegians voted for have lied about the sick child. And you know that Prime Minister Solberg. The other moral dilemma is that the politicians bring home an ISIS woman that most Norwegians do not want in their country. The politicians are putting a terrorist before the welfare of the Norwegians and the land of Norway. But then again, what else is new.

NRK asks the prime minister if she is willing to negotiate with the Progress Party, and she says all parties can bring demands before the government. Still, there is no basis for making changes to the *Granavolden-plattformen* now. The political platform was signed at Granvolden Gjæstgiveri in January 2019 and comprised of a government led by the Conservatives, the Progress Party, the Liberals, and the Christian Democratic Party. The agreement led to the Christian Democratic Party joining the Solberg government.[14]

Granavolden has an interesting past worth mentioning. Gjæstgiveri translates to guesthouse or inn. Granavolden, located in Hadeland, has been a guesthouse since 1657. In ancient times, the place was a hub with churches, a local court, and a posting station. The guesthouse provided overnight accommodation, food, and drinks. The main road to Bergen brought all sorts of travelers to *Granavøll*. In 1716 the place became known outside its borders when the District Sheriff and innkeeper, Gregers Granavolden, mobilized 50 men from Hadeland to fight a large troop of Swedish soldiers on horseback. The Battles of Harestuskogen were of great significance in the Great Northern War. Thanks to his heroic efforts, Gregers was granted a lifelong innkeeper's license for himself and his posterity by King Frederick IV himself. In April 1814, the guesthouse opened its doors to five delegates from Hordaland bound for the National Assembly at Eidsvoll.[15]

The Norwegian constitution was signed at Eidsvoll on May 17, 1814, the most important day in the history of Norway, and later designated and celebrated as Norwegian Constitution Day. *Grunnlovsforsamlingen* or the Norwegian Constitution Assembly voted for the Norwegian Constitution and formalized the dissolution of more than 400 years of a union with Demark. I wonder what those five delegates that visited Granavolden 205 years before Norwegian politicians signed the Granavolden platform would think, if they knew the current affairs in Norway. I have a feeling they wouldn't be pleased and as distraught as those men who signed the U.S. Constitution on September 17, 1787.

The Progress Party's popular member Jon Helgheim counters that the Granavolden platform did not include bringing home an ISIS woman. He claims the party can leave the government because of the case. They have agreed to help the children, but that is where the Progress Party draws the line:

> It is right that we have a platform, but it does not say anything about us bringing ISIS terrorists to Norway. When the others still do it, even if we say no, one should not surprise that we react. The ISIS woman's case is an important issue because it pulls at people's sense of justice. I must say that I respond to the fact that words about morality are spoken. I cannot see anything moral in bringing a terrorist back to Norway.[16]

Helgheim believes that the government parties that agree to pick up the family should have checked if the child is ill. "When you enter into negotiations with a terrorist, it is a minimum of what I expect.[17]

Sumaira's attorney, Nils Christian Nordhus, happier than a clam at high water, has announced a press conference after the freedom fighter set foot in Norway. He will enlighten those who care about the rescue effort from Syria and how the woman accused of terrorism now reacts to the charges. Because the world as we know it revolves around Sumaira. He is otherwise tight-lipped and will not comment on the matter further until the family has landed on Norwegian soil. A central source in the Kurdish self-government authorities in Northeast Syria tells NRK that the family has had to take DNA tests in Iraq. The results are never published in the media, not even to his day. Not that it matters. She is on her way to Norway, come hell or high water. PST has announced that the woman must expect arrest after arriving in Norway, and the 29-year-old will be taken into custody on Saturday, according to NRK's information.[18]

If the woman must face justice, she will be the first woman who actively joined ISIS facing a trial at Oslo District Court. At least eleven women traveled from Norway to Syria. *Aftenposten* and NRK found six of them. The rest are presumed dead, missing, or are in an unknown place.[19] That's beyond belief. Not that they are presumed dead, that's belief with an R, but *Aftenposten* and NRK actions. Many innocent and downright good people, both children, and grown-ups are suffering in the world and ignored. Also, in Norway. Exactly what Jon Helgheim said, and I cannot for the life of me accept why the activists in Norway's mainstream media make it their life mission to rescue terrorists. To report on a story, I understand, but that doesn't seem like their primary mission to judge from their endless propaganda to bring the ISIS women home.

Five of the women they have found have Norwegian citizenship writes NRK, and I'll bet my last dollar that all of them will eventually land their niqab clad a**es in Norway. Aisha Shazadi Kausar, also from *Bærum*, is one of them. Another jihad from the most affluent neighborhood in Norway. That flies in the face of experts claiming poverty, close quarters, exclusion, and God knows what else, for a reason, young people become extreme. They always have an excuse and look for root causes, except if you're ethnic Norwegian. On May 18, 2021, Aisha Shazadi Kausar's spokespersons at *Aftenposten* reported that she wanted help from the Norwegian authorities to come back to Norway.

Aisha Shazadi Kausar *er ikke hvem som helst*, "not just anyone", writes Hege Storhaug at HRS:

> The ISIS woman, now 29, has for about a decade emerged as a hardcore Islamist. For that reason, she ended up with ISIS and as the wife of a prominent ISIS man and convert, Bastian Vasquez from Skien. She is now begging the Norwegian authorities to be allowed to return home to Norway. Kausar uses her son as an argument. If he is not brought home with her, he will also be an extremist, she says. Will Prime Minister Erna Solberg give in to the pressure.[20]

You did not read that wrong. Ms. Storhaug writes that Kausar was married to Bastian Vasquez. And Kausar was, at the same time he was married to Sumaira Ghafoor. I believe they are allowed to take four wives. As if one isn't enough. I say that out of experience. I don't know how my husband could put up with four of me.

Aisha Shazadi Kausar, of Pakistani origin, was born in Norway and lived in Bærum, writes Ms. Storhaug. She entered into sharia marriage in Oslo with Arfan Bhatti, the notorious Prophet Ummah extremist convicted of attacking the Jewish synagogue in Oslo and who has posed with weapons in Taliban areas on the border between Pakistan and Afghanistan. She became a member of the Salafist organization Islam Net, a springboard to violent Islam. Precisely the reason why she joined the Profeten Ummah jihadists:

> We Norwegians have followed Kausar via interviews and reports in the Norwegian media from the Roj camp in Syria for a long time. She has emerged as a hardcore ISIS member and has defiantly said she would never return to Norway. She would instead move to her parent's country of birth, Pakistan.[21]

In Syria, she married the most famous ISIS fighter from Norway, Bastian Vasquez. It has come to light that Vasquez allegedly killed her first son, and Arfan Bhatti was the boy's biological father. Let me add the following says Ms. Storhaug:

> When you are married to a man like Bastian Vasquez, who was ranked high in the ISIS hierarchy, it is in my opinion that you also had slaves in the house. It is in the cards that you have been extreme to the utmost. I wouldn't be surprised if Kausar also took an active part in acts of violence. In 2012, the organization *Foreningen Les* sent Kausar on a tour of high schools in Norway to promote the "excellence" of wearing a face veil. She received support for the project from *Aftenposten's* then cultural editor, head of *Fritt Ord*, Knut Olav Åmås.[22]

Foreningen Les is a learning organization that promotes reading in all walks of life and distributes literature to children, young people, and adults. Kausar's tour caused controversy in Norway among those who saw the insanity of it.

The Excellence of Wearing a Niqab

In June 2012, NRK reported that author Morten Skårdal returns an award from Foreningen Les in protest of the lectures with Taliban sympathizer Aisha Shezadi Kausar. Along with co-author Axel Hellstenius, the author received an award for best young adult book in 2011. Mr. Skårdal is an officer in the Norwegian Armed Forces, and the novel is about a young girl's life at the officers' school. A jury of young adults selected the book as the winner of the award. "This was a prize awarded by the youth. I really appreciate that recognition and take it with me further," said Skårdal at the time.[23]

Verdens Gang, VG, had previously written that Kausar supports the Taliban, and she believes that democracy is unnecessary if one follows the Islamic law Sharia. Skårdal told NRK:

> Kausar is a speaker with controversial opinions linked to extreme Islamism. I defend her right to speak out, but I am critical that she appears in a love of reading campaign aimed at young people in the Norwegian school system, financed with public funds. VG's story shows what connection she has to the extreme Islamic environment in Norway. It would be completely wrong to use a person with such a connection for a reading campaign in Norwegian schools.[24]

Aisha Shezadi Kausar traveled around to Norwegian schools and talked about her values and why she wears the niqab after contributing the text "You, me and the niqab" in the anthology "Pure text." Kausar started wearing the veil niqab when she was nineteen. The lectures were paid for by The Norwegian Non-Fiction Writers and Translators Association and Foreningen Les. The association receives project and operating funds from the Ministry of Culture and Church Affairs.[25]

Ministry of Culture and Church affairs? Operating funds? Taliban? Niqab? It's tough for me not to comment here. I have to pry my fingers from the keyboard, as I often must do when reading the comment section in the *Huffington Post*.

The general manager for Foreningen Les thought it was a pity that he returned the price, but they accepted his opinion. However, she stressed, it would not change their attitude. They will not break out the collaboration with the Taliban sympathizer, as her mandate was clear:

> She will talk about her choice to wear the niqab, not politics. She is crystal clear that she does not speak about her political views in the classroom, where she only talks about her personal choice to wear the niqab. She does not say anything illegal. We cannot withdraw an already initiated alliance because she has different opinions. We will use her as long as there are funds left in the budget.[26]

You can't fix stupid. And now in September 2021, Taliban is the new normal. Hege Storhaug continues Kausar's story:

In 2014, she traveled to Syria and married Bastian Vasquez, who was then married to a woman now in prison for ISIS participation [Sumaira]. Kausar thus became Vasquez's second wife. The first wife, Sumaira, is the only ISIS woman brought back from Syria by Norwegian authorities so far. Kausar also uses children as her primary weapon to force herself back to Norway. The first wife allegedly used a terminally ill child as an argument, which was a pure lie by all accounts. Kausar uses the risk that her son may develop into an extremist as an argument. She fears that her son will develop 'radical tendencies':

> I admit that I have made mistakes, and I have paid a high price for those mistakes, which I deeply regret. The last thing I want is for my child to

end up on the same track. But it will be difficult to avoid if he grows up here.²⁷

Kausar has always appeared to be a diehard extremist, continues Ms. Storhaug. That she should now have second thoughts seems highly unlikely: "I am not a threat to anyone, neither to Norway nor to others," Kausar says. Then Ms. Storhaug concludes with and expresses a common-sense idea that would never, ever in a million years, come out of a politician's mouth, which is a crying shame for Norway:

> Norwegian authorities should perhaps choose to enter into negotiations with Pakistan, a country we have given billions of kroner in aid throughout the years: Either you accept Aisha Shezadi Kausar, or we turn off the *pengekranen*, the money spigot. It is time for Norway to take back the values of the country. And in that country, there is no room for either Islamists, left-wing, or right-wing extremists. It is time to put the foot down for all forms of extremism.²⁸

Terrorists' Rights Matter Too

As Progress Party leader Siv Jensen is getting ready for negotiations with Prime Minister Solberg, she tells NRK that there is nothing wrong with their moral compass:

> The ISIS woman is a crucial issue for the Progress Party to handle. It is a complex case for our entire party organization. And I can say that there is nothing wrong with our moral compass. We are, of course, very concerned about helping innocent children return to Norway, but we are also apprehensive about not negotiating with terrorists.²⁹

Earlier, she was a guest on *Politisk Kvarter*, a political debate program on NRK, and emphasized a difference between Norwegian citizens who find their way back and actively bring someone home to Norway:

> The cup is now full. The reason for people reacting, in this case, is that this woman has actively chosen to travel, joined ISIS, and distanced herself from all values we stand for in Norway. Many believe that she has used her child as a shield to return to Norway, which is not only upsetting to the Progress Party but very many Norwegians.³⁰

Sources believe that Siv Jensen, the Minister of Finance, is unlikely to promote demands that will affect the budget. Therefore, changes in legislation involving terrorism, the National Security Act, the Immigration Act, and penalty limitations covering those laws may be on the table. In particular, the proposal to make it easier to deprive people of their Norwegian citizenship.³¹

In 2018 the Progress Party and the Conservative party proposed legislation to allow the Ministry of Justice to deprive people of their Norwegian citizenship. People who are posing a threat to national interests. It would be a security measure and not a basis for punishment decided without a judgment from the court. The proposal did not get a majority, as it received neither support from the opposition parties nor from their governmental partners, the Liberal Party.[32]

After the downvote in 2018, Jon Helgheim, immigration policy spokesman for the Progress Party, accused the opposition of being more concerned with protecting potential terrorists than the country. The basis for the proposal is to act quickly if they suspect potential terrorists and foreign fighters plan to carry out terror plans against Norway. At the time, the only way authorities can revoke citizenship is if fraudulently obtained. Mr. Helgheim told NRK:

> The majority, led by the Labor Party, do not want to make it possible to deprive suspected terrorists of their citizenship. They think that the welfare of the terrorists is more important than the nation's security.[33]

"Isn't it an important principle in law and order that revocation of Norwegian citizenship shall take place by law and judgment?" asks an ambitious NRK journalist:

> Losing citizenship is a serious intervention. But if one loses citizenship administratively, one will always be able to try the case in court afterward. Nonetheless, to protect us there and then from possible terrorist acts, we must act quickly. Therefore, the trial can occur later.[34]

Heidi, Erik, and I and others know all about that. Losing citizenship is a serious intervention, especially if you follow the law.

Britain has similar laws and by mid-July 2017 had already stripped more than 100 British foreign fighters and "brides" of their citizenship, preventing them from re-entering the country legally. More than 152 ISIS recruits had lost their British citizenship since 2016 and 30 more in July 2017. All those who have lost British citizenship are dual nationals. Under international law, governments cannot revoke someone's citizenship if it would render them stateless.[35]

Perhaps Elon Musk's plan to settle on Mars isn't such a bad idea. He did say Mars isn't for wealthy people but for explorers who will probably die. "You might not come back alive. But it's a glorious adventure." The stateless terrorists can hitch a ride with Jeff Bezos on his one-way trip to space when the petition to leave him out there gets enough signatures. I kid a lot, but in this case, I am deadly serious.

Also, the Danish government agreed to propose new rules in March 2019 that would allow citizenship stripped from nationals fighting in Iraq or Syria without going through the court. The law could also deny children of fighters born abroad citizenship.[36] It cannot be confirmed if the ruling passed, but as Demark has begun cracking down on ill-advised immigration, I am confident it will. Denmark, we Norwegians always said *Det er deilig å være norsk i Danmark.* "It is always lovely to be Norwegian in Denmark." The phrase may have started as a slogan to invite Norwegians to vacation in Denmark, but today, it is a recognizable part of the Norwegian language and one we cherish. Please don't change Denmark and keep fighting.

In 2019, the Migration Policy Institute published an article titled "Foreign Fighters: Will Revoking Citizenship Mitigate the Threat?" They write that while not all returning foreign fighters pose a threat, some have perpetrated among the most lethal attacks on European soil. In Paris, the November 2015 terrorist attacks, which killed 130 people and wounded 494, were the worst loss of life in France since World War II. A Belgian citizen trained in Syria masterminded the attack. In 2014, a French citizen who had fought in Syria's civil war killed four people in a Jewish Museum in Brussels. These attacks revealed how terrorists trained and backed by ISIS can deliver exceptional harm.[37]

A municipal committee member for the Labor Party calls Jon Helgheim's comments a cheap shot and says they do not protect terrorists:

> It's about the protection of the law. Losing one's citizenship is a punishment and should be experienced as a penalty. In a society based on the rule of law such as Norway, we believe it should be the courts that decide whether you should retain or lose your citizenship.[38]

The Labor Party member upset by Helgheim's cheap shot fires one right back at Progress Party member Sylvi Listhaug, then Ministry of Justice. And whose second job is the scapegoat in Norwegian politics? He says the Labor Party believes it is wrong that a randomly elected Minister of Justice should have the authority of depriving people of their citizenship:

> Let me put it this way: I think we should all rely more on a court decision than on Sylvi Listhaug's judgment.[39]

Sylvi Listhaug, that *randomly selected* Ministry of Justice, as the Labor party labeled her, would soon find herself in deep water, making national and international headlines. Beyond their wildest dream, the hyenas in mainstream media and the left-wing politicians had finally reached their goal. They were bringing down the Trump of Norway, as the *Washington Post* once so cunningly called her. And as the *New York Times* would report, it was a single, incendiary Facebook post that had threatened to bring down the government and led to her resignation as justice minister.

Sylvi Derangement Syndrome Is Alive and Well

To the *New York Times*, she is the anti-immigration politician capable of sharp comments and, therefore, Norway's most polarizing political figure. Her party, they write, is the right-wing Progress Party, which is a junior partner in a fragile coalition. The anti-immigration Progress Party supported a bill that allowed the government to strip Norwegian citizenship from those suspected of joining terrorist or foreign militant groups without a court hearing. After the bill was defeated earlier this month, Sylvi Listhaug lashed out online the NYT writes.[40]

To NRK, she is the *Frp-kronprinsessen*, the Progress Party crown princess. Presumably a cynical label. They report that on the morning of March 8, 2018, after the terrorist bill her party had proposed was turned down, the crown princess woke up her followers on social media with a picture of terrorists from the Somali al-Shabaab militia. The text accompanied the photo:

> AP mener terroristenes rettigheter er viktigere enn nasjonens sikkerhet
> The Labor Party believes that terrorists rights are more important than the nation's security.[41]

The *New York Times* writes that the photo she attached was of two veiled and gun-toting fighters from the Shabaab militant group in Somalia, thousands of miles away. Listhaug's post hit a nerve in a country with painful memories of its worst terrorist attack in modern times, where Labor Party members were the targets. On July 22, 2011, terrorist Anders Behring Breivik, or ABB, a far-right, anti-Islam extremist, detonated a bomb outside a building in the Government Quarters in Oslo. The targeted building housed offices of the government, then led by Labor, killing eight people. He then went to a Labor youth camp on Utøya island, where he shot and killed 69 people, most of them teenagers. Sylvi Listhaug's published the Facebook post around the same time as a movie premiere about the 2011 massacre.

A social media war-of-words then followed between Ms. Listhaug's supporters and her opponents, as she first refused to back away from it and then repeatedly apologized.[42]

The Facebook post, writes NRK, was the reason why the Christian Democratic Party in March decided that they did not trust Sylvi Listhaug as Minister of Justice and threatened to overthrow the government if Listhaug did not resign:

> Of course, I had expected debate and a lot of criticism, but the way this was twisted and turned, caricatured, and portrayed as something completely different than it was. It went much further this time than it had done before. A post about depriving terrorists of citizenship turned into firing up the hatred the mass murderer Anders Behring Breivik stood for.[43]

The *New York Times* keeps focusing on the right-wing Ms. Listhaug's anti-immigration stance and her base as if that is all she and her supporters stand for. And being for controlled immigration is different than being anti-immigration, but *reasoning* is not what those on the left or the NYT are known for. And they disregard that the issue is about terrorists and their rights. Then again, they called Osama bin Laden a devoted family man. What's there to expect.

The NYT writes that a far-right Facebook group delivered piles of flowers to the Justice Ministry after the "scandal" broke. But happily, the reporters announce that the outrage over the post prompted an online campaign asking those opposed to Listhaug to donate to Doctors Without Borders. In a matter of days, the campaign raised its target figure of 15 million kroner, about $1.94 million.[44]

It is unknown if the philanthropists that donated to Doctors Without Borders were progressives on the far-left. Still, judging by their hysterical overreaction to Listhaug's post, it's a sure bet. Sylvi Derangement Syndrome is alive and well in Norway, as Trump Derangement Syndrome is still in the USA, and there is no cure. And most of the politicians in the Storting, suffering from SDS and sitting in their glass houses, made it clear, one by one, that they did not trust Sylvi Listhaug as Norway's Minister of Justice. There was a unanimous vote of no confidence from a flock of self-opinionated left-wingers, no matter what they call themselves; from the communist party Red, the Socialist Left, the Labor Party, the Christian Democratic Party, and the Centre Party. On March 20, 2018, hours before the Storting convened on the no-confidence vote, Sylvi Listhaug announced her resignation as Minister of Justice.

Yes, there is a communist party in Norway.

NRK shares a picture of Sylvi's office, where she stands in a sea of beautiful flowers. The crown princess of the Progress Party received hundreds of flowers at the door of the Ministry of Justice in the days before she left. In Sylvi's autobiography *Der Andre Tier*, "When Others Are Silent," Listhaug writes that she was hurt that the left branded those who sent flowers as Nazis and racists. She describes them as ordinary folks.[45] I agree with Sylvi Listhaug, as I do not know any racists or Nazis in Norway. Although *I* am already labeled as such writing this book. And those regular folks have no voice, and as soon as they speak up are branded by many on the left with the very same words Sylvi mentioned.

Her autobiography gives an in-depth description of how she thinks the Labor Party decided to use her Facebook post by linking it to the terror on July 22, thus attacking the Progress Party, and *her* particularly, for being extreme. She could hardly believe her ears when the labor party leader, in a speech to the national government, said, "We have a Minister of Justice who deliberately and calculatedly nurtures under exactly the hatred that took so many lives on July 22." She felt he blamed her for the reason why innocent young people were murdered in cold blood by Norway's worst mass murderer and terrorist:

> I very rarely go to the movies and pay little attention to which films premiere when. Of course, I had read in the newspapers about the Utøya film that was to come, and several already had reviews out. It was never in my thoughts or anyone around me that this was the day the film premiered. I think the Labor Party would have come up with such a link anyway.
> I was so distraught that I cried. The media, on the other hand, didn't blink an eye. It was apparently okay to compare me with Anders Behring Breivik. Støre had no scruples. It is startling that a person who claims to be so concerned with solidarity, understanding, diversity, and all the right words of praise is willing to lie, construct and demonize in the way he did in this case.[46]

The witch hunt was not why the Washington Post labeled Sylvi Listhaug Norway's Trump, but they might as well have. It is unsettling to witness the same theater play out in the USA in 2021. From the Republicans and their supporters held responsible for the storming of the U.S. Congress, as Sylvi Listhaug, the Progress Party, and their supporters are held accountable for the slaughter of innocent children on July 22. We are here in the United States witnessing the silencing of those on the right and the accusation of right-wing extremism and racism at every turn, the same as we see in "democratic" Norway. Furthermore, Norway and the rest of Europe's kid-glove treatment of terrorists, criminals, and violent protesters, have reached American shores.

There is also the prejudicial treatment of good citizens compared to those who want to hurt our country, mirroring what's happening in Norway and most of Europe. And the strangest of it all is that when there are terror attacks in the name of Islam, the politicians and media are quick to say that it has nothing to do with the religion of peace and the good Muslims. But January 6 and July 22 were the responsibility of everyone with conservative views and what they like to label right-wing extremist thoughts.

A Norwegian journalist called Trumpism a virus, and the virus had reached Norway. She should have spoken about the mainstream media she works for. The most dangerous virus of all.

I fear for the future of both my home country and my adopted country, the United States of America. I wish I could give a stark warning to those Americans indoctrinated by the progressive left that radical socialism is not the answer. And I would say, among other things; What the hell is wrong with you?

Breivik Left Us Because We Were Too Liberal

In September 2013, the Progress Party invited the international media to a press conference to clarify the party's connection with the mass murderer Anders Behring Breivik, a former party member. Several in the foreign press had linked the convicted terrorist and the Progress Party. Many journalists and photographers attended the press conference, most of them Norwegian and some foreign media. "It is easy to explain why he left the party, said the Progress Party's deputy leader Ketil Solvik-Olsen. "Breivik left us because we were too liberal."[47]

He began the press conference by drawing up the main lines of the party's history. He stressed that the party, and himself, is primarily concerned with less bureaucracy, better health, and better communication. The party is in favor of a stricter immigration policy, but it is not against immigration. Solvik-Olsen was a local chapter member where the mass murderer Anders Behring Breivik was a member but does not remember him:

> It is difficult to understand why he joined the party but easy to see why he disappeared. There is no breeding ground for his ideas in our party. I hope we can clear up some misunderstandings.[48]

The Progress Party Youth leader Himanshu Gulati was also present, and he thinks it's sad how the international media have perceived the party. He believes the party could not have had members from so many countries if it was anti-immigrant:

> I think back to our summer camp this year. People from Somalia, Sudan, Morocco, India, Myanmar, Thailand, Vietnam, and the Philippines. If only some critiques were correct, I do not think we would have seen so many immigrants who supported our party.[49]

The Progress Party issued a press release and pointed out that it is unreasonable and incorrect to use far-right, right-wing populist, and xenophobic terms about the party. Mr. Gulati continues:

> He was once a member but withdrew because he did not receive any support for his views in the party. We are a pragmatic, classical liberal, and liberal-conservative party that promotes lower taxes, free health and education choices, economic policy anchoring, and international cooperation. Cornerstones in our foreign policy are the defense of human rights, democracy, and free trade.[50]

The Progress Party fights for controlled and limited immigration, but never for a complete halt in immigration. They state there is a big difference between being for a strict immigration policy and being hostile to immigration.[51] Some good advice for the new administration here in the United States.

Today, nine years after the press conference, Sylvi Listhaug is the new leader of the Progress Party since Siv Jensen stepped down in February 2021. Ketil Solvik-Olsen, who hosted the press conference in 2013, was elected as the first deputy at the party convention in May 2021, and Sylvi Listhaug's confirmed as leader. The media they need to worry about today is most likely not the international press but rather the mainstream media in Norway and their far-left colleges in government.

CHAPTER 14
Oh, What a Tangled Web We Weave...

Gardermoen Oslo Airport, February 27, 2021,
The Homecoming of An ISIS Woman

ON JANUARY 17, 2020, Sumaira Ghafoor and her two children landed at Gardermoen Oslo Airport just before midnight. A dozen police officers and the Ministry of Foreign Affairs representatives escorted the family on the journey home to Norway. They flew out of Erbil in Iraq, where they have been staying pending transport back to Norway. They flew on a scheduled flight from Erbil, via Vienna and Copenhagen, to Oslo. During the flight, the family was kept in the back of the plane, shielded from the other passengers.[1]

Members of the Green Party must now pedal on bicycles for the rest of the year; since they donated their yearly carbon footprints to the ISIS woman, they were dying to get home. Alternatively, they could have someone else drive their limos because if someone else is behind the wheel, wasting carbon footprints doesn't count.

When the plane landed, the other passengers from Copenhagen had to leave first, to be transported by bus to the terminal. Finally, the entourage escorted the ISIS woman and her two children out of the plane. Shortly after the woman set foot on Norwegian soil, she was "arrested" by the Police Security Service. The ISIS woman and her children were then driven to Ullevål hospital by ambulance,[2] hired by the film team to shoot the first episode of the second season of *She Was Almost Left Behind*. The ambulance was followed by a car from PST, leaving nothing to chance. The movie script required the child to be carried in on a stretcher when they arrived at the children's ward.

Anonymous sources had heard officers from PST mumbling something about the kid running through the airport not looking deadly ill but rather healthy. However, the information is not confirmed. And even if it were, it would never make it to the mainstream media. After all, cherry picking is a full-time job among journalists in mainstream media Norway. As the child was hurried inside to receive lifesaving treatment put on hold for six months, the ambulance drove on to the hospital hotel, closely followed by civilian, masked police. Several police cars parked outside the hospital hotel as the ISIS woman and her daughter walked inside. Because even though PST arrested Sumaira at Gardermoen Airport, it didn't mean they would throw her in the slammer. In Norway, we treat criminals with kid gloves remember; because we are not me, me, me, as they are in the United States, according to Michael Moore. The jihad princess had just arrived, and she received a welcome fit for a queen.

Attorney Nordhus can hardly contain himself and, while burning the midnight oil waiting for the ISIS woman to arrive, took the time to write a press release and announced a press conference the following day:

> Last night I was publicly appointed as a defender for the woman arrested for participating in a terrorist organization. As soon as practically possible, I will have meetings and conduct conversations with the woman in necessary collaboration with PST.[3]

That Attorney Nordhus would act as a defender for the ISIS women once she landed in Norway rendered many Norwegians speechless. They didn't see it coming. It is still heard in conversations around the land; around water coolers and cocktail parties. And people shake their heads in disbelief.

Foreign Minister Ine Eriksen Søreide says consideration for the child was crucial for the family's homecoming. She states in a press release the children receive health care and are followed up the by child welfare service:

> Assistance for the homecoming was given on humanitarian grounds because we fear illness in one of the children. I'm glad we can now conclude this demanding consular case. I thank everyone who has contributed to this work. The children deserve peace and must be shielded. I hope this is respected.[4]

Norwegian politicians always know the words to use when faced with possibly scrutiny: Humanitarian, morals, diverse, respect, inclusion, unity, peace, multiculturalism, dialog, right-wing supremacy, islamophobia, racist, to name a few. Ethical is another one, and Attorney Nordhus, as the good lawyer he is, follows the guidelines to a tee but is still tightlipped about the case and will not comment further:

> As counsel, I am following existing ethical guidelines obliged to discuss the matter with my client as soon as possible. I will not comment on the matter further until after the meeting.[5]

And speaking of morals and ethical guidelines. NRK reports that the Norwegian Ministry of Foreign Affairs representatives had met with the Kurdish autonomous authorities in northeastern Syria regarding the ISIS woman. In a Facebook post, the self-governing authorities in northeast Syria write that Norway's Ministry of Foreign Affairs representatives and the Syrians signed a document. And signing the paper, they all assured that the children and their mother are in good health and not mentally or physically pressured during their stay in the area.[6]

Sometimes NRK surprises and asks hard-lined questions and grills the spokesperson for the Ministry of Foreign Affairs. It could have been a conservative journalist, an almost extinct species in Norwegian media, as only 1.9 % are members of the conservative Progress Party. Frightening, but true. They are now on the Norwegian endangered species list, but hope is dwindling they will survive. Cloning is one option, but it is not legalized in Norway yet.

"Why could such a document be signed, at the same time as both Prime Minister Erna Solberg and Foreign Minister Ine Eriksen Søreide have told the Norwegian public that the child is presumed ill," asks the NRK journalist? The bureaucrat and master at beating around the bush answers, "This document is a formality that marks the end of a longer dialogue with local authorities to have the family transferred to the Norwegian authorities. "What examinations of the health condition were the basis before the Ministry of Foreign Affairs signed the document?":

> The Ministry of Foreign Affairs has *not* made any assessment of the health situation of the family. That is why we have always referred to it as the *presumed* sick child.[7]

Oh, what a tangled web we weave, when first we practice to deceive!
(Sir Walter Scott, 1808, Marmion: A Tale of Flodden Field.)

Oh, My Lord. She Is Getting Rid of Her Niqab

Attorney Nordhus tells NRK he has had in-depth discussions with the 29-year-old woman, and although she does not admit criminal guilt after being charged, she does accept custody for four weeks. Phew. Do they have a choice? She has been interrogated by PST today. NRK writes that they interviewed the woman while in the al-Hol camp wearing a niqab, a tearjerker of a story we are all too familiar with. But part of the Hollywood script, of course. Since the interview last year, they did manage to keep it a secret but can now happily reveal that she had told them then that she would get rid of her niqab when, or if, she was allowed to travel:

> I will take it off then because I do not feel like wearing it anymore. I've been wearing it long enough. It is enough. I want to be free again, the way I was before.[8]

Attorney Nordhus tells NRK she got rid of her full-length niqab as soon as she was out of Syria and the al-Hol camp, and she does not need to wear it anymore. Being not just her attorney but also the woman's wardrobe consultant NRK asks him if she will continue not wearing the niqab:

> Yes, definitely. She has no need or desire to wear it. She felt immensely relieved about getting rid of this clothing and which she took the initiative to do quite immediately.[9]

"Well, isn't that special," said the Church Lady. Kidding aside, but not really, I was curious to find out if Norway allow defendants to wear the niqab in court and did some intensive research. If anyone born after 2000 reads this, research is what we called googling back in the day and often performed in a library. I did not find anything specific about niqabs in court, but interestingly I came across countries that have banned the burqa. The burqa is the full veil covering the head and body and has a grill that hides the eyes. According, to Wokepedia, there are currently 17 nations that have banned the burqa. The countries are Tunisia, Austria, Denmark, France, Belgium, Tajikistan, Latvia, Bulgaria, Cameroon, Chad, Congo-Brazzaville, Gabon, Netherlands, China, Morocco, Sri Lanka, and Switzerland.[10]

Why are you not on the list Norway? Oh, that's right. You want to go back in time to the dark ages. The hijab, burqa, and niqab are becoming more and more visible in Norway as each day passes. I could not believe my eyes the last time I was home, and it broke my heart. *Nettavisen*, who I noted conduct random surveys from their readers, asked: "Should full-coverage garments such as the niqab and the burqa be completely banned in Norway?" Ninety-three percent, 93% answered YES.[11] That would be an astonishing ninety-three percent. But if there is one thing we have learned in these pages, it is that the politicians in Norway do not give a hoot what the men and women in the streets of Norway think.

And not only that, the Government passed a law in 2020 changing passport regulations so that it will no longer be necessary to show your ears. The decision allows for passport photos with garments such as hijab and turban. The Minister of Justice acknowledged that the background for the new rules is the stubbornness of religious activists. In a country, I must add, where the politicians and mainstream media tries to move as far away as possible from their Christian heritage.

The politicians involved with the new regulations are satisfied with the decision. And it would be only fair since the United States and Great Britain have no requirements for visible ears in a passport photo, they said.[12] Okay, then, let us institute the death penalty in Norway since the United States does it. It's only fair. I am only kidding Norway. I know how you feel about the death penalty, but I still believe that ABB deserved nothing but.

But yet again, the politicians and authorities in Norway have submitted to another unreasonable demand from an immigrant community. What's next? Sharia law, FGM clinics, access to high-rises so they can throw gays and infidels from the rooftops, ban on all pork and state-owned liquor stores, niqab-clad police, and so on? It makes me think of a fable called the "Camel's Nose," in which an Arab miller allows a camel to stick its nose into his bedroom, then other parts of its body, until the camel is entirely inside and refuses to leave. The miller ends up having to leave. Permitting small, harmless acts, allowing the camel in little by little, soon allowing the entire camel in, opening the door for larger, undesirable, and irreversible situations. And who wants a big camel in their bedroom they can't get rid of? Unless they prefer camel. Although studies show that nine out of ten men who tried Camel prefer women. I am not entirely sure if that was Camel cigarettes or camels.

The phrase "to give someone an inch; they'll take a mile" has a similar meaning as the Camel's nose fable. Regrettably, the camel may have already entered the bedroom in the land of the midnight sun.

The new passport regulation, allowing hijabs, evoked strong reactions from the Norwegian public, with thousands commenting on social media and the newspaper's comment section on Facebook. The majority were against the new regulations and felt that the politician had yet again submitted to demanding immigrants, taking away their country one inch at a time. The saddest part of this story is that those Norwegians can complain until they are blue in the face. The politicians in Storting could care one iota about their opinions, and one day I think it will come back and bite them in the a**. You can only push people so much. Has anyone seen the schoolboard protesters and the brave teachers in the news lately in the United States? I am, of course, not talking about violence. I am not Antifa or Blitz. But I envision Norwegians going out there in numbers and demand that those they put in power must do good for Norway and Norwegians. If they don't, Norway, as we once knew it, will be gone forever.

After discussing Sumaira's newfound interest in Western clothing with NRK, Attorney Nordhus tells them there is nothing so far in her explanation indicating she has been actively fighting in Syria. As if she would admit to him if she did. Lying is a fulltime job among those who are accused, as it is among the mainstream media. Or should I say, lying by omission. Nordhus adds the prosecution has not accused her of that either, and the woman wants to cooperate with PST and put behind her the life she has lived in Syria for many years:

> She wants to take charge of the life that marked her years in Syria. She's had an utterly terrible time. The time in the camp has been particularly demanding, but it is clear that the time in Syria was a nightmare for her. She maintains that at an early stage, she made mistakes and judged things wrong, and that contributed to her ending up in Syria, and she is bitter about that today.[13]

Before they were decapitated and thrown in mass graves was utterly terrible for the Yazidi people, but at least they are not suffering anymore.

Norwegian authorities have justified the repatriation because the information indicated that one of the woman's children, her five-year-old son, was seriously ill, writes NRK. It must have been newly released information uncovered by NRK because that was news to me. The Government's primary wish, and original offer, was to pick up the children alone, but the mother refused to send them away. The reporter asks Nordhus why the woman insisted on being with the children back to Norway. And as usual, he is not for loss at words and nauseously stating the obvious:

> Oh, that's easy to answer. It is simply because she thought it best for the children to bring their mother home to Norway. She considered it to the point that the boy's health situation was so severe and dramatic that the best thing for him would be that she could follow and follow him safely to a Norwegian hospital. She was simply afraid that transport of the boy in itself could expose him to the danger of dying.[14]

Excuse my English, but what a bunch of nonsense. If she was so concerned about the child's health situation, why did she refuse to let the authorities take the children back to Norway? And nobody is questioning the fact that, according to Attorney Nordhus, the boy was on his deathbed in September 2020? And because of negotiations and planning, they did not arrive in Norway until February 2021. Six months later, without treatment for the mystic fibrosis, the boy appears healthy enough to walk or run through the airport. And his apparent good health is questioned by law enforcement officers. Why isn't NRK asking those questions? We all know the answer to that; it simply does not fit their agenda. And the entire story is a big fat lie.

Since arriving in Norway, the woman and the children are under guard at Ullevål hospital. The NRK reporters manage to ask Attorney Nordhus about the boy's health, but he refuses to inform the public about the boy's health condition now. Health privacy laws matter only within the Norwegian border. They do not ask follow-up questions and lets him conclude:

> No, these children have an unconditional right to complete and absolute protection, and any personal information about these children will potentially expose them to the risk of being identified.[15]

The ISIS princess has said that she does not want to appear in the prison meeting in Oslo District Court, but it is up to the district court to decide whether she must be present. PST tells NRK that they are awaiting the court's decision. "Whether the woman must appear in prison is up to the court. Further stays in hospitals are an option," says Martin Bernsen, senior adviser at PST. As Sumaira continues twisting the authorities around her little finger, Attorney Nordhus gushes about how she can't wait to tell her story and prevent others from traveling to Syria:

> She wants the time ahead to be used well and to ensure her explanation. In addition, PST will have the opportunity to check out her information with the questioning of others and through other investigations. An extensive interrogation process will take place in the near future. She is looking forward to this, and the goal is to give PST so much information that one can prevent this from happening again; that others travel to conflict areas such as Syria.[16]

Mark my words. In a few months, we will have to endure glowing reviews from mainstream media of her book *Kidnapped by the Caliphate. My Life as a Jihad Bride*. With a heartfelt foreword by Attorney Nordhus. I better get this book published fast, so she doesn't get to tell her story first.

It Wasn't a Matter of Snapping Your Fingers

The Liberal Party Leader Trine Skei Grande could barely contain her delight when news broke that they were bringing the ISIS woman home. Again, she reassures NRK that there is no doubt it was the right choice to get Sumaira to Norway. NRK meets her at the Deichman Library at Torshov, Oslo, shortly before the Progress Party's national board convenes for a meeting to decide the party's faith. She was at the library to sum up, the 2019 financial year. It was probably the same as it was the year before and the year after, enormous money spent on anything but Norway and its people. Maybe she should have picked up Hege Storhaug books about Islam or Douglas Murray's *The Strange Death of Europe* while she was there.

Even though the Progress Party may decide to leave the Government, Grande says it was not a difficult choice to bring the 29-year-old ISIS woman and her two children home. NRK reminds her that several members in the Progress Party have expressed that they think it was challenging that the Prime Minister said this was a morally correct choice:

> At least I'm sure that this was the right choice. There has been no doubt in the Liberal Party that this was the right thing to do. We always prioritize children first. And we will always prioritize those Norwegian citizens around the world ask for assistance in rescuing a sick child. That's why I think the choice wasn't so difficult. I understand it must be difficult for the Progress Party, but they need to work it out.[17]

The Progress Party continues questioning the health condition of the five-year-old boy. Now, the elephant in the room for those on the left. Tone Ims Larssen, the Oslo's Progress Party leader, questioned why the woman's attorney, Nils Christian Nordhus, would not comment on the boy's health condition yesterday. Larssen told NRK earlier, "it makes me feel that a terrorist has pressured us to get her home, and then it makes the case even worse." Trine Skei Grande, continuing the rigamarole and double-talk, has an answer that contradicts everything said before about the reason for bringing the mother home. It was never critical how sick the boy was, according to her:

> If a mother asks for assistance to come home with her children, it is not the medical category that decides. We must secure the children, which has been the Liberal Party's standpoint all along.[18]

Ms. Grande then launches into an Academy Award-worthy speech paying tribute to the Ministry of Foreign Affairs and their heroic job of retrieving the woman and her two children. It will play out in season three of *She was almost left behind*. An episode you won't want to miss. And, mind you, it wasn't just a matter of snapping your fingers to arrange something heroic like that she reminds the reporters:

> Remember that this has been a very challenging job, and I must pay tribute to the Ministry of Foreign Affairs, who carried it out. It took quite a few months [and tons of money] from the time we said yes until they managed to get them home. It's not just a matter of snapping your fingers to arrange something like that. It has been a nerve-wracking experience, and it was a relief when it actually happened.[19]

It is too bad politicians in Norway cant's show that kind of enthusiasm about pressing and important matters in the country that concerns Norway and Norwegians. I sound like a broken record, don't I? Such as monumental problems in health care, dissatisfactory elder-care, rising crime rates, loneliness, and poor finances among elders; it goes on and on, and on, and on, but geez… it's not like I am writing a book.

Nobody knows what will happen if the Progress Party leaves the Government, writes NRK. But their exit could open the way for a government that the Christian Democratic Party and the Liberal Party wanted, sounding almost wishful. "The Christian Democrats, the Liberal Party, the 'Conservative' Party. How does that sound?" the reporter gleefully asks Trine Skei Grande:

> It's a government constellation that the Liberal Party went to the polls for and wanted to achieve. The Storting we have today is challenging where there is a very fragmented opposition.
> Do you think it will work? Asks a NRK journalist, as hopeful as ever.
> I can't conclude that now. The Progress Party must decide whether they will join us, then we'll have to shuffle the cards.[20]

The politicians on the left in Norway and the mainstream news wouldn't shed a tear if the only conservative party left the scene forever. Just like the Democrats in the United States dream of, and now work diligently toward becoming a one-party state.

Incidentally, Sumaira's attorney sent a thank you note to the leader of the Green Party for her role in getting the ISIS woman and her two children to Norway. When it became known that the Progress Party was exiting the Government because of the decision, The Green Party's leader hailed it as a victory. In VG, she is quoted as saying, "I had no idea it would lead to the Progress Party leaving the Government. Two good victories in one."[21] An award ceremony for those involved is scheduled for later this year, and it may be combined with the Nobel Peace Prize sermon. Hopefully, former President Trump can take time away from his busy life and accept the prize.

And a victory for the Norwegian people would be if they didn't have to worry about radical Islam in their country. Spending millions getting an ISIS woman back to the country she betrayed is not a triumph, but as with most politicians in Norway, her priorities are way out in the left field.

Norway Extended a Hand and Not Just Once

While the left celebrates the homecoming of the ISIS princess, many Norwegians on the right side are furious that the Government caved in to a terrorist. The relentless propaganda to get a traitor back to Norway from the mainstream media and politicians has not gone unnoticed, and many feel betrayed by those they have put in office. The Progress Party did not support the decision, and dissent was their only option. Per Willy Amundsen, a party member and former Minister of Justice calls the decision a betrayal of Progress Party voters:

> I am very disappointed that the Conservatives, Liberals, and Christian Democrats opened the door to Norway for ISIS women. [Great example of the Camel's nose fable]. The Conservatives should understand that this is a problematic issue for the Progress Party. Instead, they let the micro-parties forcibly get their way while we are informed via the media.[22]

Another member, who does not tend to go against the administration, told *Aftenposten* she is ashamed of her government and thinks it is awful they picked up the ISIS woman. She calls her a terrorist. She said to TV2 that she would vote to leave the Government if there was a vote now. "Nothing can repair this," she says.

Former Minister of Agriculture Bård Hoksrud tells *Aftenposten* that the repatriation of the ISIS-accused woman is "completely unacceptable." He is disappointed with the Government's reversal in this matter:

> The state has no responsibility to help people who have left to join a terrorist organization that uses all means to fight our values and way of life. They must, of course, themselves, take responsibility for the choices they have made to leave.[23]

Prime Minister Solberg, unwavering as always, tells *Aftenposten* she thinks the Progress Party troubles are sad. Her answer reveals they did not inform the Progress Party due to security issues, audacity at its highest level. Not only do they not have morals, like herself and the social justice warriors, but they are not to be trusted.

> I think it's sad, and I know it's a complicated case within the Progress Party. But we had to focus on this one child. And I understand that it came as a surprise to many in the Progress Party. We could not inform many people in advance about this is, of course, due to security issues.[24]

Aftenposten asks the prime minister if she knows how seriously ill the child is:

> Our challenge is that this child is reportedly ill, seriously ill. It is difficult for us because we could not give the child medical assistance. The mother has not been willing to bring the child to get medical aid. The question is, how long can we accept this when she doesn't want to. We have chosen to trust that this is a sick child.[25]

Oh, what a tangled web we weave. In a recent interview in May 2021, one and a half years after they picked up the ISIS woman, she told *Nettavisen* she has no regrets, and it was the right thing to do. Elections are coming up, and they ask her if she has any regrets after her eight-year tenure as a prime minister. "I'm not so concerned about regretting things," she said.[26] And that's why she is a politician. An ordinary person would say like Frank Sinatra, "Regrets, I had a few...Then, reading the rest of Sinatra's lyrics makes me think maybe he was a politician, "Regrets, I've had a few. But then again, too few to mention..."

The Conservative party in Norway is not to be confused with, for example, the Republican party in the United States. *Høyre* is the name of the party in Norway, which translated to right. To me, their politics resemble the Democratic party here, at least in recent years. The Progress Party is the only party that comes close to a conservative party, but there are also questions among voters these days, how traditional are they? Some members are caving in to the globalists and socialists and seem conservative in name only as with the RINOs in the United States, Republican In Name Only, and who govern and legislate as Democrats. I hope that is not the case because Norway needs them sorely to challenge the left.

Smaller parties are emerging, one named *Demokratene*, which translates to Democrats in English. But they have nothing to do with the progressive socialistic ideology of the Democratic party in the United States. A party I once supported by voting for Barak Obama twice, and Hillary Clinton in 2016. Yes, I could have been one of those pink pussy hats that emerged after President Trump won. Yikes. I blame it on being indoctrinated by the media both here in the United States and Norway. I was convinced Donald Trump would start a world war and I was curled up in a fetal position on the floor the night he won. I used to read the *Huffington Post* for crying out loud. Now I just read it to troll people those who comment. Not really, but once I commented positively on an article about Trump and I have never been yelled at more in my life. You can't win. After the election in 2016, it didn't take me long to open my eyes and I thank God I did. I was never a diehard democrat. I voted for George W. Bush for his second term, the year after I became an American Citizen. The now radical democrats will never ever get my vote.

The party Demokratene in Norway and their party politics is for *Norway and Norwegians*. As in Norway first. I wish them well in the upcoming election. I still suggest they change their name.

A young Conservative party member made headlines after news broke that the ISIS woman was coming back to Norway. His opposition letter was published in the media. Undoubtedly only in the conservative press, but his words resonate with many Norwegians, including myself. What he writes pretty much sums up *Sympathy for the Evil*, and I believe the sentiment among many Norwegians who do not have a voice. The young conservative left the Conservative party in protest and joined the Progress Party. Preben Dimmen wants to know why the ISIS woman receive the help that the rest of us do not get:

> The Government has negotiated an ISIS woman back to Norway. As an ordinary citizen, if you had become ill abroad, you would not have received this luxury treatment. The Government has now made the big mistake of setting a precedent for negotiations with terrorists on their terms, thus weakening Norwegians' security abroad.
>
> As with the Progress Party (FrP) sent to the gallows and politically divided by its government, there is *nothing* wrong with my moral compass concerning this case. My party leader, the party's leadership, and Government colleagues now think differently, after an about-turn and *knefall* [kneeling, submission]. I believe it to be just tragic for all the traditional Conservative voters who now wonder why we give special treatment and negotiate with ISIS terrorists.
>
> Launching a demanding and dangerous foreign operation to retrieve the ISIS woman and her two children; was made on an independent, extrajudicial, political, and ethical basis. And the children were used as a means of pressure by her. And it's a breach of rationality.
>
> *All* parties in the Storting have wanted the allegedly sick child–who is quite possibly actually ill–returned if he suffers from a severe illness.
>
> The ISIS woman's lawyer has so far refused to confirm anything about the child. The only thing we know is that neither the Ministry of Foreign Affairs nor the Government has documentation that the child was seriously ill before arrival. Nevertheless, an accused ISIS terrorist, her

lawyer, and the left outmaneuvered them. Including some of those who are miraculously inside our conservative Government.

The ISIS woman deceived most of the Norwegian Government and the Ministry of Foreign Affairs and was ultimately willing to let her child die. The Government's position was that the child should receive local medical treatment or be brought to Norway without the mother. The fact that the child was offered several options for treatment is proof of that. Norway extended a hand, not just once, but several times.

These hands were extended, entirely voluntarily, for purely humanitarian reasons, with the support of all parties in the Government. There is no legal obligation to bring either the child or the ISIS woman home. The decision to meet her demands and thus set a precedent for future negotiations and kneel before the needs of terrorists was of the Government's own free will. And a turnaround operation rooted in morality, poor judgment, and a reversed standpoint. That is not good for children with Norwegian citizenship abroad.

The offer to guarantee medical assistance abroad is not a legal obligation. And at least not a state-funded return trip. You would not have received it if you had injured yourself or became ill on holiday abroad. The following is what the Ministry of Foreign Affairs writes on the Government's website:

Every so often, Norwegian citizens abroad expect, and even demand, that the Norwegian authorities cover medical and hospital treatment expenses and travel home. However, the Foreign Service does not have funds available for such purposes. Therefore, the foreign service missions cannot cover costs or guarantee expenses for hospitals, the return home, or the like unless there is a guarantee from the individuals themselves, relatives, employer, or others. If no one can guarantee the expenses, the foreign service missions can, in exceptional cases, provide emergency loans.

Norwegian citizens who have emigrated from Norway are not entitled to have expenses for medical treatment covered, regardless of the place of residence, as they are no longer members of the National Insurance Scheme. An emigrated person has resided or intends to live abroad for more than 12 months or more than six months per year over two years. Exceptions to this are, i.e., students with student loans from Lånekassen and persons who have voluntary membership in the National Insurance Scheme.

It is also not possible for the Foreign Service to cover any expenses for search or rescue operations for Norwegians missing after expeditions abroad. Likewise, in such cases, the assistance will have to be limited to notifying and following up with the responsible authorities in the location abroad.

Nevertheless, all parties in the Storting and the Government, including the Progress Party, have wanted to offer the innocent son of the ISIS woman help, but on the condition that it took place either locally (outside the al-Hol camp) or in Norway, without the mother returning.

This deserves recognition, not virtue signaling from those who cannot see the bigger picture or context in politics.

We have now made the big mistake of setting a precedent for negotiations with terrorists on their terms, thus weakening Norwegians' security abroad.

We have given way to our principles and made ourselves weaker. At the same time, we have also weakened the community in the nation further, and precisely the community that will pay them millions of kroner it cost to bring the ISIS woman home.

And what it will cost to drag her through trials, keeping her, a traitor who exploits our generosity, in our welfare system.

Unfortunately, this is a decision that comes from my own governing party, the Conservatives, headed by mini-parties, the Christian Democrats and the Liberals, who have turned 180 in the case and kneeled for the ISIS terrorist demands and cynical exploitation of her own child's health as a means of leverage.

I'm not just outraged at the poor judgment of my party leader, party leadership, and my party's ministers in this matter. I am also passionately frustrated with the direction in which my party is moving, faster and faster. It is not only with the neighboring party [Progress Party] that the cup has overflowed. The Conservative Party, Høyre, must make sense and move in a conservative direction as soon as possible. After all, we are supposed to be the Storting's, the Parliament's, only self-proclaimed conservative party.

And damned if this is conservative politics…[27]

An Unparalleled Soap Opera

In August 2020, Sumaira had still not gone to trial. NRK one day reports that under questioning from Police Security Service, Sumaira revealed that a Norwegian one-year-old died after abuse in Syria. Old news to the NRK activists because a year earlier, they reported that while visiting the ISIS woman in the al-Hol camp, she spoke about the boy's death. NRK write that they chose not to reveal the information at the time. Because uncovering inconvenient truths is not in NRK's job description. Did they at least notify the Police Security Service about their conversations with Sumaira that might have shed light on the mystery of how the child died?

Under questioning, Sumaira has told PST that a Norwegian foreign fighter was violent towards a child and believed the man caused the child's death. It is the first time Norwegian police had received an explanation from a person who is said to have been present when the boy died. The story gives a glimpse into the inner life of the Norwegian foreign fighters in the ISIS caliphate, writes NRK.[28]

The one-year-old boy was born in Bærum Hospital in 2013 and was a Norwegian citizen. Bærum, as previously written, is one of the most affluent areas in all of Norway. The mother of the child is Islamist Aisha Shazadi Kausar. She is also the hardcore ISIS woman who, in May 2021, has asked for assistance from the Norwegian Government to return to Norway. The same woman and Taliban supporter who went on a tour around Norway with her excellent niqab. NRK fails to mention that the boy's father is Arfan Bhatti, who we remember from the Prophet Ummah and the Oslo Synagogue shooter. And the biggest bombshell of all, which NRK also keeps out of the story, is that Bastian Vasquez, the Chilean Norwegian we know from Skien, is the foreign fighter that killed the boy.[29]

NRK goes to great lengths to protect these jihadist identities, and the million-dollar question is a big Why! Their identity is out in other news outlets, so what is their motive for the secrecy? Perhaps they look towards the future when they can hire the terrorists. Like the Iraqi that hijacked a plane to Norway with his brother, demanded asylum, was employed by NRK as a sound technician, and lives happily ever after in Norway. Not the kind of Norwegian fairytales I grew up with. As said before, you can't make this stuff up.

The story of the one-year-old boy is heartbreaking. The child was taken to Syria by his hardcore jihad mother, Aisha Shazadi Kausar, in August 2014. There, Kausar and her son moved into the same home as the ISIS fighter and the woman now charged with terrorism. That would be Sumaira and Bastian Vasquez, NRK. It is then the abuse of the one-year-old is said to have started, according to Sumaira. Vasquez used increasing violence against the one-year-old and beat the child repeatedly with blows of varying strength. In November, just four months after the boy arrived in Syria, the child died. He was then 18 months old. Sumaira said that the death happened when Bastian was alone in a room with the boy. He reportedly changed the diaper of the one-year-old, who woke up and started crying. Vasquez must have intensely disliked that. He then allegedly beat the child until the boy vomited, according to the woman's explanation.[30]

"He was crying and vomiting and due to his heavy breathing got food stuck in this throat. Then he tried to hit the boy on the back to get the food out," Sumaira told NRK in March last year. "We talked to her about the one-year-old's death," writes NRK, "but we chose not to publish these details until now." They are even so audacious admitting they waited a year to reveal the news, as if that is the most normal thing in the world. Breaking news put on hold for one year. When NRK met her in the al-Hol camp in Syria in March 2019, she and her children had just arrived there. She told them about the boy's death and that Bastian Vasquez tried to give first aid to save the child. When that did not help, he ran out to find a car to take him to the hospital. When asked back then if the foreign warrior was involved in the child's death, the woman answered "not the way she saw it."[31]

But now, trying to save her own a**, she sees it differently, and no matter what the ISIS woman tells NRK, the Police Security Service, the attorney, and all others, they take her word for it.

However, now being questioned by PST, she has opened up about her version of the death, writes NRK. During questioning, Sumaira said that she was not an eyewitness to the boy's abuse but repeatedly heard the beatings. So, if she was an earwitness, she could have opened the door and been an eyewitness. She had taken pictures of the boy's bruises. The information about the cause of death coincides with what Aisha Shazadi Kausar, the child's mother, has said. A former friend of Kausar tells NRK that Kausar had told her that her son was beaten by a Norwegian ISIS member and sent her pictures of him full of bruises. NRK, now playing private detectives, has contacted Aisha Shazadi Kausar, still detained in Syria. She will not comment on her son's death, but has previously said that his vomit suffocated her son, also noted in the autopsy report.[32]

After the boy died, ISIS accused Bastian Vasquez of killing the child, and he faced a trial in ISIS court. NRK writes that ISIS contacted two Norwegian Islamists to be character witnesses for Vasquez, an utterly laughable scenario if the case wasn't so horrendous. And even more hysterical is NRK's headline: *Norske islamister som karaktervitner,* "Norwegian Islamists as Character Witnesses." Upstanding citizens and good Norwegian Islamists Ubaydullah Hussain and Mohyeldeen Mohammad, our outspoken friends from the Prophet Ummah, were contacted to testify in favor of Vasquez. Sumaira told PST that the ISIS court dropped the case against Bastian because there were few witnesses to convict him. According to Islamic law, one female witness was not enough to convict the man. Sumaira did not testify in the case against Vasquez. The child's mother, Aisha Kausar, has previously told *Aftenposten* that she would report the foreign warrior after the death but that she did not do so because of the risk of being convicted of false accusations.[33] These women never put their children first do they?

Later, in a judgment from the Oslo District Court involving a separate case, information emerged that the ISIS court had executed the man. But Sumaira has told her comrades at NRK a different story. Bastian Vasquez died when a grenade exploded in a bomb factory. "I was never allowed to see him, but as I found out, he was in the room when the grenade exploded." Attorney Nordhus does not want to comment on what his client has said in questioning. He writes in an e-mail to NRK that "the interrogations shed light on several years of incidents that it is demanding for her to talk about. " As demanding as it must be to write about it. "My client will continue to work with PST." The father of the deceased child, Arfan Bhatti, has been informed of NRK's delayed death coverage. He will not comment on the case.[34]

Document, the online conservative news outlet, has also written about the death of the one-year-old boy but has additional information about the boy's parents, Arfan Bhatti and Aisha Shezadi Kausar. They also note the state channel does not mention Vasquez by name and refers to the Norwegian-Pakistani terror suspect woman as the "Oslo woman." Øyvind Thuestad for *Document* writes that Aisha Shezadi Kausar was first married to Arfan Bhatti. He was already married, so Kausar became his second wife in a religious marriage. The short marriage was a fiasco. Thuestad quotes from Åsne Seierstad's book *Two Sisters*:

> On her honeymoon, she took off her niqab for the first time. Hafjell's honeymoon was a disaster. In the car home, they barely exchanged a word. The Islamist had grown tired of her almost from the first moment.[35]

Shortly after the honeymoon Arfan Bhatti divorced Kausar with three words in an SMS. It was not revealed in *Document's* article what the three words were, so I did some research. According to Lexio.com, the three words are *talaq*, and I assume those were Bhatti's three words to Kausar. Or it could have been "you're fired":

> In Islamic law, divorce involves the husband's threefold repetition of the word talaq, this constituting a formal repudiation of his wife.
> In the Prophet's time, Nadvi explains, divorce took the form of the husband uttering the word talaq three times, spaced over three consecutive menstrual cycles of the wife.[36]

Alrighty then. You really do learn something new every day. And they've come a long way, baby. At least the poor women don't have to go through three menstrual cycles anymore, putting up with the abuse from their men. Abuse and discrimination that seems to be swept under the carpet by the liberal, woke, #metoo, Islamo-leftists and feminist media. Today, an SMS is all it takes.

It is strange to read about their honeymoon in Hafjell, a village and ski resort not far from where I grew up. To think of two newlywed jihadists on a honeymoon, the wife wearing the oppressive niqab, carousing around in the mountains I grew up in is frightening and depressing. And how do you ski with a niqab? Very carefully, I would imagine. And by the way, how do you drink wine? That would be a deciding factor for me to wear one or not.

PST has sent information from Sumaira's interrogation to the Oslo police district, which will decide whether to investigate the death, writes Thuestad. *Norges Røst,* Norway's Voice, commented on the *Document* article and, as usual, is dead-on.[37]

Despite all its horror, this is an unparalleled soap opera. Hold on: The synagogue terrorist, the ex-boyfriend of a well-known Norwegian TV reporter and Oslo woman, divorces from his brand-new burka wife, also an "Oslo woman" via an SMS message. This latter "Oslo woman," who now carries the child of the ex-boyfriend of the first Oslo woman (the TV reporter,) gives birth to the child at the same time as she becomes the second wife of the brother-in-arms of the TV reporter ex-boyfriend. Then the brother in arms of the TV reporter's ex-boyfriend kills the ex-girlfriend's child during a diaper change. All this is happening at the same time as those involved are shedding blood and spreading terror— unspeakable terror and horror among innocent people in the Middle East. The participants in the soap opera gain enormous sympathy and understanding among the celebrities in glamour Norway. Many of the official do-gooders in Norway are moving mountains to help them safely to Norway. An exceptionally high number of people and celebrities in culture, media, non-governmental organizations, and politicians in Norway, even a top diplomat or two, is piously lining up in a massive solidarity initiative. They demand that the Norwegian state use resources in the millions to help the "unfortunate" return to the country where they have burned all bridges. In this way, these celebrities also become part of the everlasting soap opera. They are proud participants and bask in the splendor of their "sacrificial" contribution to making the world a slightly better place.

Enormous police resources are used to map the stories of ISIS women. Millions of kroner will now be spent investigating precisely when, where, how and by whom of the ISIS people killed the ISIS child, while all the other tens of thousands of ISIS victims are long forgotten.

What's next? And what's the point? In any case, we will not learn anything from what has happened. The Norwegian police and judiciary are impoverished enough as it is. Should not therefore, the country's scarce police and investigative resources instead have been used to investigate attacks on and a crime against Norwegian women and children on Norwegian soil? The living among us? Instead of on a foreign child, who, despite tons of documentation in police quarters meter-long shelves, can no longer be awakened to life?[38]

CHAPTER 15
God Will Forgive Your Sins. The Bureaucracy Won't

AT THE END of August 2017, two months after Eric came back from his first stay in the USA, the family had yet to hear from the Immigration Appeals Board (UNE). On September 14, Heidi gets terrible news from the family attorney. While UDI handles Eric's case, they did not grant him extended time, and he had to leave the country the next day. His three months permitted stay was up. Leif dropped everything and called the immigration authorities. After hours on hold and in line to speak to a caseworker, miraculously, they put Eric's case on hold. He was, by the grace of God, allowed to stay until a decision regarding his residency.

But the celebration was short-lived, and a few days later, the family again took farewell with Eric for another three-month stay in the United States. UNE did not grant him a residence permit nor the ability to stay in Norway until his case received a final determination. A local newspaper covered their story and wrote that UNE disregarded that he had several job offers and could work as soon as he had a residence and work permit. They did not consider that he would not be a burden on society, nor that his mother Heidi guaranteed him until he became self-sufficient. The only thing that apparently mattered was the insignificant detail that his mother was a United States citizen when he was born. Ergo he was considered an American and had no right to residency in Norway. Because in Norway, it's all about WE, Michael Moore.

And kudos to the reporters at the local newspaper in Heidi's hometown who kept residents in their hometown informed on Eric's fight to stay in Norway. "I am as Norwegian as my brother and will fight for it to be accepted. I want to live in Norway where I have all my family, and not in the United States," he told them in one interview. The reporters wrote sixteen detailed articles about Eric, Heidi, and Sonja's predicament and deserved praise for their empathetic involvement in the case. Nationwide, mainstream media could have easily picked up the story. A heartbreaking story in little Norway that would have engaged many Norwegians and most men and women in the streets would have seen the injustice in UNE and UDI's treatment of the family. But unfortunately, it was not a story for the Norwegian mainstream media and their activists. And a Norwegian woman fighting for her American-born son to live in Norway was not on their agenda.

Eric's Grandmother Thinks She'll Never See Him Again

Leif, and Eric's uncle, is fighting relentlessly for his nephew Eric. He pours his heart out on Facebook:

> The UDI and UNE have decided that my American nephew, Eric, will not stay in Norway. Twenty-four years old, unskilled, and without work, housing, or network in the USA, he must travel from home, work, family, and girlfriend in Norway. He has not done anything criminal in Norway either. I think UNE's decision is wrong. Optimistically, I thought politicians in the Storting and the Government would sort this out when I notified them. So wrong one can take. They probably prefer to show up when they think they can demand the people's praise. Then I felt the national media would get involved. No, they have not shown the kind of empathy that can benefit an American youth.
>
> And you have no idea how I dread explaining to my old mother about this decision that UNE has made. I probably have to explain to my mother what is happening because I do not think the politicians will help me. The last time I visited my mother, I just had to report that my mother is ninety years old, weak and sick, but still has meanings, feelings, and wishes. Now my mother is sad. Sad that her daughter's American-born son is not allowed to be with her. Sad, she does not understand why immigration authorities do not treat her to the joy of having her grandson here. In her vicinity at the end of her life. Sad that she does not understand what wrong she has done when she has contributed to the birth and upbringing of a ruling generation that does not seem to have inherited empathy that can benefit an old lady and her American-born grandchildren.
>
> Then my mother suddenly becomes sad that she shouldn't allow herself to think like that. The authorities probably have more important things to get involved in, my mother thinks. My old mother cannot be happy. She worries that her grandson will not be allowed to be with the rest of her family. Then she only gets sad again when she thinks that Eric may have to travel to the United States where he no longer has a family. The poor boy, my mother thinks. My mother does not think it is right that the authorities divide our family. She is sad that the prime minister does not understand and agrees with her. My mother is unhappy today that she may not see Eric ever again.

Hearing Leif's account of his mother's worries is not only heartbreaking but resonates with me and is not unlike experiences I have with older members of my family and friends in Norway. I was, in a way, brought up this way too. Don't rock the boat. Don't question the Government's decisions. Don't protest anything because they know better and know what's best for us. If you complain or protest, immediately say in a bi sentence, "Who am I to think like this and question my government. The authorities probably have more important things to get involved with."

Eric is back in Norway in December 2017 after three months on an air mattress with his wardrobe in a bag. Heidi, Sonja, and the rest of the family are ecstatic to have him back in time for Christmas celebrations, and they hope he is finally home to stay. The local newspaper that continues to report on Eric's fight to stay in Norway reports that in January 2018, the family finally had an exciting occasion. Sonja and Eric got married. It was sort of a historical event, writes the paper, since they were the first to be married at the local town hall. The Norwegian Marriage Act was amended three months earlier, gave mayors the authority to marry. The mayor performed the sermon in English and Norwegian, and the beautiful couple were now husband and wife. Many will probably think you arranged the marriage, intending to give Eric residence in Norway, the journalist emphatically advises, something Eric and Sonja adamantly deny. "We have held together through thick and thin since we met and are sincerely in love with each other. We want to live our lives together, and then marriage was a natural step forward. But children we dare not think about, just dream about," said Sonja and Eric.

The young couple makes no secret that their love affair has had more deep valleys and hills than perhaps many experiences. Most of it, undoubtedly, is because of Eric's desperate situation as being unwelcome in Norway. Nothing would therefore please them more than that UDI grants him residency like his brother and mother. The injustice that Eric experiences go deep, both for him and the rest of the family. It is perceived as blatantly unfair that he should have less affiliation with Norway than his brother. Because the mother took American citizenship between the first and second birth. Eric and his family have decided to continue the fight so that one day he will be allowed to settle down and build a future in Norway together with Sonja. Last year they hired a well-known attorney to help with the "sequel."

The attorney does not take kindly to the bureaucrats' treatment of Eric write the newspaper. He tells the journalist that it is incredibly frustrating that a person who has a strong connection to the district through his mother gets such treatment. The advocate thinks this is simply unnecessary paragraph riding: Someone who meticulously, beyond reason, follows written rules and regulations. He firmly believes that UDI will allow Eric a resident permit when the citizenship law is changed next year, and he can be considered the son of a Norwegian citizen.

> Imagine the absurdity of Heidi being Norwegian for her eldest son and American for her youngest son when one has to decide the requirements for residence.

He thinks it is sad that common sense is not used in this case but predicts that Eric will eventually get permission to stay in Norway. Although Eric has to put his own and Sonja's lives on hold until the bureaucrats get their spotlight. "It is shameful," he adds.

Now that Sonja and Eric are married, Eric can apply for family reunification with his Norwegian wife. I foolishly thought the bureaucrats at UDI and UNE would allow Eric to stay in Norway while they await approval. But no such thing in we-we-we Norway, Michael Moore. He is still considered a "tourist" by the heartless paper-pushers and must return to the USA for another three months. On March 15, 2018, the family said farewell to Eric for the third time. They all hope and pray it will be the last time so that the newlyweds can start their lives together. Eric and his family are heartbroken.

It Is as Sad as The Pouring Rain…

One day while Eric is in the USA, he gets a call from Heidi. She tries to be strong but cannot help crying when she hears Eric's voice. Her mom Ingrid has passed away, and now she has to tell her son the dreadful news. Eric was strongly attached to his grandmother after many holiday visits to Norway throughout his childhood. Heidi says Eric cried on the phone when he learned that his grandmother had died. The young American felt unwanted in Norway and forcibly separated from his family during a painful and challenging time. Since Eric was in the United States under force by the UNE, he could not attend her funeral. It was difficult to cope with and has left its mark on the young man. Heidi and Leif told the local newspaper that their mother had been upset about the Norwegian authority's treatment of her grandson until her death.

This passage, by far, is the most heartbreaking story for me to relay in this book. Ingrid, 90 years old, and Eric's grandmother had finally gotten her daughter and grandsons home, and it was despair from day one. And that she died while Eric was in the USA and he could not be by her side is incomprehensible. She was afraid that she would never see him again, and she was right. And I can also relate because I have relatives who love my American husband, and I envision what would happen if he was denied residency in Norway. We have had our trials and tribulations with the Norwegian Directorate of Immigration and the U.S. Immigration and Naturalization Service. It is frightening to be on the receiving end when you face stonewalling from immigration officials. I didn't have a happy ending with my Norwegian citizenship, but it was nothing like what Eric, Heidi, and his family went through. Not even close.

On June 13, 2018, Eric was back in Norway. They can now send an application for family reunification with Sonja, and the wait begins. From what I understand, they could not apply after they got married but had to wait until after he has spent three months in the USA. "I am not exactly proud to be Norwegian when I realize how they treat Eric, Sonja, and Heidi," said a friend on Facebook. On August 30, they get more bad news from their attorney. UDI cannot process the application with his wife until after the 90-day deadline expires on October 9. It's almost too bureaucratic to understand, but that is the case, according to the attorney. And since Norway is all about, WE, Eric is not allowed to be in the country during the application period and must return to the USA. For the fourth time. On September 10, 2018, the family bid farewell to Eric again, and everyone is full of tears, frustration, disappointment, and despair.

The Norwegian Bureaucrats from Helvete

On December 10, 2018, Eric arrived at Gardermoen Airport Oslo airport back from his fourth stay in the USA. As he is going through border control, he is taken into custody and cross-examined. According to UDI's information, border control officers told him that he left Norway on December 6, five days earlier, and had therefore not been out of the country for three months. They pretty much told him that he would have to be put back on the next flight to the United States. The UDI bureaucrats from hell had registered the wrong departure date, which was September 9, and now Eric sat in custody because of it. Heidi was beyond stressed when she got the message he was detained and was afraid he would either miss his connecting plane to Molde or, worst-case, risk being sent back to the USA.

I am just reminding you all about terrorist-accused Arfan Bhatti being able to walk in and out of the airports in Norway. After being deported from who knows where. Every time he turned around; his Norwegian attorney was around to plead the "good Norwegian's" case. And not to mention all those Syria travelers under surveillance by PST. The young men seeking a holy war were allowed to travel to Syria with shitloads of money in their suitcases. The scenario Eric had to go through at Gardermoen airport displays injustice toward good people at its highest level, and Eric, Sonja, and Heidi did not stand a chance.

There were some heated phone calls writes the local newspaper before everything was "resolved" in the end. If things couldn't get any worse, airport police told Eric that UDI had denied his application for a residence permit and family immigration with Sonja. An application from Eric that had taken UDI five months to come to a decision. The letter was a week old but was never communicated to Eric or Heidi by UDI. The verdict was in a few words, writes the newspaper:

| The income requirements were not met. Sonja could not support them. |

And while they were at it, Eric receives a letter from UDI warning that he had to leave Norway and the Schengen area by December 31. The Schengen area includes 26 European countries that have officially ended all passport and other types of border control at their mutual borders. Just imagine what goes through those borders. Although they notified UDI of this incorrect information, the bureaucrats had not yet withdrawn the notification. In the meantime, Eric has stayed in Nordmøre as he can document that he has a valid tourist visa for ninety days from December 10 to March 9, 2019. He was deeply affected by the events at Gardermoen Airport and distraught when he finally arrived home to his family. But despair soon turned into temporary happiness at home with Sonja, Heidi, and everyone in the family. But I guarantee the UDI and UNE's harassment was not far from their minds, and they had no idea how it would end.

The local newspaper reports that the attorney sent a letter to UDI when he found out about UDI's unfavorable decision. On December 22, in a complaint to the immigration officials, he requests a reversal of the refusal of family immigration. The complaint is based on incorrect facts by UDI, including Sonja's ability to support herself. The attorney attached documentation that shows that she satisfies the income requirement of 260,000 kroner a year and that she has a part-time job in addition to a student loan. He also demanded that Eric is allowed to stay in the country until they complete the case. So far, they have not heard a peep from UDI, writes the journalist, using those exact words; *så langt har de ikke hørt et pip fra UDI*. When the attorney finally got UDI to speak on the phone earlier in the week, the answer was that they have four months to take a position on the attorney's complaint and allegations.

They also informed the attorney that with the strained personnel situation in the UDI, there is no reason to expect an answer any earlier than in four months. That also applies to the requirement to remain in the country until a decision on the case. Thus, Eric saw no other option but to pack his suitcase again and take the difficult trip across the Atlantic, once again. Staying in Norway past the ninety days would be too risky. In the worst case, the authorities may deny him entry on a tourist visa for the next five years. In that case, that's too high a price to pay. Hijacking a plane would be an option too, but unfortunately, Eric is not one of those good Norwegians who would do that.

On March 7, 2019, Eric once again must leave his wife and family because UDI did not take the time to look at the reversal of decision request from the attorney. Note the date is around the same time the NRK activists were carousing with the ISIS woman in the al-Hol refugee camp in Syria. And Eric's case must have consistently been put at the bottom of the document pile to make room for the thousands of family reunification and asylum seekers from MENA countries, dare I say again. Sounding like a broken record. The journalist from the local newspaper gives Heidi the last word this time around:

> I'm so incredibly disappointed, frustrated, and worried. I feel like my family is torn apart. Eric and Sonja's life is put on hold again. If there is any justice in the world, I hope that he will one day be allowed to settle in Norway and start a family with Sonja.

When The Shit Hits the Fan

Finally, Eric returned to Norway in June 2019, and the family hopes this is the last time he must leave Norway. It is time for Eric and Sonja to start a new life together. In August 2019, two months after Eric returned from the USA, Heidi writes that the verdict fell from UNE and UDI again. A final verdict! The time also happens to be the same month the Norwegian Government, politicians, and media start their campaign to get the ISIS woman back from the al-Hol camp in Syria.

It is incomprehensible, and utterly heartbreaking, but the Norwegian Directorate of Immigration has decided in Eric's family immigration case with his ethnic Norwegian wife, Sonja. And the final decision is: DENIED.

In Heidi's words:

> Then the verdict fell again. UDU and UNI have refused family reunification for Eric with his wife, Sonja. The reason is, among other things, that Sonja did not meet the income requirement and that Eric has no particular connection to Norway. We feel depressed, frustrated, and disappointed. Sonja and Eric thank everyone who has supported them here in Norway, and they are now moving to Sweden to live as a married couple. They thank everyone who has shown support and compassion.

The local newspaper that had previously covered Eric's case reports that Norway has rejected Eric, and the town's Mayor cannot understand that he is not allowed to stay. And neither can I.

Eric, Heidi, their family, and friends fought for three years for family reunification so that Eric could get a residence permit to live in Norway with his wife and family. Heidi fought her own country, men and women she thought would be on her side but had become coldhearted bureaucrats. For three long years, they fought to get media and politicians to give them as much coverage and attention as other high-profile immigration cases have. Those we have seen covered for days and weeks engaging media frenzy and politicians into changing laws.

They watched and agonized as Eric was sent out of the country involuntarily five times. He was facing months in the USA away from his family, with no job and no steady place to live. They filled out countless forms and spent excessive money on attorney fees and supporting Eric while in the United States. They were denied and not afforded a state attorney that jihad brides, terrorists, and foreign criminals demand and are entitled to. They never gave up hope and fought a good fight with decency and civility; not many in that type of situation would. They followed the rules, directions, and advice of officials from day one, never losing hope.

They followed guidance from the Norwegian consulate in New York that turned out to be ill-advised and wrong, but the heartless bureaucrats still didn't give them any leeway and understanding. Just grief. Those bureaucrats had made up their minds long ago when they, with their bureaucratic wired minds, zeroed in on Heidi's United States citizenship from 1997, and no amount of good fight could change those twisted bureaucratic minds.

I had followed their case for over a year since 2017. For some reason, busy with my own life, I had gotten away from it. My belief and hope were that Eric had finally gotten his Norwegian residency and was now living happily in Norway with his wife and family. I thought of them from time to time, and one day in late 2019, I did a Google search to see if there was any news on the case. The Facebook support page was still active, and after checking updates, I was astonished to find out that Eric and Heidi's story had not ended the way I thought. It had not ended well for the boy who many years ago brought a bottle of air from Norway to the USA so his friends could experience the fresh Norwegian air.

I was heartbroken to find out Eric and his family's fate, and even though I don't know him, Heidi, or Sonja, I could not get it out of my head that my homeland had treated them the way they did. It confirmed that the Norwegian Government and the politicians do not have their countrymen and women in mind: The ordinary Norwegian men and women in the streets of Norway. It also confirmed that honesty, decency, hard work, and a strong desire to be a good citizen did not matter. Using President Kennedys' line from his inaugural address, "Ask not what your country can do for you, ask what you can do for your country," does not interest Norwegian politicians one bit. Instead, they are looking out for strangers, their own political interests, welcoming foreigners with their hands stretched out, and asking those who may hurt Norway what they can do for them. Heidi writes in a post that there is a moving day to Sweden, and they must replant love:

> UNI and UDI do not accept that Sonja should live with her American husband, Eric. And those who can change this are more concerned with themselves and the election campaigns. The couple has shown an impressive will to survive and prove that when they look for places where love can continue to live, Sweden gives them space and hope. Thank you to our brother country. And congratulations to Sonja and Eric.

> Thank you for all the compassion and support from family, friends, and strangers they received while fighting to live together in Norway.

A few months later, Sonja shares an update from Sweden:

> Three years of struggle is finally over, and after six months in Sweden, Eric got his residence card in the mail. We both stood and looked at the residence card, cried, and hugged each other, and there were tears and joy and hugs all over the place. We can finally start to live life as a normal married couple here in Sweden. We are forever grateful for all the support we have gotten the past three years. Thank you so very much, everybody.

A Letter to the Prime Minister of Norway

I cannot end Eric, Sonja, and Heidi's story without sharing an open letter to Norwegian Prime Minister Erna Solberg. It was written by a young Norwegian man and a cousin of Eric after the first verdict fell from UDI in 2017. I'll name him Thor. An appropriate name for a young man that dares to question authority. It is an extraordinary letter and a plea to the prime minister and sums up what I and many I know would think if they knew the case. It is also remarkable because I discovered the letter after writing chapter one. It amazes me how Thor's letter mirrors what I wrote about politicians and immigration officials in that chapter. When I read Leif's Facebook posts, Heidi's brother that fought Eric's case with her, I had the same thoughts. Thor has many similarities with Leif's letter. Still, it is important to include, especially since his letter was published in a local newspaper and addressed to Norway's prime minister. I believe Thor is Leif's son, a young man wise beyond his years.

It may seem unusual for someone not from Norway to read that we expect a prime minister or politicians to act or consider such a letter. Especially in countries with a larger population. But with Norway's population a little more than five million, the size of Alabama, such personal interactions are possible, and they happen all the time. We have seen it in countless cases, including Sumaira Ghafoor and Maria Amelie. Those people politicians speak out about whether it is facing problems with immigration officials, perceived racisms, and other issues are most often non-Norwegians. As far as I know, Thor never received a reply from the prime minister, nor did anyone in the mainstream media publish his letter.

That there is something fundamentally wrong with how the Government has treated Eric's case is firmly understood when reading Thor's letter. Especially when compared to the "star treatment" jihad brides and terrorists get in Norway. He also articulately points out how the Norwegian council in New York advised his aunt and his two nephews that it was safe to leave their lives in the U.S. and wait for the approval of the applications in Norway.

Only to get the news that Eric must leave the country. And he, like his father, is concerned about relations with the United States. If only such a man or woman would run for office in Norway. Maybe there would be hope.

The letter is translated from Norwegian and published in a local paper as an opinion addressed as an open letter to the prime minister of Norway, Erna Solberg, with the headline:

What in the World Are the Norwegian Authorities Doing?

> Can you stand by such treatment of my family, Erna Solberg? I need to get an answer because there will be elections again soon.
> Yesterday, I was shocked, disappointed, and ashamed to have been involved in deciding the composition of our legislative assembly. Because what happened yesterday is utterly incomprehensible to me. Yesterday, my American cousin, Eric, 24 years old, with his Norwegian-born mother, my youngest aunt Heidi, and a deceased American father, learned that UNE would not reconsider his case. Despite his lawyer presenting a thorough and well-founded argument for a reversal of UDI's decision.
> The lawyer believed that several factors in the case had not been discussed and assessed, and UDI had shown no reasonable judgment. UNE has been blind to the fact that his mother was an American citizen when he was born. There is no consideration that he is the only one in the family not granted residency, that the decision divides the family, that he is in an established relationship and lives with a Norwegian girl, or that he has his entire family network in Norway.
> Now he must travel back to the United States alone and manage on his own without education, without housing, and without a family network. I am shocked that the Norwegian authorities divide the family in this way. I am very disappointed with the treatment of Norwegian Americans. I am ashamed to have been involved in electing people to the Storting who can make laws that do not want our own welcome home again with their closest ones.
> I understand that one must create rules that prevent the country from being 'flooded' by large flows of migrants from the third world, which can be challenging to integrate and lead to significant expenses. But that a few native Norwegians and Norwegian-Americans, fully integrated when they arrive, make sure that they will not burden the public welfare systems and want to return home with their immediate family should not be a problem. I fear that the Americans will react to their citizens being treated in this way in Norway. Meanwhile, Norwegians who have emigrated to the United States have been well received there for over a hundred years. I also fear what American soldiers, who are willing to

sacrifice their lives for our freedom, think about this. Are they welcome here only to save us in case of war, but not otherwise?

Information about the case:

I grew up close to my aunt Heidi in a small village in Norway, and even though she was far away, it was exciting when she found love and married an American after an au pair stay. They had a good marriage, had sons Robert and Eric, and made a good life in the USA. After the sons' father died suddenly a few years ago, my aunt Heidi and her two sons living at home had no remaining family network in the USA. My Norwegian-American aunt wanted to move home to Norway to an extensive family network here and to be together with and support her mother, who is now old and ill. Eric was thrilled when they finally took this step together because he has always loved Norway and has said that he would live in Norway since he was a boy. Now it is he who the Norwegian authorities reject.

Before she moved back to Norway, my aunt Heidi contacted the Norwegian consulate in New York for advice and information. They advised her that it would not present any problems for the three to stay in Norway awaiting approval, and they could safely settle everything over there and move home. All three gave up their jobs, the house and cars sold, and bank accounts were closed. They have carefully and with conscience followed all the advice they received at the consulate and have not cost the Norwegian state a penny. The Norwegian consulate advised them to contact the police within a specific time limit after arriving in Norway. They applied for family immigration, obtained Norwegian bank accounts and tax identification cards, and all three quickly found jobs.

Following an appeal to UNE, my aunt was finally granted a temporary residence permit after almost two years in Norway. They have settled a half-hour car and ferry ride from the place my aunt was born and raised, and she got a job in the healthcare services in hometown, where her 90-year-old mother, and my grandmother, is now a nursing home patient. Her eldest son, Robert, has been taught Norwegian at his own expense and is now employed in the healthcare services for the mentally disabled. He was met with less resistance from the UDI and granted temporary residence because he was born before my aunt received U.S. citizenship.

The youngest son, Eric, now denied residency, has no education but is a bright boy who is hands-on and has always been the one who has helped his mother with practical things at home and around the house. He has also worked for a local marine company and has traveled around the country to perform cleaning work in electrolysis tanks and tankers and other assignments the company receives. He has quickly integrated into the local community and got a Norwegian girlfriend, Sonja, two years younger than him, and many friends in the small town. He has learned a lot of Norwegian without formalized teaching. With an ADHD diagnosis, he has never coped with formal school very well and has no formal education. But the desire and ability to do practical work is all the greater.

The UDI and UNE have also used it against him that he has earned a living himself or worked illegally in Norway, according to UNE's terminology. Even though it was what the consulate in New York advised them to do, they had only looked at the fact that his mother was a U.S. citizen when he was born and have not been willing to see the realities of the case and exercise reasonable judgment.

My cousin is rejected in this way in Norway by the Norwegian authorities, which makes me unwell and very disappointed. The fact that the family had sought advice from the Norwegian consulate in New York before they moved and followed them with conscience and acceptance makes the refusal even more incomprehensible. How can they behave this way towards my family? How can they split a family in this way? How can they do this to my grandmother, who was so unspeakably happy when her daughter and two grandsons finally wanted to move back home? Now Eric must return to the United States alone and manage on his own without education, without housing, and without a family network.

It is entirely incomprehensible that a public servant or a public court of law can exercise such poor judgment in a case. I am so incredibly disappointed. My grandmother of 90 years is hurt and disappointed. The whole family is disappointed. Most disappointed is my aunt Heidi, and of course Eric himself and Sonja. Can you stand by such treatment of my family, Erna Solberg? I need to get an answer because there will be elections again soon.

And those elections are coming up as I write, and no matter who gets elected, sadly, it will be the same old song and dance.

CHAPTER 16
Radical Islam Will Never Leave Norway

Oslo District Court, May 04, 2021

> *I have no plans to return to Norway. It is not going to happen. I do not want to return to kuffar infidelity, zina (sex outside of marriage), haram (everything that is forbidden in Islam).*

Sumaira Ghafoor, November 2016

(("The court has concluded that the accused has participated in a terrorist organization. And that she did so with knowledge and free will. She thus meets the law's requirements for intent."

District court judge Ingemar Nestor Nilsen asks Sumaira Ghafoor to stand while he reads the verdict. She is charged with violating Penal Code 1902, section 147 (d) and Penal Code 2005, section 136 (a), and sentenced to imprisonment for three years and six months. With four hundred and two days deducted as time spent in custody. In his closing proceedings, public prosecutor Geir Evanger requested four years' imprisonment for the woman. Sumaira's attorney, Nils Christian Nordhus, had argued she should be acquitted. The ISIS woman who had denied criminal guilt appealed the verdict on both the sentencing and the question of blame. Prosecutor Evanger pointed out in his closing proceedings that an aggravating element in the case is that she went to Syria voluntarily and has glorified acts of violence committed by ISIS. In court, the accused woman said she supported a beheading her husband Vasquez is said to have performed.[1]

The verdict is the first of its kind in Norwegian legal history. Never before has a woman been charged with terrorist involvement because she cared for her home and looked after the children while her husbands fought for ISIS in Syria, cries *Nettavisen*. The woman did not fight for ISIS herself with weapons in hand, alleged by the journalist. Still, the prosecution believes her contribution at home was crucial for her three husbands to have an active role in the extremist group.²

The Progress Party's immigration policy spokesman Jon Helgheim is intense when he talks to *Nettavisen* about the verdict, just after it became known. As is well known, the party took a dissent and left the government in January last year when they brought the ISIS woman home after allegations that she had a sick child. The journalists from *Nettavisen* write that someone in court confirmed that the child *was* ill.³ It is unclear where they got the information from. Perhaps they are referring to a statement from Sumaira's attorney. Or did they make it up? There has so far not been any news documenting the child was sick, but *Nettavisen* still makes the confirmation without further explanation. And they were basically misleading their readers. It's not called fake news for nothing.

Jon Helgheim fears the verdict is no determent:

> That's what I feared. This verdict is not a deterrent if you look at the context of what this woman's actions have inflicted on other people's suffering. I will not comment on the verdict itself, but the penalty is too low. The double of four years would have been reasonable.
> It's good that we have a verdict, but unfortunately, the woman will be free in a relatively short time. Take away her time spent in custody, and she is released after a specific time. I think she can be out within a year after a final verdict. I have a big problem with that.³

It is, however, not a final verdict because the woman appealed the decision on the spot and was therefore set free. She lives in an unknown place until a possible final judgment against her is available, and she faces imprisonment.⁴ Attorney Nordhus takes the criticism from Helgheim with crushing calm. He is fresh back from Hollywood and the Golden Globe awards, where he accepted best supporting actor in a foreign film:

> When she was in Syria, she was always prepared to be arrested and remanded in custody on arrival in Norway. She has also agreed to this. She expected that there would be a trial and a possibility of being convicted. We think that the facts the court has based the case on, that she has been a stay-at-home housewife, the Court of Appeal, and other agencies should assess whether that constitutes participation in a terrorist organization.⁵

In their closing proceedings in the trial, Nordhus and his defense team argued that the ISIS woman was a victim of human trafficking. Since the court had stopped believing in urban legends and folk tales long ago the defense was thus not heard by the court:

> First and foremost, it is important to point out that she has been in a forced situation in Syria. The court briefly touched on that but did not

emphasize it. We are disappointed with that, and that is what we think of most of all.⁶

The journalist from *Nettavisen* asks if there is any reason to fear her. Jack of all trades Attorney Nordhus, part-time actor and wardrobe consultant, is unfortunately not a security expert:

> My task is not to make a security assessment, but I confirm that she is released from police custody. There is no indication she is a person who would need such evaluation. I think PST has made an absolute correct assessment.⁷

Michael Moore would be ecstatic. Lucky for her, she is not in the United States, where if the shit hits the fan, you pull yourselves up by your bootstraps. In Norway, Canada, and the third world, they are basically all in this boat and will sink or swim together. Most likely sink. So, Sumaira and her attorney await the court's decision on the appeal hearings. In the meantime, she is free to walk the streets of Oslo, footloose, and niqab free.

Jon Helgheim also claims that it is ordinary people's legal opinion that the level of punishment, in this case, was far too low, but what he fears most is that the woman will still be a danger to society on the day she is released:

> In Norway, a fundamental legal principle is that arrangements are made for everyone to become good citizens upon release. However, research has shown that strongly radicalized Islamists are difficult to deradicalize. This is a new issue for us, and we now have a phenomenon that was completely unthinkable some time ago. These are people who have ideas that are downright incomprehensible.⁸

Nettavisen, noted earlier, conducts random surveys within news articles and asks readers what they think of the three-year and six-month sentence the ISIS woman received. Seven percent thought the penalty was reasonable. Six percent agreed with the prosecutor that it should have been four years. And eighty-six percent agreed with Mr. Helgheim that the punishment is too low.⁹ Again proving that politicians, authorities, and the mainstream media's views, are far removed from many ordinary men and women in Norway.

And many Norwegians are not happy that the government forces them to pay for the state-owned-propaganda news conglomerate the Norwegian Broadcasting Corporation, NRK. The activists at NRK worried after Sumaira's sentence that the verdict is bad news for the other women and have no qualms about using the headline *Dommen er dårlig nytt for de andre kvinnene*, "The verdict is bad news for the other women.":

> The verdict against the so-called ISIS woman may make it more difficult for the other Norwegian women in Syria to return home. The court states that it is a criminal offense to have been a housewife for ISIS fighters.¹⁰

And it should be NRK! The author of the article concludes:

> The 30-year-old appealed the verdict on the spot. It was no surprise. Given the principled nature of the case, there is every reason to believe that the woman will receive a new hearing in the Court of Appeal. But whether the result will be different is probably more uncertain. Poor communication lines notwithstanding, there is every reason to believe that the news of the verdict will quickly reach the remaining women in Syria. There are currently four Norwegian women in various internment camps in the war-torn country. According to NRK's source, there are four children with them.
> If the Oslo District Court verdict stands, it will undoubtedly make it more difficult for both mothers and children to come home. The women can then count on an arrest as soon as they cross the border onto Norwegian soil. Their stories are different but yet similar to what the court has considered a crime. Thus, the verdict is discouraging reading for them as well.[11]

The poor mothers delusional NRK thinks. But don't sweat the small stuff NRK. Even though Sumaira got a couple of years in jail, if the sentence stands, you've reached your principal goal. You got the ISIS woman back on Norwegian soil. And don't worry about the other jihad women. Norway has now set a precedent; they will be back sooner than you think. And Norway doesn't leave ISIS women behind, only Norwegian women who were too "stupid" to get American citizenship. And the ISIS women that betrayed the country and that you are so worried about should be able to handle Norwegian prison life. The Taj Mahal compare to al-Hol. A high-end prison even a fourteen-year-old boy knows is so good that for some criminals, it may seem more tempting to be locked up for a couple of years than to have to struggle through a dreary life on the outside.

Our Troubles Have Just Begun

As Norway has opened the country to radical Islam and terrorists, the problem will never go away but only escalate unless a miracle happens. Those are pessimistic thoughts, but politicians and authorities have had warning signs for years, and they continue on their ill-advised paths. Norwegians do not have to look further than toward our brothers and sisters in Sweden to get a glimpse of Norway in a few years.

Just recently, in June 2021, a 16-year-old Syrian "boy" was charged with preparations for a terrorist act and participation in the terrorist organization Islamic State. The 16-year-old boy came to Norway from Syria with his family a few years ago. Sources say 2015, the same year Eric, Heidi, and Robert were preparing their move to Norway. The Syrian family has lived in a quiet residential area outside Oslo city center. When NRK was on the scene in February, the family stated they did not understand why the 16-year-old was arrested.[12]

The kid had poisonous material in the house, for crying out loud. I have a husband and a dog, and I know every move they make. I'm kidding, of course, but not really. But then again if my husband were the Unabomber or Ted Bundy, I would know if he was up to something. How do you not understand and know that a sixteen-year-old is planning terrorist attacks and has toxic materials in your house?

The young terrorist had been accused, among a host of other charges, of planning to use poison against infidels in terrorist attacks in Norway. In February, he chatted with a suspected ISIS sympathizer where the man asks the 16-year-old if he has prepared the poison for use in terrorist attacks in Norway. "I finished it yesterday and will give it a try soon," the 16-year-old wrote to the ISIS sympathizer on the encrypted messaging service Telegram. They found poisonous materials at his home. The Police Security Service believes they caught him just in time and that an attack was imminent. He may have planned terror attacks on crowded places in Norway, such as nightclubs. The indictment listed several searches the 16-year-old did on Google:

> Fight against the unbelievers who live near you. Fight against all unbelievers. Fight against them until there is no more persecution. The reward of heaven for the martyrs. Crowded, busy places in Norway. Entertainment venues in Norway. Nightclubs in Norway.[13]

NRK reports that Swedish terror expert Michael Krona will be testifying in the 16-year old's court case about the media–and the propaganda apparatus of ISIS. Mr. Krona is affiliated with the University of Malmö and has given several lectures on ISIS. In one of the lectures, he said the terrorist group has moved from open communication channels, such as Facebook and Twitter, to encrypted channels such as Telegram. He says it's a mistake to believe that ISIS has disappeared. He believes, however, that ISIS's need for solo terrorists has increased after the so-called caliphate fell in 2018 and points out that there have been several attacks with fatalities in recent years.[14]

Meanwhile, the government in Norway has passed a sweeping action plan on Islamophobia because of all those racist, right-wing extremist Norwegians. In its introduction for "Action plan against discrimination of and hatred of Muslims," *Regjeringen*.no writes:

> Research shows that hostility, prejudices, and negative attitudes towards Muslims are real and a growing problem in Norway. The same applies to large parts of the world where there has been one increase in discrimination against and attacks on Muslims. Several terrorist attacks internationally and in Norway, such as the Al-Noor Mosque in Bærum in

> August 2019, have made many Muslims feel insecure. Police Security Service (PST) threat assessment in recent years shows that it has been an increase in the threat from right-wing extremists in Norway.[15]

The mantra in Norwegian media and among those on the left in Norway that there is an increase in right-wing extremism in Norway is one repeated over and over again. Yet, there are never any concrete examples given who these right-wing extremists are. And besides the attack on the Al-Noor Mosque in Bærum, there are few examples of racists attacks on Muslims in Norway. And if you are going to have an action plan *Regjeringen*, at least name some concrete examples. And if there have been several terrorist attacks against Muslims worldwide, there have been thousands against the infidels. Research has also shown that many Muslims are hostile, prejudiced, and have negative attitudes toward the small Jewish community in Norway. And what is really the meaning of Islamophobia? When a once peaceful nation realizes what the radical Islamists in Norway mentioned in these pages can do, and they witness a violent dogma preached around their country, wouldn't the natural reaction be fear? Instead, the Norwegian politicians chastise the Norwegians into silence and submission. "Norway must be a safe and good country to live in, regardless of religious affiliation," writes *Regjerningen.no* in their action plan.

Don't Norwegians deserve a safe and good country to live in too, which they once had, and I know and lived it. Or are terrorists' right's more important than national security and the welfare of its citizens? Nobody from the Norwegian government needs to answer that question. The answer is a resounding Yes.

And speaking of trouble. Ubaydullah Hussain, Arfan Bhatti, and Mohyeldeen Mohammad are still on Norwegian soil and have continued to make the news since we left them a couple of chapters back. The last we heard from Ubaydullah was that he got acquitted from charges of indirect incitement to terrorism and multiple counts of encouraging others to commit murder. He thanked Allah for the acquittal and hoped to put the case behind him. He trusted that since the Police Security Service had suffered another defeat and spending countless resources on his case, their persecution, harassment, and intimidation propaganda against Norwegian Muslims would soon end.

An Ordinary Muslim in Norway

In November 2016, a year and a half after he begged the Norwegian Police Security Service to end their persecution against Norwegian Muslims, Ubaydullah Hussain appeared in Oslo District Court, accused of recruiting members to fight for ISIS. A terror organization that beheads kills, burns, and buries people alive. A 19-year-old Norwegian native, Johan, sat alongside Hussain in court, accused of terrorism and preparing to fight for ISIS.[16]

Johan, a fictitious name, is the Nordic version of the name John and Hebrew origin. It means "God is gracious" and is an alias for this story.

On his way to Syria, Johan was arrested on June 08, 2015, at Landvetter Airport in Gothenburg, Sweden. The two defendants reject any form of terror and deny criminal guilt. Ubaydullah Hussain appeared in court, without a Muslim headdress, in Western clothes with shaved hair, a short beard, and a regular plaid shirt. With blond half-long hair and a gray wool sweater, Johan, the young Norwegian convert, tells the court he was 18 years old when police arrested him at Landvetter Airport. He left school because he became so preoccupied with the Syrian war that he wanted to contribute with his own hands. The first time he met Ubaydullah was a coincidence, and he had already become radicalized, he claims.[17]

In June 2015, Johan and Ubaydullah uploaded a photo on Finn.no, the equivalent of Craigslist in the USA. The convert Johan dressed in combat clothing, including a bulletproof vest. They intended to sell the equipment to the highest bidder. Four days later, the police arrested the 19-year-old on his way to Syria, and they seized the equipment.[18] Ubaydullah and Johan must have missed chapter eight of *Holy War for Dummies*, specifically advising hopeful jihads not to sell combat stuff on Craigslist or any other online classified.

Johan is from Oslo and converted to Islam in 2012; he tells the court. According to public prosecutor Frederik Ranke, he intended to travel to Syria once earlier, in 2014, to "help his brothers," but that did not happen. Before becoming a Muslim, Johan did "a lot of nonsense," smoked hashish, and did a lot of drinking. Did he convert at Islam Net, I wonder? He feels being charged with joining ISIS is burdensome, not least because of the brutal methods ISIS used to establish its Islamic State. The prosecutors found evidence that Johan had chatted on Facebook with a friend about a well-known Norwegian foreign warrior in Syria, Kim Andre Ryding. Ryding went to Syria in 2012 and was wanted by Interpol in 2016 for being a member of ISIS from 2013 to 2016.[19] The ethnic Norwegian from Rygge, Østfold, was declared dead in 2018, losing his life fighting in Syria. He was 28 years old.

Prosecutor Sundet reads aloud from the Facebook chat: "Your friend asked, 'are you going to join ISIS too?' What did you answer?" "Where I end up is God's will. Syria is a large country with many groups," says Johan. The prosecutor asked Johan if he would use weapons in Syria if necessary. He answered in the affirmative and would do that against the Assad regime, but he did not support ISIS. He received advice and hints from a former foreign fighter in Syria, Mister X, about the journey to war-torn Syria. Johan talks about Thom Alexander Karlsen, another native Norwegian, killed in March 2014 fighting for ISIS. He had to pass on the death message to Thom Alexander's sister. He tells the court of seeing the dead man's picture for the first time. "It made a strong impression. It could have been me, sort of," says the young man in Oslo District Court.[20] He had himself bought a GoPro camera to document what he would do in Syria.

The prosecutors link Johan with Ubaydullah Hussain with several preparations before the trip to Syria. Ubaydullah had ordered equipment with Prophet's Ummah email address. Chapter four of *Holy War for Dummies*, Hussain! He communicated with two Turkish telephone numbers that the police believe were contact numbers for ISIS. The same phone numbers have also appeared in terrorist investigations in Italy, Australia, and the Netherlands. And multi-talented Ubaydullah helped cut the 19-year-old's hair before departure. Johan explains that this was because Hussain had become a good friend.[21]

On December 1, two weeks into the trial, a young woman entered the courtroom at Oslo District Court. She is a petit dark-haired beauty with hazel eyes and porcelain skin. She wears a grey wool sweater and dark pants and appears nervous but determined to face the accused, Ubaydullah Hussain. Her name is Mahreen, and she is the sister of Thom Alexander Karlsen, the ethnic Norwegian convert and foreign fighter killed in Syria in March 2015. Just a few months after joining the terrorist group ISIS. Ubaydullah Hussain is accused of having recruited Karlsen to ISIS:

> I started crying just before I was going to enter the courtroom. It's uncomfortable, especially considering my brother is dead. It is painful to testify about it.[22]

During the testimony, the young woman is low-key but clarifies what she thinks about Ubaydullah Hussain's role in radicalizing her brother. Hussain conveyed the death message to the family at the end of March 2015. He called Mahreen when he could not get hold of Thom Alexander's mother. Mahreen began meeting Hussain against the family's wishes to learn more about her brother:

> I intended to find out things about what had happened. There were so many questions, right. I contacted Ubaydullah Hussain and got answers to some questions.
> You said in court that he had organized the trip for your brother?
> He told me that he had fixed the trip for Thom Alexander, like the routes down to Syria, and helped him get into Syria.[23]

Mahreen had met Hussain six or seven times and had some SMS contact with the Islamist. In her first meeting with Hussain, she met the 19-year-old Norwegian convert, "Johan," at Oslo S, Oslo Central Station. Ubaydullah wanted to show a picture of Thom Alexander's dead body as proof that he was killed:

> I was so hurt to see him [Johan]. He seemed so innocent. I wanted to tell him that, for God's sake, he must not do the same as my brother.

But Mahreen never got to say this to the young man. Today he sat in court and heard what Mahreen thought about him. Johan glanced at Mahreen as she mentioned him by name while she explained herself to the judge. He immediately looked away from her and seemed unaffected. Ubaydullah Hussain, on the other hand, smiled during Mahreen's witness testimony almost the entire time.[24]

Later, outside the courtroom, Mahreen has decided to come forward. "I think it is important to stop this. I do not want others to experience what my family has experienced. It has been tough. A long process. "Who do you think brainwashed him?" asks a reporter for NRK:

> I believe Ubaydullah Hussain and the Prophet's Ummah did. Their thinking and what they stand for. I think they're the ones who made my brother travel.
> What would have happened if it were not for them?
> I do not think Thom Alexander would have traveled if it were not for the Prophet's Ummah. Then I think he still would have been an ordinary Muslim here in Norway.[25]

Johan Can No Longer Bear the Situation

In April 2017, Ubaydullah Hussain was sentenced in Oslo District Court to nine years in prison for terrorist recruitment. A first in Norway. The former front figure for the Prophets' Ummah was accused of, among other things, assisting and recruiting people to the terrorist group ISIS. In the prosecution's favor, the Oslo District Court also ruled that he recruited the 19-year-old Norwegian convert, Johan, to ISIS, who had sat alongside him in court.[26]

The court convicted Hussain of all the charges against him, except having recruited the Norwegian convert, Thom Alexander Karlsen, from Halden. Mahreen's brother. Ubaydullah's conviction entailed charges of financial or other material support to a terrorist organization. He bought combat clothing, a backpack, clothes, and gloves for a Syria "traveler" who fought for ISIS. He also transferred thousands of kroner, through several people, to another Syria traveler who was fighting for ISIS and influenced a witness in another criminal case by causing severe fear.[27]

The prosecution believes Ubaydullah intended to recruit foreign fighters and join the war himself. In a PST statement, Hussain became the spokesman for the Prophet Ummah in 2012. According to the verdict, he exposed himself vigorously in the media with explicit opinions. And the press allowed him to do that, didn't they? In August 2014, he defended ISIS and its actions in the press when several foreign fighters went to Syria to join ISIS. PST launched a covert investigation of Hussain, and after a lengthy investigation, arrested him on December 08, 2015. His sentence was ten years at the Marriot prison resort, but the court deducted the 376 days he spent in custody. Ubaydullah Hussain denied all criminal guilt except for the charge against him for possessing an electroshock weapon and agreed to confiscate the weapon.[28]

Johan, Ubaydullah's codefendant, the ethnic Norwegian, now 20-years-old got two years and ten months in prison for trying to join ISIS. Johan's attorney Javed Hussain Shah tells NRK the Norwegian will not appeal the verdict:

> My client will most likely accept the verdict. He can no longer bear the situation and wants to put it all behind him.[29]

It's The Far-Right Progress Party's Fault Says Bhatti

Arfan Bhatti continued to make news in Norway. In November 2018, headlines across the land it that the Oslo District Court sentenced the Norwegian state to pay 120,000 kroner to Arfan Bhatti for compensation and legal costs. Bhatti claimed the police and the Police Security Service unjustly prosecuted him and sued the state for redress and compensation for lost earnings. He initially demanded millions, and Bhatti was awarded 47,600 kroner in reparation and 70,245 in legal costs. The court did not believe he was entitled to compensation for lost earnings. Bhatti presented statements in court from several employers, stating that the employment relationship was terminated due to Bhatti's past, creating adverse reactions among customers.[30]

The background for the lawsuit is Bhatti's acquittal for terrorist acts and attempted murder after being in custody for 1,036 days. As we know, he was convicted in 2008 of conspiracy in attempted murder and shooting at the Jewish synagogue in Oslo, but the court did not consider this an act of terrorism. The court found him not guilty of charges of planning terrorist attacks against the U.S. and Israeli embassies. He received two years in prison for other offenses, and PST did not appeal the verdict. Bhatti demanded compensation for excess custody and loss of employment. Bhatti, the career criminal since conception, almost impossible to rehabilitate, says the state must take responsibility:

> The state must take responsibility for its mistakes. It's that simple, really. It is perfectly fine that I have incurred suspicion, but that does not justify the state's mistakes.[31]

The state rejected both claims. They believe Bhatti did not document any income since 2006 and believe he has himself to thank for a long time in custody. The government's attorney Tolle Stabell said Bhatti, with his behavior, contributed to the trial, and he is not entitled to compensation.[32] Arfan Bhatti, however, walked away with nearly 120,000 kroner from the infidel state the notorious welfare recipient isn't supposed to receive help from, according to his beliefs. A few days after the verdict, former Minister of Justice and deputy leader of the conservative Progress Party, Sylvi Listhaug, reacted strongly in an SMS sent to *Nettavisen*:

> It is contrary to people's sense of justice that a dangerous Islamist receives compensation from the state. The Police Security Service must spend considerable resources on these people because it is dangerous for Norway. He has been convicted of threats, extortion, and violence. I will discuss this matter with the Minister of Justice to see if there is anything we can do to prevent potential terrorists from receiving money from the community in this way.[33]

Bhatti's permanent attorney John Christian Elden for some odd reason threatens that such a statement from Sylvi Listhaug could mean higher compensation. Wasn't he the one boasting about the marvel of freedom of speech in Norway when defending Ubaydullah Hussain's horrendous statements and incitements to terror attacks?

> Had she been Minister of Justice or in any other power position, such a statement would have meant that the compensation would have been higher. Beyond that, I have no comments on the desire for differential treatment.[34]

Another former Minister of Justice, Per-Willy Amundsen, also from the Progress Party, believes it is wrong for Bhatti to be awarded compensation:

> I react very strongly to this and think it is unfortunate that the state does not use its opportunity to appeal. The outcome of this lawsuit is utterly incomprehensible to most people out there. It is contrary to most people's sense of justice. Arfan Bhatti does not deserve a penny in compensation from the Norwegian state.[35]

"Shouldn't there be legal certainty for everyone in Norway?" asks a meddlesome *Nettavisen* reporter:

> The rule of law must be for everyone. But if people like Arfan Bhatti can get compensation from the state, it may be that the legislation is too liberal in this field. Then there will be too many who are in a similar situation as him who will get compensation.[36]

Now on a roll, the intrusive reporter asks Mr. Amundsen, "who should not get compensation; Islamists, right-wing extremists, criminals, others?":

> We have to look more closely at where we will draw those boundaries. But it cannot go so far that it goes against people's sense of justice. Ironically, the Islamist who hates Norway uses the system to be awarded compensation. *Had Norway been created and built according to his ideology, he would never have had these rights.* Now he is happily using the rights Norway gives him.[37]

Arfan Bhatti has previously received compensation from the Norwegian authorities. In 2004, he was charged and later convicted after a shooting incident at Sognsvann in Oslo and later acquitted. According to Elden, the compensation amount was around 50,000 kroner.[38]

The next day *Nettavisen* publishes emails Islamist Arfan Bhatti has sent to the newspaper slamming the Progressive Party's politicians Listhaug and Amundsen:

> Listhaug and Amundsen, members of a far-right party, have and have had political colleagues who have admitted or charged with abuse, violence, and fraud. They should thus sweep in front of their door (*feie for egen dør*). Besides, it is not me who is dangerous for Norway, but the ideology of the Progress Party, which plays on the strings of nationalism and xenophobia.[39]

What nerve. To support Bhatti's point, *Nettavisen* then makes a point to link to a seven-year-old article concerning politicians in Norway convicted of crimes. They have taken the time to go through all the severe crimes. According to daily *Dagsavisen*, half of them were from the Progress Party.[40] Cherry picking, I guarantee. Way to go, and so typical of the left-wing rags in Norway. They go above and beyond smearing the only conservative party in Norway and siding with the jihads. Besides, Sylvi Listhaug and Per-Willy Amundsen are not criminals. Arfan Bhatti is.

Bhatti, as brazen as ever, continues his rant against Sylvi Listhaug and Per-Willy Amundsen to *Nettavisen*, and they let him:

> Listhaug should also address with the Minister of Justice the problems with elected representatives accused and convicted of crimes and deceive others with deliberate lies. It should also be a topic of whether potential criminals should work as elected representatives and enjoy the community's money. Such politicians can hardly be worthy of trust. It will be exciting to see if an amendment to the law happens and how this will be regulated, following Listhaug's and Amundsen's desired understanding of the regulations. Compensation is a must in all cases where the Norwegian state has committed injustice against individuals, regardless of who they may be and what they may be responsible for.[40]

A legal expert who specializes in human rights is in full support of the upstanding Norwegian citizen Bhatti. It's like clockwork any time politicians from the Progress Party speak out about political correctness and insane decision makings in Norway. The mainstream media, experts, and 95% of Norway's politicians jump up with their claws out, ready for an attack:

> It is fundamental in a state governed by the rule of law that everyone is subject to the law and that everyone is equal under the law, in every case, and for every person. Those who argue that this principle should not

apply to some people, need schooling and should be kept far away from positions as Minister of Justice.⁴¹

Nettavisen has conducted another random survey and asks their readers, "Should *anyone* be able to sue the state?" Sixty-one percent do not think criminal repeat offenders should be able to sue the state. Thirty-five percent say yes, the law is equal for all. Two percent do not now. And *Nettavisen* threw in an option, "No, not politicians." Two percent of Norwegians believe politicians should not be able to sue the state.⁴²

You've Invited Jihad in Norway, Now Deal with It

In October 2020, NRK wrote, "Syria traveler soon released from prison. One month ago, prison leave was not defensible." Islamist Mohyeldeen Mohammad has been transferred from prison to prison four times in the past year. Fighting, violence, and threats are the justification of transfer from the Correctional Service. In a short time, he is out on the streets. NRK has met Mohammad's attorney at the Oslo courthouse. His client has been serving a sentence of two years and six months for threats against the Liberal Party politician Abid Raja.⁴³

Mohammad's attorney Øyvind Bratlien believes the transfers were made on thin grounds without actual content. Documents NRK has received show decisions on transfer from prisons in Eastern Norway. Mohyeldeen's first transfer was from Oslo to Halden. After that, Halden prison staff found it necessary to transfer the inmate to Drammen prison based on an incident in November 2019. Violence against inmates at the K-building notes the report. At Drammen prison, they found Mohammad involved in several incidents of unacceptable behavior. In May 2020, he shouted out from a window, "you who fuck your children should be killed and burned." He also directed death threats at officers by saying, "I will kill you all," and showed extreme aggressive behavior. His last transfer to Ringerike prison was voluntary, but NRK notes they would have forced him if Mohammad opposed the transfer.⁴⁴

Mohammad has spent the last few months at Ringerike. A high wall surrounds the high-security prison, and there is a no-fly zone over the area. His last months behind bars is held under strict conditions, writes NRK. The Correctional Service denied Mohammad prison leave twice. Believing leave is not justifiable in terms of security. They also rejected an application for transfer to a lower-security prison. Mohammad, therefore, thinks that his rehabilitation in prison is not sufficient. He continues his fondness for writing letters to the media and spills his sorrows and frustrations of the Norwegian prison system in a letter to NRK. He does not dispute the decisions or episodes but believes the imprisonment has been a contributing factor to the incidents:

> It is worrying that the penal care system discriminates against inmates in Norwegian prisons by forgetting rehabilitation and not thinking about returning to society. The principle of equality should apply to everyone. You get double punishment, first by the court and then the prison service, in the form of denial of progress rights, registration in *Infoflyt* (InfoFlow) and stricter conditions of imprisonment than other prisoners.[45]

However, the prison management points out that unwanted incidents such as violence and threats in prison can directly affect progress privileges, such as parole and transfer to prison with lower security. On the other hand, Mohammad believes that he has not had opportunities for progress like others. NRK notes that he has had several incidents of violence in prison, has been in Syria and is serving a severe sentence for threats against a parliamentary representative. "Isn't it to be expected that you are treated somewhat differently?" they ask. Muhammad disagrees and wants the same treatment as everyone else:

> There are people with stricter sentences, for murder, for example, who do not even get such conditions of imprisonment. I expect to be treated like everyone else and that the decision-makers own prejudices do not affect me as a prisoner. It will work against their purpose and goal of one leaving prison and becoming a better neighbor.[46]

Muhammad's attorney is not happy with the Correctional Service's handling of his client. He believes the conditions the client has served under are a contributing factor to the episodes in prison. The entire system is at fault and Muhammad, and his lowlife client is a victim in all this, it seems.

> Punishment must include rehabilitation. I have strong doubts about what kind of rehabilitation Muhammad has had, and after all, he is serving a short sentence. He is released in six or seven months, and it is horrible that they do not facilitate a return to society more sensibly. It is a great paradox that the system set to protect society contributes to increasing the risk to the community by creating so much irritation and frustration. It appears so unfair and imprecise that the individual inmate acquires a greater grudge against society than he had when he entered. That's not how we should be.[47]

NRK confronts Attorney Bratlien about Muhammad's threats, riots, and violence in prison, but the attorney thinks it did not affect the transfers. Instead, the attorney concludes that it is the registration of Mohammad in a so-called *Infoflyt* system, which leads to the frequent prison transfers:

> It is connected with the regime he has been under, which has been very frustrating for him. *Infoflyt* (InfoFlow) is a system where the police and prosecutors communicate with the prison without us gaining insight into

> what kind of information they are sitting on and its truthfulness. There is no absolute transparency and no possibility of adversarial proceedings. It is an utterly hopeless system.⁴⁸

To the astonishment of many often subjected to NRK's softball questioning, the journalist keeps pressing the attorney and confronts him with the fact that his client has been in Syria, in addition to having received a severe sentence for threats. He must be that 1.9 percenter. "Do you not understand why he is registered in the Infoflyt system?":

> Well, that's understandable. But I criticize the ability to know what information the police and the prison are sitting and our ability to accommodate it. Especially since it is quite a long time since Muhammad was in Syria and that he has been in Norway for a long time without anything wrong happening.⁴⁹

Well, jihad attorney, he has been in prison, hasn't he? Lots of wrongdoings are happening there.

The Correctional Service rejects the criticism and lists the reasons for creating an InfoFlyt folder on Mohammad:

> First and foremost, the nature of the criminal case forms the basis for our assessment, namely threats against a parliamentary representative. Furthermore, our review of Muhammad's case is that he poses a particular risk to order and security in prison and society in general.
> The Prison and Probation Service may process personal data about prisoners in the InfoFlyt system if it is necessary to prevent and fight organized crime, terrorism, violent extremism, or other serious crime.⁵⁰

At least somebody is doing their job.

The Correctional Service does not believe that the Infoflyt system classifies prisoners. According to them, one does not get stricter conditions of imprisonment due to being under that regime. It's about sharing information around individuals to prevent one from committing a serious crime. They look at the verdict, the criminal case, behavior, and history of imprisonment.⁵¹

Mohyeldeen Mohammad's proposed release from prison is in the spring of 2021. Just over a month ago, the prison management concluded that prison leave is not safe. According to the refusal, there is reason to assume that the prisoner will commit a new criminal act, evade completion, or violate the parole conditions. Prison Manager Eirik Bergstedt is worried:

> Unwanted incidents such as violence and threats in prison will mean that progress towards release will be affected. It is worrisome, all the time, when we then send out inmates who have not been fully rehabilitated.⁵²

As I write, it is now August 2021, and there is no recent information in the news media if Mohyeldeen Mohammad is out on the streets. I have a feeling this is not the last we have heard from him.

How Much Can Norwegian Democracy Endure?

David Hansen is an associate professor at the Norwegian Correctional Services' college and education center and has researched the radicalization of prisoners. He believes that today there are no well-functioning measures to deradicalize prisoners in Norway:

> Part of the challenge is that we do not have an adequate mapping system to measure risk, as the countries we like to compare ourselves to have, which could provide a basis for implementing targeted measures against the individual radicalized prisoner.[53]

The Minister of Justice Monica Mæland says that is why the government recently presented a revised action plan against radicalization:

> Among other things, we must have procedures that assess risk based on Norwegian conditions and new methods for reintegrating the prisoners upon release. There are now separate interaction routines between the police, prison care, municipalities, and other public agencies, related to the flow of information and better work aimed at the individual. Then there are separate radicalization contacts locally in the prison service and independent coordinators who will work with this regionally.[54]

Politicians! Do you realize what a disastrous situation you have created in Norway? Read the above statement from the Minister of Justice. You are directly responsible for creating such complicated scenarios trying to reintegrate radicals, and that's just a drop in the bucket. Norway hasn't even been successful in the integration of the majority of immigrants. Yet, you spend millions trying to integrate radicals that wish nothing more than ills on Norway and its people. And if you are lucky enough to deradicalize a few, there are hundreds in line to fight the unbelievers. Hundreds that you so eagerly keep importing into Norway, no matter how many problems it creates. A quote attributed to Albert Einstein is often heard today but may not have come from him, rather a passage in a Narcotics Anonymous pamphlet. But whoever said it, it is still relevant when discussing politics in Norway. "The definition of insanity is doing the same thing over and over again and expecting different results."

Hege Storhaug of HRS wrote an opinion about NRK news article of Mohyeldeen Mohammad's troubles in prison and impending release. "He complains via his lawyer that this has made it difficult for his rehabilitation. In other words, it is more difficult to become a non-violent jihadist," Ms. Storhaug muses. "Mohammad has been at war in Syria. So, he is competent and has shown who he is. Nevertheless, it is the Norwegian judiciary he is attacking." On Mohammad's imminent release, she notes, "We do not think very many in Norway want a person like this back among us."[55]

Ms. Storhaug ends with thoughts most of us have, views and ideas scorned by the politicians, media, and those on the left. She is a true hero in the Norwegian media landscape:

> We citizens do not get information about how many such people make up the clientele in Norway's and Western Europe's prisons. But we experience over the years that they are many. And, Mohammad must be released? How many of us think that's okay? And how much of his caliber can the Norwegian democracy endure?[56]

What lies ahead we don't know, and the difficult question is: Is it too late? As a person whose glass has been mostly half full throughout my life, although anyone reading *Sympathy for the Evil* will not get that impression. I think it is too late unless there is a drastic change in the Norwegian authorities' and politicians' handling of Norway's immigration and asylum policies and the overall governing of the country. I hope I am wrong. Elections are coming up this September 2021. No matter who wins and what parties collaborate, I do not see a change in the ill-advised strategies concerning immigration and other matters that have reigned for over fifty years. As noted earlier, it will be the same old song and dance.

And again, I must clarify that I am not talking about sensible and controlled immigration, which would have been positive for Norway. But that's not the case. It's almost as those in charge are on a one-way mission to destroy a once peaceful and democratic country. A scenario already unfolding in neighboring Sweden. And they seem not to give a hoot what the ordinary Norwegians think. Just think of Norway as the state of Alabama. It has approximately the same number of inhabitants. Alabama has a small but growing immigrant population at 3% in 2018. Norway in 1983 was at 3%. Today it is at 18% growing exponentially ever year. Norwegian women do not have children at the rate as immigrants, so do the math. Alabama has 31 mosques. Norway has 220+, also growing exponentially. But since I point this out, I am a racist. There are 4.2 million ethnic Norwegians and if the trend continues, we will be in the minority in our own country. We are already a minority, being only 4.2 million. That's not a right-wing rant, there are scholars and professors in Norway who have calculated that. More on that in my next book.

I have painted a bleak picture of the future and what goes on in my home country. What if I am wrong? What if I only see the negative of a multi-cultural Norway and not the positive. Sometimes I get doubtful and think if so many politicians and the entire mainstream media give a rose-colored picture of a changing Norway, they must be right, and I'm wrong. What do I know? I am not an academic, not an expert on anything, and maybe there is something wrong with me for wanting the status quo in the peaceful country I once grew up in. And a safe future for the beautiful children in my family.

And now, I witness the same scenario play out in the United States. Along with other insanities. I have never felt guilty for being white, but at times I think I should. I apologized to Ireland for the bronze vessel found in the Viking ship, loot most likely taken by the Norsemen. I probably should extend my apologies to others, but I am not sure who they are. It was a thousand years ago. I must apologize to Christopher Columbus because I wear a Happy Leif Erikson day t-shirt. It's October 9th, by the way. But I would never have knocked your statue down, even if Leif Erikson probably came to American shores before you did. Those thugs that struck your statute down, Mr. Columbus, should be made to pay. But as that Italian American politician said, "People will do what they do," they were probably right to do that. Because today such actions are hailed and encouraged. She did just that, didn't she, speaking from the house? Cheer on such awful acts as long as they are on the left. Deplorable is a word overused today, but the only word I can come up with.

There are a few cities in the United States that have Leif Erikson statutes. If someone tries to knock them down, Thor and Odin will release *helvete* on them. I will make sure of that.

But anyway, as I was trying to say before I got on a tangent about the despicable knocking down of statues of historical figures, I have at times serious doubts about what I have written on these pages. Although 90 percent is based on newspaper accounts and 10 percent rants, or is it the other way around? Maybe I am exaggerating, and the Scandinavian utopia will never fall. And I don't even reside in my country anymore. What do I know? How about if an American was living in Norway, and we could get his point of view?

And, coincidentally, an American *is* living in Norway, and he surely does know the situation better than I do. After all, he has resided in Norway, as long as I have lived in the United States.

And that American is Bruce Bawer, a New Yorker and the author of *While Europe Slept: How Radical Islam is Destroying the West from Within*, my favorite book title on the subject of a changing Europe. A title his aunt came up with, he writes in the book's acknowledgments. I highly recommend *While Europe Slept*, an enlightening, engaging, and disturbing story from an American's perspective who traveled to Europe in 1998 and found love and a disaster he had never envisioned. Mr. Bawer is an American writer, a literary, film, cultural critic, and a novelist and poet. He has written about gay rights, Christianity, and Islam.

CHAPTER 17
The Shadow Has Fallen Upon Norway

> Meantime, beyond the hills and mountains that surround Groruddalen, the shadow that has fallen upon the valley is slowly darkening the rest of Norway.

BRUCE BAWER ENDS with those foreboding words in an article written for the *City Journal* in January 2018. Back then, he wrote a somber viewpoint on the "Islamization of Oslo,"[1] twelve years after he published *While Europe Slept*. The *City Journal* is a publication of the Manhattan Institute for Policy Research, a leading free-market think tank.

While Europe Slept is "A must-read book, timely and incisive, Bawer describes a landscape of dysfunction," writes Carlin Romano in the *Philadelphia Inquirer*. Andrew Sullivan calls the book: "A clarion call for the West to understand the radical threat to our freedoms from politized fundamentalist Islam." And described as unbelievable for most Americans in a Booklist review: "A book of the utmost importance, full of deep concern for Europe and almost unbelievable revelations for most Americans."[2]

Quoting from the back cover of his book, both on Amazon and the hard copy I own, Bruce Bawer has lived in Europe since 1999:

> His enlightening and disturbing report on anti-American and anti-Israeli sentiment in Europe and on the egregious failure of European liberals to confront Islamic extremism in their own countries. Traveling to major cities and talking with people in trains, cafes, restaurants, and street corners, Bawer came face-to-face with the peculiar mix of moralistic smugness and abysmal ignorance that feeds the rising tide of hatred toward the United States. He found, as well, a widespread refusal to grapple with problems caused by a growing Islamic presence in Europe. From the violation of immigration laws to appalling incidents of honor killings to horrific acts of terrorism, including the assassination of a prominent Dutch politician and the March 2003 bombing in Madrid. Bawer warns that Europe can no longer ignore the clash of civilizations raging on its territory and around the world. He predicts that failure to

recognize the problems and react quickly will lead to a virulent right-wing nationalism of a kind not seen since the 1930s.[3]

Bawer encountered Muslim enclaves in cities across the continent where women were abused, homosexuals persecuted, "infidels" vilified, Jews demonized, barbaric traditions (such as honor killings and forced marriage) practiced, and freedom of speech and religion repudiated. To all this, he found a continent's political and media elite turn a blind eye, selling out democratic principles to pacify radical Islamists and preserve an illusion of multicultural harmony. Those who dared to defend those liberal values were slandered as fascist bigots. Witnessing the reaction of Europe's elites to 9/11 and later atrocities, Bawer concluded that Europe was heading down a path to cultural suicide.[4]

I hope I have somehow proved Bawer's observations and predictions in *While Europe Slept* in my book *Sympathy for the Evil*. He wrote the book in 2006, a heroic effort at the time, considering the backlash it could, and did, cause. It is now 2021, and I believe Europe has not learned anything from those who saw the writing on the wall. Men like Bruce Bawer, who still resides in Norway. The City *Journal* article explains the Islamization of a suburb of Oslo and foreboding that the shadow that has fallen upon the Groruddalen valley is slowly darkening the rest of Norway. "The Islamization of Oslo" is worth a read and can be found on the *City Journal* website.[5] A stark warning from a brave American who went to Europe searching for utopia and found a continent in peril. I have taken the liberty to quote the last two paragraphs of Mr. Bawer's commentary. Nothing has changed since 2018, and as noted before, if Norway and its politicians do know change course, I am afraid the Scandinavian utopia we once knew, and love, will be gone forever:

And so, it goes. Muslims keep pouring into Groruddalen, and ethnic Norwegians keep leaving. Muslim reproduction rates put those of ethnic Norwegians in the shade. In some classrooms, only one or two children can speak Norwegian. Reports at the HRS website and *Document.no* (which also addresses Islam-related issues with a frankness rarely found in the mainstream media) make clear that violence in the valley continues to rise and is growing more intense, with more gang slugfests and Paris-type car burnings. Reports have circulated of ethnic Norwegians banding together, vigilante-style, to patrol and protect their neighborhoods. If Groruddalen isn't yet a full-fledged no-go zone, on the scale of Rinkeby or Rosengård [Sweden], it's pretty damn close. Before long, it will be fair to describe it without qualification as an Islamic dominion within a secular polity. Yet politicians and journalists continue to paint it as a paradise of integration and multicultural enrichment.

In August 2017, Hege Storhaug of HRS took note of a promotional poster for the new library in Stovner. It depicted three dark-skinned girls, two wearing hijabs, happily reading books together. "Here," commented Storhaug, "is the future." Thorbjørn Berntsen saw it coming 16 years ago. Others did, too, but most stayed silent. Even now, as Groruddalen plunges toward anarchy and full Islamization, few dare to speak up. Meantime, beyond the hills and mountains that surround Groruddalen, the shadow that has fallen upon the valley is slowly darkening the rest of Norway.[6]

A Letter to My Fellow Norwegians

In the first pages of *Sympathy for the Evil*, I dedicated the book to my fellow Norwegians. Those who see the writing on the wall but have no voice. I know who you are, and I am heartbroken for you and my country. You are James, who wrote of a gang of youths that robbed your young son, took his money and cell phone, and cut him with a knife. Your son asked you where the hatred from the Muslims came from when the thugs abused him and taunted him with racial hate speech. You are the Norwegian father who is lucky that your son came out of the hospital alive, but you say there are hundreds of others. And some do not survive, like 18-year-old Håvard Pedersen, who was almost decapitated with a box cutter while peacefully sitting down at his job at Coop Byggmax in Vadsø. The 9/11 terrorists used the same weapon. The murderer was conveniently declared psychotic, as so many others are. Or Marie Skuland, only 17 years old who was stabbed to death by a 16-year-old Afghan-Norwegian girl while Marie was at work at the Coop store at Sørlandssenteret. Her friend, also stabbed, survived, and has lasting trauma. They are only two of many innocent Norwegians murdered in cold blood. Meanwhile, politicians are working on action plans against Islamophobia and right-wing extremists.

You are also Hanne, mentioned earlier in these pages, who says goodbye to our dear country, Norway. A country that gave us so much joy. You are witnessing with great sorrow that churches are disappearing, and we are invaded by many that do not wish us well unless we change course and worship our new master and people who speak another language.

You are Mary, who remembers all the wonderful times wandering around the streets of Oslo at night. Summer nights when almost everyone had gone to bed, and you alone could take in the streets, the houses, the trees along the sidewalks all alone. You were going to a party or on your way home from a disco. Or you were wandering the streets of your beloved city, which changed mood early in the evening, and became beautiful, dark, mysterious, and intoxicating when night came. Almost wholly, completely silent. Only a faint sound of a late tram far away or someone was laughing low in another street.

It was dizzyingly beautiful freedom and a heavy, happy presence in a void in time that only took place at night, you wrote. When all the day's duties and chores are on hold until the next day, the senses are not disturbed by the sounds and noises of the day. Sometimes you were slightly intoxicated, once in a while a little too drunk after a festive evening, especially when you were very young and had not learned. You wore high heels and short skirts, other times sneakers and training clothes. But it was always the same enchantment of your quiet, beautiful city that you felt you had all to yourself. You write you can no longer do this, and many young women today have never even experienced it. Now, we only own our city during the day, you say with sorrow. At night it is given away to strangers, and we must stay at home.

I read your comment and felt a loss and sadness difficult to define. Because you described a time I remember so well, a time we will never experience again, and you told it with such emotion and beautiful words. If I could write half as wonderful as you, I would be an author.

Or you are *Norges Røst,* Norway's Voice, who recently voiced frustration over the hyper moralists' reactions to the Iman Ahmad Noor from the Norway branch of Minhaj-ul-Quran, who has posted rabid messages about Jews on Facebook calling for them to be killed. At the same time, the media and politicians are mostly silent. "Hitler saved some Jews so that the world can know how evil this nation is, and why it is necessary to kill them," he wrote. And "Israel is a devil. Hitler did not kill everyone, but let some live, so that the world can see how they endanger humanity when they are alive." You said the entire nation's hyper moralists and morally indignant anti-racists are, as usual, as silent as the grave in the face of the world's most dangerous and widespread hate and racism ideology since Hitlerism? Strange, is it not? You say. We're exposed to a theater. And if you're not mistaken, many of the activists in the media probably hide the imams' anti-Jewish attitudes. Their silence is unveiled loudly toward us and reveals *them*. Well said, Norway's Voice.

And you are Erik, who asked what does Norway's prime minister has against ethnic Norwegians? You asked that question after she said Norwegians don't have any historical rights to Norway. "That you don't have any special rights because your parents have been living here forever," were her exact words. Erik, you didn't understand why and asked readers to think about those farmers and our descendants. For centuries after centuries, they cultivated the earth. They removed stones and rocks to make life a tiny bit easier for the next generation, so they had, in turn, a little more land than their forefathers to cultivate. You asked us to think of all the volunteer hours Norwegians have put in their own country to make Norway a safe and decent country. After several hundred years of perseverance and effort, we got it pretty good here, you thought. And all this will then be given away for free to anyone? You are afraid. You think this can be roughly defined as a betrayal. And without strong nation-states, large multinational companies will take over. Those that do not care or take into consideration the human aspect.

You are all those Norwegians I dedicated this book to. And all the thousands out there that don't have a voice. Those that the media, politicians, even friends, and family quickly silence. I don't know you, but I think I know what you go through. You may have a friend or two that feel like you. Maybe even a family member. You have tried to voice your opinions to those who do not share your views, and the backlash has made you wordless. You nod and fake agreement to keep the peace, or perhaps you have lost contact with a few friends or even family members. You go to bed angry because they silenced you into submission. You read conservative news such as *Resett*, *Document*, and HRS, and because you seek the truth, you are labeled a racist, right-wing extremist, white supremacist, Islamophobe, and xenophobic. Sometimes you have doubts, and you start thinking maybe the critics are right. Perhaps you *are* all those awful names they call you and others who think like you. You feel ashamed and must come to your senses and join the hysterical flock, you think.

You watch in horror and despair a beautiful country change right before your eyes, and there is nothing you can do about it. You try to look on the bright side, but when looking around the detrimental changes in your country, you lose faith and think it is too late. You go to the polling station and put in your vote for the politicians least likely to turn your country into a sh***ole, but deep inside, you know it doesn't matter. Because those same politicians who have had years, even decades, to do what's good for Norway and Norwegians will continue to ignore their constituents and look abroad for accolades, bask in their own glory and special interests.

You worry about your children and grandchildren who you want to grow up in the same awesome land you did. But you know there is no chance in *helvete* they will. Then you feel guilty for thinking the thoughts you have. They brought you up to be a good citizen. The media and politicians, and many you know, repeatedly told you that since you were lucky to grow up in a peaceful and prosperous country, you must help everyone else in the world. It's the moral thing to do, like bringing home ISIS women and harbor terrorists. So, you work hard and let the world take advantage of you because that's your duty. Meanwhile, Norway is crumbling.

I read your thoughts almost every day in the comments sections of the Norwegian conservative news online, and I feel as helpless as you do. And as I am nearing the end of the letter and this book, I think I must have a solution. What am I trying to say? I am not even sure myself because I do not know the answer. Or maybe I do because it should not be that difficult. The problem is the politicians do not, and they don't want to. I just wanted to tell you how I have learned from you and how much I feel a connection to you nobody can take away even though I live across the ocean.

Please never give up, my Norwegian friends. You have everything to gain and a lot to lose if you give in. You have a right to your country that your forefathers and mothers built, and don't anybody let you tell you anything different. Stand up for your rights, your country, and your freedom. Go out there and protest, band together. There are strengths in numbers. And if someone tells you, you have a moral obligation to help the world, ask them what about those in Norway that need help. The Norwegians left behind, so others from faraway countries are taken care of. Also, ask them; name one thing positive mass immigration has given Norway? Name one thing?

Perverse Priorities in Norway

In March 2021, our American friend living in Norway, Bruce Bawer, wrote a commentary posted online in *FrontPage* magazine, a project of the David Horowitz Freedom Center. He is, in my opinion, a concerned observer who came to Europe seeking utopia. Now living in Norway, he sees the insanity and injustice toward good Norwegians. Bawer titled the article "Can You Say 'Death Panels'? Perverse priorities in Norway." By death panels, I assume he is referring to a term coined by former Alaska governor Sarah Palin. On August 7, 2009, she posted the following on Facebook:

> The Democrats promise that a government health care system will reduce the cost of health care, but as the economist Thomas Sowell has pointed out, government health care will not reduce the cost; it will simply refuse to pay the cost. And who will suffer the most when they ration care? The sick, the elderly, and the disabled, of course. The America I know and love is not one in which my parents or my baby with Down Syndrome will have to stand in front of Obama's "death panel" so his bureaucrats can decide, based on a subjective judgment of their "level of productivity in society," whether they are worthy of health care. Such a system is downright evil.[7]

According to Political Dictionary online, "Politifact later named Palin's death panels statement the "lie of the year" for 2009. Politifact also pointed out the Palin was not the first conservative to make dramatic claims about Obamacare and vulnerable members of society."[8] The online Political Dictionary obviously is in itself bias, and writes:

> "Death panels" was a political term that falsely referred to the supposed dangers posed by the Affordable Care Act. Some opponents of the law, better known as Obamacare, argued that government-run healthcare could lead to a kind of de-facto euthanasia if preferential treatment was given to certain tiers of society.[9]

I hate to break it to you, Politifact, and bias Political Dictionary, and all those hyenas on the left who participated in the witch hunt against Sarah Palin. She may have laid it on thick, but if universal healthcare in the United States will resemble anything like Norway's, she may not have been far from the truth. And managing universal healthcare for five million is different than managing it for 330 million. I am all for it, but today, I do not trust the government to do the right thing, not even with healthcare. There are countless stories of Norwegians not receiving healthcare because of costly procedures not approved by the government, procedures that may be someone's last hope. Many have died. Remember little 4-year-old Ulrik? He is only one of many. It was his eyesight, but it was not worth it for the "health panels. "

The Political Dictionary mentions preferential treatment given to certain tires of society. That scenario played out in Norway, in 2021, with immigrant communities in the largest cities receiving the coronavirus vaccine before those in smaller communities. Like my elderly mother. The government also gave away one million vaccines to undeveloped countries before a fraction of Norwegians were vaccinated, including the elderly and again my mother. And had the government prioritized health care and the sick instead of saving the world, my brother-in-law would have been alive today. Instead, he died alone in a hospital that could not take care of him because of cutbacks and inadequate help in a country that claims the best healthcare in the world.

Bruce Bawer's story also gives a glimpse into the world of the Nordic healthcare model and the priorities of the Norwegian government. And it does not sound anything like Bernie and AOS's fables. He writes that on paper, the almost six million citizens of Norway are among the luckiest people in the world:

> Thanks to profits from North Sea oil, the nation's sovereign wealth fund is worth over $1 trillion, which comes to about $200,000 a head. Norwegians earn good salaries, on average, and even though they shell out a lot in income taxes – as well as the world's highest taxes on gasoline and alcohol – they're supposed to receive a great deal in return, namely free education up through the graduate-school level (if they choose to go that far) and a social-welfare system that promises to serve the needs of the disabled and unemployed as well as to cover the costs of everyone's medical care from the cradle to the grave.
>
> But the promises are one thing, the reality another. In recent decades, like other countries in Western Europe, Norway has welcomed massive numbers of immigrants, an alarmingly high percentage of whom seem destined to be lifelong welfare clients. In Norway, as elsewhere, this has put a severe strain on the treasury. Priorities have had to be identified, and choices have had to be made. The nature of those priorities and choices is reflected in two recent news items from the land of the fjords.[10]

One of the news items writes Bawer, concerns a family of five in Seljord, a small town in the mountains of Telemark. The father, his wife; and their three children came to Norway from Syria about four years ago, presumably as asylum seekers:

> It's not clear from the news story,[11] which was posted on the website of NRK on March 4, whether anyone in the family has a job; all we know is that they can't afford to buy their own residence. As a rule, such families are placed in rental apartments on the taxpayers' kroner, in addition to being supplied with furniture, a car, and regular bank transfers to guarantee them a decent standard of living.[12]

A new program initiated by the Seljord municipal government, "From Renting to Owning," is designed to ensure that people like the Syrian family stay in the area and have their own "dream house." The family picked out the house themselves, and the municipality of Seljord bought it for them to live in. Seljord retains the title, and eventually, the family will own the home. They were one of the first two families in Seljord to benefit from this program. The Seljord municipality paid a total of about $500,000 for the two houses. Bawer notes that the media treated the Syrian family's new house as a feel-good story.[13] The authors' next story is the opposite of feel-good and perhaps why Bawer titled the piece "Can you say Death Panels?":

> An op-ed[14] that appeared at the end of February in the newspaper *Bergensavisen* was the opposite of a feel-good story. Under the headline "The Right to Breathe," 21-year-old David . . ., a native of Bergen, explained that he was born with cystic fibrosis (CF) and that he is expected to live to be somewhere between 40 and 50. "The question is really what will give way first – the intestines, the pancreas, or the lungs? I would bet on the lungs, because it already feels as if they're running on empty. Breathing isn't easy, and talking is usually followed by coughs and hacking. Breathing, for me, is like breathing through a straw while running at full speed up and down the stairs." And this is just one of several very unpleasant symptoms that make living with CF a painful daily struggle.
> Fortunately, there are two new medicines, Kaftrio and Symkevi, that not only could make it easier for David and other CF patients to breathe but also could prolong their life expectancy by an average of nine years. Around the world, doctors treating CF have begun prescribing both drugs for CF patients, and private and public health insurance in many countries have begun bearing the expense. Unfortunately, Norwegian authorities have ruled that the price tag for these drugs, 130,000 kroner (about $13,000) a month per patient, is too steep. As David puts it: "I can't tell you exactly how much my life is worth, but it's obviously not worth 130,000 kroner a month." So much for a healthcare system

that, like the NHS in Britain, is promoted domestically as the greatest provider of its kind in the world.

I have juxtaposed these two stories for an obvious reason. Do the math: the $500,000 that Seljord paid for those two houses could pay for three years and four months of Kaftrio and Symkevi for a single CF patient. How is it that a government that can afford to buy a house for a recently arrived foreign family refuse to give life-prolonging medication to a lifelong Norwegian citizen? It is not a question of who is intrinsically more deserving. It is a question of whether a life is worth more than a home. It is also a question of whether someone who, given that he has a Norwegian name, presumably descends from a long line of Norwegian taxpayers, has more of a right than a Syrian family does to benefit from the welfare system to which his parents and grandparents have contributed. How much has the [Syrian] . . . family cost Norway in total? How many other families in Seljord and elsewhere in Norway will be given homes under programs like "From Renting to Owning"? How much money will all that add up to – and how many of Norway's 400 CF patients could live longer and healthier lives if that money were spent on medicine rather than real estate? Further complicating this picture are anecdotes like the following: a few years ago, in another town in Norway, I had a friendly young neighbor from Kabul who was allowed to move permanently to Norway, along with his wife and two small children (and a nephew), and was instantly put on the welfare rolls, precisely so that he could receive treatment for a dire ailment of his own that would likely have taken his life had he remained in Afghanistan.

Living in this country for 20 years, I have spent years observing the priorities on display in these stories. I have seen disabled Norwegian widows stashed away in shabby public housing among druggies and jailbirds, and homeless Norwegian citizens (heroin addicts, veterans with PTSD) sleeping in the doorways of downtown Oslo businesses, even as newcomers from Syria and Iraq and Pakistan sit watching Al-Jazeera on widescreen TVs in their pleasant, centrally located apartments. Routinely, immigrants – especially those who come from certain countries and who, from the moment they arrive in Norway, are dependent on the state to feed, clothe, and house them – are given precedence over Norwegians. Nor is this pattern unique to Norway, of course.

How can priorities be so twisted? Simple. The political elites who make these decisions derive immense self-satisfaction from helping down-and-out aliens. Helping ordinary Norwegians? Not so much. All too many of the people who run this country look upon ordinary Norwegians as deplorables. Besides, it's those deplorables whose taxes fund the welfare system: how can you expect the political elites to derive any sense of self-satisfaction from giving handouts to the very people

> who paid that money in to begin with? No, in order to feel like saviors, the elites need to give that cash to foreigners – and the more foreign the better. (Europeans or North Americans, for example, need not apply.)
> Yes, the Norwegian welfare system was introduced, above all, to give Norwegians in dire straits a safety net – *not* to buy houses for immigrants. But for the elites, that's an uncomfortable truth. In order to bury it, those elites, like their counterparts in America and elsewhere, have striven to implant in the minds of the rabble the idea that putting themselves first in their own country – America First in America, and Norway First in Norway – is selfish, insular, xenophobic, racist. In short: Trumpian! So it is that the . . . [Syrian family] get their house – and every chance of living long, safe, prosperous, and happy lives in Norway – and David . . . is denied his meds, and faces an early death.[15]

Hanne, Erik, James and Mary, and *Norges Røst*, and thousands of others in Norway, your concerns are not imagined. There are people out there who see what you do and worry about our country as much as you do. Thank you so much, Bruce Bawer, for sticking up for us Norwegians. My homeland is lucky to have you.

CHAPTER 18
You Are Always in My Heart, Norway

On March 13, 2018, Maria Zähler, a reporter at the online conservative *Resett*, writes:

> Foreign fighters who travel out of the country and join groups waging war against the West, Norway, and our allies, can return to Europe and move freely here. In Britain, the authorities have proclaimed that they want to "reintegrate" the enemy soldiers. To many, this seems to be the pinnacle of self-destruction. Last week it became clear that the Labor Party does not support a proposal from the government to immediately revoke the citizenship of those who have joined groups at war with Norway and our allies. Even if they have dual citizenship.[1]

As the reader or readers, if there should be more than one, of *Sympathy for the Evil* may remember in an earlier chapter, the Labor Party incident resulted in Progress Party Sylvi Listhaug resigning as Ministry of Justice.

"But what about Norwegians who move abroad and marry foreigners and take another citizenship?" asks Ms. Zähler. Previously, the practice was to cancel Norwegian citizenship, as Norway does not allow dual nationalities. At least if you followed the rules. But what happens when they want to move back home? In fact, it may seem more difficult for them to return to their country of origin than it is for foreign fighters to enter a land they have betrayed and gone to war against.[2]

Resett has spoken to a woman whose daughter married a United States citizen in 1997. She had to renounce her Norwegian citizenship when she became an American citizen. The woman tells Resett the daughter is now divorced and wants to come back to Norway to be with her mother. Therefore, her daughter must apply for family reunification so that she can regain her Norwegian citizenship. The bureaucracy is cumbersome. "When my daughter reported moving from Norway and was going to marry her American husband, they told her to hand in her passport. She had to obtain

U.S. citizenship, both for legal, marital, and financial reasons if something were to happen."[3]

Norwegians are known for being *hjemmekjære*, home-loving. We like to travel, but we prefer to return home to Norway sooner or later. When the woman's daughter divorced her husband in the United States, she had no doubt where she wanted to live. Her mother says: "You always think love will last forever. It didn't happen that way. In November, she lost her father, and she spent a lot of time in Norway while he was ill. When it became clear that she was going to divorce, she wanted to come home to Norway."[4]

But it was not going to be as easy as the family had first thought. If you, as a Norwegian, renounce your citizenship and want it back, you have no special rights or advantages. You must seek family reunification with your family in Norway, like any foreigner who wants to live with their family in Norway, writes Ms. Zähler. The woman wants to know why Norwegians don't have any special rights:

> She was born and raised in Norway. We were born and raised in Norway, and our parents were born and raised in Norway, and so on. And now she has to apply for family reunification with me to move home again. Why don't Norwegians, who grew up in Norway and are of Norwegian descent, have any special rights?[5]

The woman *Resett* spoke to has followed the debate on foreign fighters returning from war. She reacts to the bias in allowing warriors for foreign powers, who have even raised weapons against the West, to return to Norway. At the same time, Norwegians who have been married abroad struggle to come home because they are treated the same as foreigners without the same connection to Norway:

> I think it is terribly wrong that they cannot take away the citizenship of foreign fighters and terrorists, but that they make it so difficult for a Norwegian to return home. I have tried to contact other media and presented the case to them, but they have not shown any interest in my daughters' situation.[6]

I may have mentioned this previously, but Norwegian mainstream media often cherry-pick and lie by omission. Often, meaning 24/7.

The woman talks about the time when her daughter was born. She and her husband had to get married when she became pregnant, as was the norm at the time. For six years, the couple lived with their child in a small summer cottage without running water and insulation. "Nothing was handed to us like it is today. We didn't have kindergartens either, and I had to work at night to take care of the children during the day. Today, one is entitled to so much, and immigrants coming to the country can immediately utilize the public goods Norwegians have paid taxes for. No wonder people are furious."[7]

The woman's daughter had to obtain old documentation of her parents' marriage and birth to move back to Norway. "My daughter wants to move home so she can be with her old mother. To do so, she must prove that my husband and I were married and that she is our daughter. It is absolutely hopeless. You must find copies of certificates and documents that are over 50 years old. There's a lot of digging."[8]

The woman tells *Resett* her daughter had received a strong message from an official at the UDI that she has no special rights. She must go through the same system as any foreigner who wishes to apply for family reunification with someone in Norway.

They told her that she must go through the same mill as everyone else. It does not matter that she is genuinely Norwegian, has been a citizen, or was born here. She must seek family reunification like any foreigner.[9]

The woman wants to warn Norwegians abroad who are considering renouncing their Norwegian citizenship that they should take their time and think carefully about the decision:

> I would recommend that anyone who lives abroad and is considering renouncing their Norwegian citizenship think carefully before doing so. It can be complicated and time-consuming to regain Norwegian rights. My daughter basically had to opt-out of Norwegian society to get married. But no one told us that it would be so difficult to sign up again.[10]

What In the World Were You Thinking?

I could have used the woman's warning as I became a United States citizen in 2004, and I would have followed it. My story is very similar to the woman's daughter, but like Heidi, I never knew that I would lose my citizenship when I took the oath to become a citizen of the United States. It may seem implausible to some, as in "how can you be so ignorant and not know." Others would say, "what an imbecile." Forrest Gump would have said, «Stupid is, as stupid does." And, believe me, I felt the same way when I called the Norwegian Consulate one day a few years ago. I never forget the counselor's answer when I asked about the formalities of moving back after so many years abroad. "You're not a Norwegian citizen. You have to apply for a residence permit like any foreigner." I cannot remember if I had told her I had an American passport or the authorities already knew, but the shock of hearing her words rendered me speechless. "What in the world were you thinking becoming an American citizen," she said. Albeit in a friendly way, sort of, but the word stung regardless.

A quote attributed to Albert Einstein says, "Assumptions are made, and most assumptions are wrong." He may also have said, "Two things are infinite: the universe and human stupidity, and I'm not yet sure about the universe!" Well, I'm no Einstein, and because of my stupidity, I assumed Norway allowed dual citizenship. I had no idea at the time that they didn't. And it did not even occur to me to check. I always believed Norway and the United States had a special relationship because many Norwegians emigrated to this enchanted land. Indeed Norway, with its generous immigration stance, would allow dual citizenships. And as the USA allows dual citizenship and I assumed Norway did also. According to the U.S. Department of State:

> U.S. law does not mention dual nationality or require a person to choose one nationality or another. A U.S. citizen may naturalize in a foreign state without any risk to his or her U.S. citizenship. Dual nationals owe allegiance to both the United States and the foreign country. They are required to obey the laws of both countries, and either country has the right to enforce its laws.

I had to pay a high price for making assumptions about such an important thing, and I learned a valuable lesson. Citizenship is the most precious thing we can have from our mother country, and losing is not for the faint of heart, especially when going up against the UDI.

I became an American citizen after 9/11 for several reasons. I had lived in the USA long enough to feel patriotism and pride for this country and what it stood for. When the planes of destruction hit American soil, it was unfathomable devastation that we cannot believe to this day. I recall that day as if it was yesterday. As a civilian employee at a police department, I remember watching the second twin tower falling on a large tv screen in the conference room. Police officers and civilians were staring at the screen in disbelief of what we were seeing.

I recall driving home hours later, and I heard on the radio the Pentagon was hit and thought I heard bombs go off in the distance and that America was at war. It turned to be thunder, but the feeling of despair and fear lasted for months. In the days, months, and years afterward, there was a surge in patriotism. The entire country was in mourning but also coming together as one. How about we do that again, America? I believe most Americans felt they had to do something to show love for their country. As an immigrant, I felt the same, and what better way to show your love than by pledging allegiance to the flag. And in 2004, I became the proud owner of an American passport. But even though I love the United States, I would never have given up my Norwegian citizenship had I known. Just like Heidi. The day I found out that I was not a citizen of the country I was born in, my beloved Norway was one of the worst days of my life.

My story of how I came to America is also very similar to Heidi's. I went to the United States as an au pair and met the man of my dreams, Kevin. Ever since I was a little girl, I dreamed of traveling to the beautiful land I had watched unfold on our little television at home and in the makeshift movie theater in the small town where I grew up. We had one television channel when I was a little girl, and in 1981, the monopoly of NRK, the Norwegian Broadcasting Corporation, was broken. Now, in 2021, our NRK is just broken. But it wasn't until the late eighties that satellite channels TV3 and TV Norway started broadcasting for the Norwegian audience.[11]

I firmly believed that life in America was just like in the movies. Little House on the Prairie, Dallas, Dynasty, McCloud, Gunsmoke, Grease, Saturday Night Live, Jaws. All of them. That was America. I remember babysitting for friends of my parents as a teenager. The woman had been an exchange student in the USA, and she had a yearbook from the high school she attended. I had never seen such a thing, and I studied it like it was the bible—the young women with their coiffed hair and the dapper young men. High school in America seemed so exciting (unless you were Carrie) and different from life in Norway.

I still find the United States of America captivating. I still believe it's like in the movies. "Only in America" isn't just a tired old quote, and I love this country above all, as I love Norway. And it is heartbreaking to see the rapid changes in both countries. Changes, I believe, may lead to the end of great nations as we knew them. Unless we unify and fight for the freedom, we have enjoyed as democratic countries.

On October 27, 1964, years before becoming president, Ronald Reagan delivered the Regan Freedom Speech at the Republican National Convention. Reagan.com writes the following:

> Reagan delivered the address while the country was grappling with the threat of Communism and other foreign adversaries, all while civil rights and other domestic issues were taking center stage at home. With his Freedom Speech, Reagan sought to unify the American people around the shared common goal of pursuing freedom, which he emphasized wasn't guaranteed. He aimed to motivate listeners out of complacency, to inspire them to keep fighting for the freedom he knew could be at risk if they weren't vigilant. That idea has survived for generations and serves as a clarion call to not lose sight of the value of freedom—and the risks of it dissipating from American society.[12]

The heart of Reagan's Freedom Speech, also known as 'A Time for Choosing' is:

> Freedom is never more than one generation away from extinction. We didn't pass it to our children in the bloodstream. It must be fought for, protected, and handed on for them to do the same, or one day we will spend our sunset years telling our children and our children's children what it was once like in the United States where men were free.[13]

After so many years in the United States, the decision to move back to

Norway was not an easy one. Kevin and I had reached a time in our marriage, which some would call troubled, but divorce was still out of the question. We have loved one another through thick and thin, and life without one another was a depressing thought. During the difficult time, I decided to move to Norway. Maybe a separation would be good for Kevin and me, and I felt alone and lonely and wanted to be with my family. I have a large family in Norway and had not lived in my home country since I was nineteen. I wanted to make up for the lost time. If things worked out, maybe Kevin could move with me and make a new life in Norway.

I still had my Norwegian passport and had gotten a renewal not long before I got my American citizenship. I was worried about such a big move, but I was not concerned about a residence and work permit because, in my mind, I was still a Norwegian citizen. Imagine my shock when I find out I am not, and I have no rights whatsoever in the country I was born. I cannot recall much more about my first conversation with the Consulate, only the words "What in the world were you thinking."

I must add that I believe there should be strict laws and regulations in Immigration, and my purpose for writing *Sympathy for the Evil* is not to evoke empathy for my struggles with UDI. Not being Einstein, I put myself in the situation by not checking citizenship laws. Only I made the choices I did and do not blame anybody. And I myself decided to live in the United States. And my struggles were nothing like Heidi's, and besides being childless, I didn't have a son like Eric to worry about. It's the unjust treatment of good Norwegians that is frustrating, and as the woman, *Resett* spoke to who said; "I think it is terribly wrong that they cannot take away the citizenship of foreign fighters and terrorists, but that they make it so difficult for a Norwegian to return home."

After speaking to the woman at the Norwegian General Consul in the U.S., I ventured on the Norwegian Directorate of Immigration website, trying to figure out what to do. Reading paragraph sections of the Immigration Act didn't help, likely to confuse even rocket scientists. I often wonder what compels bureaucrats to use such insanely complicated language, and having worked in government in the United States; it's a widespread problem here also. Often referred to as gobbledygook. Many politicians use it, I have noticed, especially in recent times. I can't recall who it was, but it was in response to a question about the coronavirus:

> You know, there's a, uh — during World War II, you know, Roosevelt came up with a thing that uh, you know was totally different than a, than the, you know he called it you know the, World War II, he had the war… the war production board.

No wonder they keep us constituents in the dark.

After decoding the language on UDI's website, with the help of a language expert, I learned that before I could even think of moving to Norway, I had to prove that I had enough funds to support myself. Section 58 of the Immigration Act required subsistence and accommodation. Either from a full-time job in Norway, pension or fixed benefits, a student loan or scholarship, or funds in the bank. The latter being my only option. In the end, a year went by before I had enough money saved up and could start the application process. I had to show proof of 200,000.00 kroner, which was almost $37,000.00 at those times exchange rate. I believe UDI based the amount on a years' worth of minimum wage in Norway. With the $10,000 I had saved up, Kevin and I, the privileged white couple we are, had after all these years around $40,000 in savings. Always working hard and paying our bills with no handouts. I did not want to use our savings for this endeavor, but I needed to prove that I had enough money and worried UDI would not accept our bank statement from the United States.

Of course, a full-time job in Norway would have been a better choice, but how would I commute the 7000 kilometers across the ocean? I could have hitched a ride with the *Malizia II*, the razing yacht a Swedish activist used to get to New York that uses solar panels and underwater generator turbines to avoid producing carbon emissions. But I looked into what the actual vessel was made of, and the materials used were not as Earth-friendly as I thought. Like electric cars I looked into, to show the world and those damned global warming deniers, how at least *I* care about the environment. When I saw something about mining for cobalt in Congo and child labor to make the batteries, I was like, "I'll just stick to the nearly Impossible burger, hoping no child was exploited making them." And I'll use paper straws so I can sleep well at night knowing I am saving the world. I love it when the Styrofoam and plastic cups and lids have paper straws to offset my carbon footprints. Besides, regarding the *Malizia II*, two people had to fly to New York to return the ship to Europe. That, unfortunately, was not in line with my environmental conscience now that I have fully embraced the Green New Deal. Being thoroughly indoctrinated in the GND, I contemplate living naked under a rock to get to zero carbon emission.

After having enough money in the bank to prove that I could support myself, I finally sent the application to the Norwegian Consulate here in the United States. I had already been in contact with UDI in Norway via email, and they advised me that I must apply on the basis that I was born to parents of whom at least one was a Norwegian citizen at the time of the applicant's birth. As we know with Heidi and Eric, the bureaucratic mill runs slow, and three and a half months later, I received a reply via mail. And I picture Eric going to the mailbox, probably excited finally receiving a letter from the bureaucrats, and how he must have felt when he opened it. The letter was not good news for me either. Short, but not sweet, and very official. My application was denied:

> The Consulate General refers to your application for a work and residence permit. You have submitted an application based on "born of parents, at least one of whom was a Norwegian citizen at the time of the applicant's birth," cf. Section 3 of the Immigration Regulations, cf. Immigration regulations. § 5 second paragraph.
> However, according to the Immigration Regulations § 2, there must be a concrete offer of work for the applicant that falls under the Immigration Regulations §3, first paragraph. *A job offer from a Norwegian employer must be presented* before we can further process your case.

In summary, the gobbledygook from UDI told me that even if I gave them proof of funds to support myself, I could not move to Norway unless I have a job offer. How was I supposed to apply for jobs and go on job interviews 7000 kilometers away? And full-time jobs required by UDI do not grow on trees in Norway, especially if you have no network, don't know the boss, and aren't fresh out of college. To think of Eric and Heidi, who had to endure three years of a bureaucratic nightmare, I am reminded how absolutely impossible UDI is. I had not looked at the correspondence between UDI and myself in years and had almost forgotten how utterly frustrating and distressing it was.

Besides, the immigration official at UDI in Norway had confirmed via email that I could get a work permit under the Immigration Act and whatever gibberish paragraph she had verified. She wrote that it gives me the right to apply for a work permit in Norway. The only catch is, I had ninety days to get a job, and if I didn't, I would have to return to the USA. And if anyone thinks they would give me leeway on that, remember Eric how they shipped him out of the country five times because of their senseless rules hurting good people. If I broke the law, they could deny me entry for five years. Imagine how the good Norwegian Arfan Bhatti would have felt about that? I couldn't even afford to go back and forth to Norway since I had a certain amount of money to prove to UDI. And I do not have any wealthy relatives in Norway, and contrary to what so many spew out today, I am white and I have never been privileged.

As I would later find out, it did not seem like the right hand knew what the left hand was doing at UDI.

Before I received the letter from the Consulate General, I had sent UDI all paperwork required. Copies of passports, my birth certificate, my mom's birth certificate, bank statements, applications, grocery store receipts, bar bills, old love letters, and everything else that was required. As I said before, I do understand that there are rules and regulations. But why do they have to make it so complicated? It is almost as if they want to make sure that you must atone for what you did and that you have no more rights than any foreigner that set foot in Norway. And as Heidi's attorney said, they use American citizenship for all that it's worth.

If I were the only one experiencing stonewalling because of that minor detail, I wouldn't even think of it. Heidi, Eric, and I are only one of many. I do not want to identify the woman, but she had similar problems with American citizenship and contacted the American Embassy in Norway. They told her they could not send a complaint to UDI or UNI or get involved in her case because his case is very similar to other American citizens. The American embassy said immigration officials look for *technical mistakes* on the applications, get hung up on those mistakes, and blindly stick to their decisions. The American embassy told her they think this is very sad and asked her to keep them updated about the case.

A few months after I got the letter from the General Counsel, I traveled to Norway after much back and forth and many sleepless nights. There was still uncertainty from UDI and the General Council in the U.S. about handling my case, but I had gotten confirmation that I am allowed to go to Norway and apply for a job. For ninety freaking days. They had not yet asked me for proof of living accommodations, but as Leif would put it, according to the paragraph riders at UDI: "It is a condition for obtaining a residence permit that the applicant is secured housing." Is an Igloo considered housing? I was going to live with my parents until I had a job and an apartment, and although I was relieved to set foot on Norwegian soil finally, I was constantly worried about my case and how it would end. My entire family was outraged about how UDI treats their "own," As the mother *Resett* spoke to, they noted the bias in how Norwegians are treated compared to those not born in the country. But as we all know, there is nothing you can do when you are up against the stonewalling bureaucracy.

A few weeks after I landed in Norway, my case was still up in the air, and contacting UDI was a nightmare. I had sent emails to my caseworker as soon as I arrived but never received an answer. One day, I finally got through by phone and spoke to a person at the service unit. My caseworker had moved to another department, and there was uncertainty concerning my case. I was told I would get a new caseworker but had to confirm housing, proof of financial means, and everything else to help my case. Again. My mom had already established in a letter that I could live with my parents until I got an apartment. Three weeks later, I receive a confirmation by email that my case is active, but they cannot promise completion in my case. I was never able to talk to a caseworker and was told by the service unit that is not possible. They never gave me feedback on how my case was going or whether I had done my part to complete it.

Two months after I arrived in Norway, I received a job offer. I sent the job offer to UDI, as I was required to. I called a few days later, waiting on hold for hours since I had not heard from them. Time was running out for me. I had one month left of my ninety-day stay, and if I did not receive my work permit in time, which was separate from the residence permit, I had to return to the United States. And say no thank you to the job at a municipality, which was an excellent opportunity for me. I got through to the service unit and was told the job offer was not sent to my new caseworker yet, and also that the Norwegian Consulate in the United States had sought confirmation and proof that I had a place to live. In addition, the service unit told me that I was assigned yet another caseworker, and they could not give me a completion date. It was now almost two years since I had first contacted UDI to inquire about moving to Norway, and my case was lost in the dark corridors of the UDI bureaucracy.

I struggled to understand why the Consulate that I had dealt with in the U.S. needed proof of living accommodations. And why were they still involved with my case? When I came to Norway, they told me I had to deal with UDI in Oslo. But the insanity in this is that they had given me wrong directives in the first place, and they had given me the runaround since I started the application process. Now the Consulate had nothing better to do than to make sure the traitor who gave up her citizenship had to prove that she had a place to live.

I still have a copy of the letter I sent to the Norwegian Consulate with proof of living accommodations and asking for help in my case. I was at my wit's end and thought my days in Norway were over. And I had just gotten there. Reading the letter brings back memories of how intimidated and afraid I was. I felt that they held my destiny in their hands. I was so scared they would deny me a residence and work permit. In the letter to the counselor, I am overly polite and excuse myself for taking up their time, and twice I stressed my letter was not a critique. I even told them I wasn't looking for special treatment, which I wasn't, but my time in Norway was running out, and I needed help.

A week later, I received a letter from UDI that my application was approved. I don't know if the letter to the consular officer helped "speed" up my case, but I have a feeling it did. As I told her I was not looking for special treatment, one would still expect timely handling of a work and residence permit when the applicant only has ninety days to find a job. But remembering Eric's case, there is no such thing as rational thinking in the Norwegian immigration bureaucracy. As his uncle Leif was saying, they are paragraph riders and blindly adhere to the law. Especially if dealing with native Norwegians, it seems.

As I was only a foreigner in my own country, the UDI would only grant me a temporary residence permit. The permit was valid for one year from the date of the decision. I was permitted to take a job or run a business in Norway. I was thinking of starting a consulting business helping people going through the trials and tribulations of dealing with UDI." Still, I decided against it, considering the bureaucracy of starting a business was probably no better.

As this was a temporary residence and work permit, I would have to undergo the same application procedures for three years. As noted in the Immigration Act paragraph, "The applicant is entitled to a renewed permit if the conditions for the permit are still present." That meant I would have to prove that I can support myself either through a full-time job, funds in the bank, or both, and housing. After three years, if I still meet all the requirements from UDI, I can apply for a permanent residency. And I believe after seven years; I could apply for Norwegian citizenship and get my passport back. The woman's words that *Resett* spoke to is good advice: "I would recommend that anyone who lives abroad and is considering renouncing their Norwegian citizenship think carefully before doing so. It can be complicated and time-consuming to regain Norwegian rights."

I had finally gotten the residence and work permit I had fought so hard for, and soon I had started in my new job. After a short time, I got an apartment, and I was beginning to think my life in Norway was coming together. The best part of being in my homeland was that I had my family close by, something I had missed all those years in the United States. I also enjoyed doing the things I did growing up. Skiing, hiking in the mountains, picking blueberries in the woods, eating lutefisk, drinking moonshine, even fishing for trout in mountain lakes. Activities that are possible in the U.S., except for the lutefisk part, but not in the state I live in. I did miss Kevin a lot, and we talked on the phone almost every day. I had a phone plan with unlimited calls to the U.S., or I would have been bankrupt. Absence makes the heart grow fonder is true, and as time passed, I knew we had to find a way to get back together again.

When I received the job offer, my supervisor told me that the position was a one-year project with the possibility of extension. But she could not promise me anything since it was a municipal job, and she did not decide such things. I had no alternative but to accept the job, as my ninety days were almost up. But on the other hand, it was an excellent opportunity for me in Norway, as employment in government is hard to come by. Especially in the small community, I lived in.

I loved the job and formed great friendships with my co-workers. Everything was a new experience for me since I had been away from Norway for so many years. Time flew by, and after six months in Norway, Kevin came to visit for two weeks. I think we both had realized we did not want to be apart, and we had to figure out a way to make things work. We did have a minor setback when the five-hour train ride to Bergen didn't have a dining car. Kevin, who loves Norwegian beer, not that there is anything wrong with Bud Lite, was looking forward to a Hansa or three while taking in the beautiful scenery. The longest five hours of his life, and he still talks about the traumatic experience all these years later.

We talked about him moving to Norway, and we could start a new life there. But looming over my head was, how in the world were we going to do that. We would be dealing with the bureaucracy for years, and what if things did not work out. I didn't even know if I had a job at the end of the year. And that would be my only savior when I applied for renewal before my one-year permit expires.

After Kevin returned to the United States, I started applying for other jobs. My supervisor worked hard on getting my position extended, but if it wasn't, I had to have a job. She had no say if it was since it was a government job. You can't bend their rules unless your mother is the mayor or your uncle the city manager. I had been reluctant to apply in larger cities, like Oslo. I was afraid I could not afford to live there, as renting an apartment is on par with New York City prices. But there were no jobs in the town I lived in, so I sent several applicants to prospective employees in Oslo. I even sent one to the prime minister's office but did not get a response. Thank God, as I now realize their politics, bringing ISIS women home and putting Norway and Norwegians last.

In the end, my position was not extended, and I had no job to refer to when applying for residence renewal at UDI. And I did not have enough funds in the bank. Even before that, I had started to have serious doubts if I could handle three years of uncertainty regarding my residency. I was losing all my courage. If the regulations were easier, I could have moved in with my parents and stayed there until I got a full-time secure job, but I could not do that without a residence permit. I don't know if that is possible if you apply for family reunification, but UDI had already confirmed that I could not do that in my case. Maybe they were wrong. At that point, I could not deal with it anymore. I picked up the phone one night and called Kevin. I woke him up because it was in the middle of the night where he was. "I'm coming home," I said. There was silence, and then I could hear him cry. And so, did I. And no longer after that I was home in the United States.

I cried when writing the last paragraph because it brought back memories of what I perceived as an impossible situation. I could have taken the chance to stay in Norway and fought for my residency, but after going through the ropes with UDI, I had no courage left. My anxiety level was so high, and I could barely function in the end. And I consider myself a strong person. Kevin would have had to move there if I stayed in Norway because we did not want to be apart. That meant he would have given up a good job, sold a house that was paid for, and left his homeland. He loves Norway and my family and would have had no problems fitting in, but the hurdles we would have to go through dealing with UDI and starting anew was frightening to think of. My family was devastated that I left Norway, but thankfully understood, and they all love Kevin.

Today, Norway allows dual citizenship, as the laws changed in 2020. I will send my application to UDI, and someday I will have a red Norwegian passport again. It's somewhat bittersweet because it doesn't change that Norway is harboring terrorists and treating foreign criminals and those that will hurt our country with kid gloves, while Norwegian's welfare and the country's security come in second. And so do the Norwegians themselves. It is too late for Kevin and me to start a new life in Norway, but we have a good life here in the United States, and we still have the best of two worlds. Being part of two great countries is unique, and we cannot wait for our next vacation to Norway, the land I love, which is always in my heart.

I believe that my experience with UDI is why I felt such affinity for Eric and Heidi when I read their story in the *Daily News* back in 2017. I could feel their pain, and their case was a hundred times worse than mine. And they did not give up like me and returned to the USA. They fought until the bitter end. For three years, they fought a good fight with decency and courage not many in their situation would have. And they lost. The American boy who loved Norway lost to the enormous bureaucracy that is the Norwegian Directorate of Immigration.

Does that sound like we, we, we, Michael Moore?

.

Notes

Chapter 1: The American Boy Who Loved Norway
1. https://wikitravel.org/en/M%C3%B8re_og_Romsdal

Chapter 2: You've Made Your ISIS Husband's Bed, Now Lie in It
1. Brekke, A., Zondag, M., & Døvik, O. (2021, March 02). Is-kvinnen: jeg tenkte ikke klart på den tiden. Retrieved April 12, 2021, https://www.nrk.no/norge/is-kvinnen_-_-jeg-tenkte-ikke-klart-pa-den-tiden-1.
2. Ibid.
3. Her leses tiltalen mot IS-kvinnen. VGTV. (n.d.). https://www.vgtv.no/video/214122/her-leses-tiltalen-mot-is-kvinnen.
4. Ibid.
5. Ibid.
6. Døvik, O., Olsson, S. V., Solheim, S., Zondag, M. H. W., Alayoubi, M., & Svendsen, C. (2021, March 1). Slik ble IS-kvinnen radikalisert: Her prøver hun nikab for første gang. NRK. https://www.nrk.no/norge/xl/fra-oslo-til-raqqa-1.
7. Ibid.
8. https://www.nrk.no/norge/is-kvinnen_-_-jeg-tenkte-ikke-klart-pa-den-tiden-1.15396110
9. Ibid.
10. Ibid.
11. Ibid.
12. Ibid.
13. Ibid.
14. Ibid.
15. Ibid.
16. Ibid.
17. Ibid.

18. Ibid.
19. Ibid.
20. Ibid.
21. Brekke, A., Zondag, M. H. W., & Solheim, S. (2021, March 12). Tiltalt kvinne i avlyttet samtale: – Jeg vil også ha våpen. NRK. https://www.nrk.no/norge/tiltalt-kvinne-i-avlyttet-samtale_-_-jeg-vil-ogsa-ha-vapen-
22. Wikimedia Foundation. (2021, May 26). Hegira. Wikipedia. https://en.wikipedia.org/wiki/Hegira.
23. https://www.nrk.no/norge/tiltalt-kvinne-i-avlyttet-samtale_-_-jeg-vil-ogsa-ha-vapen-
24. Ibid.
25. Ibid.
26. Ibid.
27. Ibid.
28. Ibid.
29. Ibid.
30. Wikimedia Foundation. (2021, February 22). Finlandshette. Wikipedia. https://no.wikipedia.org/wiki/Finlandshette.
31. https://www.nrk.no/norge/tiltalt-kvinne-i-avlyttet-samtale_-_-jeg-vil-ogsa-ha-vapen-
32. Ibid through 47.

Chapter 3: Do Not Return. Wait for Your Reward from Allah

1. Brekke, A., & Zondag, M. (2021, March 03). Forteller Om flukten fra IS: Ventet på Å dø. Retrieved April 12, 2021, from https://www.nrk.no/norge/forteller-om-flukten-fra-is_-_-ventet-pa-a-do-
2. Ibid.
3. Ibid.
4. Ibid.
5. Ibid.
6. Ibid.
7. Ibid.
8. Ibid.
9. Ibid.
10. Ibid.
11. Ibid.
12. Al-Shaddadah. (2021, March 20th). Retrieved May 07th, 2021, from https://en.wikipedia.org/wiki/Al-Shaddadah
13. https://www.nrk.no/norge/forteller-om-flukten-fra-is_-_-ventet-pa-a-do-

14. Ibid.
15. Ibid.
16. Ibid.
17. Raqqa. (2021, April 21st). Retrieved May 07th, 2021, from https://en.wikipedia.org/wiki/Raqqa
18. Ibid.
19. National Consortium for the Study of Terrorism and Responses to Terrorism. (2017). Annex of Statistical Information Country Reports on Terrorism 2016. Retrieved from https://www.state.gov/wp-content/uploads/2019/04/National-consortium-2016.pdf
20. https://www.nrk.no/norge/forteller-om-flukten-fra-is_-_-ventet-pa-a-do-
21. Ibid.
22. Wikimedia Foundation. (2021, June 25). Al-Baghuz Fawqani. Wikipedia. https://en.wikipedia.org/wiki/Al-Baghuz_Fawqani.
23. Sang, L. I. S. (2019, February 28). Fox News. https://www.foxnews.com/world/mass-grave-with-dozens-of-decapitated-bodies-found-in-last-isis-enclave-they-were-slaughtered.
24. Wikimedia Foundation. (2021, May 13). Denis Mukwege. Wikipedia. https://en.wikipedia.org/wiki/Denis_Mukwege.
25. Murad, N., & Krajeski, J. (2018). The last girl: my story of captivity, and my fight against the Islamic State. Amazon. https://www.amazon.com/Last-Girl-Captivity-Against-Islamic/dp/1524760447.
26. https://www.nrk.no/norge/forteller-om-flukten-fra-is_-_-ventet-pa-a-do-
27. Ibid.
28. Ibid.
29. Al-Hawl refugee camp. (2021, March 05th). Retrieved May 08th, 2021, https://en.wikipedia.org/wiki/Al-Hawl_refugee_camp
30. Ibid.
31. Ibid.
32. Ibid.
33. Callimachi, R., & Porter, C. (2019, February 20) https://www.nytimes.com/2019/02/19/us/islamic-state-american-women.html
34. Hoda Muthana. (2021, April 07). Retrieved May 09, 2021, from https://en.wikipedia.org/wiki/Hoda_Muthana
35. https://www.nytimes.com/2019/02/19/us/islamic-state-american-women.html
36. Ibid.
37. Ibid.
38. Ibid.
39. Scarborough, R. (2019, March 3). Hoda Muthana's social media

messages on MEMRI record. AP NEWS. https://apnews.com/article/f201533f796941288ce8265f2e70180d.
40. Ibid.
41. Ibid
42. https://en.wikipedia.org/wiki/Hoda_Muthana
43. https://www.nytimes.com/2019/02/19/us/islamic-state-american-women.html
44. Kimberly Gwen Polman. (2021, February 03). Retrieved May 09, 2021, https://en.wikipedia.org/wiki/Kimberly_Gwen_Polman
45. https://www.nytimes.com/2019/02/19/us/islamic-state-american-women.html
46. Ibid.
47. https://en.wikipedia.org/wiki/Hoda_Muthana
48. Ibid.
49. https://apnews.com/article/f201533f796941288ce8265f2e70180d.
50. Ibid.
51. Robinson, C., & Gray, J. (2021, April 2). Retrieved October 11, 2021, from https://www.al.com/news/2021/04/sister-of-alabama-isis-bride-hoda-muthana-arrested-with-husband-while-allegedly-trying-to-join-terrorists.html.
52. Ibid.
53. Ibid.
54. Ibid.
55. Ibid.
56. The United States Department of Justice. (2021, April 6). https://www.justice.gov/usao-sdny/pr/new-york-city-man-and-alabama-woman-charged-attempting-and-conspiring-provide-material.

Chapter 4: The Filthy Shameless Acts of Western People
1. Wikipedia. (2021, February 19). Taqiyah (cap). Retrieved April 16, 2021, from https://en.wikipedia.org/wiki/Taqiyah
2. Memri. (2013, October 31). Norwegian Islamic Leader Fahad Qureshi: All Muslims Believe in the Death Penalty for Homosexuals. MEMRI. https://www.memri.org/tv/norwegian-islamic-leader-fahad-qureshi-all-muslims-believe-death-penalty-homosexuals.
3. Ibid.
4. Ibid.
5. Ibid.
6. Slettholm, A., & Stokke, O. (2017, January 23). Stadig

Flere unge SØKER seg til bokstavtro islam. Retrieved April 12, 2021, from https://www.aftenposten.no/norge/i/9zAw/stadig-flere-unge-soeker-seg-til-bokstavtro-islam

7. Churchill, D. (2014, November 24). London Evening Standard https://www.standard.co.uk/news/london/london-university-bans-preacher-who-calls-homosexuality-a-filthy-disease-9879579.html.
8. Memri. (2018, September 20). *British Preacher "Dawah Man" Imran Ibn Mansur Advises His Listeners to Return to Muslim Lands:* MEMRI. https://www.memri.org/tv/british-preacher-dawah-man-imran-ibn-mansur-advises-listeners-return-muslim-lands.
9. Wikimedia Foundation. (2021, June 18). *Dawah.* Wikipedia. https://en.wikipedia.org/wiki/Dawah.
10. https://www.memri.org/tv/british-preacher-dawah-man-imran-ibn-mansur-advises-listeners-return-muslim-lands.
11. Memri. (2020, February 13). *British Preacher Imran Ibn Mansur "Dawah Man": Infidels in the U.K. Are So Filthy They Don't Care How Many People You Sleep with; You Can Marry Multiple Wives.* MEMRI. https://www.memri.org/tv/british-preacher-imran-mansur-dawah-man-marriage-multiple-wives-adultery-young-men.
12. https://www.aftenposten.no/norge/i/9zAw/stadig-flere-unge-soeker-seg-til-bokstavtro-islam
13. Ibid.
14. Ibid.
15. Ibid.
16. Ibid.
17. Ibid.
18. Ibid.
19. Ibid.
20. Ibid.
21. Wikipedia. (2021, March 18). Haitham al-Haddad. Retrieved April 17, 2021, from https://en.wikipedia.org/wiki/Haitham_al-Haddad
22. Change.org. (n.d.). Sign the petition. Retrieved April 17, 2021, https://www.change.org/p/university-of-westminster-stop-anti-gay-preacher-sheikh-haitham-al-haddad-speaking-on-campus
23. Ibid.
24. March 30, 2011. (2021, June 16). *Dershowitz in WSJ: Norway to Jews: You're Not Welcome Here.* Harvard Law Today. https://today.law.harvard.edu/dershowitz-in-wsj-norway-to-jews-youre-not-welcome-here/.
25. Ibid.

26. https://www.aftenposten.no/norge/i/9zAw/stadig-flere-unge-soeker-seg-til-bokstavtro-islam
27. Ibid.
28. Ibid.
29. Retrieved April 22, 2021, from https://www.ssb.no/sosiale-forhold-og-kriminalitet/artikler-og-publikasjoner/56-prosent-av-sosialhjelpsutbetalingene-gar-til-innvandrere.
30. https://www.aftenposten.no/norge/i/9zAw/stadig-flere-unge-soeker-seg-til-bokstavtro-islam

Chapter 5: The Road to Syria Was Paved with Bad Intentions

1. Rivrud, K., Jørstad, R. H., & Andersen, B. L. (2014, June 30). NRK. https://www.nrk.no/vestfoldogtelemark/_-han-ble-uthengt-i-norge-1.
2. Ibid.
3. Sandvik, S., & Omland, E. (2012, January 17). *PST etterforsker islamist-video*.https://www.nrk.no/norge/pst-etterforsker-islamist-video-1.
4. Sandvik, S. (2012, January 10). Hyller drap på Nato-soldater. NRK. https://www.nrk.no/norge/hyller-drap-pa-nato-soldater-1.
5. https://www.nrk.no/norge/pst-etterforsker-islamist-video-1.
6. Sæthre, S., & Morgenbladet. (2021, March 01). Slik BLE Bastian FRA gulset is-kriger. Retrieved April 20, 2021, from https://www.varden.no/nyheter/slik-ble-bastian-fra-gulset-is-kriger/
7. Ibid.
8. Ibid.
9. Ibid.
10. SSB. (2004). Fakta om ti innvandringsgrupper i Norge. https://www.ssb.no/a/publikasjoner/pdf/rapp_200414/rapp_200414.pdf
11. Mauren, A. (2017, July 22). Flyktninger flest kommer fra syv land. https://www.aftenposten.no/norge/i/LLwR/flyktninger-flest-kommer-fra-syv-land.
12. Telelaget of America. (n.d.). Skien Kommune. Retrieved April 19, 2021, from https://www.telelaget.com/telemark/skien.htm
13. Ibid.
14. Skien. (2021, April 05). Retrieved April 19, 2021, from https://en.wikipedia.org/wiki/Skien
15. https://www.varden.no/nyheter/slik-ble-bastian-fra-gulset-is-kriger/
16. Sundt, H. (2018, November 19). Retrieved April 21, 2021, from https://www.document.no/2018/11/19/det-storste-trossamfunnet-i-telemark-er-muslimsk/
17. Ibid.

18. Ibid.
19. Storhaug, H. (2020, December 6). Like mange moskeer i Norge som i Frankrike: Page 23. Human Rights Service. https://www.rights.no/2020/12/like-mange-moskeer-i-norge-som-i-frankrike/.
20. Ibid.
21. Thuestad, Ø. (2019, December 1). Regjeringen støtter konvertering av kirke og bedehus til moské. Document. https://www.document.no/2019/12/01/regjeringen-stotter-konvertering-av-kirke-og-bedehus-til-moske/.
22. Ibid.
23. https://www.varden.no/nyheter/slik-ble-bastian-fra-gulset-is-kriger/
24. Ibid.
25. Ibid.
26. About Zeitgeist the Movie. (n.d.). Retrieved April 21, 2021, from https://www.zeitgeistmovie.com/about
27. Zeitgeist (film series). (2021, March 14). Retrieved April 21, 2021, https://en.wikipedia.org/wiki/Zeitgeist_(film_series)
28. Ibid.
29. Ibid.
30. https://www.varden.no/nyheter/slik-ble-bastian-fra-gulset-is-kriger/
31. Ibid.
32. Ibid.
33. Ibid.
34. Ibid.
35. Ibid.
36. Ibid.
37. Ibid.
38. Ibid.
39. Ibid.
40. Ibid.
41. Ibid.
42. Ibid.
43. Ibid.
44. Norsk Islamist (24) I Terrorvideo fra grensen mellom Syria OG IRAK. https://www.vg.no/nyheter/utenriks/i/3yB7P/norsk-islamist-24-i-terrorvideo-fra-grensen-mellom-syria-og-irak
45. Ibid.
46. Ibid.
47. Ibid.

48. https://www.varden.no/nyheter/slik-ble-bastian-fra-gulset-is-kriger/
49. Zondag, M. H. W., Døvik, O., Brekke, A., & Solheim, S. (2021, March 10). Faren til Bastian Vasquez: – Jeg kjente ikke igjen min egen sønn. NRK. https://www.nrk.no/norge/faren-til-bastian-vasquez_-_-jeg-kjente-ikke-igjen-min-egen-sonn-1.

Chapter 6: Bureaucracy Is The Art of Making the Possible Impossible

1. Guardian News and Media. (2002, June 25) https://www.theguardian.com/world/2002/jun/25/iran.andrewosborn.
2. Ibid.
3. Ibid.
4. Ibid.
5. Hammerfjeld, J. (2016, December 09). Retrieved January 27, 2021, from https://www.dagbladet.no/nyheter/flykaprer-fikk-jobb-i-nrk/65815923
6. Jonassen, A. (2011, October 20). Iransk flykaprer narkotikadømt. Retrieved January 29, 2021, from https://www.aftenposten.no/norge/i/w8lnM/iransk-flykaprer-narkotikadoemt
7. Rustad, H., & Kjørholt, D. (2019, April 03). Retrieved February 09, 2021, from https://www.document.no/2019/03/26/46-arig-flykaprer-saksoker-staten-for-a-fa-opphold-pa-humanitaert-grunnlag/

Chapter 7: When Norwegian Journalists Become Social Justice Activists

1. Svendsen, C., & Alayoubi, M. (2021, February 22). – Jeg angrer – vær SÅ snill og Hjelp oss. Retrieved May 08, 2021, from https://www.nrk.no/urix/xl/_-jeg-angrer-_-vaer-sa-snill-og-hjelp-oss-
2. Ibid.
3. Ibid.
4. Rovick, A., Hansen, K. H., & Hodne, A. M. (2021, March 21). Ulrik blir blind hvis familien ikke skaffer minst åtte millioner kroner. TV 2. https://www.tv2.no/a/13888751/.
5. https://www.nrk.no/urix/xl/_-jeg-angrer-_-vaer-sa-snill-og-hjelp-oss-
6. Ibid.
7. Ibid.
8. BBC. (2020, April 24). Genocide trial: IS suspect in court in Germany. BBC News. https://www.bbc.com/news/world-europe-52409406.
9. ISIS woman stands trial in Germany for crimes against humanity. Shino, Z. (n.d.). rudaw.net. https://www.rudaw.net/english/world/05052020.

10. https://www.nrk.no/urix/xl/_-jeg-angrer-_-vaer-sa-snill-og-hjelp-oss-
11. Ibid.
12. Ibid.
13. Ibid.
14. Ibid.
15. Svendsen, C., & Alayoubi, M. (2019, August 23). IS-kvinne med syk fireåring: Vil ikke GI fra seg Barna TIL norske myndigheter. Retrieved May 10, 2021, from https://www.nrk.no/norge/is-kvinne-med-syk-firearing_-vil-ikke-gi-fra-seg-barna-til-norske-myndigheter-
16. Ibid.
17. Redaksjonen. (2020, March 29). Mulla Krekar Sendt Til ITALIA: NRK ønsket å Vite "HVOR Mye flyet kostet NORSKE SKATTEBETALERE". Retrieved May 10, 2021, from https://resett.no/2020/03/27/mulla-krekar-sendt-til-italia-nrk-onsket-a-vite-hvor-mye-flyet-kostet-norske-skattebetalere/
18. https://www.nrk.no/norge/is-kvinne-med-syk-firearing_-vil-ikke-gi-fra-seg-barna-til-norske-myndigheter-
19. Ibid.
20. Svendsen, C., Olsen, K., & Alayoubi, M. (2019, August 08). Frykter for LIVET til norsk Gutt (4) I Al Hol. Retrieved May 10, 2021, from https://www.nrk.no/norge/frykter-for-livet-til-norsk-gutt-_4_-i-al-hol-
21. Ibid.
22. Ibid.
23. Ibid.
24. Svendsen, C. (2019, September 20). Syk fireåring Mister vekt: Regjeringen endrer IKKE POLITIKK. Retrieved May 11, 2021, https://www.nrk.no/norge/syk-firearing-mister-vekt_-regjeringen-endrer-ikke-politikk-
25. Ibid.
26. Mayo Clinic Staff. (2020, March 14). Cystic fibrosis. Retrieved January 14, 2021, from https://www.mayoclinic.org/diseases-conditions/cystic-fibrosis/symptoms-causes/syc-20353700
27. https://www.nrk.no/norge/syk-firearing-mister-vekt_-regjeringen-endrer-ikke-politikk-
28. Tjørholm, V., Sølhusvik, L., & Befring, Å. M. (2019, June 26). Statsministeren med klart svar til Ropstad. NRK. https://www.nrk.no/norge/statsministeren-med-klart-svar-til-ropstad-
29. MDG vil hente hjem syk norsk gutt, og hans IS-tilknyttede mor. VG. https://www.vg.no/nyheter/utenriks/i/g7j8P5/mdg-vil-hente-hjem-syk-norsk-gutt-og-hans-is-tilknyttede-mor.

Chapter 8: The Formation of the Prophet Ummah

1. Granbo, K., & Carlsen, H. (2010, February 15). Advarte mot NORSK 11. september. Retrieved April 20, 2021, from https://www.nrk.no/norge/advarte-mot-norsk-11.-september-
2. Ibid.
3. Ibid.
4. Ibid.
5. Fria Tider. (n.d.). Fick REDA På Att bussföraren inte var Muslim: https://www.friatider.se/fick-reda-pa-att-bussforaren-inte-var-muslim-jag-ska-knulla-dina-barn.
6. https://www.nrk.no/norge/advarte-mot-norsk-11.-september-
7. Wikipedia. (2021, February 10). Profetens Ummah. Retrieved from https://en.wikipedia.org/wiki/Profetens_Ummah
8. Wikimedia Foundation. (2021, July 23). Salafi jihadism. Wikipedia. https://en.wikipedia.org/wiki/Salafi_jihadism.
9. from https://en.wikipedia.org/wiki/Profetens_Ummah
10. Ibid.
11. Wikimedia Foundation. (2020, December 19). Wikipedia. https://en.wikipedia.org/wiki/Ubaydullah_Hussain.
12. Ibid.
13. Hultgreen, G. (2016, October 21). Ekstremistens forvandling - FRA Fotball til ekstremist. Retrieved May 01, 2021, from https://www.dagbladet.no/nyheter/ekstremistens-forvandling---fra-fotball-til-ekstremist/63007106
14. Ibid.
15. Ibid.
16. https://en.wikipedia.org/wiki/Ubaydullah_Hussain.
17. Sætran, F. (2014, October 3). Ubaydullah Hussain er frifunnet. https://www.aftenposten.no/norge/i/qxoe/ubaydullah-hussain-er-frifunnet.
18. Ibid.
19. Ibid.
20. Ibid.
21. Wikimedia Foundation. (2021, June 18). Hassan Abdi Dhuhulow. https://en.wikipedia.org/wiki/Hassan_Abdi_Dhuhulow.
22. https://www.aftenposten.no/norge/i/qxoe/ubaydullah-hussain-er-frifunnet.
23. Ibid.
24. Ibid.
25. Ferguson, D. (2021, August 8). Writing on the wall.

https://missionbibleclass.org/old-testament/part2/kingdom-ends-captivity-return-prophets/writing-on-the-wall/.
26. Storhaug, H. (2020, May 26). Klage på NRK's diskriminering, islam-hvitvasking, polarisering og Human Rights Service. https://www.rights.no/2020/05/klagestorm-na-er-det-mer-enn-nok-islam-nrk/.
27. Ibid.
28. https://www.aftenposten.no/norge/i/qxoe/ubaydullah-hussain-er-frifunnet.
29. Kolberg, M., & Halsør, M. (2015, October 07). Ubaydullah Hussain frifunnet for terroroppfordring. Retrieved May 01, 2021, from https://www.nrk.no/norge/ubaydullah-hussain-frifunnet-for-terroroppfordring-
30. Ibid.
31. Wikimedia Foundation. (2021, June 12). Mohyeldeen Mohammad. https://en.wikipedia.org/wiki/Mohyeldeen_Mohammad.
32. Ibid.
33. Ibid.
34. TV 2. (2011, September 12). Norsk islamist løslatt i Saudi-Arabia. TV 2. https://www.tv2.no/a/13153914/.
35. https://en.wikipedia.org/wiki/Mohyeldeen_Mohammad.
36. Ibid.
37. Karlsen , O., & Qasim, A. (2012, January 25). Deportert fra Tunisia.https://www.abcnyheter.no/nyheter/2012/01/25/144664/deportert-fra-tunisia.
38. https://en.wikipedia.org/wiki/Mohyeldeen_Mohammad.
39. Ighoubah, F. (2018, October 22). Retrieved April 28, 2021, from https://www.nettavisen.no/nyheter/innenriks/trusseltiltalt-islamist-mohyeldeen-mohammad-motte-ikke-opp-til-rettssak/s/12-95-3423549869
40. Ibid.
41. https://en.wikipedia.org/wiki/Mohyeldeen_Mohammad.
42. Hultgreen, G. (2016, December 10). dagbladet.no. https://www.dagbladet.no/nyheter/jeg-lever-for-islam-og-hater-norske-verdier/65831673.
43. Ibid.
44. Ibid.
45. Ibid.
46. Ibid.
47. Dragland, L., & Stokke, O. (2017, January 26). Retrieved May 03, 2021, from https://www.aftenposten.no/norge/i/R0OJ/hvem-er-arfan-bhatti

48. Wikimedia Foundation. (2021, June 27). Arfan Bhatti. Wikipedia. https://en.wikipedia.org/wiki/Arfan_Bhatti.
49. https://no.wikipedia.org/wiki/Young_Guns_(gjeng)
50. Nakken, M. (2008, June 03). - Bhatti Er En rå torpedo. Retrieved May 03, 2021, from https://www.nrk.no/osloogviken/--bhatti-er-en-ra-torpedo-1.
51. https://www.aftenposten.no/norge/i/R0OJ/hvem-er-arfan-bhatti
52. https://www.nrk.no/osloogviken/--bhatti-er-en-ra-torpedo-1.
53. (2021, April 16). Retrieved May 04, 2021, from https://en.wikipedia.org/wiki/Life_imprisonment_in_Norway
54. https://www.nrk.no/osloogviken/--bhatti-er-en-ra-torpedo-1.
55. Ibid.
56. https://www.aftenposten.no/norge/i/R0OJ/hvem-er-arfan-bhatti
57. Hultgreen, G. (2016, October 31). - Vi vil at Norge skal bli en islamsk nasjon styrt etter Sharia-lover. dagbladet.no. https://www.dagbladet.no/nyheter/vi-vil-at-norge-skal-bli-en-islamsk-nasjon-styrt-etter-sharia-lover/63361979.
58. https://www.aftenposten.no/norge/i/R0OJ/hvem-er-arfan-bhatti
59. Andersen, M., Kvilesjø, S., & Mo, H. (2011, October 19) https://www.aftenposten.no/norge/i/g0mo9/skjoet-mot-synagoge
60. Jonassen, A. M. A. M. (2011, October 20). Aftenposten. https://www.aftenposten.no/oslo/i/23J6R/tiltalt-for-terror-br-planer-i-oslo.
61. Nyheter, NTB (2021, February 22). Bhatti benekter drapsforsøk, Dagsavisen. https://www.dagsavisen.no/nyheter/innenriks/2009/02/16/bhatti-benekter-drapsforsok-men-vedgar-trusler/.
62. Mener Bhatti dyrkes som en helt. Aftenposten. (2011, October 20). https://www.aftenposten.no/norge/i/rLeql/mener-bhatti-dyrkes-som-en-helt.
63. Røli, O. (2011, October 20). Bhatti pepret huset til Dame (76) med MASKINPISTOL: - Jeg angrer. Retrieved May 05, 2021, fromhttps://www.aftenposten.no/norge/i/41laR/bhatti-pepret-huset-til-dame-76-med-maskinpistol-jeg-angrer
64. Ibid.
65. Røli, O. (2011, October 20). Aktor: Ikke tvil om at Bhatti er terrorist. https://www.aftenposten.no/norge/i/aWpV2/aktor-ikke-tvil-om-at-bhatti-er-terrorist.
66. Ibid.
67. Ibid.
68. Røli, O. (2011, October 20). Bhattis alibi: Jeg røykte hasj. https://www.aftenposten.no/norge/i/O3qV3/bhattis-alibibr-jeg-roeykte-hasj.

69. Ibid.
70. Ibid.
71. Ibid.
72. Ibid.
73. Ibid.
74. Jenssen, G. K. (2015, October 6). Bhatti dømt til forvaring. NRK. https://www.nrk.no/osloogviken/bhatti-domt-til-forvaring-
75. TV 2, Ervik, K., & Berthelsen, O. (2008, June 4). - Bør endre lovverket. TV 2. https://www.tv2.no/a/12047899/.
76. Røli, O. (2011, October 20). Israels ambassadør skuffet Over Bhatti-dom. Retrieved May 05, 2021,from https://www.aftenposten.no/norge/i/aWvJ2/israels-ambassadoer-skuffet-over-bhatti-dom
77. https://en.wikipedia.org/wiki/Arfan_Bhatti
78. https://www.aftenposten.no/norge/i/R0OJ/hvem-er-arfan-bhatti
79. https://en.wikipedia.org/wiki/Arfan_Bhatti
80. https://www.aftenposten.no/norge/i/R0OJ/hvem-er-arfan-bhatti
81. https://www.nettavisen.no/nyheter/bhatti-har-dratt-til-midtosten/s/12-95-3422774584
82. Farooq, K. (2016, October 13). Bhatti stoppet på grensen til Tyrkia. https://www.dagbladet.no/nyheter/bhatti-stoppet-pa-grensen-til-tyrkia/60740380.
83. Ibid.
84. Ibid.
85. Vedeler, M. (2015, February 23). VG: Bhatti hadde BOMBEOPPSKRIFTER OG lister over "vantro" politikere. Retrieved May 04, 2021, from https://www.nrk.no/norge/vg_-bhatti-hadde-bombeoppskrifter-og-lister-over-_vantro_-politikere-
86. Ibid.
87. Ibid.

Chapter 9: I Swear By Allah I Didn't Know He Was a Terrorist

1. Svendsen, C. (2019, October 8). Norsk IS-kvinne siktet. NRK. https://www.nrk.no/norge/norsk-is-kvinne-siktet-for-deltagelse-i-en-terrororganisasjon-
2. Wikimedia Foundation. (2021, May 5). *Murders of Louisa Vesterager Jespersen and Maren Ueland*. Wikipedia. https://en.wikipedia.org/wiki/Murders_of_Louisa_Vesterager_Jespersen_and_Maren_Ueland.
3. Guardian News and Media. (2019, July 11). Mother of Danish student suspected killed by jihadists demands death penalty. https://www.theguardian.com/world/2019/jul/11/

mother-of-danish-student-suspected-killed-by-jihadists-demands-death-penalty.
4. Alnes, E. (2019, October 9). Norsk terrorsikta kvinne ber om å bli arrestert. https://www.nrk.no/norge/norsk-terrorsikta-kvinne-ber-om-a-bli-arrestert-
5. Svendsen, C. (2019, October 29). Norsk kvinne siktet. NRK. https://www.nrk.no/norge/norsk-kvinne-siktet-for-deltagelse-i-to-terrororganisasjoner-
6. Ibid.
7. Myklebustskipet. https://sagastad.no/myklebustskipet/.
8. Wikimedia Foundation. (2021, February 8). Myklebustskipet. Wikipedia. https://no.wikipedia.org/wiki/Myklebustskipet.
9. https://sagastad.no/myklebustskipet/.
10. Ntb. (2019, January 14). Somalisk fembarnsmor avviser tiltale https://www.nettavisen.no/nyheter/innenriks/somalisk-fembarnsmor-avviser-tiltale-om-terror-og-is-stotte/s/12-95-3423580048.
11. Thuestad, Ø. (2018, December 18). Somalisk fembarns¬mor var medlem av IS da hun fikk kommunal bolig i Nordfjord. Document. https://www.document.no/2018/12/17/somalisk-fembarnsmor-var-medlem-av-is-da-hun-fikk-kommunal-bolig-i-nordfjord/.
12. Ibid.
13. https://www.nettavisen.no/nyheter/innenriks/somalisk-fembarnsmor-avviser-tiltale-om-terror-og-is-stotte/s/12-95-3423580048.
14. Reporter, J. N. (2018, April 6). Somalian who 'planned attack' on Jews.https://jewishnews.timesofisrael.com/somalian-who-planned-attack-on-jews-jailed-for-trying-to-join-isis/.
15. Ibid.
16. https://www.rights.no/2018/04/fengslet-somalisk-fembarnsmor-31-for-is-tilknytning/
17. Zondag, M. H. W., & Døvik, O. (2018, April 10). Fant bombeoppskrifter på mobilen til terrorsiktet asylsøker. NRK. https://www.nrk.no/norge/fant-bombeoppskrifter-pa-mobilen-til-terrorsiktet-asylsoker-
18. https://www.document.no/2018/12/17/somalisk-fembarnsmor-var-medlem-av-is-da-hun-fikk-kommunal-bolig-i-nordfjord/.
19. https://www.nettavisen.no/nyheter/innenriks/somalisk-fembarnsmor-avviser-tiltale-om-terror-og-is-stotte/s/12-95-3423580048.
20. Myadmin. (2018, December 6). Om HRS. Human Rights Service. https://www.rights.no/om-hrs/.

21. Wikimedia Foundation. (2021, April 25). Hege Storhaug. Wikipedia. https://en.wikipedia.org/wiki/Hege_Storhaug.
22. Ibid.
23. Dahle, J. (2021, March 18). Terrordømt, utvist IS-kvinne utgjør sikkerhetsrisiko ble løslatt. Human Rights Service. https://www.rights.no/2021/03/terrordomt-utvist-is-kvinne-utgjor-sikkerhetsrisiko-ble-loslatt/.
24. Ibid.
25. Ibid.
26. Ibid.
27. Ibid.
28. Ibid.
29. Ibid.
30. Ibid.
31. Lillealtern, R., & Saugestad, K. (2019, March 8). Maria Amelie - NRK. https://www.nrk.no/dokumentar/maria-senket-nesten-regjeringen-
32. Knudsen, S. Ø. (2015, October 6). 10 sentrale fakta om Amelie-saken. NRK. https://www.nrk.no/norge/10-sentrale-fakta-om-amelie-saken
33. https://www.nrk.no/dokumentar/maria-senket-nesten-regjeringen-
34. Ibid.
35. Ibid.
36. Ibid.
37. Staude, T., Birhane, D. K., & Moxnes, A. (2015, October 6). - https://www.nrk.no/kultur/--mikrofonstativ-for-maria-amelie-
38. Ibid.
39. Ibid.
40. Ibid.
41. Ibid.
42. Uncle Buck Five Year Plan. https://youtu.be/QDnfNzmV0FM
43. Lilleås, H. (2017, January 12). 2016: Retrieved April 07, 2021, from.https://www.nettavisen.no/nyheter/2016-15-580-fikk-familiegjenforening/s/12-95-3423301615
44. Schei Lilleås, H. (2018, January 10). Retrieved April 07, 2021, from.https://www.nettavisen.no/nyheter/udi-14-432-fikk-familiegjenforening/s/12-95-3423404965
45. Noahalbert7886. (2018, May 25). Michael Moore: Norway is unbelievable for Americans - VIDEO DAILYMOTION. Retrieved April 07, 2021, https://www.dailymotion.com/video/x6kbab0
46. Ibid.

47. Ibid.
48. Ibid.
49. Presse, A. F. P.- A. F. (2021, May 26). Sweden Tops Europe In https://www.barrons.com/news/sweden-tops-europe-in-fatal-shootings-report-shows-01622034913.
50. https://www.dailymotion.com/video/x6kbab0
51. Norske fengsler er for gode. Aftenposten. (2015, April 7). https://www.aftenposten.no/meninger/sid/i/30Be/norske-fengsler-er-for-gode.

Chapter 11: Beating Up Jews Awakened Young Muslims Politically

1. 2008–2009 Oslo riots. (2020, October 3). Retrieved April 24, 2021. https://en.wikipedia.org/wiki/2008%E2%80%932009_Oslo_riots
2. Ibid.
3. Ibid.
4. Ibid.
5. Ibid.
6. Ibid.
7. Ibid.
8. Ladegaard, I. (2013, January 02). Opptøyene I Oslo Vekket UNGE muslimer politisk. Retrieved April 30, 2021, from https://forskning.no/krig-og-fred/opptoyene-i-oslo-vekket-unge-muslimer-politisk/667300
9. Ibid.
10. Ibid.
11. Ibid.
12. Ibid.
13. Rustad, H. (2010, February 19). Varige SKADER AV GAZA-VOLD i Oslo. Retrieved April 30, 2021, from https://www.document.no/2010/02/19/varige_skader_av_gaza-vold_i_o/
14. Ibid.
15. Ibid.
16. Suissa, M. R. (2011, October 17). Jon Gunnar Aksnes er død. sma. https://sma-norge.no/jon-gunnar-aksnes-er-.
17. Law, T. (2019, October 27). What to know about DEAD Islamic state LEADER AL-BAGHDADI. Retrieved April 23, 2021, from https://time.com/5711809/al-baghdadi-islamic-state-isis-dead/
18. Ibid.
19. Ibid.
20. Ibid.
21. Ibid.

22. History.com Editors. (2017, July 10). ISIS. Retrieved April 23, 2021, from https://www.history.com/topics/21st-century/isis
23. Ibid.
24. Ibid.
25. https://time.com/5711809/al-baghdadi-islamic-state-isis-dead/
26. Wikimedia Foundation. (2021, July 4). Death of Abu Bakr al-Baghdadi. https://en.wikipedia.org/wiki/Death_of_Abu_Bakr_al-Baghdadi.
27. https://time.com/5711809/al-baghdadi-islamic-state-isis-dead/
28. Svendsen, C. (2019, May 13). PST: Ytterligere Ti norske fremmedkrigere TROLIG DREPT. Retrieved April 23, 2021, https://www.nrk.no/norge/pst_-ytterligere-ti-norske-fremmedkrigere-trolig-drept-
29. Døvik, O., & Svendsen, C. (2018, June 15). Retrieved April 27, 2021, from https://www.nrk.no/norge/fire-av-ti-norske-is-domte-er-loslatt-1.14082372
30. Ibid.
31. Ibid.
32. Ibid.
33. Capatides, C. (2016, January 27). Which European countries have produced the most ISIS fighters? Retrieved April 23, 2021, from https://www.cbsnews.com/news/isis-terror-recruiting-europe-belgium-france-denmark-sweden-germany/
34. Ibid.
35. Ibid.
36. Soufan Group. (2015). Hotbed for Recruitment. Retrieved April 25, 2021, from https://www.jstor.org/stable/resrep10784.6

Chapter 12: The World Needs Another Osama bin Laden

1. Denne verden trenger en ny Osama. VG. (n.d.). https://www.vg.no/nyheter/innenriks/i/8nlw1/denne-verden-trenger-en-ny-osama.
2. Ibid.
3. Wikimedia Foundation. (2021, July 5). Innocence of Muslims. https://en.wikipedia.org/wiki/Innocence_of_Muslims.
4. https://www.vg.no/nyheter/innenriks/i/8nlw1/denne-verden-trenger-en-ny-osama.
5. Hirsti, K., Honningoy, K., & Grosvold, O. (2015, October 06). Norske muslimer Mot muhammed-film. Retrieved April 25, 2021, from https://www.nrk.no/norge/norske-muslimer-mot-muhammed-film-
6. Hirsti, K. (2015, October 7). Unge muslimer vil støtte Muhammed. NRK. https://www.nrk.no/norge/unge-muslimer-vil-stotte-muhammed-
7. Ibid.

8. Foss, A. (2012, October 19). Retrieved April 25, 2021, from https://www.aftenposten.no/norge/i/dOk31/baade-bhatti-og-mohyeldeen-er-i-syria
9. Ibid.
10. Lurås, H. (2021, May 2). SIAN med aksjon mot Islam Nets planer om "aktivitetssenter": – Oslo jihadistsenter. Resett. https://resett.no/2021/05/02/sian-med-aksjon-mot-islam-nets-planer-om-aktivitetssenter-oslo-jihadistsenter/.
11. Ibid.
12. A. R. (2021, May 1). Politikere fra høyre til venstre fordømte Islam Nets planer så ble det stille: Urovekkende. Resett. https://resett.no/2021/04/30/politikere-fra-hoyre-til-venstre-fordomte-islam-nets-planer-sa-ble-det-stille-urovekkende/.
13. Ibid.
14. https://www.aftenposten.no/norge/i/dOk31/baade-bhatti-og-mohyeldeen-er-i-syria
15. Ibid.
16. Ibid.
17. Ibid.
18. Solheim, S., & Zondag, M. (2012, November 06). – ER der FOR å FORSVARE sivlie. Retrieved April 26, 2021, from https://www.nrk.no/norge/_-er-der-for-a-forsvare-sivlie-
19. Ibid.
20. Ibid.
21. Ibid.
22. Grosvold, Ø, & Solheim, S. (2015, October 07). Retrieved April 26, 2021, from https://www.nrk.no/urix/norsk-mann-drept-i-syria-
23. Ibid.
24. Hultgreen, G., & Borgos Hjelle, T. (2016, October 21). Islamist truer med å DREPE JØDER i Norge. Retrieved April 25, 2021, from https://www.dagbladet.no/nyheter/islamist-truer-med-a-drepe-joder-i-norge/63005275
25. Ibid.
26. Ibid.
27. Ibid.
28. Solheim, S., & Olsson, S. V. (2015, October 7). Truende Facebook-melding.https://www.nrk.no/norge/truende-facebook-melding-mot-joder-1.8371012.
29. Zondag, M. (2015, October 06). Retrieved April 25, 2021, from https://www.nrk.no/norge/ekstreme-islamister-tar-jegerkurs-

30. Ibid.
31. Ibid.
32. Helljesen, V., Skille, O., & Alayoubi, M. (2015, October 06). Vil DEMONSTRERE mot norsk heksejakt. Retrieved April 26, 2021, from https://www.nrk.no/norge/vil-demonstrere-mot-norsk-heksejakt-
33. Svendsen, C., & Skille, Ø. B. (2015, October 6). Tidligere Profetens Ummah-talsmann utvist fra Norge: Krever å få komme tilbake. NRK. https://www.nrk.no/norge/tidligere-profetens-ummah-talsmann-utvist-fra-norge_-krever-a-fa-komme-tilbake-
34. https://www.nrk.no/norge/vil-demonstrere-mot-norsk-heksejakt-
35. Ibid.
36. Ibid.
37. Ibid.
38. Foss, A. B., Andreassen, T. A., Aspunvik, S. G., & Dokka, Å. G. (2014, May 1). Norsk islamist drept i Syria. Aftenposten. https://www.aftenposten.no/norge/i/8VaW/norsk-islamist-drept-i-syria.
39. Norsk-algerisk IS-kriger: "Det er en drøm som går i oppfyllelse". https://www.vg.no/nyheter/innenriks/i/nzj9m/norsk-algerisk-is-kriger-det-er-en-droem-som-gaar-i-oppfyllelse.
40. Aspunvik, S. G. (2016, January 22). Norsk-algerisk IS-kriger (49) drept i Irak. NRK. https://www.nrk.no/norge/norsk-algerisk-is-kriger-_49_-drept-i-irak-1.
41. TV 2, Andersen, K., & Zaman, K. (2013, February 19). Nav-penger SKAPER Splittelse BLANT islamister i Norge. Retrieved April 26, 2021, from https://www.tv2.no/a/13630315/
42. Ibid.
43. TV 2, Zaman, K., & Ervik, K. (2012, October 25). Islamisten Langer ut mot skatt - HEVER Selv dagpenger. Retrieved April 26, 2021, from https://www.tv2.no/a/3909520
44. https://www.tv2.no/a/13630315/
45. Ibid.
46. TV 2, Zaman, K., & Persen, K. (2012, November 08). Dette Får Arfan bhatti i Nav-stønad. Retrieved April 26, 2021, from https://www.tv2.no/a/3920003
47. Ibid.
48. Pettersen, E. (2013, February 20). - Det er en hån mot det norske folk. Nettavisen. https://www.nettavisen.no/nyheter/det-er-en-han-mot-det-norske-folk/s/12-95-3574323.
49. Ibid.
50. https://www.nrk.no/norge/carl-i.-hagen-om-blitz-1.8057152

51. Ibid.
52. Ibid.
53. Wikimedia Foundation. (2021, April 13). Blitz house. Wikipedia. https://en.wikipedia.org/wiki/Blitz_House.
54. Ibid.
55. Ibid.

Chapter 13: Sometimes a Government Has To Make Moral Decisions
1. Svendsen, C., & Alayoubi, M. (2020, January 14). Norge henter tilbake IS-siktet mor og to barn fra Syria. NRK. https://www.nrk.no/norge/norge-henter-tilbake-is-siktet-mor-og-to-barn-fra-syria-
2. Ibid.
3. Ibid.
4. Ibid.
5. Ibid.
6. Berge, J. (2020, February 1). Tre av fem nordmenn sier nei til å https://www.nettavisen.no/nyheter/tre-av-fem-nordmenn-sier-nei-til-a-hente-hjem-flere-is-familier/s/12-95-3423916846.
7. Ibid.
8. Ibid.
9. Ibid.
10. Olsson, S. V., Owing, N., Brekke, A., & Vigsnæs, M. K. (2020, January 17). Erna Solberg: – Jeg ville ikke risikere at en syk https://www.nrk.no/norge/erna-solberg_-_-jeg-ville-ikke-risikere-at-en-syk-norsk-femaring-dode-i-syria-
11. Ibid.
12. Ibid.
13. Ibid.
14. Ibid.
15. About Granavolden Guesthouse - granavolden Gjæstgiveri. Granavolden. (n.d.). https://www.granavolden.no/eng/About-Granavolden-Guesthouse.
16. https://www.nrk.no/norge/erna-solberg_-_-jeg-ville-ikke-risikere-at-en-syk-norsk-femaring-dode-i-syria-
17. Ibid.
18. Vigsnæs, M. K., Svendsen, C., & Alayoubi, M. (2020, January 16). IS-kvinnen kommer trolig til Norge fredag. NRK. https://www.nrk.no/norge/is-kvinnen-kommer-trolig-til-norge-fredag-1.
19. Ibid.

20. Storhaug, H. (2021, May 18). Truer med at sønnen blir terrorist om hun ikke får komme tilbake. Human Rights Service. https://www.rights.no/2021/05/truer-med-at-sonnen-blir-terrorist-om-hun-ikke-far-komme-tilbake-til-norge/.
21. Ibid.
22. Ibid.
23. Jappee, G., & Trulsen, O. N. (2018, June 1). Returnerer pris i islamist-protest. NRK. https://www.nrk.no/kultur/returnerer-pris-i-islamist-protest-1.
24. Ibid.
25. Ibid.
26. Ibid.
27. https://www.rights.no/2021/05/truer-med-at-sonnen-blir-terrorist-om-hun-ikke-far-komme-tilbake-til-norge/.
28. Ibid.
29. Helljesen, V., Kinn, E., & Vigsnæs, M. K. (2020, January 17). Siv Jensen: – Ikke noe i veien Med FRPS moralske kompass. https://www.nrk.no/norge/siv-jensen_-_-ikke-noe-i-veien-med-frps-moralske-kompass-1.
30. Brekke, A., & Grønli, H. (2020, January 16). Siv Jensen: Frps kravliste blir klar i dag. NRK. https://www.nrk.no/norge/siv-jensen_-frps-kravliste-blir-klar-i-dag-1.
31. Fossen, C. H., Olsson, S. V., & Berge, K. M. (2020, January 17). Kilder til NRK: Frp vurderer omkamp om lovforslaget som ledet til Listhaugs avgang. NRK. https://www.nrk.no/norge/kilder-til-nrk_-frp-vurderer-omkamp-om-lovforslaget-som-ledet-til-listhaugs-avgang-
32. Ibid.
33. Helljesen, V., Strand, T., & Svaar, P. (2018, March 26). https://www.nrk.no/norge/regjeringen-far-ikke-la-justisdepartementet-frata-fremmedkrigere-statsborgerskapet-
34. Ibid.
35. Dettmer, J. (2017, July 30). Britain Strips More Than 100 Islamic State Fighters of Citizenship. Voice of America. https://www.voanews.com/europe/britain-strips-more-100-islamic-state-fighters-citizenship.
36. Meghan , M., & Banulescu-Bogdan, N. (2019, April 23). Foreign Fighters: Will Revoking Citizenship Mitigate the Threat? https://www.migrationpolicy.org/article/foreign-fighters-will-revoking-citizenship-mitigate-threat.
37. Ibid.
38. https://www.nrk.no/norge/

regjeringen-far-ikke-la-justisdepartementet-frata-fremmedkrigere-statsborgerskapet-
39. Ibid.
40. Libell, H. P., & Martyn-hemphill, R. (2018, March 20). Norway's Justice Minister Resigns in Storm Over Facebook Post. NYT. https://www.nytimes.com/2018/03/20/world/europe/norways-justice-minister-resigns-in-storm-over-facebook-post.html.
41. Fossen, C. H., Sættem, J. B., & Sølhusvik, L. (2018, October 23). Listhaug forsvarer terror-utspillet: Hevder Støre fikk henne til å gråte.https://www.nrk.no/norge/listhaug-forsvarer-terror-utspillet_-hevder-store-fikk-henne-til-a-grate-
42. https://www.nytimes.com/2018/03/20/world/europe/norways-justice-minister-resigns-in-storm-over-facebook-post.html.
43. https://www.nrk.no/norge/listhaug-forsvarer-terror-utspillet_-hevder-store-fikk-henne-til-a-grate-
44. https://www.nytimes.com/2018/03/20/world/europe/norways-justice-minister-resigns-in-storm-over-facebook-post.html.
45. https://www.nrk.no/norge/listhaug-forsvarer-terror-utspillet_-hevder-store-fikk-henne-til-a-grate-
46. Ibid.
47. Berge, J. (2013, September 17). - Breivik forlot oss fordi vi var for liberale. https://www.nettavisen.no/nyheter/breivik-forlot-oss-fordi-vi-var-for-liberale/s/12-95-3679976.
48. Ibid.
49. Ibid.
50. Ibid.

Chapter 14: Oh, What Tangled Web We Weave
1. Helljesen, V., Kinn, E., Hotvedt, S. K., Bruland, R. S., Rønneberg, O., & Vigsnæs, M. K. (2021, February 28). IS-kvinnen pågrepet rett etter hjemkomst. NRK. https://www.nrk.no/norge/is-kvinnen-pagrepet-rett-etter-hjemkomst- Ibid.
2. Ibid.
3. Ibid.
4. Ibid.
5. Ibid.
6. Ibid.
7. Ibid.
8. Kinn, E., Fjeld, I. E., & Helljesen, V. (2020, January 19). Nordhus:

Min klient erklærer ikke straffskyld. NRK. https://www.nrk.no/norge/nordhus_-_-min-klient-erklaerer-ikke-straffskyld-
9. Ibid.
10. Wikimedia Foundation. (2021, August 1). Hijab by country. Wikipedia. https://en.wikipedia.org/wiki/Hijab_by_country.
11. Stavrum, G. (2020, June 17). Selvsagt helt uaktuelt å tillate Bruk av nikab Og hijab blant UNIFORMERTE POLITIFOLK. Nettavisen. https://www.nettavisen.no/okonomi/selvsagt-helt-uaktuelt-a-tillate-bruk-av-nikab-og-hijab-blant-uniformerte-politifolk/s/12-95-3423983721.
12. Skaug, C. (2020, October 2). Regjeringen tillater PASSBILDER m/ hijab. https://www.document.no/2020/10/02/regjeringen-tillater-passbilder-med-hijab/.
13. https://www.nrk.no/norge/nordhus_-_-min-klient-erklaerer-ikke-straffskyld-
14. Ibid.
15. Ibid.
16. Ibid.
17. Grønli, H., & Lydersen, T. (2020, January 20). Grande om henting av IS-kvinna: Veldig sikker på at det var eit riktig val. https://www.nrk.no/norge/grande-om-henting-av-is-kvinna_-_-veldig-sikker-pa-at-det-var-eit-riktig-val-
18. Ibid.
19. Ibid.
20. Ibid.
21. Une Bastholm om Frp-exit: To gode seiere i ett. VG. (n.d.). https://www.vg.no/nyheter/innenriks/i/y3nzyK/une-bastholm-om-frp-exit-to-gode-seiere-i-ett.
22. Ntb, Ruud, S., Sørenes, K. M., & Ask, A. O. (2020, January 16). Sinne I frp:Jeg SKAMMER Meg over å sitte I regjering. https://www.aftenposten.no/norge/politikk/i/dOBdwj/frp-i-opproer-etter-at-regjeringen-henter-hjem-is-kvinne-med-sykt-barn.
23. Ibid.
24. Ibid.
25. Ibid.
26. Heldahl, H. (2021, May 15). Erna Solberg om is-kvinnen: – Det Riktige å gjøre. https://www.nettavisen.no/nyheter/erna-solberg-om-is-kvinnen-det-var-det-riktige-a-gjore/s/12-95-3424127753.
27. Dimmen, P. (2020, January 19). IS-kvinnen I norge: – Hvorfor Får hun HJELP som VI Andre Ikke får?

Human Rights Service. https://www.rights.no/2020/01/is-kvinnen-i-norge-hvorfor-far-hun-hjelp-som-vi-andre-ikke-far/.
28. Svendsen, C., Alayoubi, M., Frøysa, K., Bulai, E. M., & Kolseth, H. I. M. (2020, October 26). Terrorsiktet kvinne i avhør: NRK. https://www.nrk.no/norge/terrorsiktet-kvinne-i-avhor_-norsk-ettaring-dode-etter-mishandling-i-syria-1.
29. Ibid.
30. Ibid.
31. Ibid.
32. Ibid.
33. Ibid.
34. Ibid.
35. Thuestad, Ø. (2020, August 17). IS-kvinnen i avhør: Document. https://www.document.no/2020/08/17/is-kvinnen-i-avhor-norsk-ettaring-dode-etter-mishandling-i-syria/.
36. Lexico Dictionaries. (n.d.). Talaq english definition and meaning. https://www.lexico.com/en/definition/talaq.
37. Ibid.
38. Ibid.

Chapter 16: Radical Islam Will Never Leave Norway

1. Ighoubah, F. (2021, May 4). Is-kvinnen dømt til fengsel i tre og https://www.nettavisen.no/nyheter/is-kvinnen-domt-til-fengsel-i-tre-og-et-halvt-ar-for-terrordeltakelse/s/12-95-3424122968.
2. Ibid.
3. Torres, M., & Ighoubah, F. (2021, May 4). Frp-helgheim reagerer sterkt etter dommen mot is-kvinnen. Nettavisen. https://www.nettavisen.no/nyheter/frp-helgheim-reagerer-sterkt-etter-dommen-mot-is-kvinnen/s/12-95-3424123159.
4. Ibid.
5. Ibid.
6. Ibid.
7. Ibid.
8. Ibid.
9. Ibid.
10. Rønneberg, O. (2021, May 5). Dommen ER Dårlig nytt for De andre kvinnene. NRK. https://www.nrk.no/ytring/dommen-er-darlig-nytt-for-de-andre-kvinnene-1.
11. Ibid.

12. Zondag, M. H. W., Døvik, O., & Olsson, S. V. (2021, May 14). Mener ANGREP var nært FORESTÅENDE: Terrortiltalt 16-https://www.nrk.no/norge/mener-angrep-var-naert-forestaende_-terrortiltalt-16-aring-har-fortsatt-ikke-forklart-seg-for-pst-1.
13. Ibid.
14. Ibid.
15. Handlingsplan mot diskriminering av og hat mot muslimer. https://www.regjeringen.no/contentassets/b2a6fd21c6a94bae83d5a3425593da30/handlingsplan-mot-diskriminering-av-og-hat-mot-muslimer-2020-2023.pdf. (n.d.).
16. Stokke, O. (2016, November 07). Terrortiltalt 19-åring: Var beredt til å krige mot is. Retrieved May 01, 2021, from https://www.aftenposten.no/norge/i/O72qA/terrortiltalt-19-aaring-var-beredt-til-aa-krige-mot-is
17. Ibid.
18. Ibid.
19. Ibid.
20. Ibid.
21. Ibid.
22. Ansari, A., Døvik, O., & Zondag, M. (2016, December 01). Ubaydullah hussain hjernevasket Min bror. Retrieved May 02, 2021, from https://www.nrk.no/norge/lillesosteren-til-drept-jihadist_-_-ubaydullah-hussain-hjernevasket-min-bror-1.13253912
23. Ibid.
24. Ibid.
25. Ibid.
26. Brustad, L., & Nordahl Finsveen, J. (2017, April 04). Ubaydullah Hussain dømt til NI års Fengsel for Terrorrekruttering. from https://www.dagbladet.no/nyheter/ubaydullah-hussain-domt-til-ni-ars-fengsel-for-terrorrektruttering/67458637
27. Ibid.
28. Ibid.
29. Røset, H. H. (2017, April 6). Ubaydullah Hussain anker terror-dommen. NRK. https://www.nrk.no/norge/ubaydullah-hussain-anker-terror-dommen-1.
30. Skille, &., & Kalajdzic, P. (2018, November 08). Staten må betale over 100.000 kroner Til Arfan Bhatti. Retrieved May 04, 2021, https://www.nrk.no/norge/staten-ma-betale-over-100.000-kroner-til-arfan-bhatti-1.
31. Ibid.
32. Ibid.
33. Ighoubah, F. (2018, December 13). Retrieved May 04, 2021, from

https://www.nettavisen.no/nyheter/innenriks/sylvi-listhaug-raser-over-at-arfan-bhatti-far-118-000-kroner-i-erstatning/s/12-95-3423568631
34. Ibid.
35. Ibid.
36. Ibid.
37. Ibid.
38. Ibid.
39. Ighoubah, F. (2018, December 13). - sylvi listhaug burde være den siste som peker på andre. Retrieved May 04, 2021, from https://www.nettavisen.no/nyheter/innenriks/sylvi-listhaug-burde-vare-den-siste-som-peker-pa-andre/s/12-95-3423568675
40. Ibid.
41. Ibid.
42. Ibid.
43. Alayoubi, M., & Tahir, A. I. (2020, October 26). Trøblete Fengselsopphold for syria-farer: Bråk, vold OG TRUSLER. NRK. https://www.nrk.no/norge/troblete-fengselsopphold-for-syria-farer_-_-brak_-vold-og-trusler-1.
44. Ibid.
45. Ibid.
46. Ibid.
47. Ibid.
48. Ibid.
49. Ibid.
50. Ibid.
51. Ibid.
52. Ibid.
53. Ibid.
54. Ibid.
55. Storhaug, H. (2020, October 14). Syria-kriger SLIPPES Snart UT av norsk fengsel. Fryktes av... Retrieved April 28, 2021, from https://www.rights.no/2020/10/is-kriger-slippes-snart-ut-av-norsk-fengsel-fryktes-av-myndighetene/
56. Ibid.

Chapter 17: The Shadow That Has Fallen Upon Norway
1. Bawer, B. (2019, June 18). *The Islamization of Oslo*. City Journal. https://www.city-journal.org/html/islamization-oslo-15686.html.

2. Bawer, B. (2007). Back Cover. In While Europe slept: How radical Islam is destroying the west from within. essay, Anchor Books.
3. Bawer, B. (2007). While Europe slept: How radical Islam is destroying the west from within. Amazon. https://www.amazon.com/While-Europe-Slept-Radical-Destroying/dp/0767920058.
4. Bawer, B. (2007). Back Cover. In While Europe slept: How radical Islam is destroying the west from within. essay, Anchor Books.
5. https://www.city-journal.org/html/islamization-oslo-15686.html.
6. Ibid.
7. Bawer, B. (2021, March 17). Can you say 'death panels'? Frontpagemag. https://www.frontpagemag.com/fpm/2021/03/can-you-say-death-panels-bruce-bawer/#commento.
8. Ibid.
9. Torstveit, M. (2021, March 4). Seljord kommune kjøpte hus til barnefamilie. https://www.nrk.no/vestfoldogtelemark/seljord-kommune-kjopte-hus-til-barnefamilie-1.
10. Instebø Vang, D. (2021, February 28). Retten til Å puste. Bergensavisen. https://www.ba.no/retten-til-a-puste/o/5-8-1559428.

Chapter 18: You're Always In My Heart Norway

1. Zähler, M. (2018, April 24). https://resett.no/2018/03/13/skilt-norsk-kvinne-i-usa-sliter-med-a-fa-statsborgerskapet-i-norge-tilbake-na-som-hun-skal-flytte-hjem/.
2. Ibid.
3. Ibid.
4. Ibid.
5. Ibid.
6. Ibid.
7. Ibid.
8. Ibid.
9. Ibid.
10. Ibid.
11. Fordal, J. A. (2020, August 17). Fjernsynets historie. NRK. https://www.nrk.no/organisasjon/fjernsynets-historie-1.6512060.
12. Ronald Reagan Freedom Speech. Reagan.com. (n.d.). https://www.reagan.com/ronald-reagan-freedom-speech.
13. Ibid.

Made in the USA
Monee, IL
07 November 2021